GILLINGHAM PARISH CHURCH.   Royal Arms.   Probably 1618

AN INVENTORY OF
HISTORICAL MONUMENTS
IN THE
COUNTY OF
DORSET

VOLUME FOUR
NORTH DORSET

ROYAL COMMISSION ON
HISTORICAL MONUMENTS (ENGLAND)
MCMLXXII

SBN 11 700460 X*

Printed in England for Her Majesty's Stationery Office
by Butler & Tanner Ltd, Frome and London

TABLE OF CONTENTS

PARISHES DESCRIBED IN THE INVENTORY

(see map in pocket at end of volume)

1 ASHMORE

2 BOURTON

3 BUCKHORN WESTON

4 CANN

5 CHETTLE

6 COMPTON ABBAS

7 EAST ORCHARD

8 EAST STOUR

9 FARNHAM

10 FIFEHEAD MAGDALEN

11 FONTMELL MAGNA

12 GILLINGHAM

13 IWERNE MINSTER

14 KINGTON MAGNA

15 LANGTON LONG BLANDFORD

16 MARGARET MARSH

17 MELBURY ABBAS

18 MOTCOMBE

19 PIMPERNE

20 SHAFTESBURY

21 SILTON

22 STOUR PROVOST

23 SUTTON WALDRON

24 TARRANT CRAWFORD

25 TARRANT GUNVILLE

26 TARRANT HINTON

27 TARRANT KEYNESTON

28 TARRANT LAUNCESTON

29 TARRANT MONKTON

30 TARRANT RAWSTON

31 TARRANT RUSHTON

32 TODBER

33 WEST ORCHARD

34 WEST STOUR

LIST OF ILLUSTRATIONS

(Prefixed numerals in brackets refer to the monument numbers of the Inventory)

Sixteenth-century wood carving in
Fontmell Magna Church

PREFACE

Volume four of the Commission's Inventory of Dorset describes the Monuments of thirty-four parishes, extending from the extreme north of the County south-eastwards to include the Tarrant Valley. The Monuments (other than Roman Roads and 'Celtic' Fields) are listed in the following order under the names of the Civil Parishes in which they occur : (1) Ecclesiastical Architecture, (2) Secular Architecture, (3) Mediaeval and Later Earthworks, (4) Roman and Prehistoric Monuments, (5) Undated Earthworks etc. 'Celtic' Fields are described extra-parochially at the end of the volume. Roman roads do not appear, being reserved for a comprehensive survey of the Roman roads of the County in the final volume. The parishes are arranged alphabetically, and each parish is prefaced by a short topographical and historical synopsis.

The scope of the Dorset Inventories and the method of their compilation have been explained in preceding volumes (*Dorset* II, xix–xxi ; III, xxi–xxii). Every Monument included in the Inventory has been inspected by one or more of our investigators and the entries relating to Monuments of major importance have been verified in the field ; after this the typescript and line-drawings have been scrutinised by my fellow Commissioners ; finally the descriptions of important Monuments have been submitted to the incumbents of churches and to the owners of large houses or other property, as appropriate, for comment. Within the limits prescribed by the Royal Warrant, I am confident that no significant Monument dating from before 1850 has been omitted.

I hope that the Commission's decision to provide more line-drawings and correspondingly to shorten the verbal descriptions of certain Monuments will add to the value of the Inventory. In most instances architectural plans, at a uniform scale of 24 ft. to the inch, are hatched to indicate the dates of the various parts of the buildings ; key plans of lesser buildings are drawn without hatching at a scale of 48 ft. to the inch. With few exceptions the surveys upon which the maps and plans are based have been made by our investigators. Nearly all the half-tone illustrations are from photographs taken by the Commission's photographers.

Our thanks are due to many public authorities and private persons who have helped in the compilation of the volume. Individual acknowledgements will be found in our twenty-sixth Report, a copy of which appears on pp. xix–xxii below.

The Inventory was checked in the field during 1969 and changes that have taken place since that date are not taken into account. No work of this kind can escape the intrusion of some mistakes, and the Commission will welcome any corrections that may be sent to the Secretary with a view to amendment in a future edition of the Inventory ; meanwhile such corrections will be added to the record cards. These records are open for consultation by accredited persons, due notice being given to the Commission's Secretary.

SALISBURY

LIST OF COMMISSIONERS

THE ROYAL WARRANTS

WHITEHALL,
2ND OCTOBER, 1963

The QUEEN has been pleased to issue a Commission under Her Majesty's Royal Sign Manual to the following effect :

ELIZABETH R.

ELIZABETH THE SECOND, by the Grace of God of the United Kingdom of Great Britain and Northern Ireland and of Our other Realms and Territories, QUEEN, Head of the Commonwealth, Defender of the Faith,

To

Our Right Trusty and Entirely-beloved Cousin and Counsellor Robert Arthur James, Marquess of Salisbury, Knight of Our Most Noble Order of the Garter ;

Our Trusty and Well-beloved :

Sir Albert Edward Richardson, Knight Commander of the Royal Victorian Order ;
Sir John Newenham Summerson, Knight, Commander of Our Most Excellent Order of the British Empire ;
Nikolaus Pevsner, Esquire, Commander of Our Most Excellent Order of the British Empire ;
Christopher Edward Clive Hussey, Esquire, Commander of Our Most Excellent Order of the British Empire ;
Ian Archibald Richmond, Esquire, Commander of Our Most Excellent Order of the British Empire ;
Henry Clifford Darby, Esquire, Officer of Our Most Excellent Order of the British Empire ;
Donald Benjamin Harden, Esquire, Officer of Our Most Excellent Order of the British Empire ;
John Grahame Douglas Clark, Esquire ;
Howard Montagu Colvin, Esquire ;
Vivian Hunter Galbraith, Esquire ;
William Abel Pantin, Esquire ;
Stuart Piggott, Esquire ;
Courtenay Arthur Ralegh Radford, Esquire ;
Arnold Joseph Taylor, Esquire ;
Francis Wormald, Esquire ;

GREETING !

Whereas We have deemed it expedient that the Commissioners appointed to the Royal Commission on the Ancient and Historical Monuments and Constructions of England shall serve for such periods as We by the hand of Our First Lord of the Treasury may specify and that the said Commissioners shall, if The National Buildings Record is liquidated, assume the control and management of such part of The

National Buildings Record's collection as does not solely relate to Our Principality of Wales and to Monmouthshire, and that a new Commission should issue for these purposes :

Now Know Ye that We have revoked and determined, and do by these Presents revoke and determine, all the Warrants whereby Commissioners were appointed on the twenty-ninth day of March one thousand nine hundred and forty six and on any subsequent date :

And We do by these Presents authorize and appoint you, the said Robert Arthur James, Marquess of Salisbury (Chairman), Sir Albert Edward Richardson, Sir John Newenham Summerson, Nikolaus Pevsner, Christopher Edward Clive Hussey, Ian Archibald Richmond, Henry Clifford Darby, Donald Benjamin Harden, John Grahame Douglas Clark, Howard Montagu Colvin, Vivian Hunter Galbraith, William Abel Pantin, Stuart Piggott, Courtenay Arthur Ralegh Radford, Arnold Joseph Taylor and Francis Wormald to be Our Commissioners for such periods as We may specify in respect of each of you to make an inventory of the Ancient and Historical Monuments and Constructions connected with or illustrative of the contemporary culture, civilisation and conditions of life of the people in England, excluding Monmouthshire, from the earliest times to the year 1714, and such further Monuments and Constructions subsequent to that year as may seem in your discretion to be worthy of mention therein, and to specify those which seem most worthy of preservation.

And Whereas We have deemed it expedient that Our Lieutenants of Counties in England should be appointed ex-officio Members of the said Commission for the purposes of that part of the Commission's inquiry which relates to ancient and historical monuments and constructions within their respective counties :

Now Know Ye that We do by these Presents authorize and appoint Our Lieutenant for the time being of each and every County in England, other than Our County of Monmouth, to be a Member of the said Commission for the purposes of that part of the Commission's inquiry which relates to ancient and historical monuments and constructions within the area of his jurisdiction as Our Lieutenant of such County :

And for the better enabling you to carry out the purposes of this Our Commission, We do by these Presents authorize you to call in the aid and co-operation of owners of ancient monuments, inviting them to assist you in furthering the objects of the Commission ; and to invite the possessors of such papers as you may deem it desirable to inspect to produce them before you :

And We do further authorize and empower you to confer with the Council of The National Buildings Record from time to time as may seem expedient to you in order that your deliberations may be assisted by the reports and records in the possession of the Council : and to make such arrangements for the furtherance of objectives of common interest to yourselves and the Council as may be mutually agreeable :

And We do further authorize and empower you to assume the general control and management (whether as Administering Trustees under a Scheme established under the Charities Act 1960 or otherwise) of that part of the collection of The National Buildings Record which does not solely relate to our Principality of Wales or to Monmouthshire and (subject, in relation to the said part of that collection, to the provisions of any such Scheme as may be established affecting the same) to make such arrangements for the continuance and furtherance of the work of The National Buildings Record as you may deem to be necessary both generally and for the creation of any wider record or collection containing or including architectural, archaeological and historical information concerning important sites and buildings throughout England :

And We do further give and grant unto you, or any three or more of you, full power to call before you such persons as you shall judge likely to afford you any information upon the subject of this Our Commission ; and also to call for, have access to and examine all such books, documents, registers and records as may afford you the fullest information on the subject and to inquire of and concerning the premises by all other lawful ways and means whatsoever :

And We do by these Presents authorize and empower you, or any three or more of you, to visit and personally inspect such places as you may deem it expedient so to inspect for the more effectual carrying out of the purposes aforesaid :

And We do by these Presents will and ordain that this Our Commission shall continue in full force and virtue, and that you, Our said Commissioners, or any three or more of you, may from time to time proceed in the execution thereof, and of every matter and thing therein contained, although the same be not continued from time to time by adjournment :

And We do further ordain that you, or any three or more of you, have liberty to report your proceedings under this Our Commission from time to time if you shall judge it expedient so to do :

And Our further Will and Pleasure is that you do, with as little delay as possible, report to Us, under your hands and seals, or under the hands and seals of any three or more of you, your opinion upon the matters herein submitted for your consideration.

> Given at Our Court at Saint James's the Twenty-eighth day of September, 1963, in the Twelfth Year of Our Reign.
> By Her Majesty's Command,
> HENRY BROOKE

By Royal Warrant dated 23rd October, 1964, William Francis Grimes, Esquire, C.B.E., and by Royal Warrant dated 21st March, 1966, both Maurice Willmore Barley, Esquire, and Sheppard Sunderland Frere, Esquire, were appointed Members of the Royal Commission on Historical Monuments (England)

By Royal Warrant dated 2nd April, 1968, Richard John Copland Atkinson, Esquire, and Arthur Oswald, Esquire, were appointed Members of the Royal Commission on Historical Monuments (England), and Henry Clifford Darby, Esquire, having completed his term of office, was reappointed a Member of the Commission.

By Royal Warrant dated 31st December, 1969, Sir John Betjeman, C.B.E., and John Nowell Linton Myres Esquire, were appointed Members of the Royal Commission on Historical Monuments (England) ; and Courtenay Arthur Ralegh Radford, Esquire, and Sir John Newenham Summerson, C.B.E., having completed their terms of office were reappointed Members of the Commission.

Mediaeval floor-tiles in
Shaftesbury Abbey Church

ROYAL COMMISSION ON THE ANCIENT AND HISTORICAL MONUMENTS AND CONSTRUCTIONS OF ENGLAND

REPORT to the Queen's Most Excellent Majesty

MAY IT PLEASE YOUR MAJESTY

We, the undersigned Commissioners, appointed to make an Inventory of the Ancient and Historical Monuments and Constructions connected with or illustrative of the contemporary culture, civilisation and conditions of life of the people of England, excluding Monmouthshire, from the earliest times to the year 1714, and of such further Monuments and Constructions subsequent to that year as may seem in our discretion to be worthy of mention therein, and to specify those which seem most worthy of preservation, do humbly submit to Your Majesty the following Report, being the twenty-sixth Report on the work of the Commission since its first appointment.

2. With regret we have to record the retirement from the Commission upon expiry of term of office of Professor John Grahame Douglas Clark, Fellow of the British Academy, Fellow of the Society of Antiquaries, and the resignation of Arthur Stanley Oswald, Esquire.

3. We have to thank Your Majesty for the appointment to the Commission of Sir John Betjeman, Knight, Commander of the Order of the British Empire, and of John Nowell Linton Myres, Esquire, Fellow of the British Academy, Fellow of the Society of Antiquaries ; also for the reappointment of Courtenay Arthur Ralegh Radford, Esquire, Fellow of the British Academy, Fellow of the Society of Antiquaries, and of Sir John Newenham Summerson, Knight, Commander of the Order of the British Empire, Fellow of the British Academy, Fellow of the Society of Antiquaries, Associate of the Royal Institute of British Architects. These appointments and reappointments took place on 1st January 1970 under the terms of Your Majesty's Warrant dated 31st December 1969.

4. We have pleasure in reporting the completion of our Survey of the Monuments in the northern part of the County of Dorset, an area comprising thirty-four parishes, containing 857 Monuments of sufficient significance to demand separate enumeration and some 200 minor Monuments.

5. Following our usual practice we have prepared a full, illustrated Inventory of the Monuments in North Dorset, which will be issued as a non-Parliamentary publication (*Dorset* IV). As in the Inventory of Central Dorset (*Dorset* III), accompanying the twenty-fifth Report, we have adopted the terminal date 1850 for the Monuments included in the Inventory.

6. The methods adopted in previous Inventories have in general been adhered to and attention has again been paid to topography and to the form and development of the landscape in which the Monuments are set. Introductory notes are designed to suggest the natural features of each parish and to indicate the history of settlement.

7. The method of presenting 'Celtic' Field Groups and associated Monuments follows that of *Dorset* III. Since many of these Monuments extend beyond the boundaries of a parish they are described extra-parochially in a part of the Inventory following the Inventory by parishes.

8. Important entries in the Inventory of North Dorset have been submitted in draft to the incumbents of parishes and to the owners of houses, as appropriate, and we believe that no significant Monument dating from before the year 1850 has been omitted.

9. Our special thanks are due to incumbents and churchwardens and to owners and occupiers who have allowed access by our staff to the Monuments in their charge or ownership. We are indebted to the Directors and Curators of many institutions for their ready assistance to us, particularly to Mr. R. N. R. Peers, Curator of the Dorset County Museum, to Miss M. Holmes, the County Archivist, and to Miss P. K. Stewart, assistant Diocesan Archivist in Salisbury. We have to record our indebtedness to the Director General of the Ordnance Survey for access to his archaeological records, for assistance in the preparation and printing of maps, and for valuable work done by the Air Surveyors of his Department. We have also to thank the Director in Aerial Photography in the University of Cambridge for air photographs taken specially for us.

10. We humbly recommend to Your Majesty's notice the following Monuments in North Dorset, as being Most Worthy of Preservation :

ECCLESIASTICAL :

BUCKHORN WESTON
: (1) THE PARISH CHURCH of St. John, in which the chancel and nave are of 14th-century origin and the N. aisle is of the 15th century ; the chancel contains an interesting late 14th-century tomb with a recumbent effigy.

CHETTLE
: (1) THE PARISH CHURCH of St. Mary, with a 16th-century W. tower, and with chancel, nave and transeptal chapels of 1849.

COMPTON ABBAS
: (2) THE OLD PARISH CHURCH of St. Mary, disused and in ruins, but retaining a late 15th-century W. tower.

EAST STOUR
: (1) CHRIST CHURCH, wholly rebuilt in 1842, an interesting example of Victorian Romanesque architecture.

FARNHAM
: (1) THE PARISH CHURCH of St. Lawrence, with a nave perhaps of 12th-century origin, and a 15th or 16th-century S. porch and tower.

FIFEHEAD MAGDALEN
: (1) THE PARISH CHURCH of St. Mary Magdalen, with chancel, nave and S. tower of the 14th century, and with a N. chapel containing an important 18th-century wall-monument.

FONTMELL MAGNA
: (1) THE PARISH CHURCH of St. Andrew, with a 15th-century W. tower, interesting parapets of 1530 reset on the 19th-century N. aisle, and an important 12th-century font.

GILLINGHAM
: (1) THE PARISH CHURCH of St. Mary, with an early 14th-century chancel, and with nave and aisles of 1838.

IWERNE MINSTER
: (1) THE PARISH CHURCH of St. Mary, an important monument retaining a mid 12th-century nave and N. aisle, and probably part of a S. tower, also a late 12th-century S. aisle, a 13th-century N. transept, a 14th-century chancel, W. tower and S. porch, and a 15th-century spire.

KINGTON MAGNA
: (1) THE PARISH CHURCH of All Saints, with a fine late 15th-century W. tower.

MARGARET MARSH
: (1) THE PARISH CHURCH of St. Margaret, with a 15th-century W. tower.

PIMPERNE
: (1) THE PARISH CHURCH of St. Peter, with a 12th-century doorway reset in the 19th-century S. aisle, a 12th-century chancel arch and a 15th-century W. tower.

SHAFTESBURY
: (1) THE ABBEY CHURCH, razed to the ground at the Dissolution, but retaining the foundations of an important late 11th-century church with 12th-century and 14th-century additions, together with the valuable collection of architectural fragments recovered during the excavation of the Monument.
: (2) THE PARISH CHURCH of St. Peter, with a 15th-century nave, N. aisle and W. tower, and a 16th-century S. aisle.
: (3) HOLY TRINITY CHURCH, by Gilbert Scott, 1841.

SILTON
: (1) THE PARISH CHURCH of St. Nicholas, largely rebuilt in the 15th century, but incorporating a late 12th-century nave arcade ; within the nave is the important monument by Nost of Sir Hugh Wyndham (1692).

STOUR PROVOST
: (1) THE PARISH CHURCH of St. Michael, of 14th-century origin, with a 15th-century S. tower and a 16th-century N. aisle.

SUTTON WALDRON
: (1) THE PARISH CHURCH of St. Bartholomew, of 1847, with a well-proportioned W. tower and spire.

TARRANT CRAWFORD

 (1) THE PARISH CHURCH of St. Mary, with a chancel of 12th-century origin and a 13th-century nave, the walls retaining important 14th and 15th-century paintings.

TARRANT GUNVILLE

 (1) THE PARISH CHURCH of St. Mary, with a 14th-century W. tower, and interesting wall-arcading of *c.* 1100, discovered in 1843 and reset.

TARRANT HINTON

 (1) THE PARISH CHURCH of St. Mary, with a 14th-century nave, a 15th-century S. aisle and W. tower, and an important 16th-century Easter Sepulchre.

TARRANT MONKTON

 (1) THE PARISH CHURCH of All Saints, of 15th-century origin, with 18th-century restorations.

TARRANT RAWSTON

 (1) THE PARISH CHURCH of St. Mary, probably of 14th-century origin, and with 16th and 18th-century additions.

TARRANT RUSHTON

 (1) THE PARISH CHURCH of St. Mary, of 12th-century origin, with 14th-century additions.

TODBER

 (2) CROSS-SHAFT of the late 10th or early 11th century.

WEST STOUR

 (1) THE PARISH CHURCH of St. Mary, with a 13th-century chancel.

SECULAR :

CHETTLE

 (2) CHETTLE HOUSE, of *c.* 1710, an interesting building with baroque characteristics, probably designed by Thomas Archer.

IWERNE MINSTER

 (3) WEST LODGE, with a handsome 18th-century S.E. front.

 (7) 'THE CHANTRY', a small early 17th-century house.

KINGTON MAGNA

 (7) LOWER FARM, a late 17th-century house with a well-proportioned S. front.

MARGARET MARSH

 (4) HIGHER FARM, a 15th-century farmhouse with the hall originally open to the roof, but chambered over in the 16th century.

MOTCOMBE

 (3) NORTH END FARM, an early 17th-century farmhouse retaining interesting original features.

SHAFTESBURY

 (51) THE SHIP INN, a small 17th-century town house.

 (68–75) GOLD HILL, a picturesque thoroughfare flanked on the W. by the mediaeval boundary wall of the abbey, and on the E. by 17th and 18th-century cottages.

STOUR PROVOST

 (4) CHURCH HOUSE, an early 17th-century dwelling with interesting interior fittings.

 (5) DIAMOND FARM HOUSE, of the early 17th century.

TARRANT CRAWFORD

 (3) TARRANT ABBEY HOUSE, incorporating a small early 15th-century building, presumably part of the former abbey.

 (5) FARM BUILDINGS of the late 15th century.

TARRANT GUNVILLE

 (2) EASTBURY HOUSE, incorporating the remains of an 18th-century mansion, a monumental archway and park gate-piers, all designed by Vanbrugh.

TARRANT HINTON

 (3) THE OLD RECTORY, of *c.* 1850, in the revived 'Tudor' style by Benjamin Ferrey.

MEDIAEVAL AND LATER EARTHWORKS :

 Note: The rapid and widespread destruction of field monuments continues to be a cause of anxiety. All field monuments listed in the Inventory of North Dorset should be treated with care, not only on account of their increasing rarity, but also because the extent and impressiveness of surface remains do not by themselves indicate a monument's archaeological importance ; this can be revealed only by excavation. Destruction should never be allowed until competent archaeological investigation has taken place.

MOTCOMBE

 (20) MOAT AND BANKS, remains of an early 13th-century royal hunting-lodge.

SHAFTESBURY

 (138) CASTLE, remains of a small 12th-century fortification.

TARRANT GUNVILLE

 (30) PARK PALE.

ROMAN AND PREHISTORIC MONUMENTS :
 See note under Mediaeval Earthworks.

FONTMELL MAGNA

 (33, 34) CROSS-DYKES, on the crest of Fore Top, notable for their good state of preservation.

IWERNE MINSTER

 (15) IRON AGE SETTLEMENT SITE and ROMAN VILLA.

TARRANT GUNVILLE

 (32) HILL FORT, of Iron Age date, the only example to survive in the area covered by this Report.

TARRANT HINTON

 (24) PIMPERNE LONG BARROW, perhaps the finest Neolithic long barrow in Wessex.

TARRANT KEYNESTON

 (16) BUZBURY RINGS, an unusual enclosed settlement of Iron Age and Romano-British date.

11. Our criteria in compiling the foregoing lists have been architectural and archaeological importance (subject to the reservation expressed in the note to *Earthworks* above), rarity, and the degree of loss that would result from destruction, always bearing in mind the extent to which the Monuments are connected with or are illustrative of the culture, civilisation and conditions of life of the people, as required by Your Majesty's Warrant. We have taken no account of such circumstances as cost of maintenance, usefulness for present-day purposes, or difficulty of preservation.

12. We wish to express our appreciation of the work done by our executive staff in the production of this Inventory : by the editor, Mr. G. U. S. Corbett, and by our investigators, Messrs. R. W. McDowall, N. Drinkwater, H. C. Bowen, T. W. French, W. E. Mercer, J. E. Williams, C. F. Stell, D. J. Bonney, C. C. Taylor, Dr. B. E. A. Jones, and Mr. J. N. Hampton ; also by our illustrators, Mr. A. L. Pope and Mrs. G. M. Lardner-Dennys, and by our photographers, Messrs. W. C. Light, R. E. W. Parsons, and C. J. Bassham. The index was compiled by Miss M. Meek.

13. We also wish to acknowledge the valuable and constant assistance rendered by our Secretary and General Editor, Mr. A. R. Dufty, whom Your Majesty has lately been pleased to appoint a Commander of the Most Excellent Order of the British Empire.

14. It is hoped that the final Inventory in the Dorset series, recording the Monuments of twenty-five parishes in the eastern part of the County, may be submitted to Your Majesty in 1974.

Signed :

SALISBURY (*Chairman*)	A. J. TAYLOR
J. W. WELD	W. F. GRIMES
H. C. DARBY	M. W. BARLEY
C. A. RALEGH RADFORD	S. S. FRERE
JOHN SUMMERSON	R. J. C. ATKINSON
FRANCIS WORMALD	J. BETJEMAN
H. M. COLVIN	J. N. L. MYRES
D. B. HARDEN	
W. A. PANTIN	A. R. DUFTY (*Secretary*)

Mediaeval floor-tiles in
Shaftesbury Abbey Church

ABBREVIATIONS USED IN THE VOLUME

Ant. J.	*The Antiquaries Journal.*
Arch.	*Archaeologia.*
Arch. J.	*The Archaeological Journal.*
B.A.P.	Abercromby, J., *Bronze Age Pottery* (1912).
Barrow Diggers	Wools, C., *The Barrow Diggers* (1839).
B.M.	The British Museum.
Cambridgeshire I	R.C.H.M., *Inventory of Cambridgeshire*, Vol. I (1968).
C.T.D.	Warne, C., *Celtic Tumuli of Dorset* (1866), in three parts, each separately paged : Pt. 1, *My own Personal Researches* ; Pt. 2, *Communications from Personal Friends* ; Pt. 3, *Tumuli Opened at Various Periods.*
C.U.A.P.	Air photographs taken by Dr. J. K. S. St. Joseph for the Committee for Aerial Photography, Cambridge University.
Cunnington MS.	Notes by E. Cunnington, *c.* 1890, in D.C.M. ; published in part in *Dorset Procs.*, XXXVII (1916).
D.B.	Domesday Book ; *V.C.H., Dorset III.*
D.C.M.	Dorset County Museum, Dorchester.
D.C.R.O.	Dorset Record Office, Dorchester.
Dorset I, II etc.	Other volumes of the present work.
Dorset Barrows	Grinsell, L. V., *Dorset Barrows* (Dorchester, 1959).
Dorset Procs.	*Proceedings of the Dorset Natural History and Archaeological Society* (Dorchester, 1879–).
Durden Catalogue	Payne, G., *Catalogue of the Museum of Local Antiquities Collected by Mr. Henry Durden* (Lewes, 1892).
Eyton	Eyton, R. W., *A Key to Domesday* (1878).
Fägersten	Fägersten, A., *Place Names of Dorset* (Upsala, 1933).
Feudal Aids	*Feudal Aids, 1284–1431* (H.M.S.O.).
Hutchins	Hutchins, John, *History and Antiquities of the County of Dorset*, 3rd edition (Westminster, 1861–70). When reference is necessary to the 1st and 2nd editions (1773 and 1803) this is specified, otherwise the 3rd edition is to be understood.
I.P.M.	*Inquisitions Post Mortem*, P.R.O. ; published in *S.D.N.Q.*, VIII–XXII.

J.B.A.A.	*Journal of the British Archaeological Association.*
J.R.S.	*The Journal of Roman Studies.*
L. & P.	*Letters and Papers, Foreign and Domestic* (H.M.S.O.).
Meekings	Meekings, C. A. F., *Dorset Hearth Tax Assessments* (Dorchester, 1951).
Nightingale	Nightingale, J. E., *Church Plate of Dorset* (Salisbury, 1889).
N.M.R.	The National Monuments Record.
Notes & Queries	*Notes and Queries for Readers . . .* (London, 1850–).
O.D.	Ordnance Datum ; mean sea-level.
O.S., 1811	Ordnance Survey, *Map of Dorset*, scale 1 inch to 1 mile, edition of 1811.
Oswald	Oswald, A., *Country Houses of Dorset* (1959).
P.P.S.	*Proceedings of the Prehistoric Society.*
P.R.O.	The Public Record Office, London.
P.S.A.	*Proceedings of the Society of Antiquaries of London.*
Raven	Canon Raven, *Church Bells of Dorset* (Dorchester, 1906) ; see also Walters, H. B., *Dorset Procs.*, LX, 97–120.
R.C.H.M.	The Royal Commission on Historical Monuments (England).
Sarum Dioc. Regy.	Salisbury Diocesan Registry.
S.D.N.Q.	*Notes and Queries for Somerset and Dorset* (Sherborne, 1890–).
Subsidy Rolls	*Lay Subsidy Rolls, 1327, 1333* ; P.R.O., E/179/103/4 and E/179/103/5 ; MS. copy in D.C.M. Generally, in this Inventory, the dates 1327 and 1333 may be taken to refer to these sources without further indication.
Sumner	Heywood Sumner, *The Ancient Earthworks of Cranborne Chase* (London, 1913).
V.C.H.	*The Victoria History of the Counties of England.*
W.A.M.	*The Wiltshire Archaeological and Natural History Magazine* (Devizes, 1854–).
Wessex from the Air	by O. G. S. Crawford & A. Keiller (Oxford, 1928).

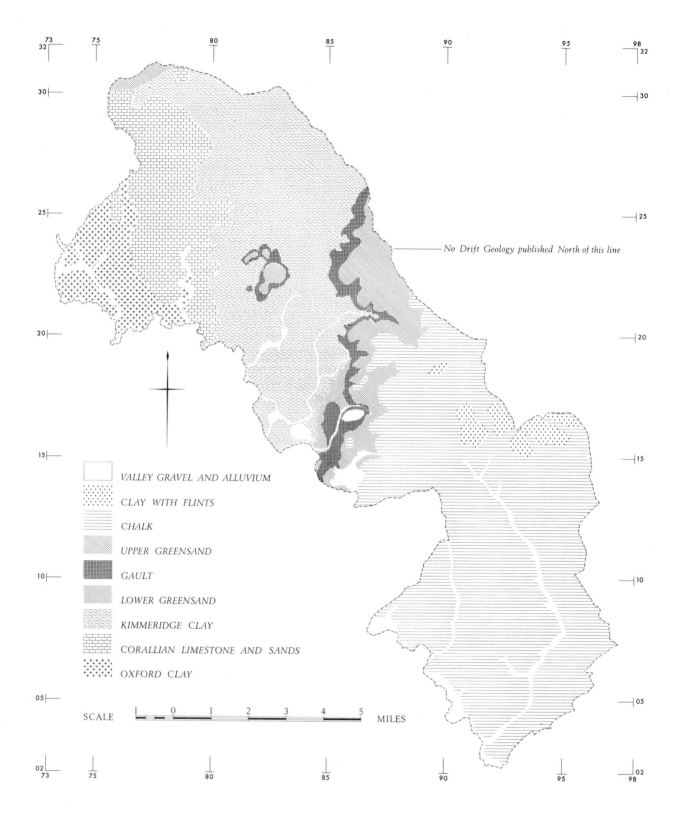

No Drift Geology published North of this line

VALLEY GRAVEL AND ALLUVIUM

CLAY WITH FLINTS

CHALK

UPPER GREENSAND

GAULT

LOWER GREENSAND

KIMMERIDGE CLAY

CORALLIAN LIMESTONE AND SANDS

OXFORD CLAY

SCALE   1   0   1   2   3   4   5   MILES

GEOLOGICAL MAP OF NORTH DORSET

DORSET IV

SECTIONAL PREFACE

In the preface, numbers in square brackets refer to the Plates ;
those in round brackets denote the Monuments in the Inventory.

TOPOGRAPHY AND GEOLOGY

THE FOURTH VOLUME of the Dorset County series, somewhat smaller than the preceding volumes, describes the ancient and historical monuments of thirty-four parishes in an area of 102 square miles
lying on or near the N.E. boundary of the county, between its northernmost point and Cranborne Chase,
and thence extending southwards to include the parishes of the Tarrant valley.

The underlying geological formation (map opposite) gives rise to two distinct geographical areas
divided by the Chalk Escarpment, which here runs almost due N.–S. The Jurassic Beds in the western
area are generally low-lying ; most of the land is Kimmeridge and Oxford Clays, rarely exceeding 250 ft.
in altitude. In only two places are there higher and more marked physical features. One, an outcrop of
Corallian Limestone near the W. extremity of the area, forms a clearly defined westward-facing scarp,
extending from N. to S. and rising to an altitude of 440 ft. The other, Duncliffe Hill, a massive Greensand
outlier of the main escarpment, rises almost to 700 ft. above sea-level some 2 miles W. of Shaftesbury.
The western area is drained by the south-westward flowing R. Stour, and its tributaries, the R. Lodden
and the Filley, Chiverick, Manston and Fontmell brooks.

The eastern area comprises the Chalk lands of Cranborne Chase, defined on the W. by the 300-ft. high
Chalk and Greensand Escarpment, which rises on Melbury Hill to a maximum altitude of 862 ft. above
sea-level. Eastwards, on the dipslope, the land falls gradually to about 200 ft., where Eocene deposits
overlie the Chalk. The dipslope is intersected by a series of southward flowing streams, giving rise to a
rolling landscape of broad, open valleys with high, rounded interfluves. The smaller of these valleys,
and also one major valley in Pimperne, are dry ; the others have permanent watercourses.

BUILDING MATERIALS

Most of the building materials noted in Central Dorset occur also in North Dorset and the general
remarks in the former volume (*Dorset* III, xxxv) apply also in the present area. In the Jurassic zone on
the W., rubble and ashlar of Corallian Limestone are the commonest materials for the walls of all buildings.
Original roof-coverings were of stone-slate or thatch, although many buildings have been reroofed with
other materials. In Gillingham, where the land is partly Corallian Limestone and partly Clay, all early
buildings are of rubble, but brick appears to have come into use early in the 18th century. In Motcombe,
where both Clay and Greensand are plentiful, older houses are of squared Greensand rubble ; brickwork
was being used as a ' show ' material for façades [29] by about 1750. In the parishes which lie astride the
Chalk escarpment, buildings are almost all of Greensand ashlar or squared rubble, occasionally with ornamental banding of flint ; notable exceptions to this rule are the Roman villa at Iwerne Minster, which is
wholly of flint [48], and a few 16th-century houses in the same parish and in Fontmell Magna which have

timber-framed walls. Timber-framework, however, is rare in North Dorset and a 15th-century building at Tarrant Crawford (3), in the extreme S. of the area, is the only other example noted.

Above the escarpment, on the Chalk dipslope, the walls of 'vernacular' buildings are usually of cob, or of flint with rubble or brick quoins; roofs generally are thatched. A mansion erected at Chettle in *c.* 1710 is of brick [36], and several 18th-century brick cottages are found in the same parish, presumably because the kilns set up to make bricks for the great house continued to be worked for a time. Churches and other large buildings in the area usually have flint walls with dressings of Greensand ashlar; cottages at Tarrant Gunville have walls of reused ashlar, no doubt salvaged from the demolition of Vanbrugh's mansion at Eastbury, *c.* 1782. Lower down the Tarrant valley the commonest building materials are cob and flint, the latter with quoins of rubble or of brickwork. Heathstone is occasionally found in the S. of the valley.

ROMAN AND PREHISTORIC MONUMENTS
(*See* Distribution Map in end-pocket)

ROADS

The Roman road from Badbury Rings to Bath traverses several parishes in the east of the area. It is reserved for description in the fifth volume, where the Roman roads of the county will be treated integrally.

SETTLEMENTS AND ENCLOSURES

Twenty-two such sites are known in the area, nearly all of them levelled, or at least severely damaged by ploughing. The majority are enclosures, not certainly all settlements, ranging in size from one to twenty acres and so far undated by excavation or surface finds. Probably most of them are of the Iron Age, or at least are in the native Iron Age tradition, although some may well have continued in use in the Roman period or may even have been constructed then. All these sites lie on the Chalk, between 200 ft. and just over 400 ft. above O.D.; seven of them occupy spurs, a position much favoured by Iron Age settlements, the others are on or near hill-tops.

Of the sites which have yielded datable material, most lie on the Chalk, on or near hill-tops, and are comparable both in elevation and aspect with the undated enclosures. On the other hand the Roman villa, Iwerne Minster (15), on a site already occupied in the later Iron Age, lies in a valley-bottom on the Upper Greensand, and the Romano-British settlement Gillingham (100) lies on the top of a low ridge of Corallian Limestone. Only one site, the eleven-acre enclosure Pimperne (15), can be ascribed with certainty to the Iron Age alone, and probably to the earlier part of that period; here, recent excavations have produced remarkably clear evidence of a large timber roundhouse similar to that of Little Woodbury, but without central posts. Presumably the hill-fort at Bussey Stool Park, Tarrant Gunville (32), is also of the Iron Age.

Five settlements have yielded evidence of both Iron Age and Romano-British occupation. Of them, only the Iwerne villa has been dated by large-scale excavations; the others are dated almost entirely by surface finds. At Iwerne, occupation was continuous from the later Iron Age to the 4th century A.D., and the limited evidence suggests that the same is true of the other sites. Morphologically the sites all differ to some extent one from another. Buzbury Rings, Tarrant Keyneston (16), comprises two roughly concentric enclosures, the inner enclosure containing the main occupation area. Tarrant Hinton (18) has two oval enclosures linked by a length of bank and ditch. At Tarrant Hinton (19) an open occupation area adjoins two or more enclosures. The settlement Chettle (14), now levelled by ploughing, appears to have been without enclosures. The extensive but sadly mutilated settlement on Blandford Race Down, Tarrant Launceston (14), has yielded no datable material, but is almost certainly Romano-British, possibly with Iron Age antecedents. Of exclusively Roman date is the large settlement on Barton Hill, Tarrant Hinton (17); it is as yet little understood, but it must surely be more than a villa.

DYKES

Seventeen dykes are known in the area, all on the Chalk; geographically they fall into two groups. In the north, in the parishes of Ashmore, Compton Abbas and Fontmell Magna, seven dykes, mostly cross-dykes, lie on spurs and ridges of the higher ground along and near the edge of the Chalk escarpment. Each dyke consists of a single bank and ditch, between 30 ft. and 45 ft. across, overall, with the bank-top rarely more than 6 ft. above the ditch-bottom. An exception is Ashmore (14), where the ditch is up to 8 ft. deep and is separated from the bank by a wide berm. None of these dykes has been examined by excavation and only Ashmore (16), which is cut by a Roman road, bears any obvious relationship to another monument. Vestiges of ' Celtic' fields survive in the vicinity of the dykes, but as yet no settlements are known. The other ten dykes lie to the south on the lower, more gently rolling downland of the parishes bordering the Tarrant brook. Nearly all of them are linear dykes between 600 yds. and 2,000 yds. in length; many have been flattened or severely damaged by ploughing, but where they survive they too are of modest dimensions. They tend to lie nearer settlements, enclosures and ' Celtic' fields than do the seven northern dykes, especially Tarrant Rawston (5) and the group in Tarrant Keyneston (17–21). The dykes of the last named group, unlike the other dykes, consist of twin banks flanking medial ditches; they are clearly associated with the Iron Age and Romano–British settlement at Buzbury Rings and with the ' Celtic' fields surrounding it.

It is obvious that these dykes were originally boundaries, and from their dimensions it is probable that they were peaceful boundaries between estates or units of land. None of them has the dimensions of a frontier work like Combs Ditch (*Dorset* III, 313), or Bokerly Dyke (*Dorset* V), but some of the cross-dykes may have served to control movement along the spurs and ridges.

FLAT BURIALS

In addition to the Bronze Age cremation cemetery in Tarrant Launceston, examined by C. Warne in 1840, which was probably flat, inhumation burials unmarked above ground have been found at four places in North Dorset. A burial in a lead coffin near Cann is certainly Roman, as are an unspecified number of inhumations near Melbury Hill, Melbury Abbas; the former burial was certainly on the Upper Greensand, the latter probably so. A single inhumation at Langton Long Blandford is probably Roman. Of greater interest, however, is a cemetery found in 1868 during the quarrying of the Corallian Limestone at Langham near Gillingham. At least one hundred extended inhumations were found, all with heads to the west. Their number and orientation, and the almost total lack of recorded grave goods, suggest affinity with several sub-Roman Christian cemeteries in eastern Somerset, all within forty miles of this site.[1]

BARROWS

As in the two previous volumes, the barrows in each parish are described as far as possible in topo-graphical order from S.W.–N.E.; barrow-groups are given names of local derivation.

Eight Neolithic *Long Barrows* are recorded in the area, all on the Chalk except for Gillingham (102), which lies on Corallian Limestone. The long barrows vary in orientation between S.S.E. and E.N.E. and are sited either on the crests of ridges or on slopes facing generally eastwards. They differ markedly in length: four are a little over 100 ft., one is nearly 200 ft. and three are over 300 ft.; the latter are situated in the adjoining parishes of Chettle and Tarrant Hinton. Generally the mounds are well preserved, except

[1] P. A. Rahtz, ' Sub-Roman Cemeteries in Somerset ', *Christianity in Britain, 300–700* (ed. M. W. Barley and R. P. C. Hanson), 193–5.

for Tarrant Hinton (25) which has suffered from heavy ploughing. Ploughing, too, has obscured most of the side ditches, but they are well preserved at Tarrant Hinton (24) and at Tarrant Rawston (6). At least five of the long barrows were opened in the 18th and 19th centuries, with comparatively little result as far as it is possible to tell from the inadequate surviving records of these activities.

There are at least one hundred and thirty *Round Barrows* in the area, but nearly three-quarters of them have been damaged or levelled, mainly by ploughing. They all lie on the Chalk, the majority between 200 ft. and 400 ft. above O.D., on the low rounded interfluves of the dipslope. Two-thirds of the barrows and eight of the nine barrow-groups lie in the adjoining parishes of Pimperne, Tarrant Hinton and Tarrant Launceston. The groups are small, the largest comprising thirteen barrows. The Telegraph Clump group in Tarrant Hinton is the only one to include a long barrow.

The round barrows are all bowl-barrows, where their form may be determined at all, except Pimperne (22) and Tarrant Hinton (41) which are double-barrows, and Tarrant Launceston (46) which is a disc-barrow.

Several of the barrows have been dug into in the past, but such records of these activities as have been kept (chiefly of 19th-century date) are usually too brief to provide useful information; indeed it is seldom possible to relate an early excavation record with any certainty to an existing barrow. The excavations undertaken by S. and C. M. Piggott in 1938 on barrows in Tarrant Launceston are the only ones that have been adequately recorded; they yielded evidence of a variety of burials ranging from the late Neolithic to the Middle Bronze Age or later.

A small number of barrows appear from their contents, size or position to have pagan Saxon affinities. Three barrows in Tarrant Launceston, (17), (43) and (44), all on the parish boundary, have yielded burials which are probably pagan Saxon. Two groups of small mounds, now destroyed, Pimperne (31–35) and Tarrant Hinton (54), lay on either side of the parish boundary close to Pimperne Long Barrow; it has been suggested (*Dorset Barrows*, 125, 134) that they too are pagan Saxon.

MEDIAEVAL SETTLEMENT
(*See* Distribution Map in end-pocket)

The pattern, siting and morphology of mediaeval and later settlement in North Dorset is largely determined, as already observed for Central Dorset, by the two distinct physical landscapes of the area.

THE JURASSIC LANDS OF THE NORTH-WEST.

Generally, the settlements in this low-lying area are large nucleated villages, often surrounded by a scatter of outlying hamlets and farms. Geology to an exceptional degree has controlled the siting of the major, and also of many minor settlements. The spring-line at the foot of the Chalk and Greensand escarpments gives rise to a chain of nucleated villages from Iwerne Minster in the S. to Motcombe in the N.; among them, Shaftesbury alone is sited at the top of the scarp, probably because of its defensive role in Saxon times. To the W., the broad belt of Kimmeridge Clay is empty of major settlements; the two Orchards and Margaret Marsh, although now parishes, have never been more than scattered hamlets. The major villages of Gillingham and Milton-on-Stour owe their existence to river terraces. The Corallian Limestone escarpment, on the other hand, gives rise to two chains of major settlements; one, at the junction of the dipslope and the Kimmeridge Clay on the E., extends from Todber in the S. to Bourton in the N.; the other, at the western foot of the scarp, includes Fifehead Magdalen and Buckhorn Weston. These settlements have no common plan and most of them are irregular concentrations of lanes and cottages.

The outlying farmsteads and hamlets result mainly from a process of secondary settlement associated with piecemeal clearance of the waste beyond the open fields of the nucleated villages ; the process was certainly in operation before the 11th century. A remarkable example of piecemeal secondary settlement is seen in the Royal Forest of Gillingham, which extended in mediaeval times over the whole of what is now Motcombe parish and also over part of Gillingham parish. Hamlets and farms with small irregular fields in this area represent mediaeval encroachments along the edge of the Forest. The Royal Forest was finally disafforested in 1624 (*see* introduction to MOTCOMBE, p. 48, and map [56]).

THE CHALK LANDS OF THE SOUTH-EAST.

Until recently, settlement on the Chalk has been largely confined to the valleys of the dipslope. The only exception is Ashmore, perched high on the downs and drawing its water from a pond ; its siting, comparable with that of known Romano-British settlements in the region, may indicate that it too originated in the Roman period. Elsewhere the village plans, the earthwork remains of deserted settlements, and documentary evidence combine to show that the early mediaeval settlement-pattern consisted of chains of villages, hamlets and farmsteads spaced out along the bottoms of the valleys. In some cases, like Luton Farm in Tarrant Monkton, the original settlements have never grown ; in others the settlements, formerly larger, have been reduced ; yet others have developed extensively, resulting in long, linear villages like Farnham and Tarrant Keyneston. In narrow valleys the linear settlements consist of a single street parallel with the stream, as in Tarrant Gunville and Chettle ; in wider valleys two parallel streets are sometimes found, one on each side of the stream, as in Tarrant Monkton. As noted before (*Dorset* III, xliii), these chalk-land settlements are always associated with narrow strips of land running back from the watercourse, on one or on both sides of the valley. The boundaries of the strips are often preserved as continuous hedge lines.

MEDIAEVAL AND LATER EARTHWORKS

As in Central Dorset, the monuments of North Dorset under this heading are divided into three groups : settlement remains, cultivation remains, and miscellaneous mediaeval and post mediaeval remains. In preparing this volume, the limitations on documentary research have been as before (see *Dorset* III, footnote on p. xliv).

SETTLEMENT REMAINS

Without excavation, only documents can show the periods of shrinkage and desertion of mediaeval settlements, and such documents as exist are generally vague in this matter. Nowhere has reliable evidence for a substantial reduction of population been found ; in most of the sites, desertion appears to result from a slow process of shrinkage and gradual abandonment over a long period. Dated desertion occurs only at Tarrant Gunville, where cottages were removed early in the 19th century for the improvement of Eastbury Park. Almost all the settlement remains have the form of long closes bounded by low banks, with the house-site, where preserved, at the lower end of the close.

CULTIVATION REMAINS

Because of the geological background, fewer traces of mediaeval cultivation remain in North Dorset than in any other part of the county except the eastern heathlands (*Dorset* V). In the rolling downland of the Chalk dipslope, declivities are usually not steep enough for the development of strip lynchets ; it is only in parishes along the escarpment that these features are found. In the low-lying Jurassic area of the N.W. the remains of mediaeval cultivation are almost always ridge-and-furrow. Much of this evidence has been destroyed, or is now being destroyed, by modern methods of agriculture.

MISCELLANEOUS EARTHWORKS

The earthworks of Shaftesbury Castle appear to be the remains of a temporary fortification of 12th-century date. King's Court Palace in Motcombe is of interest, being the remains of a 13th-century royal residence ; its history and many details of its buildings are well recorded (*History of the King's Works*, II, 944-6). Extensive earthworks in Tarrant Gunville result from the abandoned formal gardens at Eastbury, laid out by Charles Bridgeman in the first half of the 18th century [72].

MEDIAEVAL AND LATER BUILDINGS

ECCLESIASTICAL BUILDINGS

The most important pre-conquest church in North Dorset must have been Shaftesbury Abbey, but it was rebuilt after the Conquest and nothing remains of the original structure ; the museum on the site of the later church contains a few stone fragments [3] with interlace carving, perhaps from the Saxon building. Built into the N. wall of Gillingham vicarage are two fragments, of unknown provenance, with 9th-century interlace ornament. Until 1838 Gillingham parish church may have retained the nave arcades of a Saxon church, but if so they were destroyed in that year. At Todber the remains of a stone cross with interlace and other enrichment of the late 10th or early 11th century came to light in 1879 and have been re-erected in the churchyard [2]. An important carved stone from a cross-shaft of about the same period, formerly at East Stour, has recently been taken to the British Museum.

The late 11th-century Abbey Church of Shaftesbury, demolished at the Dissolution and now repre-sented by little more than its foundations [60], was certainly the most important church of its period in North Dorset ; it was a cruciform building with an apsed presbytery, apsed N. and S. chapels, and apsed transepts. The work of building continued in the 12th century with the construction of an aisled nave, the finished church being larger than either Sherborne or Wimborne. Excavation of the abbey has been confined to the area of the church itself and a small part of the cloister ; nothing is known of the monastic buildings.

Iwerne Minster church, 5 miles S. of Shaftesbury and an ancient possession of Shaftesbury Abbey, appears to be of the mid-12th century ; the original church was probably cruciform, and of this early structure there remain the nave, part of the N. transept, the N. aisle and a building on the S. which is likely to have been a tower ; a S. aisle was added at the end of the century. Fragments of small 12th-century churches survive at Tarrant Crawford and Tarrant Rushton ; Tarrant Gunville retains a section of early 12th-century arcaded decoration [8], discovered when the church was rebuilt in the 19th century, and reset. The nave arcade at Silton [6] is of the late 12th century.

In the 13th century the parish church of Tarrant Crawford [68] was remodelled and enlarged, doubt-less in connection with the development of the abbey which had been established there at the end of the 12th century. The nuns' original cell may have been beside the old parish church, but there can be little doubt that a separate convent church was subsequently built on another site, in addition to the work undertaken at the parish church ; the convent church, however, has disappeared altogether. The N. transept at Iwerne Minster [6] and the chancel at West Stour have 13th-century features.

In the 14th century a large chancel, which still exists [4], was added to the presumed Saxon nave at Gillingham. The churches of Fifehead Magdalen, Buckhorn Weston [33] and Stour Provost in the westernmost part of the area also date from the 14th century, and in the Tarrant valley Hinton and Rushton have significant remains of the same period. The tower of Iwerne Minster church [49] is distinguished 14th-century work.

As in other parts of the county, the 15th and 16th centuries saw many improvements to churches. A fine tower was built at Kington Magna [1]; that of Iwerne Minster was crowned with a spire. Fontmell Magna church was embellished with carved parapets [10] and also with a tower; Tarrant Hinton church was enlarged and partly rebuilt. Church towers were built at Stour Provost, Farnham and Compton Abbas [33]. St. Peter's at Shaftesbury [7] is largely of this period. At Silton a small N. chapel was built and the S. aisle was rebuilt. The tower of Tarrant Crawford church is probably of 1508, and the S. transept and S. porch of Tarrant Rawston [5] appear to be later 16th-century work.

During the 17th century no significant church building took place in the area. In the 18th century Tarrant Rawston and Tarrant Monkton churches were repaired and to some extent rebuilt, in each case with care to preserve the 'mediaeval' character of the building; other examples of the 18th-century 'Gothic' style are the east window in the church at West Stour and a window in the church at Tarrant Keyneston, now reset in the vestry.

Little early 19th-century church building occurs in the area; the church consecrated at Bourton in 1813 was pulled down and rebuilt in 1880. In 1838 an ambitious project of enlargement at Gillingham caused the destruction of the nave, presumed to have been Saxon; the spacious building which took its place was the first attempt in North Dorset at the revival of Gothic church architecture. St. Rumbold's at Shaftesbury and the nave of West Stour church were built in 1840. Essays in the Romanesque style at East Stour in 1842 and at Enmore Green, Shaftesbury [5] in 1843, yielded interesting results, and already in 1841 Gilbert Scott had demonstrated the possibilities of the Gothic style at Holy Trinity, Shaftesbury [63]. George Alexander's churches at Motcombe and Sutton Waldron [63], both of 1847, appear to profit from Scott's example; Sutton Waldron, indeed, recaptures the mediaeval style as successfully as any 19th-century church in the county.

CHURCH ROOFS

Mediaeval stone vaults occur only at Shaftesbury and at Silton, both of small size. The Shaftesbury vault [10] is in the W. porch of St. Peter's church and has lierne tracery with carved bosses of late 15th-century date; that at Silton covers the N. chapel and has fan tracery of *c.* 1500.

A 16th-century oak ceiling with fretted panels on moulded intersecting beams [66] survives at Stour Provost. At Silton the nave, S. aisle and S. porch have wagon roofs of *c.* 1500. In St. Peter's, Shaftesbury, the nave and N. aisle have low-pitched 16th-century roofs with moulded and cambered beams, and moulded wall-plates and ridge-beams; these members have recently been incorporated in a modern concrete roof.

Plain 18th-century barrel-vaulted ceilings are found in the churches at Tarrant Monkton and Tarrant Rawston.

CHURCH FITTINGS ETC.

Altars: Mediaeval stone altar slabs remain at Gillingham and at Todber.

Bells: The oldest bell in the area, the 4th at Iwerne Minster, is probably of the early years of the 14th century and from a London foundry (*Dorset Procs.*, 60 (1938), 99). Three bells at Chettle are of *c.* 1350, as probably is a small bell at Gillingham with 'GABREEL' in Lombardic letters. The Kington Magna tenor, probably of the second half of the 14th century, has an invocation to St. George in crowned Lombardic letters. Interesting 15th-century bells include the 5th and 6th at Fontmell Magna, the 4th at Tarrant Keyneston, and the 2nd and 3rd at Stour Provost. The Salisbury bell-founders of the late 16th and 17th centuries, Wallis, Danton, Tosier and the Purdues, are well represented in the area (Raven, 149–154).

Brasses: There are only two notable brasses [14]. Langton Long Blandford has the inscription plate, figures and shield-of-arms of John Whitewood and his two wives, probably engraved soon after 1467 and preserved in a 19th-century indented slab. Pimperne has a rectangular brass plate in memory of Dorothy Williams, 1694, with a quaint representation of the soul rising from the death-bed ; the engraver was Edmund Culpeper.

Chandeliers : Fifehead Magdalen church has four 18th-century hanging brass chandeliers, each with sixteen sconces on scrolled arms radiating from globular pendants [39].

Carved Stonework : Apart from the pre-conquest carvings mentioned above, the earliest architectural sculpture in the area is at Shaftesbury Abbey. Noteworthy in the large collection of carved fragments collected there during the excavations is the base of a small 11th-century Purbeck marble attached shaft, with cable enrichment and delicately carved cinquefoil brattishing (drawing, p. 61) ; there also are numerous simpler bases and voluted capitals from other small columns.

A carving on the lintel of the S. doorway in Tarrant Rushton church, depicting an *Agnus Dei* flanked by throned figures [8], is probably of the early 12th century. Of the late 12th century are the S. doorway and the chancel arch at Pimperne [51], both reset in the 19th-century church ; in form the elaborately carved door-head resembles those of a group described in the preceding volume (*Dorset* III, xlviii) ; the chancel arch, with chevron ornament, springs from admirably carved shaft capitals [9].

The most notable 13th-century carving in the area is a small attached shaft with a stiff-leaf capital [9] and a hold-water base, set between two round-headed windows in the N. chapel at Iwerne Minster ; the windows are typical of the 12th century and the conjunction of styles is perplexing.

Of the 14th century are moulded corbels with ball-flower enrichment supporting the twin arches leading to the chapel on the N. side of the chancel at Gillingham ; externally the chancel has moulded string-courses similarly enriched, and a few 14th-century gargoyles.

Notable 14th-century stone carvings include small traceried panels [10] set in openings to squints in Tarrant Rushton church. Parapets at St. Peter's and at St. James's, Shaftesbury, include late 15th-century traceried stone panelling with bosses with heraldic and other devices. The parapet [10] reset in the N. wall of Fontmell Magna church, peopled with reliefs of armed men, also has heraldic devices and the letters of an inscription, now confused, which formerly included the date 1530. Several 15th and 16th-century church tower parapets are ornamented with carved gargoyles.

Communion Rails : The most noteworthy communion rails are in the parish church at Tarrant Hinton. Elaborately carved with flower-festoons and cherub-heads, and with turned and twisted balusters [21], they originally formed part of a larger set of rails made *c.* 1665 for Pembroke College chapel, Cambridge. They were transferred to Tarrant Hinton in *c.* 1880, when the chapel furnishings were rearranged.

Communion Tables : St. Peter's, Shaftesbury, has two interesting communion tables, neither of them now is in use as such ; one has heavy bulbous legs with acanthus enrichment and carved rails with the date 1631 on a cartouche ; the other is of *c.* 1700 and has arcuated rails, tapering legs with claw feet, and scrolled diagonal stretchers with a turned finial at the intersection. Tables of similar form have been noted at Winterborne Stickland and at Charlton Marshall in Central Dorset (*Dorset* III, l). Another notable 17th-century communion table is at West Stour [22].

Easter Sepulchre : One of the most important monuments in North Dorset is the finely carved stone setting for the traditional Easter arrangements in Tarrant Hinton church. Dating from *c.* 1536 it is embellished with Renaissance arabesques and other details, full of freshness and grace [77].

Effigies : The earliest effigy is a late 13th-century recumbent figure of a priest, discovered early in the 19th century on the site of Shaftesbury Abbey and reset in the S. porch of Holy Trinity church, Shaftesbury [15]. Buckhorn Weston has a 14th-century tomb with an interesting recumbent effigy of a man in civil dress [15]. A noteworthy tomb in Gillingham church has the recumbent effigies of Thomas and John Jesop (see *Monuments* and *Floorslabs*, below).

Floor Tiles : An important collection of inlaid tiles of the ' Wessex school ', dating probably from the second half of the 13th century, is preserved in Shaftesbury Abbey museum (drawings, pp. xviii, xxiii) ; other examples less well-preserved survive *in situ* on the floor of the abbey church and chapter-house. These tiles appear to have been manufactured locally ; they are associated stylistically with the tiles made at Clarendon Palace, Salisbury, *c.* 1250. Specimens of similar tiles are preserved in Tarrant Rawston church.

Fonts : [11, 12] The most important font in the area is the 12th-century example at Fontmell Magna ; its tub-shaped stone bowl is enriched externally in high relief with a meandering scroll, with birds among the branches. A similar font at Compton Abbas is either a modern reproduction or an original monument entirely recarved. Pimperne has yet another font bowl of the same form, carved in relief with tendrils and scroll-work, with large flowers in the interstices and with bands of pellets above and below ; the sculpture is sharp and appears to have been extensively reworked, presumably in the 19th century ; the 19th-century tent-shaped stone font-cover is interesting.

East Stour, Tarrant Hinton and Tarrant Monkton have plain 12th-century fonts with square bowls with shallow round-headed panels on the sides, each bowl raised on a stout centre shaft and four small corner shafts. The parish church of Cann, dedicated to St. Rumbold and situated in Shaftesbury, has a well-preserved font of *c.* 1200, with a stout cylindrical stem, and a scalloped capital incorporated with the base of the bowl. Plain 14th-century fonts are found at Margaret Marsh and Motcombe. Buckhorn Weston, Stour Provost and St. Peter's at Shaftesbury have octagonal 15th-century fonts with trefoil-headed panelling on the sides. An unusual font, probably of 17th-century date, with a tub-shaped bowl, reeded in the upper part and gadrooned below, on a cylindrical shaft with octagonal mouldings above and below, has recently been installed in the Congregational chapel at Shaftesbury ; it came to light during the demolition of the Shaftesbury Poor-Law Institution and its history is unknown. Ashmore and Farnham have 18th-century stone fonts with baluster-shaped stems. At Fifehead Magdalen an 18th-century baluster supports a 15th-century bowl.

Gallery : A panelled gallery-front, formerly at the W. end of the nave in Buckhorn Weston church (Hutchins IV, 117), appears to be of the 18th century ; its six panels, with paintings of saintly figures, a Nativity and two landscapes, have been reset on the tower walls.

Glass : A few fragments of mediaeval stained glass survive in Margaret Marsh and Tarrant Crawford churches. Holy Trinity, Shaftesbury has a small stained glass panel with an epitaph of 1646, reset and extensively restored. A glass reliquary unearthed at Shaftesbury Abbey in *c.* 1902, dating perhaps from the 9th–11th century, though it may be later, is now in Winchester Cathedral (D. B. Harden in *Ant. J.,* XXXIV (1954), 188).

Images : At Buckhorn Weston church a small mediaeval figure, of stone, much eroded, is set in a niche in the gable of the S. porch. Reset in the S. aisle at Motcombe church is the lower part of a late mediaeval figure, probably the heavily draped legs of St. Catherine of Alexandria in traditional posture with an emperor as her footstool [15].

Lecterns : [13] Buckhorn Weston church has an oak lectern with a turned shaft and an inclined desk to which is chained an incomplete copy of *Reliquiae Sacrae Carolinae,* presented to the church in 1696. At East Stour the lectern desk rests on the wings of a finely carved pelican-in-piety [21], perhaps a finial from an 18th-century sounding-board (cf. Charlton Marshall, *Dorset* III, 58). It has been thought right to include in this inventory the unusual *art-nouveau* lectern at Tarrant Hinton, dated 1909.

Monuments and *Floorslabs :* The earliest named funerary monument in the area is the floorslab from the grave of Alexander Cater, with an inscription in Lombardic capitals, found during the excavation of Shaftesbury Abbey and now in the abbey museum ; it appears to be of the late 14th or early 15th century.

From the same site comes the floorslab of Thomas Scales, 1532, with an incised black-letter inscription. The epitaph of Thomas Daccomb, rector of Tarrant Gunville, 1549–1567, with deeply cut Roman lettering [23], is reset in the S. wall of the church.

Noteworthy 17th-century monuments include that of the brothers Thomas and John Jesop, 1615 and 1625, in the N. chapel of Gillingham church [42]; it comprises a mural table-tomb with the brothers' effigies side-by-side, Thomas under a wall-arch with his epitaph, now gone, painted in a small panel, John towards the front of the table-tomb under a separate stone archivolt, with his epitaph on a marble tablet suspended from the keystone [23]. Other 17th-century monuments include the glass panel of William Whitaker, 1646, and the heavily enriched cartouche [18] of John Bennett, 1676, both in Holy Trinity, Shaftesbury. The stone wall-monument of Robert Fry, 1684, in Iwerne Minster church [16], has carving of distinguished quality. The most important funerary monument in North Dorset, however, is the grand work [65] by Nost in Silton church, in memory of Sir Hugh Wyndham, 1684, in which a statue of the judge, flanked by mourning figures, stands under a rich canopy supported on spiral columns; the monument was transferred in 1869 from the chancel to a newly-built niche on the N. side of the nave.

An interesting 18th-century wall-monument is that of Sir Henry Dirdoe, 1724, in Gillingham church [17]; it is signed by John Bastard, the architect of Blandford Forum parish church (*Dorset* III, 19). Another fine wall-monument at Gillingham is in memory of Frances, 1733, the youngest of Sir Henry Dirdoe's ten daughters [43]. The most impressive 18th-century wall-monument in the area is that of the family of Sir Richard Newman in Fifehead Magdalen church [41]; by an unknown sculptor, it is of white and coloured marbles and has admirable busts of the baronet, his wife and son, and portrait medallions [20] of his three daughters; it occupies one wall of a 'chapel' on the N. side of the chancel and appears to have been erected some time between 1747 and 1763. Other noteworthy 18th-century wall-monuments are those of Samuel and Ann Clark, 1761, 1764, in Buckhorn Weston church [17], and of Elizabeth and George Chafin, 1762, 1766, in Chettle church [38].

Paintings: Tarrant Crawford church has wall paintings of the 14th and 15th centuries, including a series of early 14th-century panels depicting the acts of St. Margaret of Antioch, and a beautiful Annunciation of about the same date [67, 69]. Buckhorn Weston church has some 18th-century panels (see *Gallery*).

Plate: The paten at Buckhorn Weston [24], one of only three pieces of pre-reformation church plate to survive in Dorset, dates perhaps from between 1510 and 1520 (Nightingale, 85); it is punched with a mark having a circle in which is a cross with a pellet between each limb. The same parish has the oldest communion cup remaining in North Dorset, with the assay mark of 1562. Of numerous Elizabethan cups, that of Gillingham [24] is important for its large size and also for giving the name by which a group of similar vessels, by the same anonymous silversmith, is known (*Dorset* III, liii); the Gillingham vessel is the earliest and that at Tarrant Monkton [24] is the latest of this group. Gillingham also has two fine silver flagons, one [25] with the assay mark of 1681, the other of 1735.

Royal Arms in churches: [27] The three-dimensional representation of the arms of James I in Gillingham church, carved and painted with equal virtuosity on both front and back, is the oldest and also the most magnificent example in the area [*Frontispiece*]. St. James's, Shaftesbury, has a well-carved cartouche of the Stuart royal arms, designed to be seen from one side. Wooden panels painted with the arms of the Stuart kings are found at Motcombe, Kington Magna, Stour Provost and Todber. Other churches have panels painted with royal arms of the Hanoverian period, notably Ashmore, Holy Trinity in Shaftesbury, Iwerne Minster and Tarrant Rushton; the Shaftesbury example is signed 'M. Wilmot, 1780', that at Ashmore 'K. Wilmot, 1816', but they are closely similar in style. A pleasing 19th-century example occurs at Bourton.

Tables of Creed, etc. : Recently rediscovered and now reset in the chancel of Silton church are two slabs of Purbeck marble carved with the Lord's Prayer and the Creed, with well-proportioned and well-spaced lettering ; the inscriptions appear to be of the late 17th or early 18th century [23]. St. Peter's, Shaftesbury, is the only church in the area to retain an 18th-century reredos with shaped panels inscribed with Decalogue, Lord's Prayer and Creed [7].

Woodwork in churches : In addition to the communion-rails and communion-tables already discussed, North Dorset churches contain some other notable woodwork : Gillingham parish church retains a series of oak benches, probably of the 16th century, many with carved bench-ends with blind tracery and poppy-head finials, others square-headed [22] ; the backs of some of these seats are formed with oak panels carved to represent trefoiled niche-heads with elaborately crocketed finials. Similar panels are reused in the communion-table at Gillingham, and in a gallery front in the church at West Stour. St. Peter's church, Shaftesbury, has a few 15th-century square-headed bench-ends with blind tracery decoration ; it also possesses a small early 17th-century oak alms-box attached to the wall, with a bracket below, with foliate carving and an inscription ' Remember the Poore '.

Several churches retain polygonal oak pulpits of 17th and early 18th-century date [13], with panelled sides, some with chip-carving or with moulded rails ; an example at Iwerne Minster has neat reticulate carving on the panels.

Reset in the tower archway at Fontmell Magna is a 16th-century oak screen with linenfold panels below and traceried open woodwork above, enclosing busts in wreath surrounds (drawing, p. xii). The same church has ten early 17th-century carved oak panels incorporated with modern woodwork to form a closet.

PUBLIC BUILDINGS

There are few public buildings of note in the area. Shaftesbury Town Hall [61], in the revived Gothic style, dates from 1826-7 and appears originally to have comprised open arcaded market loggias in the ground and basement storeys, and rooms for civic purposes on the upper floor, but at a later date, probably in 1879 when a clock-tower was added, the arcades of the upper loggia were filled in to provide additional indoor accommodation. Gillingham retains a small early 19th-century stone lock-up, rectangular on plan.

The Free School of Gillingham, mentioned by the Commission for Charitable Uses in 1598, is represented by a room with a late 16th-century ceiling in a house with no other datable characteristics near the parish church. Nineteenth-century schools are noted at Ashmore, Melbury Abbas, Motcombe [28], Stour Provost and Shaftesbury.

Almshouses noted at Sutton Waldron and at Shaftesbury are of the 19th century and of small architectural importance. At Motcombe a late 17th or early 18th-century range of cottages (13) is called ' The Old Workhouse ', but its history is not recorded. The large 19th-century Poor Law Institution at Shaftesbury (99) has recently been demolished.

DOMESTIC BUILDINGS

In volume II of the Dorset Inventory, to lighten the task of cataloguing a multitude of 16th to 18th-century ' vernacular ' dwellings, a system of classification of typical ground-plans was provisionally set out (*Dorset* II, lxi-lxiv). The system was adopted in volume III and is again used in the present volume. For explanation of the several classes of plan the reader is referred to volume II, to the Inventory of Cambridge County (*West Cambridgeshire*, xlv-xlviii), and to P. M. G. Eden, in *East Anglian Studies* (1968), pp. 72-88. In the present volume the plan-types most commonly found are as follows :

Class F comprises a range of three rooms and a through-passage, with a fireplace in the middle room

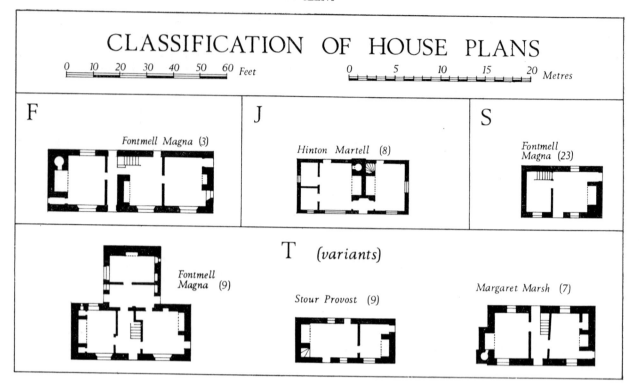

CLASSIFICATION OF HOUSE PLANS

0 10 20 30 40 50 60 *Feet*   0   5   10   15   20 *Metres*

F

Fontmell Magna (3)

J

Hinton Martell (8)

S

Fontmell Magna (23)

T *(variants)*

Fontmell Magna (9)

Stour Provost (9)

Margaret Marsh (7)

(hall) backing against the through-passage. A smaller fireplace often occurs on the gabled end-wall of the room (parlour) adjoining the middle room. The third room, separated from the middle room by the through-passage, is for service and is sometimes subdivided (pantry, buttery, kitchen etc.).

Class J houses are often more modest than those of class F, having a similar three-unit plan, but without the through-passage. Few examples survive in North Dorset.

Class S, the commonest type of 'vernacular' dwelling found in the area, consists of two rooms: a general living-room with an open fireplace set against one gabled end-wall of the range, and a room at the other end which may combine the functions of service-room and entrance-lobby, or it may be an unheated parlour.

Class T, distinguished by having a chimneystack on each gabled end-wall and none in the middle of the range, is in general a later form than those described above; in North Dorset the plan became common in 18th-century building, but earlier was not often used. Occasionally the T-class plan has an original wing at the rear of the range.

No complete example of a *mediaeval* dwelling place survives in North Dorset. 'King's Court Palace', a 13th-century royal hunting-lodge in the Forest of Gillingham, is now a rectangle of earthen mounds and ditches (Motcombe (20)). Of the Benedictine nunnery at Shaftesbury, once the richest in the land, practically nothing remains except the foundations of the church. The Cistercian nunnery at Tarrant Crawford is represented by the flint and stone outer walls of a small mediaeval building, presumably some part of the former abbey, with a timber-framed upper storey perhaps of somewhat later date. A cottage at Todber (5) incorporates part of a 15th-century building, but the remains are insufficient for analysis. At Margaret Marsh, a remote and secluded village where several interesting early farmhouses survive, Higher Farm (4) is of 15th-century origin; from the remaining parts of its original roof it appears to have comprised a small two-bay hall with an open hearth, with service rooms perhaps in two storeys at one end and presumably with a parlour at the other end, although all traces of the latter have gone. The construction of a central chimneystack and the chambering-over of the hall in the 16th century have, as usual, resulted in a class-F plan. Margaret Marsh has interesting 16th-century farmhouses at Church Farm (2) and at Gore Farm (7), the former with an unclassified plan, the latter of class T. A small town house at Shaftesbury (81) with a class-F plan is probably of c. 1500.

Noteworthy *16th-century* domestic buildings include Cross House, Fontmell Magna (9), in which the plan is a version of class T, with an original wing set at right-angles at the rear of the class-T range. It is not clear at Cross House if the wing was designed to contain a parlour, or service-rooms as at present, but in a comparable house at Shaftesbury (77) the rooms on both floors of the wing were clearly the best rooms in the house, having elaborate chimneypieces, carved panelling on the walls and an enriched ceiling ; many of these features were destroyed in recent ' improvements ', but they are recorded in the Commission's files. At Hope Farm, Buckhorn Weston (2), an original rear wing again appears in a 16th-century house, but this time in conjunction with a class-J plan.

An interesting early *17th-century* farmhouse is found at North End Farm, Motcombe (3), formerly called ' Easthaies ' and noted by that name on a map of c. 1624. The plan clearly derives from the mediaeval kitchen-hall-parlour arrangement, evolved through the class-F plan, but further formalised by the removal of the hall fireplace and the staircase to a turret at the rear of the range. Great care has been taken in the design of this house to achieve symmetry in the main elevations [53], providing a nice example of the application of classical principles to a building which in other respects retains traditional mediaeval characteristics. At Iwerne Minster (7), ' The Chantry ' provides another example of early 17th-century innovation. Basically the plan is the humble class I (see *Dorset II*, lxiii), enlarged to make it suitable for a well-to-do owner, and with a comparatively spacious staircase accommodated in a projecting wing ; advantage is taken of the sloping terrain to site the service rooms in a half-underground lower storey. Again the designer has been at pains to achieve a symmetrical elevation [52].

Lower Hartgrove Farm, Fontmell Magna (18), has an unusual L-shaped plan in which the original function of the rooms is perplexing ; the presence of two original staircases and perhaps even of two ovens implies occupation by two families, even though there is no solid wall to divide the tenements. Church House, Stour Provost (4) is a good specimen of a superior class-F house in which the kitchen and parlour are defined on the main front by gabled projecting bays. A town house in Shaftesbury (102) has an unusual plan, a variant of class F wherein the positions of parlour and service-rooms are interchanged. Lastly among 17th-century houses may be mentioned a handsome farmhouse at Lower Farm, Kington Magna (7), which has a sophisticated symmetrical façade with classical embellishments [53] ; the house has been gutted and the plan is lost, but the two end-wall chimneystacks imply that it was of class T, with a projecting wing at the back for the main staircase, as in Motcombe (3).

The most important *18th-century* house to survive is Chettle House [36], a large building of c. 1710 with a baroque plan, almost certainly by Thomas Archer ; although the house was remodelled in 1846 and again in 1912 the elevations are as originally designed, except in one particular, and the house retains a fine 18th-century staircase. Of even greater importance than Chettle was Eastbury (Tarrant Gunville (2)), a vast baroque mansion by Vanbrugh, built between 1717 and 1738. Most of the building had been pulled down by the end of the 18th century and there remain only some relatively minor parts of two stable ranges, adapted to form a smaller country house [70], also a splendid archway [80], the park gateway [70], minor fragments of buildings, and traces of the 18th-century gardens designed by Bridgeman. West Lodge, Iwerne Minster (3), a house with a tetrastyle façade [44], is of 18th-century origin if not earlier, but enlarged and much altered during the second half of the 19th century. Smaller 18th-century houses in the area include Pensbury House, Shaftesbury (126) ; Higher Langham House, Gillingham (59) ;

and Gunville House, Tarrant Gunville (3). Comfortable 18th and 19th-century parsonages are noted at Ashmore (3), Pimperne (4) and Shaftesbury, St. James (100), also [74] at Tarrant Gunville (4) and Tarrant Hinton (4).[1]

Of large *19th-century* houses in the classical style only two fall within the Commission's purview: Fifehead House, Fifehead Magdalen (5), of 1807, and Langton House, Langton Long Blandford, of 1827–33. Both houses have been demolished, but the former [44] was recorded before demolition and is described in the inventory. We give no account of Langton House,[2] but the stables and other outbuildings are recorded. Wyke Hall, Gillingham (58) incorporates a small 17th-century house, but the greater part of the building is of 1853 and later.

FITTINGS IN SECULAR BUILDINGS

Ceilings : Higher Farm, Margaret Marsh (4), supplies evidence of an early type of ceiling in the form of wattles fastened to the under side of the common rafters in the roof of the 15th-century hall. The hall is now chambered over and ceiled at a lower level than originally, and the early ceiling is preserved in the roof-space.

Few 16th-century moulded plaster ceilings are found. An example occurred at Ox House, Shaftesbury (77), where the ceiling of the chamber in the N. wing had embossed sprays of foliage and Tudor roses in the angles of the moulded cornice, but this ceiling perished during recent 'improvements'. A fragment of an enriched ceiling of about the same date occurs in an 18th-century cottage at Bourton (21) ; it has embossed corner-pieces representing pomegranates, and strips of raised vine-scroll decoration on the margins ; pieces from a similar ceiling, possibly the same one, are reset in a cottage at Gillingham (75).

A plaster ceiling at Abbey House, Shaftesbury (89) is moulded in the late 16th-century manner with vine-scrolls, roses, thistles and various kinds of foliage ; the same ceiling, however, includes foliate scrolls of 18th-century aspect, suggesting that the whole work may be comparatively modern, possibly of the school of Ernest Gimson. If Chettle House had any 18th-century plasterwork it has perished, and all the enriched ceilings in the house today are of mid 19th-century date.

Moulded or chamfered ceiling beams with corresponding wall-plate cornices, often intersecting to form ceilings of four, six or nine panels, are found in many 16th or 17th-century farmhouses in the area ; the examples at Gore Farm, Margaret Marsh (7), have elaborate mouldings.

Doorways : A mediaeval stone doorway with a two-centred head remains, blocked up, in a cottage at Todber (5) ; no other mediaeval doorway survives in a secular building in North Dorset. The traditional stone doorway with a pointed head, modified stylistically first to a four-centred form and later to a shallow triangle, persisted well into the 17th century in stone-built dwellings in this area. The four-centred door-head from Tarrant Hinton rectory, with a 16th-century inscription (Hutchins I, 318), has been reset in the stable-yard of the house, rebuilt *c.* 1850. An early example of a square-headed doorway of classical form is seen at Lower Farm, Kington Magna (7), a late 17th-century building [53]. Among 18th-century houses, Higher Langham, Gillingham (59), and Pensbury House, Shaftesbury (126), have dignified door-ways with pediments etc. in classical style.

Fireplace Surrounds : The earliest decorated fireplace surround in the area is in a 16th-century cottage (5) at Fontmell Magna. It is of oak, with a moulded four-centred head, and probably with continuous jambs although the latter are obscured by modern fittings ; the spandrels of the head are filled with

---

[1] A rectory designed by W. J. Donthorn for Fontmell Magna (R.I.B.A. collection, W.13, pp. 48–9) is not found and perhaps was not built; the present Old Rectory is of 1871.
[2] Pouncy publishes a view of Langton House from the W. (*Dorset Photographically Illustrated*, 2, pl. 13).

triangular panels of foliate carving, one of them incorporating the monogram IP. A 16th-century stone fireplace surround with trefoil and quatrefoil panelled decoration is in an inn at Shaftesbury (20). Two interesting early 17th-century chimneypieces were formerly at Ox House, Shaftesbury (77); their stone surrounds with ogee-moulded and hollow-chamfered four-centred heads and continuous jambs ending at shaped stops, of mediæval pattern, were surrounded by plain friezes and projecting stone mantelpieces with classical mouldings; the stone jambs were flanked by Ionic pilasters of carved oak supporting panelled overmantels with arabesques, coupled colonettes and vine-scroll friezes. Elaborate early 17th-century carved oak overmantels are found at Wyke Hall, Gillingham (58), and at Chettle Lodge, Chettle (3), both of them brought from elsewhere. In Church House, Stour Provost (4), the chamber over the S. parlour retains a small original stone fireplace of *c.* 1600 with a moulded four-centred head, continuous jambs and shaped stops. At Diamond Farm, Stour Provost (5), the parlour has a fine 17th-century stone fireplace surround with a moulded four-centred head composed of large voussoirs. The hall in the same house has an open fireplace with a deep oak bressummer, slightly cambered and with an ovolo-moulding, and stone jambs with the same moulding.

The Old House, Gillingham (76), retains a 17th-century stone fireplace with a frieze carved in low relief and a moulded stone mantel-shelf with classical enrichment; Wyke Hall, Gillingham (58), has a stone fireplace of perhaps somewhat later 17th-century date, with rather more correct classical features, but retaining a 'mediaeval' four-centred head and shaped stops in vestigial form. Well-proportioned 18th-century stone fireplaces with good classical details are noted at Pensbury House, Shaftesbury (126), and at Higher Langham House, Gillingham (59). Fireplaces, overmantels, doorcases and other carved fittings of 18th-century date in the late 18th-century house at Eastbury, Tarrant Gunville (2), are thought to have been brought from Yorkshire during the 19th century. A late 18th-century fireplace and overmantel at Barton Hill House, Shaftesbury (38), is said to have been salvaged from William Beckford's 'Fonthill Abbey'.

Staircases : The 17th-century circular example at North End Farm, Motcombe (3), is probably the earliest domestic staircase to survive in N. Dorset. Other noteworthy 17th-century staircases with turned oak balusters and stout newel-posts with ball finials occur at Holyrood House, Shaftesbury (92), at ' The Chantry ', Iwerne Minster (7), and at Great House, East Orchard (5); Ox House, Shaftesbury (77), formerly had a good example with vase-shaped finials. Houses at Shaftesbury (37) and at Chettle (4) have 17th-century staircases in which the balustrades are formed with flat boards profiled to resemble balusters.

The most impressive staircase in the area is that of *c.* 1710 in Chettle House [40]; a central upper flight which formerly doubled back from the half-landing was removed in 1845, but in other respects the original woodwork is little altered. The staircase at Chettle Lodge, Chettle (3), closely resembles that of Chettle House and is probably of the same date; so also is the staircase in a house in Shaftesbury High Street (14). An early 18th-century staircase with spirally-fluted balusters, bolection-moulded panelling and a dog-gate occurs at Adcroft House, Bourton (4), and another noteworthy 18th-century example is found at Abbey House, Shaftesbury (89). The fist-shaped handrail volute noticed several times in Central Dorset (*Dorset* III, lxii) is not found in this area.

The staircase at Fifehead House, built in 1807 and demolished in 1964, had oak steps, a mahogany handrail, and a balustrade with iron uprights enclosing delicately wrought panels of foliate scrollwork cast in lead.

PLATE 1

KINGTON MAGNA CHURCH. W. Tower. Late 15th century

SAXON STONE CARVING

Late 10th or early 11th century

S. side.

N. side

E. side.

W. side.

TODBER. (2) Cross-shaft.

PLATE 3

SAXON STONE CARVING

EAST STOUR. Part of cross-shaft, formerly at E. Stour, now in the British Museum.

GILLINGHAM (2).
Fragment reset in Vicarage.

SHAFTESBURY ABBEY.
Fragment (2).

SHAFTESBURY ABBEY.
Fragment (4).

SHAFTESBURY ABBEY.
Fragment (1).

PLATE 4   CHURCH EXTERIORS

GILLINGHAM CHURCH, from S.E.   Early 14th century and 1838

TARRANT HINTON CHURCH, from S.   15th century and 1874

TARRANT RAWSTON CHURCH, from S.W.   Mainly 16th century

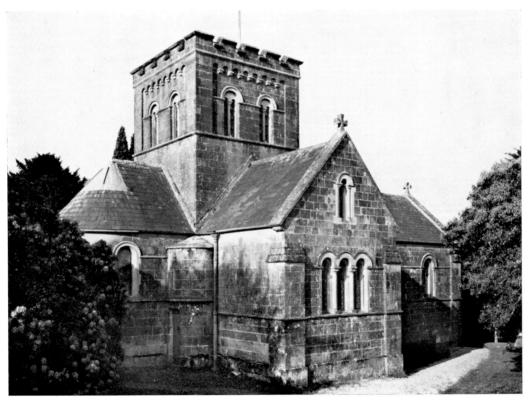

SHAFTESBURY. (5) St. John's Church, Enmore Green, from N.E.   1843

PLATE 6   CHURCH INTERIORS

SILTON CHURCH. Nave and chancel, looking S.E.   Late 12th century and later

IWERNE MINSTER CHURCH. N. transept, from S.E.   12th to 14th century

SHAFTESBURY. (2) St. Peter's Church. E. part of nave.   Late 15th and 18th century

PLATE 8

EARLY MEDIAEVAL STONEWORK

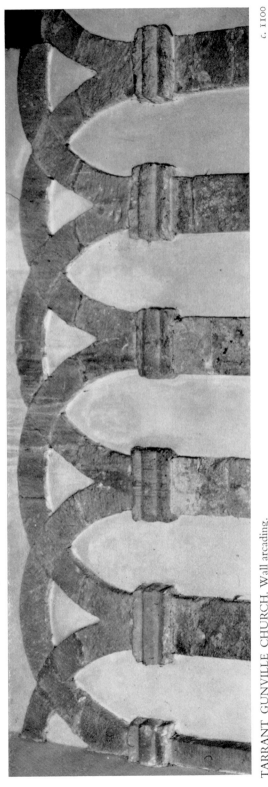

TARRANT GUNVILLE CHURCH. Wall arcading.

c. 1100

TARRANT RUSHTON CHURCH. Carved door-head.

Early 12th century

PLATE 9

EARLY MEDIAEVAL STONEWORK

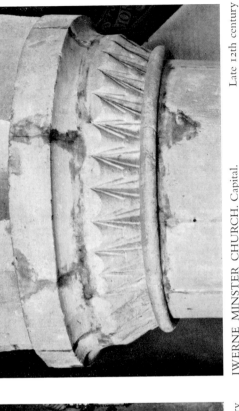

IWERNE MINSTER CHURCH. Capital.   Late 12th century

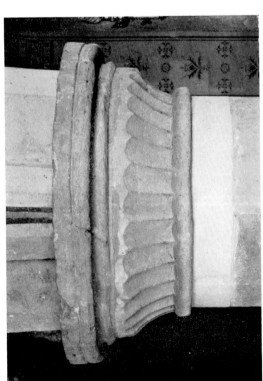

SILTON CHURCH. Capital.   Late 12th century

PIMPERNE CHURCH.
Respond capital of former chancel arch.   Late 12th century

IWERNE MINSTER CHURCH.
Capital in N. transept.   13th century

PLATE 10   LATER MEDIAEVAL STONEWORK

FONTMELL MAGNA CHURCH. Parapet reset on N. wall.   1530

SHAFTESBURY. (2) St. Peter's Church. Vault in W. porch.   Late 15th century

TARRANT RUSH-
TON.   14th century

SILTON CHURCH. Spandrel of porch arch.
Early 16th century

TARRANT RUSHTON.
14th century

SHAFTESBURY. (6) St. Rumbold's Church.
                                             c. 1200

FONTMELL MAGNA CHURCH.
                                      Mid 12th century

PIMPERNE CHURCH.
   12th century; cover and base, 19th century

TARRANT HINTON CHURCH.
      12th century; cover, 17th century

PLATE 12   PISCINA AND FONTS

TARRANT RUSHTON CHURCH.
Piscina.   14th century

SHAFTESBURY. (2) St. Peter's Church.
                                   15th century

SHAFTESBURY, (6A) Congregational Chapel.
                    17th century

FIFEHEAD MAGDALEN CHURCH.
                 15th and 18th century

TARRANT RAWSTON.   Early 17th century   IWERNE MINSTER.   Mid 17th century

BUCKHORN WESTON.   1696   FONTMELL MAGNA. 19th cent.   TARRANT HINTON.   1909

PLATE 14

BRASSES

SILTON CHURCH. Sir Hugh Wyndham.   1684

PIMPERNE CHURCH. Dorothy Williams.   1694

LANGTON LONG BLANDFORD CHURCH. John Whitewood.   c. 1467

PLATE 15

EFFIGIES etc.

BUCKHORN WESTON CHURCH. Monument (1).

Late 14th century

MOTCOMBE CHURCH.
Fragment.   15th century

SHAFTESBURY. (3) Holy Trinity Church. Monument (10).

Late 13th century

PLATE 16

WALL MONUMENTS

1684

IWERNE MINSTER CHURCH.
Monument (1) of Robert Fry.

1627

MOTCOMBE CHURCH.
Monument (2) of Elizabeth Webbe.

PLATE 17

WALL MONUMENTS

1779

GILLINGHAM CHURCH.
Monument (5) of Edward Read.

1761

BUCKHORN WESTON CHURCH.
Monument (2) of Samuel Clark.

1724

GILLINGHAM CHURCH.
Monument (1) of Sir Henry Dirdoe.

PLATE 18   WALL MONUMENTS

SHAFTESBURY. (3) Holy Trinity Church.
Monument (4) of John Bennett.   1676

CHETTLE CHURCH.
Monument (4) of Thomas Chafin.   1691

GILLINGHAM CHURCH.
Monument (14) of Mary Read.   1764

SHAFTESBURY. (3) Holy Trinity Church.
Monument (2) of Abraham Gapper.   1733

TARRANT KEYNESTON CHURCH. Monument of the Bastard family.   1731

SHAFTESBURY. (3) Holy Trinity Church. Monument (11) of Margaret Swyer.   1745

SILTON CHURCH. Monument (1) of Sir
Hugh Wyndham; weeper.   1684

GILLINGHAM CHURCH.
Monument (4) of Mrs. Francis Dirdoe; centre panel.   1733

GILLINGHAM CHURCH.
Monument (1) of Sir Henry Dirdoe; top roundel.   1724

FIFEHEAD MAGDALEN. Monument (2)
of the Newman family; medallion.   c. 1750

EAST STOUR CHURCH.
Pelican-in-piety reused in lectern.   18th century

TARRANT HINTON CHURCH.
Communion rails.   c. 1665

SHAFTESBURY. (7) The 'Byzant'.   18th century

PLATE 22

CARVED WOODWORK

WEST STOUR CHURCH. Communion Table.   17th century

SUTTON WALDRON CHURCH. Chest.   17th century

GILLINGHAM.
Bench-end. 16th cent.

GILLINGHAM
Bench-end. 16th cent.

FIFEHEAD MAGDALEN CHURCH. Door.   1637

PLATE 23

LETTERING

1625

GILLINGHAM CHURCH.
Monument (6) of John Jessop.

1567

TARRANT GUNVILLE CHURCH.
Monument (3) of Thomas Daccomb.

SILTON CHURCH.
Paternoster inscribed in Purbeck marble.

Late 17th or early 18th century

1638

SILTON CHURCH. Monument (3)
of Dorothy Kingeswell.

BUCKHORN WESTON. Paten.   *c.* 1510

BUCKHORN WESTON. Cup.   1562

GILLINGHAM. Cup and cover-paten.   1574

TARRANT MONKTON. Cup and cover-paten. 1607

ASHMORE. Cup and cover-paten.   1576   FIFEHEAD MAGDALEN.
                                                     Cup and cover-paten.   1573

GILLINGHAM. Flagon.   1681

PLATE 26

CIVIC PLATE

Detail of arms-plate.

Detail of arms-plate.

Mace.

Probably 16th century

Mace.

1604

SHAFTESBURY. (7) Civic maces.

PLATE 27

ROYAL ARMS IN CHURCHES

SHAFTESBURY.
(3) Holy Trinity Church.
1780

TARRANT RUSHTON CHURCH.
1825

IWERNE MINSTER CHURCH.
1814–1820

BOURTON CHURCH.
1814–1837

SHAFTESBURY.
(4) St. James's Church.
c. 1700

MOTCOMBE CHURCH.
17th century

PLATE 28   HOUSES

SHAFTESBURY. (76) Castle Hill House, from S.E.   18th century

MOTCOMBE. (2) School, from S.   1839

MOTCOMBE. (14) Cottages, from S.E.

18th and 19th century

SHAFTESBURY. St. James's Street, looking N.E.

Late 18th and early 19th century

PLATE 30

HOUSES

WEST STOUR. (4) Manor Farm.   c. 1800

BOURTON (53).   Late 18th or early 19th century

FIFEHEAD MAGDALEN. (7) Middle Farm.   17th century

GILLINGHAM (24).   Late 18th or early 19th century

PLATE 31

BUILDINGS FOR RURAL INDUSTRIES

SILTON. (8) Waterloo Mill and Cottage.   c. 1815

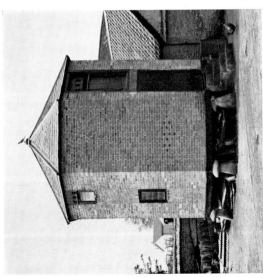

GILLINGHAM. (63) Granary.   19th century

MARGARET MARSH. (7) Gore Farm.   16th and 18th century

BOURTON. (5) Cloth Mill.   1820

PLATE 32

ASHMORE. Air view of Monuments near the centre of the village, from W.

AN INVENTORY OF
THE ANCIENT AND HISTORICAL MONUMENTS
IN NORTH DORSET

Arranged by Parishes

The group of four figures following each parish heading gives the position of the parish church on the National Grid, permitting easy location of the place on the one-inch O.S. map at the end of the volume. The next line indicates the sheets of the six-inch O.S. map (edition of 1960) which relate to the parish. Each Monument in the Inventory is located by a six or eight-figure reference to the National Grid.

In architectural descriptions of churches, the parts of the building are taken in the order E. to W. and N. to S.; in descriptions of houses the exterior precedes the interior. Architectural plans have a uniform scale of 24 ft. to the inch, except for a few key-plans at approximately 48 ft. to the inch. Hatching symbols used to indicate dating are uniform throughout the volume. All construction since 1850 is termed modern.

Information now impossible to verify and derived from literary sources, usually Hutchins, is enclosed in square brackets. The date given in the description of a funerary monument is that of the death of the person first commemorated; if known, the date of erection of the monument is added; surnames in round brackets are maiden names. The final volume of the Dorset Inventory will contain a general Armorial of the County.

'Celtic' Field Groups are described extra-parochially in a separate section (see p. 118); Roman Roads will be dealt with as a whole in the final volume of the Dorset series. These exceptions apart, the Monuments of North Dorset are listed below, under the names of the thirty-four Civil Parishes in which they occur.

1 ASHMORE (9117)

(O.S. 6 ins. ST 91 NW, ST 81 NE)

Ashmore, covering some 2,700 acres, lies entirely on Chalk above which in the S. and S.E. are extensive areas of Clay-with-flints. The land slopes down from 856 ft. above sea-level on Ashmore Down, at the N. corner of the parish, to less than 400 ft. in the S., dry valleys draining S. and S.W. into Stubhampton Bottom on the W. boundary. Extensive woods in the W. and S. are part of Cranborne Chase. The village (Plate 32) occupies a high spur between two of the valleys, at an altitude of 700 ft.; it is centred upon and takes its name from a large pond, rarely dry and probably the main reason for settlement; the situation resembles that of several Romano-British sites in the area (O. G. S. Crawford, *Antiquity*, II (1928), 184). The open fields, finally enclosed in 1859, lay around the village; until recently most of the land beyond the area of the fields was open down and woodland. Well Bottom, a small settlement in the S.E., appears to have existed in 1333; it lies beyond the former open fields and probably is secondary to Ashmore. In the E. of the parish, cutting through a pre-existing linear ditch, a well-preserved stretch of Roman road leads towards Badbury Rings. (E. W. Watson, *Ashmore, Co. Dorset, A History of the Parish*, Gloucester, 1890.)

ECCLESIASTICAL

(1) THE PARISH CHURCH OF ST. NICHOLAS was rebuilt in 1874. A two-centred archway of two plain orders with continuous jambs, opening into the N. vestry from the E. end of the N. aisle in the rebuilt church, is said to be the old chancel arch, reset. The arch may be of the 13th century, but since Hutchins (III, 370) says that the former chancel arch did not correspond with its piers, the responds must be of 1874. Fittings from the old church are incorporated in the present building.

Fittings—Chest: for registers, of cast-iron with panelled sides and top, early 19th century. *Communion Table:* of oak, with turned legs and moulded rails with chip-carving, 17th century. *Font:* with hemispherical bowl, stout baluster-shaped stem and round convex base, 18th century.

Monuments and *Floorslabs. Monuments:* Reset in vestry, (1) of Rev. George Chisholm, 1825, marble wall tablet with painted shield-of-arms; (2) of Elizabeth (Cary) Barber, 1738, baroque wall-monument with cherub-heads and drapery surround, surmounted by shield-of-arms. In churchyard, immediately S. of chancel, (3) of George Barber, 1662, stone slab with shield-of-arms; adjacent, (4) probably of Elizabeth Barber, 1738, stone slab. *Floorslabs:* In N. aisle, leaning against wall, (1) of John Mullens, 16.., broken and defaced. Reset as threshold at entry to vestry, (2) of [John Ca]rver, [1753], Purbeck marble slab with bold lettering, preserved in part.

Plate: includes Elizabethan silver cup and cover-paten (Plate 25), with assay-marks of 1576, cover-paten inscribed 1577. *Royal Arms:* painted on wood panel, in moulded surround, by K. Wilmot, 1816.

SECULAR

(2) SCHOOL (91321783), of one storey, with rubble and ashlar walls and slated roofs, was built in 1842. The original range has modern additions on the N.E. and S.W.

(3) OLD RECTORY (91301774), of two storeys, has walls of flint and rubble with ashlar dressings, and tiled roofs; it is of early 18th-century origin, with later enlargements and alterations. The N. front is symmetrical and of five bays; in the lower story an original doorway is flanked by coupled sashed windows of c. 1870, with chamfered jambs and segmental heads; in the upper storey are corresponding square-headed sashed windows. The doorway has a moulded stone architrave and a segmental broken pediment on scroll consoles. Inside, the plan is of class T. The staircase and chimneypieces are of c. 1870 or later, except for a chimneypiece of c. 1750 which has recently been brought from elsewhere.

(4) MANOR FARM (91051779), house, of two storeys with attics, has walls of ashlar and of squared rubble, and tile-covered roofs. The S.W. range is of uncertain date; the walls are up to 4 ft. in thickness and might be mediaeval, but there is no other feature to confirm this assessment; the unusual thickness of masonry could be the result of refacing a rubble or cob structure with ashlar. The demolition of Eastbury, c. 1782, must have made worked stone readily available locally. The S.W. front is two-storeyed and of four bays, with plain sashed windows and with a square-headed doorway; first-floor level is marked by a weathered string-course. The gabled S.E. elevation has a similar string-course, and, at the base of the gable, an ornamental corbel-table similar to that of the archway in the stable court at Eastbury (Plate 80). Projecting N.E. at the N.W. end of the range is an addition of c. 1800, originally built as a Wesleyan meeting room (F. Lyle Uppleby, Ashmore (1949), 8). Some rooms in the S.W. range have chamfered beams, probably of the 17th century.

(5) COTTAGE (91311778), of one storey with an attic, has walls of banded flint and rubble, and a thatched roof; probably it is of the 17th century. Inside, a large open fire-place has a chamfered bressummer, and there are chamfered beams with shaped stops.

(6) COTTAGE (91331777), of one storey with an attic, with walls of flint and rubble and with a thatched roof, is of the 17th century and has a class S plan. Inside, a chamfered beam with ogee stops is exposed. An addition with brick walls probably is of the early 18th century.

(7) COTTAGES (91351774), two adjacent, of one storey with attics, have walls of banded flint and ashlar, and thatched roofs; they are of the 17th century and perhaps originated as a single house. The S.W. elevation has an original stone doorway with a chamfered segmental head, and a stone window of three square-headed lights with hollow-chamfered jambs and heads. Inside, there are plank-and-muntin partitions and a chamfered beam.

(8) COTTAGE (91401768), of two storeys with rubble walls and a thatched roof, is of the 17th century. Inside, the plan is of class S, with a modern addition on the S.W. The original ground-floor room has two stop-chamfered beams.

MONUMENTS (9–12)

Unless otherwise described, the following late 18th and early 19th-century monuments are of two storeys and have walls of rubble, flint and brickwork, and thatched or slate-covered roofs.

(9) Cottage (91341788), has walls of flint and rubble, with ashlar quoins. The W. front is symmetrical and of three bays. Inside, one room has a chamfered ceiling beam, and an open fire-place, now blocked.

(10) Cottages (91191778), pair, have brick and rubble walls and thatched roofs. In each tenement, the S.E. front is of Flemish bonded brickwork and has two bays with segmental-headed casement windows, and a central doorway. A stone plaque is inscribed G.C. 1802.

(11) Cottage (91181776), with brick, rubble and rendered walls and with a slated roof, has a date-stone inscribed A.W. 1837.

(12) Cottages (91361773), pair, of one storey with attics, have walls of squared rubble. Each tenement has a class S plan.

MEDIAEVAL AND LATER EARTHWORKS

(13) CULTIVATION REMAINS. The open fields were enclosed in 1859 (Map and Award, D.C.R.O.). There were three fields: North Field, on the N. of the village, and Broadridge and Sandpit Fields, on the S.; they were approximately equal in size and their combined area was only 380 acres. In addition, there was a large area of enclosed fields which, even in 1590, covered 240 acres (S.D.N.Q., x (1907), 65). Fragmentary strip lynchets which exist ¼ m. N. of the village (911184) were formerly in North Field. Other strip lynchets E. of the village (915178) lie in an area which was enclosed before 1859.

ROMAN AND PREHISTORIC

The Roman Road from Badbury Rings to Bath passes through the E. part of the parish (see Dorset V).

'CELTIC' FIELDS, see p. 120, Group (78).

(14) CROSS-DYKE (90101854–90111886), near Hatt's Barn, lies across a ridge between 700 ft. and 800 ft. above sea-level and faces E.; it is cut by the modern road running S.W. from Win Green in Wiltshire. South of the road the dyke runs S.S.E. for 175 yds. and then, in Hatt's Copse, turns to run S.S.W. for a further 200 yds.; it ends halfway across a shallow combe falling south-eastward. North of Hatt's Copse the earthwork comprises a ditch some 8 ft. deep and 30 ft. across, with a modern hedge-bank along the W. edge. A main bank 28 ft. across and up to 2½ ft. high lies some 25 ft. back from the W. edge of the ditch, but it extends S. for only 100 yds. and ends immediately inside the copse. The ditch continues, but towards the S. end of the copse it is blocked by a modern track and cut into by a pond. Further S. the ditch reappears on a smaller scale, about

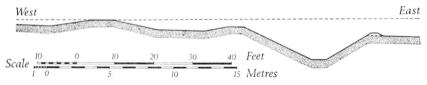

West   East

Scale
10   0   10   20   30   40   Feet
1 0   5   10   15   Metres

ASHMORE. (14) Cross-dyke near Hatt's Barn.

15 ft. across and up to 4 ft. deep, and disturbed by digging; it has no bank, and lynchets on either side of it have accentuated the profile. On the N. side of the modern road, as noted by Sumner (*Cranborne Chase*, 66), the dyke appears to have continued as far as the shoulder of the slope to a very steep-sided combe. This section, now followed by the boundary between Compton Abbas and Melbury Abbas, is marked by a large hedge-bank, 15 ft. across and up to 4 ft. high, with a slight dip which probably marks the line of the ditch along the N.E. side.

(15) DYKE (90721601–91071625), near Deadman's Coppice, 1 mile S. of the village, extends from S.W. to N.E. obliquely across a S.-facing slope, between 550 ft. and 600 ft. above sea-level. It is some 480 yds. long, but it has been almost entirely obliterated by cultivation and trackways, except at the S.W. end where, in Deadman's Coppice, it is well-preserved for a length of some 80 yds., comprising a bank 15 ft. across and 1½ ft. high, with a ditch 16 ft. across and 2 ft. deep on the N.W. side.

(16) DYKE (91931675–92531725), in Mudoak Wood, extends from S.W. to N.E. for some 900 yds. across a low spur and a dry valley, at altitudes between 500 ft. and 600 ft. above sea-level; at its N.E. end it crosses the boundary with Wiltshire. The earthwork is best preserved for a distance of about 300 yds. in

South-East   *North-West*

Scale   10   0   10   20   30 *Feet*
      1   0   5   10   *Metres*

Mudoak Wood, where the bank is 20 ft. across and 2 ft. high, and the ditch, lying along the N.W. side of the bank, is 25 ft. across and 2½ ft. deep. A so-called 'barrow' on the line of the dyke at 92131698 is almost certainly part of the bank. Between Mudoak Wood and the county boundary the dyke has almost been destroyed by ploughing, but it is clearly earlier than the agger of the Roman road, which crosses it. At the S.W. end the earthwork has been disturbed by a track.

MONUMENTS (17–18), ROUND BARROWS

A round barrow, from which bones were recovered when it was removed during the 19th century, lay near 897168 on the boundary with Fontmell Magna (Watson, *op. cit.*, 3, 20). A group of four small mounds N. of Well Bottom (91631670 centre), which Watson thought were barrows, are probably the remains of the lynchetted angles of 'Celtic' fields, elsewhere destroyed by more recent cultivation. Apart from these, two barrows are noted:

(17) *Bowl* (91511628), S.W. of Well Bottom on a S.E.-facing slope, lies at about 560 ft. above O.D.; diam. 45 ft., ht. 1½ ft.

(18) *Bowl* (91531629), immediately N.E. of (17); diam. 30 ft., ht. 1 ft.

UNDATED

(19) POND (91291780), at the centre of the village (Plate 32), is circular and some 40 yds. in diameter. Of its origin nothing is known; it may be partly natural, but enlarged artificially, perhaps in Roman times (Crawford, *Antiquity*, II (1928), 184).

2 BOURTON (7630)

(O.S. 6 ins. ST 72 NE, ST 73 SE)

This parish, the northernmost in Dorset, was regarded as part of Gillingam until the 19th century. It has an area of 922 acres between 350 ft. and 600 ft. above sea-level and falls into two parts. That in the S. is roughly oval and comprises more than two-thirds of the whole area; it lies mainly on Corallian Limestone and is drained by a small tributary of the R. Stour. The other part, a projection on the N.E., lies mainly on Greensand; it is intersected by the R. Stour, flowing S.E.

The early history of the district is bound up with that of Gillingham; the name is first recorded in 1212 (Fägersten, 3). It is possible that there were two original settlements, West Bourton and Bourton, corresponding with the two parts described above. West Bourton is still a small agricultural hamlet, but Bourton village (map, p. 4) has grown to occupy much of the N. and N.E. part of the parish, with a relatively dense scatter of dwellings resulting from industrial development. Although in Dorset, the parish lies in the area of the Wiltshire and Somerset textile industry, and the manufacture of linen was already flourishing early in the 18th century. Yarn was imported from Holland to supplement flax, locally grown and spun, and by the end of the 18th century weaving was the main occupation of the community; in 1811 three-quarters of the population was so engaged. At first the work was done on hand-looms in the scattered cottages; the first mill was established in 1720 and other mills were built early in the 19th century, some of them drawing power from the R. Stour. Later in the 19th century the industry declined in the face of competition from the North.

ECCLESIASTICAL

(1) THE PARISH CHURCH OF ST. GEORGE (76843030) stands in the W. part of the village. The walls are of squared and coursed rubble with Greensand ashlar dressings; the roofs are slated. A church was consecrated in 1813, but it was entirely rebuilt in 1880, reusing the old foundations (Faculty, Sarum Dioc. Regy.).

Fittings—*Chest*: of oak, with wrought-iron angle clasps, beaded top and moulded base, originally with three locks, inscribed 'BP 1794', recently acquired. *Monuments*: In nave, reset on N. wall, (1) of Henry Biging, 1839, marble tablet with draped urn by Chapman of Frome; (2) of John Burfitt, 1840, marble tablet by Chapman of Frome. *Plate*: includes silver cup, cover-paten, paten and flagon, all of 1810, inscribed 'The gift of Sir Richard Colt Hoare Bart. to the Chapel of Bourton, A.D. 1811'. *Royal Arms*: In nave, on N. wall, painted on small wood panel, with crowned scutcheon of Hanover, 1814–37 (Plate 27).

SECULAR

(2) CHAFFEYMOOR HOUSE (76153024) is of two storeys with attics and has walls of rubble with ashlar dressings, and slated roofs. The house originated probably in 1700, and it has additions on the W. of the early and late 19th century. The S. front was remodelled early in the 19th century.

The N. front of the original range is of five bays, with a central doorway flanked by casement windows of two square-headed lights, with moulded stone surrounds and weathered labels, and with similar windows in the upper storey. The centre bay is masked by a late 19th-century two-storey porch. At the W. end of the N. front a wing projecting northwards is probably of the early 19th century. The S. front of the original range is symmetrical and of three bays. At the centre, on the ground floor, is an original square-headed doorway with a moulded stone surround and a moulded label ; it is sheltered by an early 19th-century porch with trellised uprights and a concave lead roof ; set in the wall above the porch are two stones inscribed respectively 17 and 00. On the first floor, over the porch, is an early 19th-century sashed window. On each floor, the side bays of the S. front have early 19th-century bay windows of three sashed lights. The attic has modern dormer windows. To the W. is a two-storeyed extension, probably of the middle of the 19th century.

Inside, the first-floor room at the E. end of the original range has 18th-century pine panelling with fielded panels and moulded rails and stiles. In the attic, the roof trusses have plain tie-beams, and collar-beams with slightly raised centres.

Stables, some 30 yds. to the N., are of the early 19th century.

(3) CHAFFEYMOOR GRANGE (76223038) is of two storeys and has walls of rubble with ashlar dressings, and tiled roofs. The main range is modern, but part of a small 17th-century house is incorporated at the rear.

(4) ADCROFT HOUSE (76973018), of two storeys and a cellar, has rubble walls and tiled roofs with stone-slate verges ; it dates probably from early in the 18th century. The W. front is of three bays, with a central doorway and with sashed windows symmetrically disposed in each storey ; the N. front has casement windows informally arranged. The drawing room, in the angle between the W. and N. ranges, is of the first half of the 19th century ; its doorway probably replaces a former window.

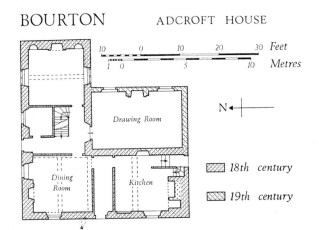

BOURTON   ADCROFT HOUSE

BOURTON
POSITION
OF
MONUMENTS

Monuments numbered and described in the Inventory

Cottages *c*.1800–1850

Buildings after 1850

··· Parish boundary

SCALE OF YARDS
100 50 100 200 300

Inside, the arrangement of ceiling beams suggests that the partition on the S. side of the present dining-room is secondary whereas that between the passage and the kitchen is original. The staircase has a dado with bolection-moulded panels with fielded centres, step spandrels with simple scroll decoration, and columnar balustrades with spiral fluting on alternate shafts ; at the foot of the staircase is a matching dog-gate. The E. ground-floor room has two round-headed niches with moulded surrounds and shaped shelving.

(5) CLOTH MILL (77713087), single-storeyed with basements, has walls of rubble with ashlar dressings, and tiled roofs (Plate 31) ; it was built in 1820. The main range has a symmetrical E. front of five bays with segmental-headed openings ; the doorway at the centre has 'WIJ 1820' inscribed above the keystone ; below, the basements have segmental-headed windows. On the W. front the falling ground allows the basement to be open, with three large round-headed archways and one segmental-headed archway. Adjoining the N. end of the main range is the former machine-house, with openings for a water-race which led to an overshot water-wheel, now removed.

(6) IVY LODGE (77743084), house, adjacent to (5), is of two storeys with walls of rubble and of ashlar and with a thatched roof ; it dates from the 18th century, with additions probably of 1834. The original range had a S. front of two bays with a central doorway, and three-light casement windows. In the 19th century the range was extended westwards and a french window was inserted in place of an original ground-floor window. At the same time a new range was built on the N., parallel with the first, with a further extension at right-angles ; the date of the extensions is suggested by a lead rain-water head of 1834. Inside, on the first floor, several 19th-century rooms have three-panelled doors with enriched beading.

(7) BULLPITS (77513117), house, is of two storeys, with walls partly rendered and partly of rubble, and with tiled and slated roofs. The main S. and E. ranges are largely of the 19th century, but incorporated in them, to N. and W., are the walls of a former *Cloth Mill*, dating from *c.* 1720. The 19th-century S. front has a symmetrical façade of three bays with a central doorway under a porch with round-headed arches and Roman-Doric corner pilasters ; originally all the windows had sashed lights, but some of these have been replaced by modern casements. To the E., slightly set back, is the S. end of the 19th-century E. range, with a Palladian window on the ground floor and with a pair of round-headed lights above. On the N. the walls of the former mill are exposed ; it appears to have been L-shaped in plan and to have had rubble walls and slated roofs ; a few large casement windows are preserved. Inside, the house has been extensively modernised. Documents and pictures relating to the history of the building are preserved by the owner.

(8) COTTAGES (76123051), two adjacent, are two-storeyed and have rubble walls and tiled roofs. The cottage on the S.E. is of late 16th or early 17th-century origin ; that on the N.W. is of the 18th century. Inside, the S.E. ground-floor room has a four-panel ceiling with heavily moulded intersecting beams and corresponding wall-plates.

(9) COTTAGES (76333027), two adjacent, are two-storeyed and have walls partly of rubble and partly rendered ; the roofs are thatched. The building is probably of the late 18th century.

(10) CHAFFEYMOOR FARM (76453020), house, two-storeyed, with rubble walls and slated roofs, dates probably from the first half of the 18th century. The original range is of four bays ; on the W. is a late 18th-century extension of one bay ; on the E. is

a similar, but slightly lower extension, probably of the early 19th century.

(11) GROVEHOUSE FARM (76383035), house, is two-storeyed and has rubble walls and tiled roofs. The main range is of the 18th century and there are 19th-century extensions on the N. and N.W. The W. front of the main range has a central doorway with a flat hood resting on moulded timber brackets. Casement windows in each storey have timber lintels and wrought-iron casements with leaded glazing. Inside, at the N. end of the original range is an open fireplace with a moulded stone surround, probably of the 18th century.

(12) COTTAGES (76753033), two adjacent, are two-storeyed and have walls of coursed and random rubble, and thatched roofs. The building is of the 18th century and has an L-shaped plan, the N. cottage standing at right-angles to that on the S. Inside, several rooms have ceiling beams with narrow chamfers.

(13) MARVIN'S FARM (76923007), house, of three storeys, has rubble walls and slated roofs ; it is of 18th-century origin, with a late 19th-century third storey. The W. front is symmetrical and of three bays, with a central doorway and with sashed windows. Inside, some rooms have panelled softwood partitions.

(14) THE RED LION INN (76933038), is two-storeyed and has walls of squared rubble with ashlar dressings, and slated roofs. It dates from *c.* 1830.

(15) COTTAGE (77203059), with rubble walls and thatched roofs, is of the late 18th century.

(16) SANDWAY HOUSE (77253069), of two storeys with attics, has rendered walls and tiled mansard roofs ; it is said to date from *c.* 1795. Extensions on the N. are of the 19th century.

(17) COTTAGES (77243071), two adjacent, have walls of coursed rubble, and thatched roofs. Originally single-storeyed with dormer-windowed attics, they have recently been heightened to make two storeys and they have also been combined as one dwelling. The building appears to be of 18th-century origin.

(18) DOVEHAYES FARM (77423089), house, is two-storeyed and has walls of coursed rubble and tiled roofs ; it dates from the late 18th century. The S. front of the main range is symmetrical and of three bays, with a central doorway flanked by sashed windows of three lights and with corresponding openings in the upper storey. Adjacent on the W. is a single-storeyed outbuilding, contemporary with the main range ; on the E. is a somewhat later addition.

(19) DOVEHAYES FARM COTTAGES (77323085), two adjacent, are two-storeyed and have rubble walls and slated and tiled roofs ; they are of the 18th century.

(20) COTTAGES (77583076), pair, are two-storeyed with rubble walls and tiled roofs ; they date from late in the 18th century. The W. front is symmetrical and of three bays, with coupled doorways at the centre and with casement windows of three and of four lights arranged symmetrically in each storey.

(21) MALTHOUSE COTTAGES (77883079), range of three and one adjacent, are two-storeyed and have rubble walls and are roofed with tiles and corrugated iron ; they date from early in the 18th century. Inside, the middle cottage of the range has a ceiling with reset fragments of moulded plasterwork of late 16th-century origin (cf. GILLINGHAM (75)).

(22) THE WHITE LION INN (77863093), of two storeys, comprises a row of three former houses of *c.* 1800 and, at the back, a cottage of *c.* 1750. The walls are of coursed rubble and the

roofs are slate-covered. The southernmost house of the row has a symmetrical E. front of three bays with a central doorway ; on the N. is a pair of two-bay houses. The cottage of 1750 stands adjacent to that first mentioned, on the N.W. ; it is roofed with pantiles.

(23) COTTAGE (78193121), single-storeyed with an attic, with rubble walls and a thatched roof, dates from early in the 18th century. Adjacent on the S. is a two-storeyed extension, with walls of coursed rubble, probably of the late 18th century. The S. gable has an ashlar coping with shaped ashlar kneelers and, at the apex, an ashlar chimney-stack.

WEST BOURTON

(24) MANOR FARM (76592927), house, is two-storeyed and has rubble walls with heavy rubble quoins, and tiled roofs. It is probably of the 18th century and a moulded stone label over the E. doorway is presumably reset. All windows have casements and are spanned by timber lintels. The plan is L-shaped.

(25) WEST BOURTON FARM (76632923), house, is two-storeyed and has rubble walls and tiled roofs with stone-slate verges ; it is of the 17th century. All windows have casements and the openings are spanned by rough timber lintels. The S. doorway has an 18th-century lead-covered segmental hood resting on scroll-shaped timber brackets. Inside, the plan is of class F, with two original open fireplaces, now blocked. A plank-and-muntin partition flanks the through-passage on the side opposite the central chimneybreast. The bressummer of the E. fireplace is cambered and deeply chamfered. The first floor rests on deeply chamfered beams, one with shaped stops.

(26) BLACKWATER FARM (76442925), house, is two-storeyed and has rendered walls and a slated roof. The symmetrical E. front is of two bays with a central doorway and with casement windows in each storey ; to the S. is an added bay. The N. gable has a date-stone inscribed 'RP 1738', probably the date of the house.

(27) FARMHOUSE (76582935), is two-storeyed and has rubble walls and a tiled roof ; it dates from about the middle of the 18th century. The E. front is symmetrical and of three bays, with a central doorway and casement windows. The N. and W. elevations retain original casement windows of two, three and four square-headed lights, some of them blocked. Inside, one room has an open fireplace, now blocked.

(28) COTTAGES (76632937), two adjoining, are two-storeyed and have coursed rubble walls and tiled roofs ; they are of the 18th century. In each cottage the W. front is symmetrical and of two bays, with a central doorway and with sashed windows in each storey.

MONUMENTS (29–53)

Dispersed in the village of Bourton, as shown on the map on p. 4 are twenty-five small two-storeyed houses, similar to one another in character. They date from the late 18th or early 19th century and have coursed rubble walls and thatched or tile-covered roofs. The façades are of three bays, each with a central doorway and with symmetrically disposed windows ; a few have casements, but in most the windows are sashed. In several of these monuments, notably (53), (Plate 30),

the three-bay façade is designed to mask two independent dwellings (cf. Milton Abbas (7), *Dorset* III, 197).

NINETEENTH-CENTURY MONUMENTS

Monuments of the first half of the 19th century include fifteen *Ranges of Cottages*, of two, three or four tenements, and four isolated *Cottages* ; the location of these monuments is shown on the map on p. 4.

3 BUCKHORN WESTON (7524)
(O.S. 6 ins., ST 72 NE, ST 72 SE, ST 72 SW)

Buckhorn Weston, with an area of 1,705 acres, lies in the extreme W. of the area described in this volume. The N.E. third of the parish is on the Corallian Limestone escarpment, at altitudes of 300 ft. to 400 ft. above sea-level. The rest of the land is Oxford Clay, almost flat, between 190 ft. and 230 ft. above sea-level ; this area is drained by the R. Cale and its tributary the Filley Brook, forming the parish boundaries on the W. and S. The village stands at the foot of the escarpment. In Domesday times *Westone* was of fair size (*V.C.H., Dorset* iii, 141), with a recorded population of 26, but little is known of its subsequent history. An isolated farmhouse (3) in the S.W. appears to stand in an area of former open fields ; it existed in 1641, showing that enclosure had taken place before that date (Hutchins IV, 116).

ECCLESIASTICAL

(1) THE PARISH CHURCH OF ST. JOHN THE BAPTIST, near the centre of the village, has walls of squared rubble with ashlar dressings, and tiled roofs (Plate 33). The *Chancel* and *Nave* are of 14th-century origin, but were extensively restored and altered in the 19th century. The N. arcade of the nave is of 15th-century origin, as also is the *South Porch*. The *West Tower* was taken down and rebuilt in 1861 ; the *North Aisle* was enlarged and rebuilt in 1870.

The fittings include a 14th-century recumbent effigy, a mediaeval silver paten, and a communion cup of 1562.

Architectural Description—The *Chancel* was extensively re-built in the 19th century, but the N. wall is original and contains a late 14th-century window of two trefoil ogee-headed lights with quatrefoil tracery in a two-centred head ; the rear-arch is two-centred. The S. wall has, reset, two restored windows similar to that on the N. and, between them, a doorway with a chamfered segmental-pointed head and continuous jambs, perhaps original. The chancel arch, of one chamfered order and of 14th-century origin, was partly rebuilt in the 19th century with reuse of original material ; cutting-away of some of the lower voussoirs indicates the position of a former rood-loft. Above the chancel arch, on the E. gable of the nave, is a mediaeval apex finial with leaf enrichment.

BUCKHORN WESTON　*The Parish Church of St. John*

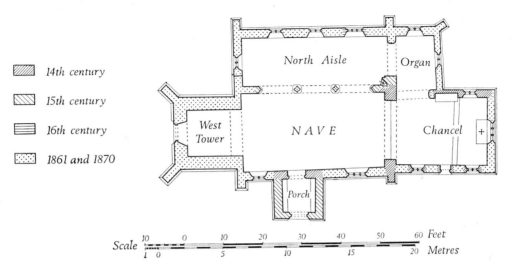

14th century

15th century

16th century

1861 and 1870

North Aisle　　Organ

West Tower　　N A V E　　Chancel

Porch

Scale

In the *Nave*, the N. arcade has piers and responds with attached shafts alternating with hollow chamfers, and moulded capitals and polygonal bases. The W. pier is of the 19th century ; that on the E., and both responds, are of the 15th century, the W. respond having been moved to its present position in 1870 when the arcade was extended from two to three bays (plan in Sarum Dioc. Regy.) ; the capitals, however, and the two-centred arches with ogee mouldings and hollow-chamfers are wholly of the 19th century. At the E. end of the S. wall is a 14th-century two-stage buttress with ogee weathering. The S. doorway has a three-centred head with a broad recessed chamfer, and continuous jambs ; it is of 14th-century origin, but rebuilt and perhaps heightened. The two S. windows are of the 19th century.

The *North Aisle* is largely of 1870, but at the E. end, on the S., are three steps and part of the doorway of the 15th-century rood-loft vice. A three-light window in the eastern part of the N. wall has trefoil-headed lights and a moulded label ; it is of the late 16th century and was transferred in 1870 from the former N. wall.

The *West Tower*, of 1861, is of two stages, with three-stage buttresses in the lower stage, an embattled parapet, and angle pinnacles with crocketed finials.

The *South Porch* has an archway with a four-centred head, with ovolo and hollow-chamfered mouldings continuous on the jambs ; above the arch is a weathered and hollow-chamfered hood-mould.

Fittings—*Bells* : six ; 1st modern ; 2nd by William Knight, inscribed 'WK, BF 1727' ; 3rd dated 1845 ; 4th by John Wallis, inscribed 'Praise the Lord IW 1602' ; 5th with black-letter inscription 'In multus annis risoent campana iohannis baptiste' (*sic*), 15th-century ; 6th by William Knight, inscribed 'The gift of George Pitt of Shroton Esq. 1727, WK, BF'. *Book :* attached to oak lectern (*q.v.*) by iron chain, *Reliquiae Sacrae Carolinae*, incomplete, leather-bound, with brass clasps and mounts, brass roundel on cover inscribed 'This book given by Steven Thos 1690, John Sampson Rector, set up 1696, Christr Thomas, Thos Davidg churchwardens. Beata Benefactoris Memoria'. *Chest :* of cast iron, for registers, 1813, on oak stand made up with carved 17th-century members. *Font :*

of stone, octagonal, with quatrefoil panel and central boss on each face, below, spaced leaf-bosses, moulded octagonal stem, and base with shaped stops, 15th-century. *Image :* see *Niche*. *Lectern :* (Plate 13) of oak, with turned stem on shaped cross foot, shaped cross-piece at top and two back-to-back desks with beaded edges, probably 1696 (see *Book*) ; roughly incised on desk, 'IE 1701'.

Monuments and *Floor-slabs*. *Monuments :* In chancel, in N. wall, (1) recess with two-centred, ovolo-moulded, hollow-chamfered and cusped head, containing recumbent effigy of man in late 14th-century dress (Plate 15) with short jupon with tippet and hood, tight hose, belt with purse ; hair long, hands together in prayer, feet resting on unidentifiable beast ; head on tasselled pillow with angel supporter on N., S. angel gone ; late 14th century. Above the foregoing, (2) of Samuel Clark, rector, 1761, and Ann Clark, 1764, marble wall monument with enriched border and pediment, with pelican-in-piety as finial, flanked by urns with flame finials (Plate 17). In churchyard, 8 paces E. of chancel, (3) table-tomb of John Davidge, 166—, with heavily moulded top slab and oval panels in sides. *Floor-slabs :* In chancel, (1) of John Samp[so]n, rector, 1715, slate slab with foliate border ; (2) of [Joseph Bannister, 1731] ; (3) of Samuel Clark, 1761.

Niche : In gable of S. porch, with polygonal base, plain sides, canopy with cusped arcading, pinnacles and crocketed finials, probably late 15th century. Within niche, worn figure said to represent St. John the Baptist, with oblong pillow behind head, probably 15th century. *Paintings :* six, on panels, formerly comprising front of W. gallery (Hutchins IV, 117), now reset in W. tower, two depicting landscapes with angels blowing trumpets, one with Nativity, three with saintly figures, paint badly deteriorated ; 18th century.

Piscina : reset in chancel, round stone basin with cusped outlet, probably 14th century. *Plate :* includes silver cup (Plate 24) with hallmark of 1562 and maker's mark, letter 'a' at centre of sun-burst ; silver paten of *c.* 1510 (Plate 24), cusped bowl with IHS in black-letter, cusps with leaf decoration, diameter 5 ins. ; maker's mark a circle divided into four quarters, each quarter with a pellet ; also 17th-century pewter flagon and 18th-century brass almsdish, the latter perhaps part of a warming-pan. *Seating :*

Small bench with turned legs and beaded stretchers, early 18th century. *Sundial*: reset on S. wall of tower, square stone plate with arabic numerals and inscription ANNO DO 1599.

SECULAR

(2) HOPE FARM (75192463), house, of two storeys with attics, has walls of rubble and coursed rubble with some brickwork, and is roofed with tiles and stone-slates; it is of late 16th-century origin with early 18th-century alterations.

The plan is a variant of class J, but L-shaped, having an original wing on the N. In the S. front the three western bays are symmetrically arranged, with casement windows of three

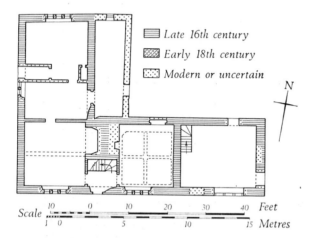

Late 16th century
Early 18th century
Modern or uncertain

N

Scale
10　0　10　20　30　40　Feet
1　0　5　10　15　Metres

square-headed lights flanking the doorway, corresponding windows in the upper storey, and with a two-light window over the doorway. The ground-floor windows have stone mullions and moulded stone surrounds under brick relieving arches and are probably of the early 18th century; a similar window occurs in the gabled N. wall of the N. wing. Inside, the central room of the S. range has deeply chamfered wall-plates and ceiling beams, intersecting at carved bosses enriched with shields bearing the monograms 'W', 'RC' and 'ST'. In elevation the E. bay is slightly lower than the rest of the S. range. Although formerly used for storage, this bay has now been made into a separate dwelling. There appears to be no doorway from the E. room to the rest of the range and it may have been a separate dwelling originally.

(3) PELSHAM FARM (74512355), house, is two-storeyed and has walls of ashlar and of rubble, and slate-covered roofs. The plan is L-shaped and the principal range, on the N., is of the late 17th century; the S. wing is perhaps of the first half of the same century. The N. front is symmetrical and of five bays, with a central doorway and uniform casement windows, each of two square-headed lights with moulded architraves; the windows of the lower storey have plain aprons rising above offsets in the moulded plinth. A plat-band marks the level of the first floor. Inside, the N. range has a class-T plan, with the earlier S. range constituting a service wing. The roof has original collar-beam trusses. At the S. end of the S. range is a 19th-century extension.

MONUMENTS (4–10)

Unless otherwise described the following buildings are of the second half of the 18th century; they are two-storeyed, with rubble walls and with tiled or slated roofs.

(4) *Caggypole Farm* (75292353), house, is L-shaped in plan. The S. range has a symmetrical S. front of three bays, with a doorway at the centre, sashed windows on each side of it, and casement windows in the upper storey.

(5) *Court Farm* (75682479), house, is of two dates: the original range on the N.E. is of the 18th century; added to it is an ashlar-fronted 19th-century block with a S.W. façade of three bays, with a central doorway and with large sashed windows in both storeys.

(6) *Hill Farm* (75882482), house, is of the late 18th century.

(7) *Newhouse Farm* (76912524), house, is L-shaped in plan and has walls of coursed rubble with ashlar quoins. The S. front is of two bays with a central doorway.

(8) *House* (75632463) is of the early 19th century; the walls are partly of brick and partly rendered. In the symmetrical S.W. front the central doorway, with a porch with wooden Roman-Doric columns, is flanked by sashed windows; three similar windows occur in the upper storey. Adjacent on the W. is a former *Smithy*, probably of the late 18th century.

(9) *Inn* (75652462), comprises buildings of two dates. The main range is of the 19th century and has a rendered N.W. front of three bays, with a central doorway under a Roman-Doric porch, flanked by three-sided bay windows, and with sashed windows in the upper storey; the extremities of this façade are marked by pilasters. Adjacent, on the N.E., is an 18th-century range, originally a stable or coach-house, but now incorporated in the dwelling; the rubble walls retain traces of former coach-house doorways.

(10) *House* (75542463), of two storeys with attics, with ashlar and rubble walls and with a tile-covered roof, is of the early 19th century. The N. front is symmetrical and of three bays, with a central doorway and with square-headed sashed windows.

Minor buildings of the late 18th and early 19th century, with rubble walls and generally with thatched, tiled or slated roofs, are dispersed in the parish, as follows: *Cottage* (76612648); *Cottage* (76542620), now two tenements; *Cottages* (76542615), two adjacent, that on the E. being the earlier, now combined as one dwelling; *Cottage* (76542611); *Cottage* (76512613); *Cottages* (75892554), two adjacent; *Cottage* (76312540), with a symmetrical S. front of two bays with a central doorway; *Cottage* (76442540); *Cottages* (76962470), pair; *Cottage* (76292436); *House* (75342467); *Cottages* (75332469), pair; *Cottage* (75302470), adjacent to the foregoing.

MEDIAEVAL AND LATER EARTHWORKS

(11) CULTIVATION REMAINS. Little is known of the enclosure of the open fields in the parish. Pelsham Farm (3), which appears to lie within the area of the open fields, was in existence in 1641 (Hutchins IV, 116) and some enclosure, if not all, presumably had been effected by that date. Ridge-and-furrow of the open fields, arranged in interlocking furlongs of curved and reversed-S type, exist all over the S. and E. of the parish; in places it is associated with flat strips, slightly lyncheted (R.A.F. CPE/UK 1924 : 2236 and 4235-7).

PLATE 33

BUCKHORN WESTON CHURCH. Exterior, from S.   14th century and later

CHETTLE CHURCH. W. tower.   16th century

COMPTON ABBAS.
(2) Old St. Mary's Church.   15th century

PLATE 34

TARRANT CRAWFORD. Air view of Abbey site and Parish Church, from W.

PLATE 35

FONTMELL MAGNA. (34) Cross-dyke on Fore Top, from N.E.   Iron Age

CHETTLE. (14) Area of former settlement, from S.   Iron Age and Roman

PLATE 36

CHETTLE. (2) Chettle House.   *c.* 1710 and later

PLATE 37

Exterior, from E.   Mainly *c.* 1710

First-floor room, formerly billiards-room.   Decorations, *c.* 1846
CHETTLE. (2) Chettle House.

PLATE 38

In Memory of
Mr. JAMES FARQUHARSON,
of London, Merchant
a Man of strict probity, unwearied Diligence,
and unbounded Beneficence.
By his extensive and correct knowledge of Commerce,
He acquired an ample fortune:
His judicious disposition of which
has raised many to Opulence;
who join with his Relict ANN FARQUHARSON,
who erected this Monument
in lamenting the loss
of the tender Husband, the good Father
and the zealous Friend.

He died at Camberwell in Surry
on the 15th Day of May 1795,
in the 69 Year of his Age.

LANGTON LONG BLANDFORD CHURCH. Monument (3).   1795

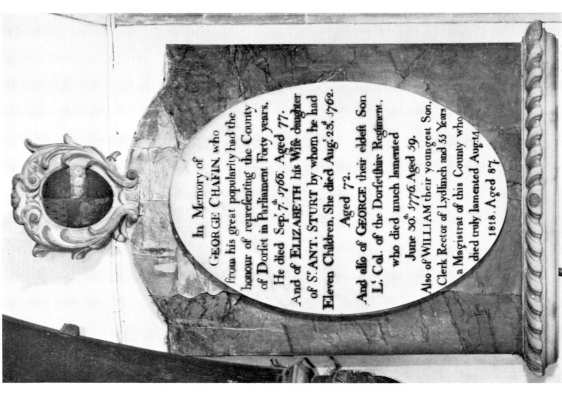

In Memory of
GEORGE CHAFIN, who
from his great popularity had the
honour of reprefenting the County
of Dorfet in Parliament Forty years.
He died Sep.t 7th 1766. Aged 77.
And of ELIZABETH his Wife daughter
of St ANT. STURT by whom he had
Eleven Children, She died Aug.t 23.d 1762.
Aged 72.
And alfo of GEORGE their eldeft Son
Lt Col. of the Dorfethire Regiment,
who died much lamented
June 30th 1776. Aged 59.
Also of WILLIAM their youngeft Son,
Clerk Rector of Lydlinch and 55 Years
a Magiftrat of this County who
died truly lamented Augt.14
1818. Aged 87

CHETTLE CHURCH. Monument (3).   1766

PLATE 39

18th century

Chandelier

Probably 1744

Monument (4) of the Davidge family.

FIFEHEAD MAGDALEN CHURCH. Fittings.

PLATE 40

CHETTLE. (2) Chettle House, staircase.

c. 1710

4 CANN (8521)

(O.S. 6 ins. ST 81 NW, ST 82 SW, ST 82 SE)

The parish, with an area of some 2,600 acres, straddles the escarpement immediately S. of Shaftesbury. In the E. the Greensand rises sharply to more than 600 ft. above the sea ; near the S. boundary in the eastern part, a deep re-entrant valley exposes the Gault Clay below the Greensand ; in the W. part of the parish the land undulates on Kimmeridge Clay at altitudes of 200 ft. to 400 ft. The present boundaries result from recent alterations. Formerly, Cann comprised the eastern third of the present area together with a narrow northern projection on the E. of Shaftesbury, now included in that borough ; the western two-thirds of the present parish were formerly part of St. James's, Shaftesbury (Hutchins III, 55). The village stands on the side of the deep valley mentioned above and contains no note-worthy monuments ; the parish church of St. Rumbold (Shaftesbury (6)) stands outside the parish. Cann is not mentioned in documents until early in the 12th century (Fägersten, 20), but almost certainly it is older. Of the open fields nothing is known. The Greensand plateau in the E. remained open common until enclosure in 1812 (Award, D.C.R.O.), after which houses and cottages were built on and along the edges of the common. The low-lying western part of the parish contains isolated farmsteads, fields of irregular shape, and much unenclosed common ; the farms here prob-ably represent secondary settlement and assarting in an area formerly of waste land.

ECCLESIASTICAL

THE PARISH CHURCH OF ST. RUMBOLD—see Shaftes-bury (6), p. 65.

SECULAR

(1) BLYNFIELD FARM (83832188), house, of two storeys with coursed rubble walls and stone-slated roofs, dates in its present form from 1812 although a manor house has existed in this place since the 14th century (Hutchins III, 78). The house has a class-U plan, with a symmetrical W. front of three bays, with wood-framed casement windows of two and of three lights ; the central doorway, however, is now blocked. A date-stone in the N.W. chimneystack is inscribed MW 1812. An undated inscription on a panel of slate fixed to the N. wall records that the manor of Blynfield belonged formerly to the Grammar School of Bruton, Somerset.

The Barn, on the N. side of the farmyard to the E. of the house, has brick walls with weathered brick buttresses, and a tiled roof ; a date-stone in the gabled W. wall is inscribed MW 1809. The Stables on the E. of the farmyard are of brick with ashlar dressings ; they have a symmetrical W. front with a door-way with an ovolo-moulded segmental-pointed head and con-tinuous jambs ; the flanking windows are each of two lights, with two-centred heads and a central spandrel light. Above the doorway is a loft doorway with a segmental-pointed head. Other farm buildings on the E. and S. of the farmyard have rubble walls.

(2) COTTAGES (87492097), range of four, now combined to form two dwellings, are two-storeyed, with rubble walls and tiled roofs, and are perhaps of the late 17th century. Two of the original doorways have been partly blocked and made into windows. At the S. end of the W. front two original windows retain moulded stone surrounds.

(3) COTTAGE (84301991), at Guy's Marsh, is two-storeyed, with rubble walls and a tiled roof ; it appears to be of the early 18th century. The W. front is symmetrical and of two bays, with a central doorway. Inside, some roughly chamfered beams are supported on rubble brackets.

MONUMENTS (4–8)

Unless otherwise described, the following late 18th or early 19th-century monuments are two-storeyed, with rubble walls and slate-covered roofs.

(4) *White's Farm* (87602116), house, has a thatched roof. The symmetrical S. front is of three bays, with square-headed sashed windows and with a central doorway.

(5) *Wilkins' Farm* (87182124), house, has walls of squared and coursed rubble and a symmetrical three-bay S. front, with sashed windows in the lower story and with casement windows above.

(6) *French Mill* (86672095), house, of three storeys on the W. front and of two on the E., has rubble walls with ashlar dressings. It was advertised in the *Salisbury Journal*, 7 July 1828, as 'lately rebuilt'.

(7) *Guy's Marsh Farm* (84392097), house and outbuildings, have thatched and slated roofs, and some brickwork in later walls. The house is of the 18th century ; inside is an open fireplace, now blocked.

(8) *Cole's Lane Farm* (84652177), house, with a tiled roof, has a date-stone of 1822. The S. front is symmetrical and of three bays, with a central doorway and with casement windows of two and of three lights.

Other late 18th or early 19th-century monuments, mostly with rubble walls and with thatched roofs, are as follows— *Mayo Farm* (87482222), house, with an adjacent *Barn* in which is reset a date-stone of 1736 ; *Cottage* (88152118) ; *Cottage* (88222086), with a date-stone of 1799 ; *Cottages* (88232083), range of four ; *Cottage* (88262080) ; *Farmhouse* (88432087) ; *Cottage* (87682140), with an open fireplace and adjacent bake-oven ; *Cottage* (87642134) ; *Cottage* (87172104), with an in-scription of 1847 ; *Cottage* (87172106) ; *Bozley Farm* (87272126), comprising two cottages ; *Cottage* (84231994) ; *Rose Cottage* (84352037), two adjacent dwellings, now combined as one ; *Green's Farm* (83922254), house, formerly two cottages, one of the 18th and one of the 19th century, the latter with brick walls.

MEDIAEVAL AND LATER EARTHWORKS

(9) ANKETIL'S PLACE (857222), the site of a mediaeval manor house, lies near the N. boundary of the parish, 150 yds. S. of

St. James's Church, Shaftesbury, at the crest of a narrow spur with extensive views to E., S., and W. The house was demolished *c.* 1770, but from the mid 13th century until 1739 it was the seat of the Anketil family. Hutchins (1st ed. II, 35) describes it as a large handsome house, the W. part dating from 1680, the other part more ancient. Part of a wall still remained in 1868 (Hutchins 3rd ed. III, 61). The site has been built over and nothing now remains ; a few sherds of mediaeval and later pottery from the area are in Shaftesbury Museum. On the W. of the site and due S. of St. James's Church are fragmentary remains of several small rectangular closes, bounded by banks and scarps up to 2½ ft. high ; they probably represent the manor farm.

ROMAN

(10) INHUMATION BURIAL (88362112), of a child in a lead coffin, was found at Cann Common in 1916. The undecorated coffin, set in a cement tray, measured 3½ ft. in length by 10 ins. to 12 ins. in width and was 7 ins. high ; the lid was slightly larger. As well as the skeleton the coffin held leaves, apparently of box and perhaps from a funerary wreath, and sherds of pottery ; a sherd of New Forest ware was found near by. Coffin and tray are now in Shaftesbury Museum (*Dorset Procs.* XXXVIII (1917), 68–73).

5 CHETTLE (9513)

(O.S., 6 ins. ST 91 SE, ST 91 SW)

This parish, roughly quadrilateral on plan and with an area of 1,124 acres, lies at the head of the dry valley which lower down is drained by the Crichel Brook. The village stands in the bottom of the valley and formerly was surrounded by its open fields ; these were still in existence in the 16th century, together with enclosed pasture (Hutchins III, 569), but the dates of enclosure are unknown. The land in the N.W. of the parish was open downland until recent years. Chettle House, an early 18th-century mansion attributed to Thomas Archer, is the principal monument in the parish.

ECCLESIASTICAL

(1) THE PARISH CHURCH OF ST. MARY, near the S. end of the village, has walls of banded flint and ashlar, and tiled roofs. The *West Tower* is of the early 16th century ; the *Chancel, Nave, Vestry* and *Organ Chamber* were built in 1849 to replace mediaeval buildings, then demolished. (View of former church : Hutchins 2nd ed. III, 170.)

Architectural Description—The 19th-century parts of the church have windows and other details generally in the 'Decorated' style. The 16th-century *West Tower* (Plate 33) is of two stages, with a moulded plinth, weathered string-courses and an embattled parapet. The buttresses are of two weathered stages, the offsets occurring about half-way up each main stage ; there is no vice. The tower arch is two-centred and of two orders, the outer order chamfered, the inner order with ogee

mouldings ; the mouldings of both orders continue on the responds and end at low chamfered plinths. The W. doorway has a four-centred head of two chamfered orders continuous on the jambs, with chamfered stops ; above is a partly restored window of three trefoil-headed lights under plain tracery in an elliptical head. The belfry has four uniform windows, each of two elliptical-headed lights with spandrel lights in a four-centred head ; below the W. belfry window is a small light with an elliptical head.

Fittings—*Bells* : three ; 1st and 2nd with 'ave gratia' in black-letter, 3rd with 'Sanc Te Pe Ter' ; all from Salisbury foundry, *c.* 1350. *Chairs* : two, of oak, heavily enriched, each with panelled back with shell cresting and two turned finials, richly carved legs and stiles, and stuffed seats ; early 17th-century material reassembled in 19th century. *Coffin-stools* : two, of oak, with turned legs, enriched rails and stretchers and beaded tops, early 17th century. *Monuments* : In chancel, (1) of Rev. John West, 1845, and others of his family, sarcophagus-shaped marble tablet by Hellyer of Weymouth ; (2) of Rev. John Napier, 1819, and Catherine his wife, 1833, marble tablet with slate surround. In nave, on N. of chancel arch, (3) of George Chafin, 1766, Elizabeth (Sturt) Chafin, 1762, and others of their family, oval tablet on variegated marble backing piece, with gadrooned sill, and finial painted with shield-of-arms of Chafin impaling Sturt (Plate 38) ; on S. of chancel arch, (4) of Thomas Chafin, 1691, and Ann (Penrudock) his wife, 1705, marble tablet in shaped stone surround with drapery enrichment, cherub heads, emblems of mortality and achievement-of-arms

CHETTLE
The Parish Church of St. Mary

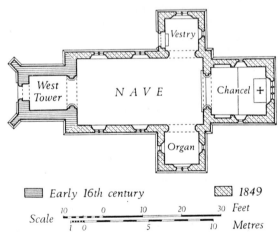

▦ *Early 16th century*	▨ *1849*

Scale

of Chafin impaling Penrudock (Plate 18). In tower, (5) of Ann Brewer, 1803, and others of her family, marble tablet with fluted grey pilasters. In churchyard, 5 paces S. of organ chamber, (6) of Henry Newman, 1717, headstone with scrollwork finial. *Pavement* : of nave and W. tower, of diagonally jointed stone flags, said to be from old church and to date from *c.* 1710 (*Illustrated London News*, 1849, 285). *Plate* : includes silver cup, perhaps late 17th century, with stem and foot renewed in 18th century ; stand-paten, perhaps late 17th century, adapted to form cover for cup ; flagon, with assay-mark of 1681 and inscription of E. Lowe, rector 1690–1693.

CHETTLE HOUSE

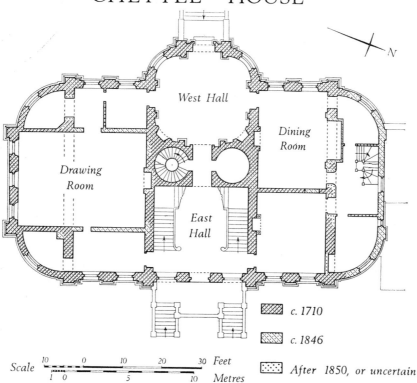

West Hall

Dining Room

Drawing Room

East Hall

N

▨ *c. 1710*

▧ *c. 1846*

▨ *After 1850, or uncertain*

Scale   10   0   10   20   30   Feet

1   0   5   10   Metres

SECULAR

(2) CHETTLE HOUSE (95141318), of two principal storeys with basements and attics, and with a three-storeyed central pavilion, has walls generally of finely coursed red brickwork with ashlar dressings, and roof-coverings of lead and of slate (Plate 36). The house was built *c.* 1710 for George Chafin, M.P. 1713–1747, the architect in all probability being Thomas Archer (Oswald, 153). An 18th-century drawing once belonging to Colen Campbell and now in the R.I.B.A. Library, here reproduced, shows the original plan of the lower

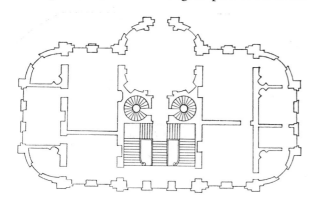

main floor.[1] That the rounded N. and S. end bays originally occurred in the upper storey, as well as at the level shown, is indicated by the description of the house in a Bill of Sale dated 1825, where 'four circular-fronted dressing rooms' are listed on the bedroom floor. After the death in 1818 of George Chafin's son, the Rev. William Chafin, the house stood empty for many years. It suffered severely while vacant and in restoring it, *c.* 1845, the new owner, Edward Castleman, remodelled the lower main floor as shown on the plan above, and removed the N. and S. bays in the upper storey; it is said that he also removed a cupola which formerly crowned the central pavilion. J. Pouncy's view of the house as it was *c.* 1856 (*Dorset Photographically Illustrated,* III, pl. 3) shows the rounded bays rising only one storey above the basement, the curved walls then being capped with parapets and urns. In 1912 the rounded upper storeys were reinstated; they were furnished with balustraded parapets in imitation of the parapets of the central part of the building, features which they cannot have had in the original design since the remains of the original parapets are still seen above the roofs,

[1] Oswald, in *The Country Seat* (Studies presented to Sir John Summerson, ed. Colvin and Harris), p. 85.

returning on the line of the outside pilasters of the main fronts.

Architectural Description—The W. front (Plate 36) is symmetrical and of nine bays, the three central bays projecting in a rounded pavilion one storey higher than the lateral bays. The basement storey forms a podium with a moulded stone capping and has windows with ashlar architraves ; above, the bays of the façade are defined by brick pilasters which support an ashlar entablature above the window heads of the upper main storey. The pilaster bases are of brick ; the capitals are of Chilmark stone and of unusual pattern, having astragals decorated with guttae, and fluted rectilinear bells wider at the bottom than at the top. The entablature has a plain frieze with modillions. The tall sashed windows have segmental heads of gauged brickwork and those of the first floor have brick aprons. Above the entablature the attic storey of the central pavilion is crowned by a balustraded parapet with finials representing castles, the rebus of the Castlemans. The lateral bays have solid parapets interrupted by balustrading in correspondence with the windows ; the bill of sale of 1825 implies that these parapets masked dormer-windowed attics containing servants' bedrooms. The doorway in the central pavilion has a stone surround with Roman-Doric enrichments, a round archivolt, and a large scrolled keystone supporting a cornice.

The E. front (Plate 37) is similar to that on the W. except that the central pavilion does not project, and in the two principal storeys it has round-headed instead of segmental-headed openings ; the piers between the windows are rusticated, bands of ashlar alternating with brickwork. The central doorway is approached by double flights of balustraded stone steps leading to a terrace. The attic storey is crowned by a balustrade, as before, with finials in the form of eagles. Pouncy's view shows these birds on pedestals flanking the W. doorway.

The S. elevation is of five bays (including the rounded corner bays). The three central bays are set between square pilasters and have capitals, entablatures and parapets as described above, but of Ham Hill instead of Chilmark stone. In the basement and lower main storey the brickwork is original ; above first-floor level the brickwork of 1912 is less closely jointed and less regular in colour than the original work. Carved on the stone window heads of the lower main storey are the dates 1710, 1845, 1912. The N. elevation is similar to that on the S., with rebuilding of 1912 in the upper storey. The lower main storey appears to have been partly rebuilt during the 19th-century restorations.

Above roof level, masked by the parapets of 1912, the original N. and S. parapets are partly preserved. They are balustraded as on the E. and W. fronts and they return, at right-angles to those fronts, above the pilasters which divide the curved end bays from the flat part of the façades. The returning parapets are only one bay long finishing in brick piers. The interrupted mouldings of the coping suggest that the parapets continued straight through from E. to W. ; a turn to bring them out to the plane of the N. and S. fronts cannot be ruled out, but the wall-thicknesses below argue against this. In any case the quadrant rooms, if not the whole of each end bay, must originally have been roofed at a level below the main entablature ; the form of the roofs is unknown.

Inside the house, the basement storey, containing the kitchen and other service rooms, has brick vaulting throughout. On the ground floor, the West Hall has bolection-moulded panelling and architectural details of the Roman-Doric order, probably of c. 1846 ; the doorways here and in the E. hall have tympana with bas-reliefs reputedly by Alfred Stevens. In the two-storeyed East Hall (Plate 40) the original stairs are preserved ;

they are of oak and have turned balusters, three to each tread, and newel posts in the form of small fluted columns. The stairs rise in two flights to meet at a landing on the W., whence a single flight leads to a circular billiards room on the first floor above the W. hall (Plate 37). According to the 18th-century plan, another flight of stairs originally connected the E. side of the same landing with the gallery at first-floor level on the E. side of the hall. The sale-bill of 1825 records that 'the sides are painted to resemble a rich cornice, frieze and fluted pilasters dividing the panels', but no trace remains of this decoration. The first-floor galleries on the N. and S. of the hall are of c. 1846.

The passage between the E. and W. halls is flanked by circular stone staircases which rise from the basement to the attics. In the S. staircase the stone stairs and iron handrails are preserved ; those on the N. were removed c. 1846.

The large Drawing Room was formed by removing a main cross-wall in the original plan and resiting other walls ; it has a mid 19th-century marble fireplace surround with caryatid pilasters. According to a tradition in the Castleman family the wall paintings were executed by Alfred Stevens's father. Generally, except for the stairs, the fittings and embellishments throughout the house are of the mid 19th century.

(3) CHETTLE LODGE (95021354), of two and three storeys with attics, has walls partly of ashlar and partly rendered, and slate-covered roofs. It appears to be of the 18th century, with 19th-century additions, but a thick wall inside suggests that an earlier building is incorporated. The western part of the N. range has a symmetrical N. front of three bays, with a central doorway now enclosed in a 19th-century porch, and with sashed windows in the two main storeys ; a third storey takes the place of a former attic. Adjacent on the E. is a 19th-century extension. The S. range is wholly of the 19th century, as are the domestic offices on the W. Inside, the hall in the original range has an 18th-century oak staircase with details closely resembling those of the main staircase at Chettle House (2). Reset as finials on the newel-posts are three carved wood figures, probably of the 16th century. The small room on the W. of the hall has a stop-chamfered beam. The dining-room in the S. range has 17th-century panelling brought from elsewhere, including an overmantel of three panels with strapwork decoration, caryatid pilasters and a figure, perhaps of Justice ; the panelling is made up with modern work. The doors and window shutters comprise some 16th-century oak panels with arabesques and medallions, made up with modern work.

(4) ST MARY'S FARM (95201330), house, of two storeys with attics, with brick walls and tiled roofs, is of the 17th century ; a single-storeyed extension on the N.E. is of the 18th century. Inside, the stairs from the first floor to the attics are of oak, with closed strings, square newel-posts, moulded handrails, and flat balusters of serpentine profile.

(5) COTTAGE (94971357), single-storeyed with attics, with walls of rubble, flint and brickwork and with a thatched roof, is of the 17th century.

(6) COTTAGE (95101353), single-storeyed with attics, with brick walls and a thatched roof, is of 18th-century origin. A modern wing has been added on the W.

(7) COTTAGES (95131355), two adjacent, are single-storeyed with dormer-windowed attics and have walls of rubble and brick, and thatched roofs ; they are of the late 17th century. Inside, there are chamfered beams and plank-and-muntin partitions.

(8) COTTAGE (95141358), single-storeyed, with walls of

rubble and of brick and with a thatched roof, is of the 17th century. Until recently the roof retained a cruck truss.

(9) COTTAGE (95141351), of two storeys with rendered walls and a thatched roof, is of the late 17th century.

(10) COTTAGE (95181350), single-storeyed with an attic, was originally two tenements. It has rendered walls and a thatched roof and is of the 17th century. Inside, one room has a chamfered beam with beaded stops.

(11) COTTAGE (95211338), of one storey with an attic, has walls of rubble, flint and brickwork, and a thatched roof; it is of the late 17th or early 18th century. Adjacent on the N. is an outbuilding of similar materials to the cottage and probably contemporary. A Barn, further N., has weather-boarded walls and a thatched roof and may be of the late 18th century.

(12) COTTAGES (95291343), range of three, are two-storeyed and have brick walls and thatched roofs; they are of the 18th century. In one tenement the windows have stone hood-moulds.

(13) COTTAGES (95371342), two adjacent, are single-storeyed with attics and have walls of rubble, flint and brickwork, and thatched roofs. They are perhaps of 16th-century origin.

ROMAN AND PREHISTORIC

(14) IRON AGE AND ROMAN OCCUPATION DEBRIS, the remains of a settlement which now has been largely flattened by cultivation, occur over an area of 5 acres on Chettle Down (Plate 35). The site (94501490) occupies a S.-facing Chalk slope, about 330 ft. above sea-level, within an area of 'Celtic' fields. Finds made at various times, including material from trial trenches cut across an earthwork thought to be a pond, include a La Tène III bronze brooch, Durotrigian pottery, samian ware, and New Forest and other coarse pottery (*Dorset Procs.*, LI (1929), 194–203; 82 (1960), 83).

(15) CHETTLE LONG BARROW (93741355), on the boundary with Tarrant Gunville, lies on a gentle E.-facing slope at 375 ft. above sea-level. The mound is orientated S.E.–N.W. and is 190 ft. long, 65 ft. wide and 9 ft. high. An oval hollow, 165 ft. by 48 ft. by 2 ft. deep, in an arable field along the N.E. side of the mound, probably represents a side ditch; a shallower hollow is just visible along the S.W. side. Numerous human bones were found when part of the barrow was removed to make a grotto some time before 1767. (*C.T.D.*, Pt. 3, p. 1; *Dorset Procs.*, XXI (1900), 144.)

(16) LONG BARROW (95061280), S. of Chettle House, lies at the top of a gentle S.E.-facing slope on a low spur at 275 ft. above sea-level. The mound is orientated E.N.E.–W.S.W. and is 320 ft. long, 65 ft. wide and 8 ft. high. The W. end has been much reduced by ploughing and no side ditches are visible. When the barrow was opened, c. 1700, 'a great quantity of human bones were found, and with them heads of spears and other warlike instruments', possibly indicating pagan Saxon intrusive burials. A further secondary or intrusive burial was found in 1776. (*C.T.D.*, Pt. 3, p. 2; *Dorset Procs.*, XXI (1900), 144–5; Hutchins III, 567.)

'CELTIC' FIELDS, see p. 119, Group (75).

6 COMPTON ABBAS (8616)
(O.S., 6 ins. ST 81 NE, ST 81 NW)

The parish, a narrow strip of some 1,450 acres, lies across the Chalk escarpment, about 2½ m. S. of Shaftes-bury. The eastern extremity and the N. and S. sides of the central part of the parish lie on Chalk at altitudes approaching 800 ft. The centre of the parish is a deep valley bounded on N., E. and S. by scarps 300 ft. high; the valley floor, only 400 ft. above sea-level, is on Upper Greensand. In the W. part of the parish the land inclines gently downwards across Upper Greensand, Gault and Lower Greensand to the Twyford Brook, which crosses the parish near the 250 ft. contour; to the S. rises a Chalk outlyer, Elbury Hill. To the W. of the brook the land is Kimmeridge Clay, about 300 ft. in altitude. The twin villages of East and West Compton probably represent original settlements. Twyford and Crocker's Farm, in the less favoured Kimmeridge Clay area, appear to be secondary settlements, but nothing is known of their history. Crocker's Farm is dated 1660.

ECCLESIASTICAL

(1) THE PARISH CHURCH OF ST. MARY, near the centre of West Compton, was built in 1866 and fittings from the former church in East Compton (see (2)) were transferred to it.

Fittings—Bells: five; 3rd by John Wallis, inscribed 'Searve God IW 1616'; 4th inscribed 'Maria' in black-letter, late 15th or early 16th century; 5th by John Danton, inscribed 'Remember God ID RT 1624'; others modern. *Brass*: reset in chancel, of Thomas Lawrence [d. 1640], plate, 12 ins. by 17 ins., with Latin inscription. *Communion Table*: of oak, with turned legs, plain stretchers and scrolled end rails, c. 1700. *Font*: with circular tub-shaped bowl with raised foliate scroll decoration, perhaps of 12th-century origin, but recut probably in 1866; shaft and pedestal, 1866. *Monument*: In S. aisle, of Edith Broughton, 1830, and John Broughton, 1827, marble tablet with pediment, by Willson, London. *Plate*: includes plain silver cup inscribed 'The parish cupp of Cumpton Abbies 1665', and paten inscribed 'The plate of the Parish Church of Compton Abbas', undated, probably 18th century.

(2) THE CHURCH OF ST. MARY (87561880), ruined, stands in East Compton. Only the late 15th-century *West Tower* and the W. wall of the former nave remain.

Architectural Description—The *West Tower*, of rough ashlar, is of two stages, with a moulded plinth and the remains of a parapet (Plate 33); the stages are defined by a weathered string-course and the parapet has a hollow-chamfered and moulded string-course with gargoyles at the centre of each side and on the angles. At the S.E. corner is a polygonal vice turret, staged in correspondence with the tower and capped with weathered stonework. At the S.W. corner is a diagonal buttress of four weathered stages; the N.W. corner has no buttress; at the N.E. corner, the projecting W. wall of the former nave has a low diagonal buttress of one weathered stage. The two-centred tower arch is walled up and the mouldings are partly hidden; it appears to be of two orders, an ogee moulding outlined by a hollow chamfer. The vice doorway and the W. doorway have chamfered two-centred heads with continuous jambs. Above the W. doorway, the W. window is of two trefoil-headed lights with a tracery light, now gone, in a two-centred head with a moulded label. In the upper stage the S. side has a chamfered ogee-headed loop ; above this, each side of the tower has a belfry window of two chamfered, trefoil-headed lights under a square label.

COMPTON ABBAS   *Remains of old church*

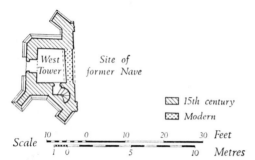

☒ *15th century*
☒ *Modern*

Scale 10   0   10   20   30 *Feet*
       1 0   5   10 *Metres*

Fittings—*Bell-cage :* much decayed, with inscription 'T.P. 1742'. *Cross :* of stone, in churchyard, some 10 paces S.E. of tower, with square stepped base, lower step with hollow-chamfered capping, chamfered square pedestal, and lower part of octagonal shaft with pyramidal stops ; probably 15th century. *Doors :* of tower vice, with iron studs and strap-hinges, late 15th century ; of W. doorway, similar to foregoing, perhaps 16th century. *Monuments :* In churchyard, adjacent to cross, (1) of Robert Thomas, 1703, headstone with wreath border to inscription panel ; 2 paces S.W. of tower, (2) of John Gould, 1716/7, headstone ; 11 paces N.E. of tower, (3) of Elizabeth Bennett, 1795, headstone with shaped top and shield-of-arms of Bennett ; adjacent to foregoing, (4) of Jenevorah Bennett, 1711, headstone. *Miscellanea :* Enclosing churchyard, rubble wall, perhaps partly mediaeval, with 18th-century coping.

SECULAR

(3) CROCKER'S FARM (84641968), house, of two storeys with attics and with ashlar walls and thatched roofs, dates from 1660. The original stone windows are of four, three and two square-headed lights under weathered labels with square stops. The plan is L-shaped, with the main range lying N.–S. and a gabled W. wing at the N. end. The main doorway is near the middle of the N. wall and a W. doorway opens near the re-entrant angle ; the latter has a chamfered four-centred head and continuous jambs. Incised on ashlar blocks over the W. doorway and the adjacent window are 'TD 1660' in an ornamental margin, and 'ID 1660'. Inside, several rooms retain plank-and-muntin partitions. Fireplaces occur on the S. end wall of the range and on the W. wall of the wing. Adjacent to the farmhouse on the S.W. is a *Granary* on staddle stones, with timber and ashlar walls, and a thatched roof.

(4) HOUSE (87061845), with rubble walls and thatched and slated roofs, is of 18th-century origin. An early 19th-century extension on the S., originally a dairy, is now incorporated in the dwelling. The W. front is of one storey with dormer windows above ; the E. front is two storeyed and has square-headed casement windows of two and of three lights ; the S. extension has similar windows.

(5) HOUSE (86821840), of two storeys, with squared rubble walls and thatched roofs, is of the 18th century. Inside, one room has a large open fireplace and a stop-chamfered ceiling beam.

(6) WHITEHALL COTTAGE (86971913), of two storeys, with coursed rubble walls and a thatched roof, is of the first half of the 18th century. The rubble walls have ashlar quoins. At the centre of the plan is a large open fireplace with a timber bressummer.

(7) MANOR FARM (87591885), house, of two storeys, with coursed rubble walls and a slate-covered roof, is of the late 18th century. The S.E. front is symmetrical and of three bays, with a central doorway in a small porch with a pediment, and with uniform sashed windows in both storeys. Inside, the plan is of class T. The S. room has a stone fireplace surround with egg-and-dart enrichment.

(8) COTTAGES (87571876), two adjacent, of one storey with attics, with squared rubble walls and thatched roofs, are of c. 1750. Each tenement has a class-S plan, the fireplaces being set back-to-back.

(9) HOUSE (87011836), of two storeys, with walls of ashlar and rubble, repaired in brickwork, and with slated roofs, is of late 18th-century origin, but it was extensively altered in the 19th century. Adjacent on the W. is a boundary wall of rusticated ashlar with gate-piers with pyramidal finials ; a low doorway in this wall has an elliptical head and a shaped stone lintel.

(10) HOUSE (86981838), of two storeys with rubble walls and a thatched roof, is of the late 18th century. The S. front is symmetrical and of three bays. The plan is of class T.

Other late 18th and early 19th-century monuments are as follows. In East Compton : a two-storeyed *Farmhouse* (87541869) of c. 1840. In West Compton : a *Cottage* (87281859) of c. 1800 ; *Tucker's Farm* (87141857), house, formerly two adjacent cottages ; a pair of *Cottages* (87081850) ; a *Cottage* (86941831). In Twyford : *Prystock Farm* (85501831), house, comprising two late 18th-century cottages ; *Twyford Farm* (85351903), house, of the mid 19th century, with a symmetrical E. front of three bays.

MEDIAEVAL AND LATER EARTHWORKS

(11) CULTIVATION REMAINS. The date of enclosure of the open fields is unknown. A late 18th or early 19th-century map (D.C.R.O.) shows nine separate open fields, all apparently in the last stages of piecemeal enclosure ; they existed substantially unaltered in 1844 (Tithe Map). Well preserved contour and cross-contour strip lynchets in four places in the parish represent some of these fields : those on the N. and N.E. slopes of Elbury Hill (863183) were in Hawkam Field ; those on the W. of Melbury Hill (868192) were in Incombe Field ; those on the S. and E. of Melbury Hill (871195) were in Forked Bridge Field ; those on the N.W. slopes of Fontmell Down (877182) were in Culverland Field.

ROMAN AND PREHISTORIC

(12) CROSS-DYKE (87781979–87701953), running from N.N.E. to S.S.W. across a ridge which rises steeply westwards to the summit of Melbury Hill, lies at an altitude of over 600 ft. and extends across the parish boundary into Melbury Abbas. It is some 300 yds. in length and comprises a bank with a ditch on the uphill side. At each end the dyke runs out on the shoulder of the slope above a combe. A gap of 30 yds. occurs where the dyke crosses the parish boundary ; it is probably an original

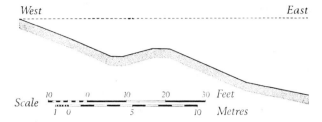

West   East

Scale
10   0   10   20   30   Feet
1   0   5   10   Metres

entrance, but disturbance makes this difficult to prove. Some 57 yds. S. of the boundary the ditch suddenly deepens and here, where the earthwork is best preserved, the ditch is 16 ft. wide and 5 ft. deep ; the bank is 20 ft. across, and 8 ft. high from below and 2 ft. high from above. Near the N. end the dyke is cut by a deep hollow-way coming from Compton Down.

(13) BOWL BARROW (88511894), over 700 ft. above sea-level, on the neck of the spur of Compton Down, lies in arable land. Diam. 45 ft., ht. 1½ ft.

'CELTIC' FIELDS, see p. 120, Group (79).

7 EAST ORCHARD (8317)

(O.S. 6 ins., ST 81 NW)

The parish, of some 950 acres, lies 3½ m. S.W. of Shaftesbury. The land is entirely Kimmeridge Clay and slopes gently down from 380 ft. above sea-level in the N. to 170 ft. in the S. ; it is drained by the Orchard Water, a small brook on the E. boundary of the parish. Until the 19th century East Orchard was a parochial chapelry of Iwerne Minster ; it included Hartgrove, now part of Fontmell Magna. The houses are dispersed and there is no village nucleus. An early mention of the settlement, *Archet*, occurs in the 15th-century Register of Shaftesbury Abbey (B.M., Harley MS. 61, f. 51v.), reciting pre-conquest matter.

ECCLESIASTICAL

(1) THE PARISH CHURCH OF ST. THOMAS, then a chapel-of-ease to Iwerne Minster, was built in 1859, and the former chapel on another site (see (11)) was demolished (Sarum Dioc. Regy., 1859). A font was transferred from the old to the new building.

Fitting—*Font* : of stone, with circular bowl with slightly tapering sides, chamfered below and with cuttings in rim for locked cover, now gone ; probably late 12th or early 13th century, with 19th-century retooling ; stem and base, 19th century.

(2) METHODIST CHAPEL (83491823), with walls of ashlar and of rubble and with a slated roof, is probably of late 18th-century origin ; it was enlarged on the S. in 1824. The gabled S. front has a segmental-headed doorway and, above, a round-headed window with a cast-iron lattice ; two similar windows occur in each of the E. and W. walls ; the N. end is masked by a cottage, perhaps contemporary with the original chapel. In the

S. part of the E. wall are two tablets, one recording the date of enlargement, the other with 'Ebenezer. Sam. VII, 12'. Inside, the meeting room (33½ ft. by 17 ft.) has a plain gallery at the S. end.

SECULAR

(3) BRIDGE (83441643), across the Orchard Water, of brick with one semicircular arch, is of the first half of the 19th century.

(4) GULLIVER'S FARM (83371660), house, of two storeys with rubble walls and a thatched roof, is of late 17th or early 18th-century origin with late 18th-century alterations and additions. The original range has a symmetrical S. front of three bays, with casement windows of two and of three lights, some retaining wrought-iron frames. The extension at the W. end of the range is of two bays. A stone at the base of a brick chimneystack on the E. gable is inscribed L.G. 1785. Inside, one room has a heavily chamfered beam with run-out stops.

(5) GREAT HOUSE (83461649), of two storeys, with walls of ashlar and brickwork and with thatched roofs, is of the 17th century, with an 18th-century service wing on the E. In the original W. range the three-bay W. front and the gabled S. wall are of ashlar, with weathered and hollow-chamfered first-floor string-courses. The W. front has casement windows of four square-headed lights in the upper storey ; in the lower storey the windows probably were once uniform with those above, but they now have 19th-century sashes ; the central doorway has a plain stone surround. The gabled S. wall has a small blocked oval window on the ground floor and blocked square-headed openings above ; the gabled N. wall is of brick-work and has no openings. The E. wing has walls of chequered flint and stonework in the lower storey and of brick above. Inside, the plan of the W. range appears formerly to have been of class F, but the range has been shortened and the presumed N. bay has gone. The main ground-floor room has an open fire-place and a six-panel ceiling with deeply-chamfered intersecting beams. The stairs, in the through-passage on the S. of the chimneybreast, are of the 17th century and have moulded close strings, square newel posts, moulded handrails and turned balusters.

(6) WHITEGATE FARM (83641660), house, of two storeys with attics, has walls of squared and coursed rubble and thatched roofs. The three-bay S. range is of the late 17th or early 18th century and the N. wing, with brick walls, was added later in the 18th century. Inside, one room has a stop-chamfered beam.

(7) BOWLING GREEN FARM (83101743), house, demolished in 1962, was single-storeyed with dormer-windowed attics and was of late 17th-century origin. In the 18th century the southern two-thirds of the range was heightened to two storeys. The walls were partly of rubble, partly of brick, and partly of cob; the roofs were thatched. The doorways at each end of the

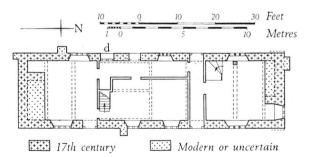

N
10   0   10   20   30   Feet
1   0   5   10   Metres

d

▨▨▨ *17th century*   ▨▨▨ *Modern or uncertain*

through-passage had heavy chamfered timber frames, as also had the southern doorway in the E. wall. A window (d) in the W. wall, nearly opposite the last-named opening probably replaced a former doorway. At the N. end of the range, rounded timber wall-plates projected externally below the eaves. Several casement windows had chamfered wooden mullions of stout cross-section, probably original. Intersecting ceiling beams in the central room retained mortices for former partitions. The open fireplaces against the N. and S. end walls had been blocked up.

(8) TRAPDOOR FARM (83351775), house, of two storeys with walls of rubble and of brick and with a slated roof, is of the early 19th century. The brick-faced S.W. front is symmetrical and of three bays, with a round-headed central doorway and with uniform sashed windows in both storeys.

(9) SWAINSCOMBE FARM (83621780), house, of two storeys with brick walls and tiled roofs, is of the early 19th century. The S.E. front is symmetrical and of five bays, with a central doorway and with uniform sashed windows in both storeys.

(10) COTTAGE (83751772), of two storeys with brick walls and a thatched roof, is of the late 18th century.

MEDIAEVAL AND LATER EARTHWORKS

(11) PLATFORM AND ENCLOSURE (84211822) of the former chapel-of-ease (see (1)), lie near the N. boundary of the parish. On the Tithe Map of 1840 the building appears as a rectangle with a projection, perhaps a porch, at the centre of the S. side. The building now is represented by a sunken platform, some 30 ft. by 40 ft., orientated E.–W.

(12) CULTIVATION REMAINS. Nothing is known of the date of enclosure of the open fields. Remains of ridge-and-furrow, 5 yds. to 9 yds. wide and arranged in interlocking furlongs, extend over a wide area in the central and southern parts of the parish (R.A.F., V.A.P., CPE/UK 2018 : 3178–3208).

8 EAST STOUR (7922)

(O.S. 6 ins., ST 82 SW, ST 72 SE, ST 82 NW)

East Stour, with an area of 1,786 acres, lies on the E. bank of the R. Stour. The western third of the area is on Corallian Limestone at an altitude of about 300 ft., sloping W. to the river; the other two-thirds are on Kimmeridge Clay, undulating between 300 ft. and 370 ft., except in the S.E. where the land rises steeply to 655 ft. on Duncliffe Hill, an outlying Greensand promontory surrounded by Gault Clay.

The history of settlement is ill-documented and largely unknown, but the pattern of field boundaries indicates slow expansion eastwards across the area of Kimmeridge Clay from a nucleus in the W. East Stour village, one of the *Sture* holdings of Domesday (*V.C.H., Dorset* iii, 82–3), was certainly the original settlement. Fields of irregular shape immediately E. of the village represent early encroachment on the waste. The larger and more rectilinear fields to N. and N.E. indicate post-mediaeval development; to judge by the date of the farmhouses at New House (14)

and Cole Street (15) this development is of the late 18th century. The S.E. part of the parish with rigidly geometrical field boundaries was enclosed from the waste in 1804 (Enclosure Map, D.C.R.O.), and the buildings in this area are of the early 19th century.

ECCLESIASTICAL

(1) THE PARISH CHURCH, CHRIST CHURCH, stands in the S. of the village. The walls are of local limestone ashlar with Greensand dressings and the roofs are slate-covered. The church was built in 1842 to the design of G. Alexander, in the Romanesque style on a cruciform plan with a central tower. The former church was demolished and some fittings from it were transferred to the new building.

EAST STOUR · CHRIST CHURCH

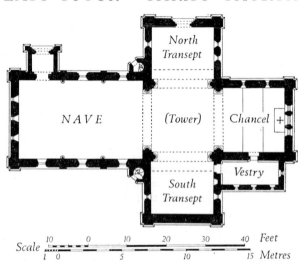

Scale   10   0   10   20   30   40   Feet
        1   0   5   10   15   Metres

Fittings—*Bible-box :* of oak, with foliate carving on front panel, 17th century. *Chests :* two, of oak ; one with fielded panels and ball feet, 18th century ; another with moulded and fielded panels, beaded corners, and three locks, late 18th century, on modern legs. *Font :* with square Purbeck marble bowl with shallow round-headed arcading, on cylindrical stone centre shaft and four coarsely moulded corner shafts, with plain rectangular base, 12th century. *Lectern :* comprising carved and gilt pelican-in-piety (Plate 21), perhaps reused finial from former sounding-board or reredos ; 18th century (cf. *Dorset III*, Plates 47, 98).

CROSS SHAFT, fragment, now in the British Museum (1969/4-1) was recovered during the demolition of a house in East Stour in 1939. The stone is 10 ins. to 11 ins. square and 2 ft. 4 ins. high (Plate 3). Each face is richly decorated with vine-scroll, inter-lace and palmette ornament, probably of the late 10th or early 11th century (*Arch. J.*, CXVII (1960), 82–87).

SECULAR

(2) CHURCH FARM (79832285), house, a few paces W. of the church, is of two storeys and has walls of rubble and ashlar, and

tiled roofs ; it is of the early 19th century. The N.E. front is symmetrical and of three bays, with a central doorway and with uniform sashed windows.

(3) ORCHARD HOUSE (80182327), of two storeys with rubble walls and thatched roofs, is of the early 17th century. A stone inscribed 1600 appears to be of the 19th century, but doubtless is a replica of an original date-stone. Inside the house, two large fireplaces have stone jambs and chamfered timber bressummers ; the W. chimneybreast formerly had a stair beside it. Two stop-chamfered beams are exposed.

(4) COTTAGE (80232330), of one storey with attics, with rubble walls and a thatched roof, is of the 17th century. Inside, one room has an open fireplace with chamfered stone jambs and a chamfered oak bressummer ; a plank-and-muntin partition and some chamfered beams are preserved.

(5) COTTAGE (80372347), of two storeys with rubble walls and a thatched roof, is of the late 17th or early 18th century ; inside, three chamfered beams are exposed.

(6) HIGH GROVE FARM (81462397), house, of one storey with dormer-windowed attics, has rubble walls and tile-covered roofs. Above the S. doorway is a date-stone with T.S. 1620 in relief, probably the date of the house. Inside, the through passage is flanked by original timber partitions. The middle room

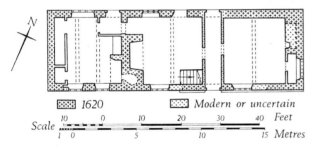

1620   Modern or uncertain

Scale

no doubt originally the main living-room of the farmhouse, has a large open fireplace ; the oven now opens to a fireplace in the W. room, but this is probably a modification; the N. window in the middle room retains an original moulded timber surround. The stairs are modern.

(7) COTTAGES (80902305), range of three, with rubble walls and thatched roofs, are of the late 17th century.

MONUMENTS (8–15)

Unless otherwise described the following houses and cottages are of the late 18th or of the first half of the 19th century ; they are two-storeyed, with rubble walls and tiled or slate-covered roofs.

(8) *Fir Tree Cottage* (82242352), with a symmetrical S. front of three bays, dates from shortly after 1804 when the land on which it stands was enclosed.

(9) *Cottages* (82242348), pair, 30 yds. S. of the foregoing, similarly date from *c.* 1804.

(10) *Manor Farm* (80552303), house, is largely modern, but it incorporates an 18th-century cottage on the S.

(11) *Cottages* (79962295), range of three, comprise two late 18th-century dwellings ; the S. dwelling is of the early 19th century.

(12) *The Crown Inn* (80422354), originally a late 18th-century range of three cottages, became an inn in the 19th century.

(13) *Cottage* (80502369), of late 18th-century origin, has a symmetrical S. front of two bays with a central doorway. Adjacent on the E. a 19th-century range, now ruinous, was used in the late 19th century as a Methodist Chapel ; its original purpose is uncertain.

(14) *New House Farm* (80132499), house, dates probably from *c.* 1800 and has a symmetrical S. front of three bays with a central doorway.

(15) *Cole Street Farm* (81782502), house, is of the late 18th century. At the centre of the three-bay S. front is a 19th-century ashlar porch with a round-headed opening.

9 FARNHAM (9515)
(O.S. 6 ins., ST 91 NE, ST 91 NW, ST 91 SE, ST 91 SW)

The parish has an area of 1,420 acres, wholly on Chalk, and occupies the head of the valley of the Gussage Brook at altitudes between 250 ft. and 500 ft. above sea-level. In some places deposits of Clay-with-flints overlie the Chalk. Woods in the W. and N. are part of Cranborne Chase. The history of settlement is obscure ; Domesday has five entries for *Fern(e)ham*, not all relating to the present settlement (*V.C.H., Dorset* iii, 83, 100, 101, 102, 105) ; one entry almost certainly concerns Minchington in Sixpenny Handley (*Dorset* V), another probably relates to Tollard Farnham and a third may well refer to Hookswood Farm (4). The boundaries shown on O.S., 1811 and the blocks of land recorded in the Tithe Map of 1843 are comparable in complexity with the Domesday record.

Although not itself a Monument, mention must be made of the Pitt-Rivers Museum, 500 yds. S. of the parish church. At the time of the Commission's survey it contained an important archaeological and ethnographical collection, including material recovered by General Pitt-Rivers during his researches in the Cranborne Chase region.

ECCLESIASTICAL

(1) THE PARISH CHURCH OF ST. LAWRENCE, near the E. boundary of the parish, has walls of flint, of Greensand ashlar, of squared rubble, and of ashlar banded and chequered with knapped flint ; the roof-coverings are of tile and slate. The *Nave* is of uncertain date, but probably of the 12th century. The *South Tower*, incorporating a *Porch*, is of the late 15th or early 16th century. The *North Aisle* was added in 1835, and the *Chancel* and *North Vestry* are of 1886.

Architectural Description—The E. wall of the *Nave* with the chancel arch is of 1886. The N. wall was removed when the N. aisle was built, in 1835, and two iron columns with moulded

FARNHAM
The Parish Church of St. Lawrence

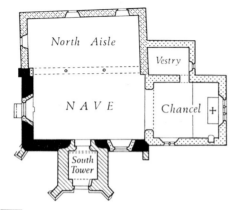

Probably 12th century

Late 15th or early 16th century

1835　　　　1886, or uncertain

Scale | 10 | 0 | 10 | 20 | 30 Feet
| 1 | 0 | | 5 | 10 | Metres

capitals were inserted. The S. wall appears to be largely original ; it is rendered, but where the rendering has fallen away the structure is seen to be of flint. Internally a pronounced ledge some 2 ft. below the wall-plate indicates heightening, perhaps in the 18th century. At the S.E. corner is a weathered ashlar buttress of one stage. Adjacent is a window of uncertain date with a double-chamfered two-centred head and continuous jambs, partly of brickwork ; it is probably of mediaeval origin with 19th-century alterations which involved the removal of a mullion and tracery. The S. doorway has a moulded four-centred head and continuous jambs with run-out stops. At the S.W. corner is a diagonal buttress of two weathered stages. The W. wall has a stout central buttress of ashlar, in one stage with a weathered head ; it is of uncertain date, but perhaps original. Further N. is a low ashlar pilaster-buttress, also with a weathered head. Over the central buttress is a window with chamfered ashlar jambs and a four-centred head ; the latter is of brickwork and probably of the 19th century, but it retains fragments of a late mediaeval label with square stops.

The *North Aisle* has rendered walls with ashlar quoins ; the windows have plain two-centred heads.

The *South Tower* has two stages. The lower stage is of ashlar partly banded with flint ; the upper stage is of chequered ashlar and flint. A chamfered plinth at the base of the tower occurs on the S., but not on the E. and W. sides. Each stage is capped by a weathered and hollow-chamfered string-course, and at the top is an embattled parapet with a moulded coping and with small 17th-century corner pinnacles. In the lower stage, diagonal buttresses of three weathered stages occur at the S.E. and S.W. corners. The S. doorway of the porch has a moulded four-centred head and continuous jambs with run-out stops. In the W. wall of the tower a square-headed loop gives light to a chamber over the porch. In the upper stage the N., E. and S. sides of the tower have each a two-light belfry window with a central mullion intersecting a four-centred head at the apex.

The *Roofs* of the nave and N. aisle are masked by plain plaster barrel vaults, probably of 1835.

Fittings—Bells : two ; treble with 'Ora Mente Pia' in black-letter, c. 1450 ; tenor with 'Mr Clvtterbook Wm Tosier, 1732'. *Door :* in S. doorway of porch, with beaded vertical planks and wrought-iron studs and strap-hinges, 18th-century. *Fonts :* two, of stone ; one with twelve plain sides continuing as chamfers on stem and dying into hollow-chamfered square base, late mediaeval ; another of crude baluster form with gadrooned bowl and stem, moulded base, and gadrooned stone cover, late 17th century. *Inscription :* In N. aisle, on E. wall, marble tablet recording building of N. aisle, 1835.

Monuments and *Floorslabs. Monuments :* In chancel, on S. wall, (1) of Alexander Bower, 1616, slate tablet with marble border. In N. aisle, near W. wall, (2) of Rev. Phillip Rideout, 1834, and others of his family, panelled stone pedestal with inscription on sides, and small shield-of-arms, by Simmonds of Blandford ; reset on N. wall, (3) of Rev. Phillip Rideout, 1814, and others of his family, marble tablet. *Floorslabs :* In nave, (1) of Thom[as Potticar]y, [1689] ; (2) of Christophe. . . . , stone slab with foliate border, partly covered by font ; adjacent, (3) of Christopher, 1708, John, 1711/2, and their mother Lucy Potticary, 1745, large slate slab with fine lettering and foliate border.

Plate : includes silver cup, without assay marks, probably early 18th century, and silver-plated paten and flagon, both unmarked, probably early 19th century. *Pulpit :* of oak, polygonal, with three sides with fielded panelling in two heights, with beaded stiles and rails, and moulded cornice, early 18th century. *Wall-paintings :* In nave, on W. wall, two roundels enclosing texts, one Ephesians IV, 31, the other indecipherable, probably 17th or early 18th century.

SECULAR

(2) STOCKS (95881510), of oak, with chamfered posts and with an iron hasp, are of the 18th century. The monument is protected by a modern brick kerb and a lead-covered timber hood.

(3) BUSSEY STOOL LODGE (93161629), cottage, of one storey with attics, has brick walls and tiled roofs. The central part of the range dates from early in the 18th century and comprises two rooms, one with an open fireplace and oven, the other unheated ; it is built with unusually large bricks. Inside, the rooms have lightly chamfered beams with ogee stops. Later in the 18th century the range was extended to N.E. and S.W., the N.E. extension containing a larder with ceiling hooks, perhaps for venison, the S.E. extension containing a living room, a stable and a loft.

(4) HOOKSWOOD FARM (94781510), house, is partly of one storey with attics and partly two-storeyed. The single-storeyed part has walls of rubble and flint with squared rubble quoins and dates from the late 16th or early 17th century ; the two-storeyed range is of the late 18th century. Inside, the older range contains two ground-floor rooms, each with an open fireplace ; one room has a chamfered beam with splayed stops. In the 18th-century range several rooms have walls panelled in two heights, with beaded stiles and rails, and fielded panels.

(5) SOUTH FARM (96041501), cottage, of one storey with attics, has walls of rubble, flint and brickwork, and thatched roofs ; it is probably of 16th-century origin. In the S.E. room the ceiling has four stop-chamfered beams resting on a central post ; the fireplace has chamfered stone jambs and an elm bressummer. In the N.W. room the fireplace is similar to that

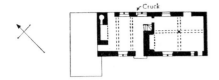

described and the ceiling has two stop-chamfered beams. Part of a cruck truss remains in the N.E. wall.

(6) COTTAGE (95951507), of one storey with an attic, has flint and rubble walls, partly rendered, and a thatched roof; it was built probably in the late 17th or early 18th century. Inside, a stop-chamfered beam is exposed, and one room has an open fireplace with a chamfered bressummer.

MONUMENTS (7–11)

Unless otherwise described the following cottages are two-storeyed, with walls of rubble, flint and cob, partly rendered, and with thatched roofs.

(7) *Cottage* (95981510), with a S. front of two bays with a central doorway, is probably of the early 18th century. The gabled W. wall is of banded brickwork and flint.

(8) *Cottage* (95961510), probably of the first half of the 18th century, has a later extension in brick and flint on the E.

(9) *Cottage* (95871504), containing an exposed chamfered beam and an open fireplace with a chamfered bressummer, probably is contemporary with the foregoing.

(10) *Cottage* (95661545), of one storey with an attic, is of the late 18th century.

(11) *Cottage* (95651547), is of the early 19th century.

ROMAN AND PREHISTORIC

'CELTIC' FIELDS, see p. 119, Group (75).

10 FIFEHEAD MAGDALEN (7821)
(O.S. 6 ins., ST 72 SE, ST 71 NE)

The parish of Fifehead Magdalen has an area of 973 acres and lies on the N. bank of the R. Stour. The northern and central parts occupy a ridge of Corallian Limestone, rising to 320 ft. above sea-level. Below the ridge the land is Oxford Clay, inclined E. and S. to the Stour and W. to its tributary the Cale. The two rivers flow together at the S.W. corner of the parish, 170 ft. above sea-level. The village stands on the ridge, the houses flanking a street which runs W. from the parish church. Manor Farm and Middle Farm, beyond the W. end of the street, are on Clay and appear to represent an extension of settlement from the original nucleus, presumably following enclosure of the open fields. Manor Farm (8) has a late 16th-century house, indicating that enclosure occurred at that period, or earlier.

ECCLESIASTICAL

(1) THE PARISH CHURCH OF ST. MARY MAGDALEN has walls of squared and coursed rubble with ashlar dressings, and stone-slated roofs. The *Chancel*, *Nave* and *South Tower* are of 14th-century origin. The *North Chapel* appears to have been designed as a setting for monument (2) and therefore in its present form is presumably of *c*. 1750; the wording of monument (3), however, implies that it replaces a chapel or burial vault of 1693. The church was restored in 1905 (Faculty, Sarum Dioc. Regy.).

FIFEHEAD MAGDALEN
The Parish Church of St. Mary Magdalen

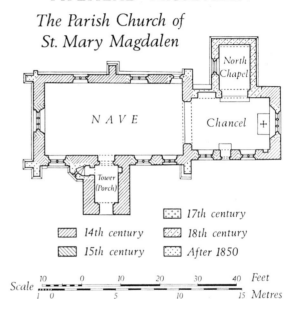

Scale

Architectural Description—The E. window of the *Chancel* is modern. In the N. wall, a vertical joint on the E. of the N. chapel indicates the position of a former window. The opening to the N. chapel has a chamfered segmental arch of rubble springing from chamfered imposts on lightly chamfered jambs. Further W. is a blocked window with a segmental rear-arch, of uncertain date. In the S. wall are two restored 15th-century windows, each of two cinquefoil-headed lights in a hollow-chamfered square-headed surround; between them is a 14th-century doorway with a chamfered two-centred head and continuous jambs; the rear-arch is two-centred and chamfered.

The *North Chapel* has walls of ashlar and of coursed rubble with plain square plinths. Internally, a moulded trefoil wall-arch at the head of the gabled N. wall springs from shaped corbels, forming a recess for the Newman monument (2). In the W. wall is a square-headed window with a moulded surround, probably of the 17th century, reset.

The *Nave* has, on the E., a two-centred chancel arch of one order, lightly chamfered, the chamfers continuing on the jambs and ending at broach stops. A straight joint in the N. spandrel is probably the jamb of a former rood-loft doorway. The N. wall has been extensively restored. At the E. end is a modern buttress; at the centre is a 14th-century buttress of two weathered stages; at the W. end is a small modern buttress of old masonry reused. The window at the E. end of the N. wall, with a chamfered round head and a wooden lintel in place of a rear-arch, is of the 17th century; further W. is a restored 15th-century window of two cinquefoil-headed lights in a square-headed casement-moulded surround; the western window is of 14th-century origin, with two ogee-headed lights under tracery in a square-headed surround; the heads and the tracery are modern. The S. wall has, on the E., a rebuilt buttress of two weathered stages on a plinth which suggests that the original buttress was larger than at present. At the S.W. corner is a modern angle-buttress in which each wing is capped with reset 15th-century weathering. Of the two windows between the E. buttress and the S. tower, that on the E. is similar to the westernmost opening in the N. wall; that on the W. is similar to those in the S. wall of the chancel. The S. doorway is of the late 14th century and has a chamfered two-centred head and continuous jambs; the rear-arch is segmental and chamfered. The western part of the S. wall has been rebuilt above window-sill level, with a restored and reset 15th-century window of two cinquefoil-headed lights. The W. wall has a 15th-century window of three cinquefoil-headed lights, with vertical tracery in a casement-moulded two-centred head with continuous jambs; the head and tracery have been renewed. At the N. end of the W. wall is a modern square-set buttress with reset 15th-century weathering.

The *South Tower* is of two stages, with moulded string-courses and an embattled parapet; the upper stage was rebuilt in 1905. In the lower stage, the *Porch* archway has a chamfered two-centred head and continuous jambs; above is a modern trefoil-headed loop. The vice turret is modern.

Fittings—*Bells*: three; treble by John Wallis with inscription 'Prayse God IW 1595'; 2nd by Thomas Purdue, inscribed 'Anno Domini 1683, EG TM CW TP'; tenor inscribed 'ave maria' in black-letter, Salisbury foundry, 15th century; *Chandeliers*: four, of brass, with globular pendants supporting two tiers of sconces on scrolled arms, with vase-shaped upper and gadrooned lower finials (Plate 39); 18th century. *Chair*: of oak, with turned front legs, enriched rails, shaped arm-rests, panelled back with flower enrichment and large fleur-de-lis in central lozenge, and scroll cresting; 17th century. *Chest*: of oak, with panelled sides; late 18th century. *Churchyard Cross*: S.E. of chancel, with chamfered stone base with shafted angles, 15th century, reset on modern plinth and with modern shaft and head. *Coffin Stools*: two, of oak, with turned legs and enriched rails; 17th century. *Communion Table*: of oak, with turned legs, enriched rails and plain stretchers; late 17th century, top modern. *Doors*: two; one in S. doorway, of oak planks hinged at centre, with enriched border and cover-fillets and two-centred head (Plate 22); planks carved with letters W T B, O I T, each letter occupying shield-shaped recess or boss, and 1637 in sunk panel; another in porch archway, with plain boards and beaded fillets, late 17th century. *Font*: (Plate 12) with octagonal stone bowl with two trefoil-headed panels on each face, 15th century, on gadrooned and fluted baluster-shaped pedestal, with moulded octagonal base and cable moulding at top, early 18th century. *Font-cover*: of oak, octagonal, with turned finial, 18th century.

Monuments: In N. chapel, reset on E. wall, (1) of Thomas Newman, 1649 [by a misprint Hutchins (IV, 58) gives 1602], and his son Richard, 1664, marble tablet in segmental-headed moulded stone surround, surmounted by three cartouches-of-arms of Newman; tablet, 17th century, surround probably

18th century; on N. wall, (2) of Sir Richard Newman Bart., 1721, his wife Frances, 1730, his son Samwell, 1747, and his daughters, Frances, 1775, Barbara, 1763, and Elizabeth, 1774 (Plate 41), large wall monument of white, grey, pink and yellow marbles, with busts of Sir Richard, his wife and his son, medallions (Plate 20) of his daughters, foliate brackets, wreaths, inscription tablet, cartouche, and obelisk-shaped back-plate; voids left in inscription for dates after 1747, subsequently filled in, hence monument probably *c.* 1750; reset on W. wall, (3) of Richard Newman, [1683], stone tablet recording transfer of coffin, 1693. In nave, on N. wall, (4) of George Davidge, 1772, his wife Joan, 1759, their children John, 1744, Hester, 1758, George, 1772, tablet in stone surround with enriched architrave and entablature, and broken segmental pediment with urn finial (Plate 39). In churchyard, 10 paces S. of chancel, (5) of Maximilian Marsh, 1642, table-tomb; 12 paces S.W. of porch, (6) of Thomas Newman, 1668, table-tomb; adjacent to the foregoing, (7) table-tomb, anonymous.

Niche: In S. porch, in E. wall, rectangular recess with segmental head, probably mediaeval. *Piscina*: In chancel, in S. wall, 14th-century stone bowl with quatrefoil sinking, in square recess with chamfered two-centred head. *Plate*: includes Elizabethan silver cup and cover-paten (Plate 25) with assay marks of 1573, and the same date inscribed on cover-paten; also silver paten of 1822. *Royal Arms*: in relief, gilded, late 18th-century. *Miscellanea*: Cherub head with wings, carved in softwood, 18th century.

SECULAR

(2) BRIDGE (79012061), over the Stour, of coursed rubble with two elliptical arches, dates probably from the late 18th or early 19th century.

(3) BRIDGE (76702014), over the Stour, of coursed rubble with two main arches and two subsidiary arches for floodwater, all round-headed, is of the first half of the 19th century.

(4) INSCRIPTION (75911999), on a stone built into a modern bridge over the Cale, 'Here End[s the S]talbridge Road', is of the late 18th century.

(5) FIFEHEAD HOUSE (78362161), some 50 yds. S.E. of (1), was demolished in 1964; it was of three storeys, with ashlar walls and slate-covered roofs (Plate 44). It was built in 1807 and had a class-U plan. The E. front was symmetrical and of three bays, with large sashed windows in each storey and with an elliptical-headed central doorway sheltered by a portico with four unfluted Corinthian columns and an enriched entablature. The ground-floor windows flanking the doorway were set in shallow segmental-headed recesses. A slender plat-band marked the first floor; an entablature above the second-floor windows had a triglyph frieze and a moulded cornice capped by a low parapet wall; the corners of the façade had rusticated quoins. The N. and S. elevations of the main building were each of three bays, with architectural details as described; the W. elevation was masked by a two-storey service range. Inside, the principal rooms had ceilings with enriched plaster cornices, doorways with moulded and reeded surrounds, and carved marble chimneypieces. The open-string stairs had balustrades with panels of foliate trellis-work in cast lead, set between plain iron uprights; the handrails were of mahogany.

(6) THE VICARAGE (78052152), about 275 yds. W. of (1), is of two storeys and has rubble walls, in part rendered, with ashlar dressings, and a thatched roof; it is probably of 17th-century origin, with 18th-century alterations and enlargement. The 18th-century S. front is of six bays, with a plain string-course at

first-floor level and with plain quoins at the S.E. and S.W. corners, that on the S.W. partly obliterated. The lower storey has four french windows and two two-light casement windows, all with moulded stone architraves ; the upper storey has six uniform two-light casement windows. A wing projecting northwards at the E. end of the S. range has a heavy stone quoin, indicating that this part of the house is of earlier date than the S. range. The N.W. wing is of the 18th century. Inside the house, some chamfered and stop-chamfered beams are exposed.

(7) MIDDLE FARM (77662125), house, of two storeys with rubble walls and tile-covered roofs, was built on an L-shaped plan in the 17th century. The S. front (Plate 30) is approximately symmetrical and of three bays, with a central doorway with a chamfered four-centred head, and casement windows of two, three and four square-headed lights with rebated and hollow-chamfered stone surrounds ; the windows in the lower storey have labels. The N.E. wing was added late in the 18th century. Inside, the S. range has a central through-passage flanked by moulded plank-and-muntin partitions.

(8) MANOR FARM (77472114), house, of two storeys with rubble walls and tiled roofs, is probably of late 16th-century origin. The N. front is of four bays, with stone windows of two, three and four square-headed lights, with moulded labels in the lower storey. The doorway is square-headed, with stout timber posts and lintel. A small round-headed mezzanine window near the E. end of the N. front, now blocked, indicates the position of an original staircase. In the western part of the S. elevation is a stone doorway with a moulded four-centred head, continuous jambs with run-out stops, a moulded square surround, and small blank shields in the spandrels. Elsewhere, the S. elevation has three-light and four-light windows uniform with those of the N. front. Internally the original plan has been obliterated, but the entrance vestibule retains the ends of truncated, heavily moulded beams and wall-plates.

(9) COTTAGE (77492117), of two storeys with rubble walls and a thatched roof, is of the early 17th century. The N. front has casement windows of two and of three lights with plain timber surrounds and leaded glazing. Inside, the plan is a variant of class F, with two ground-floor rooms instead of three ; the S. part of the through-passage has been turned into a store room. The living room, on the W., has a chamfered beam with moulded stops and chamfered wall-plates ; the open fireplace has a cambered and chamfered bressummer.

(10) COTTAGE (77312109), of two storeys with rubble walls and a thatched roof, is of the 17th century. Although the building was at one time divided into two tenements it appears originally to have been a single dwelling with a class-F plan. The living room has an open fireplace with a chamfered, four-centred timber bressummer and chamfered stone jambs, and a ceiling of four panels formed by deeply chamfered intersecting beams and wall-plates.

(11) LOWER FARM (76582041), of three storeys, with ashlar and rubble walls and slate-covered roofs, dates from the early part of the 19th century and probably is the property advertised in the *Salisbury Journal* on 6 Feb. 1826, as ACourt's Mill, a newly erected flour and grist mill with a dwelling house adjoining.

The S.W. and N.E. fronts are uniform, each being symmetrical and of three bays, with a central doorway and large segmental-headed sashed windows ; plain plat-bands occur at first-floor level, the corners are defined by rusticated quoins, and the eaves have brick dentil cornices. A two-storey wing on the S.E. has a lean-to roof masked by swept parapets ; the

details of the wing are similar to those of the main building. Single-storeyed outbuildings extend the range to S.W. and S.E.

The *Post Office* (78122151), a single-storeyed cottage with dormer-windowed attics, with rubble walls and a slate-covered roof, is probably of the late 18th century. *The Villa* (78232151), a two-storeyed house with rubble walls and a slate-covered roof, and with a symmetrical N. front of three bays with a central doorway and segmental-headed casement windows, is of the mid 19th century. Two two-storeyed *Cottages* (77952150 and 77822134), with rubble walls and thatched roofs, are of the first half of the 19th century.

MEDIAEVAL AND LATER EARTHWORKS

(12) CULTIVATION REMAINS. The date of enclosure of the open fields is unknown, but it appears to have taken place by the end of the 16th century since Manor Farm (8) came into existence after enclosure. Air photographs show that ridge-and-furrow of the fields formerly extended over much of the southern half of the parish (R.A.F. CPE/UK 1925 : 1311–12). It was arranged in furlongs, sometimes with reversed-S curves.

11 FONTMELL MAGNA (8617)

(O.S. 6 ins., ST 81 NE, ST 81 NW)

The parish, covering some 3,200 acres, occupies a narrow strip of land extending E.–W. across the Chalk escarpment. The E. extremity, on the dip-slope beyond the top of the escarpment, falls eastwards from 700 ft. to 420 ft. above sea-level. To the W. the almost precipitous Chalk scarp stands 300 ft. high and has two dry re-entrant valleys cutting into it, Longcombe and Littlecombe Bottoms. From the foot of the scarp the land slopes gently W., on Upper Greensand and Gault, into the valley of the Fontmell Brook which flows from N. to S. about 200 ft. above sea-level. Further W. the land rises to a low N.–S. ridge of Lower Greensand and then falls to the valley of the Twyford Brook. N.W. of the latter, a roughly circular area of land named Hartgrove is joined with the rest of the parish by a narrow neck ; it is entirely on Kimmeridge Clay and lies between 180 ft. and 380 ft. above sea-level. Although considered part of the parish for civil purposes during the 19th century, Hartgrove was originally a division of East Orchard, itself formerly a chapelry of Iwerne Minster ; the scattered settlement, the irregular field shapes, and the existence of Blackven Common all indicate late occupation of the area, and this is supported by the fact that the name Hartgrove does not appear in documents until as late as 1254 (Fägersten, 30).

Fontmell Magna village stands at the foot of the escarpment and is undoubtedly the earliest settlement in the parish. Bedchester, a scattered hamlet on the Lower Greensand ridge, is almost certainly of pre-conquest origin (Fägersten, 23). Hill Farm, on the Chalk dip-slope, first recorded in 1333, is a later settlement than Bedchester.

ECCLESIASTICAL

(1) THE PARISH CHURCH OF ST. ANDREW, near the middle of the village, has walls of Greensand ashlar and lead-covered roofs. The lower stages of the *West Tower* are of the second half of the 15th century. The *Nave, South Aisle* and *South Porch* are probably of mediaeval origin, but they were rebuilt in *c.* 1862 and no original work remains. The *Chancel, North Vestry* and *North Aisle* are of 1862. When the N. aisle was built a carved parapet of 1530 (Plate 10) was transferred to it from its former position on the old S. aisle and S. porch (Hutchins III, plate opp. 557). The architect for these works was G. Evans of Wimborne (Faculty, Sarum Dioc. Regy.).

Architectural Description—Reset in the N. wall of the N. aisle are four restored 15th-century windows, presumably from the former nave ; each is of two trefoil-headed lights with a central quatrefoil in a two-centred head under a moulded label. Above each buttress the string-course is interrupted by a gargoyle, and above the gargoyles are pinnacles with panelled sides and crocketed finials. The reset parapet of 1530 has two heights of square stone panelling between a moulded string-course and a moulded coping ; the merlons shown in Hutchins's engraving have gone. The lower height of the parapet is blind ; the upper height is pierced. Many of the lower panels enclose carved figures of men with weapons or implements; others enclose quatrefoils with foliate bosses or with shields charged with heraldic emblems, or words in black-letter composing an inscription. The words are no longer in order, and even in their former position on the S. aisle were only partly intelligible (Hutchins III, 558) ; nevertheless Hutchins noted the date 1530. The heraldic devices include roses, a portcullis, two stags, a knot, a heart, a fret, arms of Milton Abbey and arms of Stourton. One of the lower panels has a three-line black-letter inscription ' O man kyn bare tho' y' min '. In the upper height of the parapet each square panel has four triangular openings with cusps. Inside, the E. pier of the N. arcade has a reset 15th-century base, probably from the original S. arcade. A turret at the S.E. corner of the N. aisle probably survives from a former rood-loft vice turret, but it has been rebuilt and altered to accommodate a stair leading to the pulpit.

The *West Tower* is of four stages, with a moulded plinth, moulded string-courses between the stages and an embattled

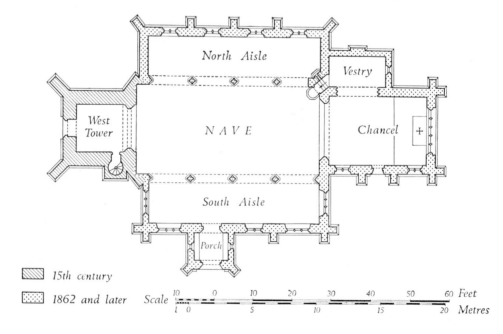

FONTMELL MAGNA *The Parish Church of St. Andrew*

15th century

1862 and later Scale

parapet with pinnacles. The top stage and parapet are of 1862, but the three lower stages are original; they have diagonal buttresses of five weathered stages, and a rectangular vice turret on the S. The tower arch is two-centred and of two orders, the inner order ogee-moulded, the outer order with a casement moulding, both continuous on the responds and ending at hollow-chamfered plinths. The W. doorway has a moulded four-centred head and continuous jambs and a four-centred label with square stops. The W. window has a hollow-chamfered two-centred head and continuous jambs, partly original; the three transomed lights and the vertical tracery are of 1862. The vice doorway has a chamfered two-centred head and continuous jambs; higher up, rebuilt masonry indicates a former doorway to a W. gallery, now gone. In the second stage a small quatrefoil loop opens eastwards into the nave, and square-headed loops occur on the N. and W. In the third stage each side of the tower has a window of two cinquefoil-headed lights with a central quatrefoil under a two-centred casement-moulded head with continuous jambs; the moulded labels have square and head stops. These were originally belfry windows, but they now are glazed and the belfry has been transferred to the 19th-century top stage. Reset in the fourth stage are fragments of capitals representing angels bearing scrolls, perhaps from the former nave arcades.

Fittings—*Bells:* six; 2nd inscribed 'Prayes ye the Lord. I.W. 1618'; 4th by W. Purdue, inscribed 'In God is my' (*sic*) in crowned letters alternating with 'Thomas Redout, William Vinson, 1641, W.P.'; 5th with black-letter inscription 'In Ter Sede Pia Pro Nobis Virgo Maria', *c.* 1450; 6th with 'Ave Maria' in crowned Lombardic letters, 15th century; others modern. *Chest:* of oak, with beaded stiles and rails, and three locks, late 17th century. *Clock:* perhaps 18th century. *Coffin stools:* four, with turned legs and plain stretchers, 17th and 18th century. *Communion Table:* In N. aisle, with turned legs, moulded stretchers and enriched top rail, mid 17th century. *Font:* of Greensand, with cylindrical stem, and round bowl carved in high relief with foliate scroll and birds (Plate 11), mid 12th century; base modern. *Font-cover:* of oak, with enriched border, probably 17th century. *Lectern:* with eagle, stand and base of cast-iron, mid 19th century (Plate 13).

Monuments: In vestry, reset on N. wall, (1) of Ann Bowles, 1696, small marble tablet. In W. tower, (2) of Jeremiah Sharp, 1787, oval marble tablet on pyramidal backing. In churchyard, set against S.E. corner of S. aisle, (3) of William Ridout, 1665, stone with oval inscription panel with scrolled surround, originally part of table-tomb.

Panelling: In vestry, made up to form closet, ten panels, each carved with arched surround enclosing finial with leaf and scrollwork, early 17th century; stiles, rails and additional panels modern. *Plate:* includes silver cup with plain conical bowl, stout knopped stem and moulded foot, mid 17th century, date-marks obliterated; silver stand-paten, probably 1666; pewter flagon 1¼ ft. high, with moulded base, handle shaped to be held in both hands, and domed cover with acorn finial, late 18th century, no marks; pewter almsdish, *c.* 1800.

Royal Arms: In W. tower, on canvas, of George III. *Screen:* reset under tower arch, of oak, with moulded stiles and rails enclosing carved and pierced panels in two heights; lower height linenfold, upper height with cusped tracery and with male and female busts in wreath surrounds (drawing, p. xii); moulded cornice with banded wreath frieze, incised on reverse of cornice 'Water Kin'; first half of 16th century. *Tables of Creed, Decalogue and Lord's Prayer:* In tower, four canvases,

inscribed 'Richard Bishop, John Bennett, Ch. wardens, 1817'. *Miscellanea:* Near E. gate of churchyard, loose fragment of gargoyle, mediaeval.

(2) CHAPEL, Methodist (86651707), with ashlar and rubble walls and with a tiled roof, was built in 1831 in enlargement of a building of 1797. The N. front has a round-headed doorway

METHODIST CHAPEL · FONTMELL MAGNA

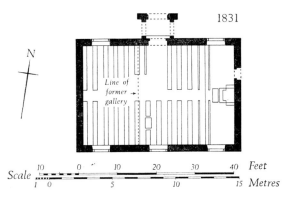

flanked by round-headed sashed windows; similar windows occur in the S. wall. A stone tablet over the doorway, partly obscured by a late 19th-century porch, records the dates given above. Inside, there is evidence of a former W. gallery, now removed. A schoolroom on the E. was added in 1874, and probably at this time the chapel roof was rebuilt and some internal fittings were renewed.

Fittings—*Clock:* by Mansfield, Shaftesbury, *c.* 1831. *Coffin stools:* two, with turned legs and moulded rails, 17th century. *Collecting shovels:* two, *c.* 1831. *Pulpit:* now in schoolroom, of two stages, *c.* 1831. *Seating:* now in schoolroom, two benches with open backs and shaped ends, perhaps *c.* 1797; on rostrum, chair with pointed back with septfoil panel, early 19th century.

SECULAR

(3) MANOR FARM (86921776), house, of two storeys with attics, with walls of ashlar and of rubble and with tiled roofs, dates from the 17th century; the plan is of class F. In the lower storey the W. front has stone windows of four square-headed lights with hollow-chamfered surrounds and moulded labels;

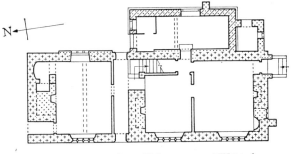

17th century   *Perhaps 18th century*   *Modern*

the doorway has a chamfered square head and continuous jambs ; in the upper storey the windows are modern. The E. doorway is similar to that on the W. Inside, a chamfered ceiling beam is exposed in the N. ground-floor room. The main partition walls are of uncertain date, but presumably occupy original positions if they are not themselves original. The partition between the middle room and the staircase is of reset 17th-century oak panelling in four heights ; above, the stairs have 18th-century trellis balustrading and a dog-gate at the top. Added to the E. side of the original range is a small service building, perhaps of the 18th century.

(4) MAYO'S FARM (86611721), house, has rubble walls with brick dressings and a thatched roof ; it is of early 17th-century origin and was formerly single-storeyed, with a class-I plan. Probably in the 18th century the range was extended southwards by one bay, and it was heightened to two storeys in brickwork in the 19th century. The S. room of the original building has a four-panel ceiling formed by deeply chamfered beams which intersect at a shaped boss.

(5) COTTAGE (86641720), No. 8, North Street, is of one storey with dormer-windowed attics and has walls partly of rubble and partly of timber-framework with herring-bone brick nogging, and a thatched roof ; it is of 16th-century origin, but has been considerably altered. The W. front is of two bays with a central doorway and has square-headed wooden casement windows of three lights, with leaded glazing, perhaps of the early 18th century. In the northern bay the brick nogging below eaves level is probably of the 17th century ; that above is modern, as also is the brickwork in the S. gable. Coursed brickwork immediately above the rubble plinth replaces a former wall-plate. Inside, an open fireplace has a timber surround with a moulded four-centred head with carved spandrels and a square surround ; one spandrel has foliate decoration, the other contains the letters IP.

(6) COTTAGE (86671714), No. 9, North Street, is single-storeyed with a dormer-windowed attic and has rubble walls and a thatched roof. It is of 17th-century origin with a later bay on the E. The main room has stop-chamfered beams and an open fireplace.

(7) COTTAGE (86851687), of one storey with an attic, has rubble walls and a thatched roof. It is of 17th-century origin, but was altered and repaired in the 18th and 19th centuries. The plan is of class T.

(8) COTTAGES (86771689), three adjacent, formerly an inn, are of one storey with dormer-windowed attics and have walls of timber-framework above rubble plinths ; the roofs are thatched. The middle part of the range is of the late 15th century and retains three bays of a cruck roof. The central cruck is chamfered, suggesting that it originally spanned an open-roofed two-bay hall. In c. 1600 a chimneystack and an upper floor with deeply chamfered beams were inserted in the former hall, and a bay was added at the N. end of the range. The E. wall retains original square-headed casement windows, now blocked, with chamfered timber mullions.

(9) CROSS HOUSE (86661690), of two storeys with attics, has walls of ashlar and of rubble, and a tiled roof. The original house, with a variant T-class plan, was built about the end of the 16th century ; extensions on the S.E. and N.E. are of the 19th century. The S.W. front is symmetrical and of three bays, with a central doorway with a chamfered four-centred head and continuous jambs ending in shaped stops, and square-headed casement windows of four and three lights with moulded labels. The porch and the stone-fronted attic dormers are modern. Inside,

the S.E. ground-floor room of the original building has moulded wall-plates and beams intersecting to make a ceiling of four panels. The middle compartment of the main range, originally a through passage, was widened and the plank-and-muntin partitions were in part reset when the staircase was built. An exposed beam in the N.E. wing, with deep hollow-chamfered and ovolo mouldings, is of c. 1500 ; presumably it comes from elsewhere.

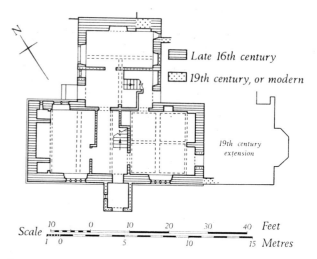

Late 16th century

19th century, or modern

19th century extension

Scale   10   0   10   20   30   40   Feet
          1   0   5   10   15 Metres

(10) BROOK HOUSE (86631692), of one storey with attics, has walls of timber-framework and of rubble, and thatched roofs. It is of late 16th-century origin with additions of the 17th and of the 18th century. In the L-shaped plan the N.E. range represents the original building and contains two rooms ; the N.W. room has a nine-panel ceiling formed by the intersection of four deeply-chamfered beams ; the same room has an open fireplace with a cambered timber bressummer. In the N.W. range, two 17th-century rooms have recently been combined by the removal of a partition ; they have chamfered ceiling beams, in part renewed. The room at the S.W. end of the N.W. range is of the 18th century.

(11) GABLE COTTAGE (86581688), with walls of timber-framework and with a thatched roof, is of 15th-century origin and consisted originally of a single-storeyed three-bay range with the roof supported on two cruck trusses. In c. 1600 a chimneystack was built close to the W. cruck, and upper floors were inserted in all three bays. In c. 1800 a bay was added on the E., and the S. front of the original range was modified, the original timber-framework in the lower storey being replaced by rubble, and a large window being inserted in the upper storey. Inside, the two original crucks have cambered collars, and the E. cruck retains arched braces resting on projecting tongues, integral with the crucks. In the E. bay of the original range the inserted floor of c. 1600 rests on two stop-chamfered beams. The corresponding floor has been removed from the middle bay, but the ends of the 17th-century joists remain.

(12) HOUSE (86471686), of two storeys, has rubble walls and a modern roof ; until 1926 it was thatched. The building dates from the 17th century and has a class-T plan. The N. front is symmetrical and of three bays, with 19th-century wooden casement windows. Inside, the W. ground-floor room has a four-panel ceiling with deeply chamfered intersecting beams.

PLATE 41

FIFEHEAD MAGDALEN CHURCH. Monument (2) of the Newman family.   *c.* 1750

PLATE 42

Finial.

Shield-of-arms on spandrel.

Head of Thomas Jesop.

General view from S.E.

GILLINGHAM CHURCH. Monument (6) of Thomas and John Jesop.

1615, 1625

PLATE 43

GILLINGHAM CHURCH. Monument (4) of Frances Dirdoe.

1733

PLATE 44

IWERNE MINSTER. (3) West Lodge, S.E. front.   18th and 19th century

FIFEHEAD MAGDALEN. (5) Fifehead House, E. front.   1807

PLATE 45

GILLINGHAM. (59) Higher Langham House, S.E. front. 1770

GILLINGHAM. (60) Bainly House, S. front. 18th century

PLATE 46

FONTMELL MAGNA. (28) Piper's Mill, from S. Probably 1795

FONTMELL MAGNA. (26) Woodbridge Mill, from S.E. Early 19th century

PLATE 47

LANGTON LONG BLANDFORD. (2) Stables of Langton House, courtyard.   1832

GILLINGHAM. (11) Town Mill, from S.   18th and early 19th century

PLATE 48

General view from S.W.

S.W. room, from S.

IWERNE MINSTER. (15) Roman Villa, as seen in 1897.

c. A.D. 300

(13) COTTAGE (86441689), of two storeys with rubble walls and a thatched roof, originated in the 17th century as a single-storeyed dwelling with an attic. The plan is of class T. The W. ground-floor room has a large open fireplace and a stop-chamfered ceiling beam. The casement windows in the S. front are of the 19th century.

(14) BEDCHESTER FARM (85011766), house, perhaps of late 17th-century origin, but extensively rebuilt, has ashlar walls and thatched roofs. Some original windows have iron casements with leaded glazing.

(15) SIXPENNY FARM (84381690), house, of one storey with attics, has rubble walls and a thatched roof. It was built in the 17th century, probably with a class-T plan, a further bay being added later on the E. A dormer window retains an ovolo-moulded wooden surround. Inside, some chamfered beams are exposed.

(16) COTTAGES (84251902), two adjacent, of one storey with attics, have rubble walls and thatched roofs; they are of 17th-century origin and probably originated as a single dwelling. Later, a bay with a second fireplace was added on the N.E. of the original range.

(17) BLATCHFORD'S FARM (83821854), of one storey with attics, has rubble walls and tiled roofs and was built c. 1600, probably with a class-F plan. The S. front has been refaced and all windows and doorways are new. Inside, the middle room, subdivided by modern partitions, retains a nine-panel ceiling with four intersecting beams, and a large open fireplace.

(18) LOWER HARTGROVE FARM (83301874), house, of one storey with dormer-windowed attics, has rubble walls with ashlar dressings, and thatched roofs. No longer a dwelling, the building is now used for animals. It was built in the 17th century, and heightened and altered internally, probably in the 19th century. There is evidence for two original staircases. The N. front has a doorway with a chamfered, four-centred head surmounted by a window, lighting the ground-floor passage, with

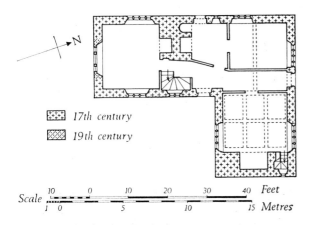

17th century
19th century

Scale [10 0 10 20 30 40 Feet / 1 0 5 10 15 Metres]

three square-headed lights under a moulded label. Flanking the doorway are stone windows of four square-headed lights with labels; the mullions have dated scratchings of 1681 and later. The N. windows in the upper storey are of the 19th century. The W. front has stone windows and a doorway, as on the N. except that the doorway has no window above it. The E. front has similar openings; the window adjacent to the E. doorway is set at a high level, showing that the stairs which it lights are in

the original position. The S. window of the S. wing is of the 19th century.

Inside, the E. room has a six-panel ceiling with intersecting chamfered beams, and a large open fireplace; an original stair-case window on the N. of the chimneybreast shows that there always was a stair in this position although the present narrow wooden stair is of the 19th century. The window above the N. doorway proves that the passage is original. The S. room has a dado of 17th-century oak panelling with beaded stiles and rails. The chamber over the E. room has a stone fireplace surround with a chamfered four-centred head and continuous jambs with shaped stops.

(19) GREEN FARM (82851916), of two storeys with attic, has coursed rubble walls and a thatched roof; it is of the late 17th century. Inside, some rooms have plank-and-muntin partitions and exposed chamfered ceiling beams. Adjacent on the N.W. is an 18th-century cottage with rubble walls with brick quoins, and with a thatched roof.

MONUMENTS (20–24)

The following houses and cottages are of the 18th century and unless otherwise described are two-storeyed with rubble walls and thatched roofs.

(20) Cottages (86671707), three adjoining, have class-S plans; the S. dwelling is somewhat later than the others. (Demolished.)

(21) House (86591702), of two storeys with brick walls and a tiled roof, is of the early 18th century and has a class-I plan. The W. front has a plat-band and some diagonal patterning in blue headers; the N. end wall has the initials KS worked in the blue headers. The chimneystack has round-headed panels of brickwork.

(22) Cottages (86571691), three adjoining, comprise two early 18th-century dwellings on the E. and one of the late 18th century on the W. The two older cottages retain original casement windows, as in (23). Inside, some stop-chamfered beams and plank-and-muntin partitions are preserved.

(23) Cottage (84201849), with a class-S plan, retains original windows with timber frames and iron casements with leaded

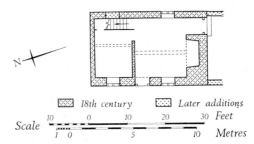

18th century   Later additions

Scale [10 0 10 20 30 Feet / 1 0 5 10 Metres]

glazing. The main room has an open fireplace with a timber bressummer. Reset in the N. room is a 17th-century beam. The stairs are not in the original position.

(24) Cow Grove Farm (83751853), house, of two storeys with brick walls and a thatched roof, is of the late 18th century. The N. front is symmetrical and of three bays, with a central doorway and with plain sashed windows. The plan is a variant of class T, having the fireplaces set against the rear wall instead of the end walls.

MONUMENTS (25–31)

Unless otherwise described the following mills and associated buildings are of the early 19th century.

(25) *Woodbridge House* (84731840), of two storeys, has walls of ashlar and of rubble, and slate-covered roofs. The S. front is symmetrical and of three bays, with a round-headed central doorway and with large square-headed sashed windows in both storeys.

(26) *Woodbridge Mill* (84661827), a corn mill of three storeys, has rubble walls and slate-covered roofs (Plate 46).

(27) *Bridge* (84621809), near Woodbridge Mill, is of ashlar and has one semicircular arch with squared rubble parapet walls and ashlar coping.

(28) *Piper's Mill* (85771703), a corn mill of two storeys with attics, has ashlar walls and a tiled roof (Plate 46). It is likely to be the building advertised as 'new-built' in the *Salisbury Journal* of 9 Nov. 1795. The ashlar is of good quality, with a plain plinth and a moulded eaves cornice. The mill-race has segmental-headed openings on the N. and S. ; other openings have flat arches. Inside, the water-wheel has gone, but much of the original machinery remains. The mill-pond, now dry, has ashlar retaining walls.

(29) *Cottage* (85791700), some 50 yds. S.E. of Piper's Mill, has rubble walls and a thatched roof, and a class-S. plan ; it is perhaps of the late 18th century.

(30) *Piper's Mill Bridge* (85751698), of the late 18th or early 19th century, has one semicircular arch of ashlar, and spandrels and parapet walls of rubble, the latter with rounded ashlar coping.

(31) *Springhead Mill* (87311691), house, of two storeys, has rubble walls and a thatched roof. The corn mill, adjacent, of two storeys with brick walls and a tiled roof, has been disused since 1881 and now forms an extension to the house.

The following monuments are of the late 18th century or the first half of the 19th century : *Millbrook House* (86691689), with brick walls and slated roofs, incorporates a 15th-century niche-head on which the date 1846 is inscribed. *Moore's Farm* (86571711), house, with brick and rubble walls, has a slated roof and a symmetrical three-bay façade. *Cottages* (86531687), two adjacent, have rubble walls and thatched roofs. A *Cottage* (86561688), with rubble walls and a slated roof, has a symmetrical three-bay N. front. A *Cottage* (86601697), with rubble walls and a thatched roof, incorporates older timbers. *Hurdle's Farm* (85611684), incorporating the remains of an earlier building, is said to have been formerly a mill. *Cottages* at (85241751) and (85061767) have rubble walls and thatched roofs. A *Cottage* (85211755), with brick walls and a tiled roof, has a symmetrical S. front. *Cottages* (84881771), three adjacent, have brick walls and thatched roofs. A *Cottage* (85281747) of *c.* 1800, with rubble walls and a thatched roof, has a class-S plan. *Gupple's Farm* (84241938), has ashlar walls and tiled roofs. *Cottages* (842198), two, with ashlar and rubble walls, and with thatched roofs, have class-T plans and symmetrical three-bay S.E. fronts.

MEDIAEVAL AND LATER EARTHWORKS

(32) CULTIVATION REMAINS. The date of enclosure of the open fields of Fontmell Magna is unknown, but open fields still existed N. and E. of the village late in the 18th century (Map of Fontmell Magna, 1774, D.C.R.O.) ; they included large fields named Netton, New, Upp, Little Combe and Long Combe, and small fields named Shortlands, Quarrendon and Fort Hill. Well preserved contour strip lynchets occur on the slopes of the re-entrant valleys in the E. of the parish ; in 1774 they formed part of the open fields. The strip lynchets around the sides of Fore Top (876179) lay in New Field ; those S. of Springhead (874166) were in Netton Field.

ROMAN AND PREHISTORIC

(33) CROSS-DYKE (87901814–88281805), in the E. of the parish and more than 650 ft. above O.D., extends obliquely from W.N.W. to E.S.E. across the crest of Fore Top, a spur which projects S.W. from the Chalk escarpment. The W. end is in Compton Abbas. The dyke is about 480 yds. long and runs in a straight line from one shoulder of the spur to the other, separating

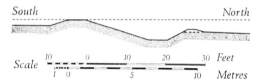

the top of the spur from the land on the N. It comprises a single bank with a ditch on the N. ; in the best preserved part the bank is 3 ft. high and 24 ft. across, and the ditch is 18 ft. across and 2 ft. deep. A gap at the centre, some 40 yds. wide, results from a later trackway and is not an original entrance. (Sumner, *Cranborne Chase*, 67.)

(34) CROSS-DYKE (88191839–88391822), on the crest of Fore Top, lies some 250 yds. N.E. of (33) and at the same altitude ; the N.W. half is in Compton Abbas. The dyke (Plate 35) is 300 yds. long and runs from shoulder to shoulder of the spur, generally from N.W. to S.E., but changing direction to E.S.E. at a point 50 yds. S.E. of the centre. It faces N.E. up the spur

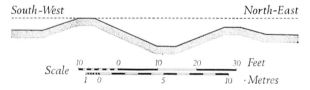

and comprises a bank with a ditch on the N.E. and a counter-scarp bank beyond. Where well preserved the bank is 21 ft. across and 3½ ft. high, the ditch is 20 ft. across and 3½ ft. deep, and the counterscarp bank is 15 ft. across and up to 2 ft. high. Gaps are obviously secondary, that in the centre having been cut by a later trackway. (Sumner, *Cranborne Chase*, 67.)

(35) TENNERLEY DITCH (88431756–89091725), cross-dyke, extends from N.W. to S.E. for a distance of 800 yds. or more across the brow of the Chalk escarpment. On the summit some 300 yds. of the earthwork has been destroyed by a track which

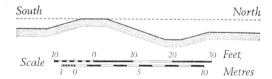

follows the same line, but the dyke survives on the W. and on the E. The western part, 260 yds. long, extends from near the top of the escarpment down a steepening slope towards

Longcombe Bottom ; the eastern part is about the same length and runs down a gentle eastward inclination inside Fontmell Wood. In the best-preserved parts the bank is 16 ft. wide and 1½ ft. high ; the ditch is 17 ft. across and 2½ ft. deep. A copse bank on the N. edge of the ditch in the eastern part of the dyke has the deceptive appearance of a counterscarp bank.

(36) BOWL (?) BARROW (88381836), on the neck of Fore Top, over 700 ft. above O.D., lies on the parish boundary with Compton Abbas ; diam. 30 ft., ht. 1 ft.

(37) MOUND (88901821), perhaps a barrow, in Gore Wood near the parish boundary with Ashmore, lies at 750 ft. above O.D. on a gentle W. slope near the summit of the escarpment. The mound is about 12 ft. in diameter and 1 ft. high, and is separated by a 9 ft. berm from an encircling bank 7 ft. wide and less than 1 ft. high ; beyond the bank is a ditch 8 ft. across and less than 1 ft. deep.

12 GILLINGHAM (8026)

(O.S. 6 ins., ST 72 SE, ST 72 NE, ST 73 SE, ST 82 SW, ST 82 NW, ST 83 SW)

Gillingham is a large parish, with an area of 7,738 acres. The land undulates gently at altitudes between 200 ft. and 450 ft. above the sea and is drained by the R. Stour and its tributaries, the Lodden and the Shreen Water. The E. half of the parish is on Kimmeridge Clay ; in the W. it is partly on Oxford Clay and partly on Corallian Limestone.

The parish lies within the area of the mediaeval Royal Forest of Gillingham. Until the 19th century the lands which now form the parishes of Motcombe, East Stour, West Stour and Bourton were regarded as parts of Gillingham, which covered more than 15,000 acres. The town stands at the confluence of the three streams named above. Dispersed around it are a number of hamlets and farms: Domesday Book mentions Gillingham, Milton-on-Stour, and Wyndham Farm ; a document of 1156 mentions Langham;[1] the settlements of Bugley, Eccliffe, Madjeston, Pierston, Sandley, Thorngrove and Wyke were certainly in existence early in the 14th century, and it is probable that some of them correspond with some of the nine Domesday entries for Gillingham (V.C.H., Dorset iii, 65 (bis), 74, 83, 90, 110 (ter), 113) ; others probably came into being with the gradual clearance of the Royal Forest, a process recorded in the Forest Eyres of 1258,[2] and which continued into the 17th century.[3]

In 1694 the town was devastated by fire,[4] and the Inventory has few entries for monuments of the 17th

century or earlier. At the end of the 18th century silk weaving was an important local industry.[1]

ECCLESIASTICAL

(1) THE PARISH CHURCH OF ST. MARY (Plate 4) stands near the middle of the town. It has walls generally of ashlar and roof-coverings of slate and of lead ; in the chancel the walls are of coursed rubble with ashlar dressings. The *Chancel* and *North Chapel* are of early 14th-century origin, with restorations of 1840 (*S.D.N.Q.* XV (1917), 73, 208). The *Nave, North* and *South Aisles, West Tower* and *North* and *South Porches* were built in 1838. According to a letter of 1838 from the vicar (quoted by A. F. H. Wagner, *The Church of St. Mary, Gillingham* (1956), 17), the antecedent nave, only 12 ft. wide, was separated from the aisles by ' heavy Saxon or Norman arches only 11½ ft. in height, supported by large masses of stone which so shut out the aisles . . . as to render them . . . of little use ', a description which suggests comparison with the pre-conquest nave at Canford (*Dorset*, II, 197). The value of the advowson, 40 shillings, in Domesday (*V.C.H., Dorset* iii, 83) suggests a foundation which might well be that of a Saxon minster ; it was given to Shaftesbury Abbey in exchange for the land on which Corfe Castle was built (*Dorset* II, 58, notes 1, 2). The W. tower, originally within the area of the nave, but rebuilt in 1838 some 20 ft. further west, was heightened and considerably altered in 1908. The South Chapel was added in 1921.

Architectural Description—The *Chancel* retains a 14th-century moulded plinth, stout ashlar buttresses of three weathered stages and, on the N. and S., coved and moulded string-courses with 14th-century ball-flower ornament and some original gargoyles. The E. window, of 1840, has four cinquefoil-headed lights set two on each side of a large central mullion with curvilinear tracery in a two-centred head. The N. wall has two windows, each with two trefoil ogee-headed lights with a curvilinear central tracery light in a two-centred head ; the stonework is of 1840, but possibly reproducing the original design. Adjacent, on the W., two 14th-century arches open into the N. chapel. They are uniform and of two chamfered orders ; the outer orders continue on the E. and W. responds and end at broach stops ; the inner orders spring from polygonal attached shafts with moulded capitals with ball-flower enrichment. Centrally the two arches rest on a Purbeck marble shaft with a moulded octagonal capital and a chamfered stone plinth. The plinth and capital are of the 19th century ; the date of the shaft is uncertain. The S. side of the chancel has five windows uniform with those on the N.; the stonework is evidently of 1840, but windows of similar design are shown on a drawing made by James Buckler in 1829 (B.M. Add. MS. 36361, f. 144). In the three western bays the wall below the windows is pierced by modern openings to the S. chapel and vestry. The chancel arch, of 1840, is four-centred and of one

---

[1] Fägersten, 7.   [3] Hutchins III, 649.
[2] P.R.O., E/32/10/7.   [4] Hutchins III, 619.

[1] S.D.N.Q. XIV (1915), 289–92.

GILLINGHAM

The Parish Church of St. Mary

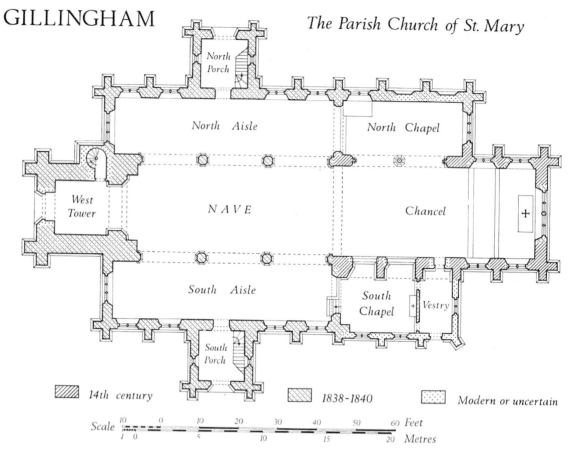

North Porch

North Aisle

North Chapel

West Tower

NAVE

Chancel

South Aisle

South Chapel

Vestry

South Porch

▨ *14th century*   ▨ *1838-1840*   ⬚ *Modern or uncertain*

Scale

10   0   10   20   30   40   50   60 *Feet*

1   0   5   10   15   20 *Metres*

chamfered order resting on moulded brackets with leaf enrichment.

The *North Chapel* is largely of 1840. The plinth is chamfered and the buttresses are uniform with those of the chancel; there is no string-course. The E. window has a two-centred head and three cinquefoil ogee-headed lights below vertical tracery. The N. wall has a window uniform with those in the side walls of the chancel; the two eastern bays have blocked windows with two-centred heads. The archway to the N. aisle has a chamfered two-centred head and continuous jambs.

The *Nave* has N. and S. arcades with two-centred arches of one chamfered order, carried on octagonal piers and responds with moulded capitals and plinths. Above, each wall has six single-light clearstorey windows with cinquefoil two-centred heads. The E. gable has a weathered coping and a large foliate finial.

The *North* and *South Aisles* have chamfered plinths and buttresses similar to those of the N. chapel. The E. window of the S. aisle was uniform with that of the N. chapel, but it now has a raised sill to make room for the archway to the S. chapel. The N. and S. windows are uniform with those of the chancel; the W. windows are uniform with the E. window of the N. chapel. The N. and S. doorways have chamfered two-centred heads and continuous jambs.

The *North* and *South Porches* have chamfered plinths, buttresses of two weathered stages, and gabled N. and S. fronts with shaped kneelers, weathered copings and foliate finials. The

date 1838 is carved on the gable of the N. porch. Both porches have external doorways with chamfered two-centred heads and continuous jambs; above each doorway is a single-light window uniform with those of the clearstorey; the E. and W. walls have similar windows. Inside, the porches are two-storeyed, the upper storeys originally forming galleries which opened into the N. and S. aisles through wide archways with shallow four-centred heads; these openings are now walled up.

The *West Tower* is of three stages. In the lower stages it has three-stage buttresses with weathered offsets. At the base is a chamfered plinth. The lower stages are defined on the W. side by a moulded and hollow-chamfered string-course; in the N. and S. sides there is no division into stages. The tower arch is two-centred and of one chamfered order with continuous responds. In the E. wall, above the nave roof, the intermediate stage of the tower has a round window of 1908. On the N. side is a vice turret of 1908, with a gabled head of weathered stonework and several square-headed loops; the turret partly masks a blind recess with a two-centred head; above, level with the round window of the E. wall is a shallow circular recess.

The W. doorway, remodelled in 1908, has a two-centred head with wave-mouldings which die into plain jambs. The W. window is of 1838 and has three trefoil ogee-headed lights, with curvilinear tracery in a two-centred head. In the second stage is a small square-headed window of two ogee-headed lights and, above, a round window of 1908. The S. face of the tower has a large blind recess, as on the N., and a clock at the level where round windows appear on the other sides. The top stage, with belfry windows, embattled parapets and corner pinnacles was rebuilt in 1908 (Faculty, Sarum Dioc. Regy.).

The *Roof* of the nave has tie-beam trusses with cusped scissor-bracing, and curved braces resting on head-corbels. In the tower, the floor of the ringing chamber rests on reset 16th-century moulded beams with hollow-chamfers enriched with leaf bosses ; the beams are arranged to form six compartments with 19th-century traceried panels.

Fittings—*Altar* : Loose, against S. wall of tower, broken slab of Purbeck stone, chamfered on under side, with three surviving consecration crosses, mediaeval. *Bells* : eight and sanctus ; 1st and 2nd modern ; 3rd by William Cockey, inscribed ' Thos. Freke Esq., Mr. Edward Reeves, Ch. Wds. 1726 W.C.' ; 4th by John Wallis, inscribed ' Voce mea ad Dominum, IW, 1607 ', recast 1909 ; 5th by Thomas and James Bilbie, with church-wardens' names : 'Ambrose Heale, John Read, 1793, Thomas Mathews, John Jupe, 1794-5 ' ; 6th by William Cockey, 1722, Thomas Freke and Henry Jukes, churchwardens, recast 1894 ; 7th by Kingston of Bridgwater, 1826, J. Read and T. Matthews, churchwardens ; tenor with same inscription as 3rd and ' Wm. Cockey Bell Founder 1726 ' ; sanctus inscribed ' † GABREEL ', probably *c.* 1350.

Chest : of oak, with moulded lid and with chip-carving on rail, early 17th century. *Coffin Lid* : forming step from chancel to N. chapel, of Purbeck stone, mediaeval. *Coffin Stools* : pair, with turned legs and moulded rails, late 17th century ; also one with turned legs and fretted top, *c.* 1700. *Communion Table* : In N. chapel, with heavy turned legs, moulded stretchers, and moulded rails, 17th century, top hinged to form locker. *Font* : of Purbeck stone, with octagonal bowl, hollow-chamfered on under side and decorated on each face with cusped hexagonal panel, much worn and fissured horizontally, resting on octagonal stem with quatrefoil panel in each face and with moulded octagonal base, 15th century. *Hatchment* : with arms of Dirdoe impaling White, and escutcheon of White, 18th century. *Inscriptions and Scratchings* : see *Royal Arms.*

Monuments and *Floor-slabs. Monuments* : In chancel, on N. wall, (1) of Sir Henry Dirdoe, 1724, and others of his family, marble monument (Plates 17 and 20) with scrolled brackets, apron with arms of Dirdoe impaling White, panel with Latin inscription flanked by composite pilasters, rounded pediment enclosing relief of cherub heads, and urn finial ; on upper fillet of apron, 'Iohn Bastard & Co. Feᵗ' (Gunnis, *Country Life*, 1948, p. 1283) ; (2) of John Pern, vicar, 1770, and others of his family, marble wall tablet with pilasters, broken pediment, urn finial, and apron with arms of Pern impaling Fisher ; on S. wall, (3) of Jane (Card) Dawson, 1812, tablet with verses, by T. King of Bath. In N. chapel, on N. wall, (4) of Mrs. Frances Dirdoe, 1733, large marble wall monument (Plates 43 and 20) with inscription on dado, above, gadrooned sarcophagus surmounted by relief of Three Graces, flanking panels with flower enrichment, open pediment and cartouche-of-arms of Dirdoe impaling White ; (5) of Edward Read, 1779, and others of his family, white marble tablet with slate surround (Plate 17), scrolled cheek-pieces, draped urn finial, and apron with shield-of-arms of Read, by Lancashire of Bath ; tablet below records benefactions and later amendment thereof. Also in N. chapel, (6) of [Thomas and] John Jesop, [1615], 1625, stone table-tomb (Plate 42) with panelled sides with strapwork decoration and enriched capping ; above, recumbent effigies of two bearded men in academic dress : N. effigy, presumably Thomas, in round-headed recess with panelled back wall and panelled intrados, inscription on central panel reported by Hutchins (III, 639) now

gone ; on each spandrel, shield-of-arms of Jesop ; above, strap-work frieze and cornice surmounted by shaped panel with reclining angels and small figure of Time with scythe and shield : S. effigy, presumably of John, vicar of Gillingham, spanned by independent stone arch with, below, marble inscription tablet with scrolled border (Plate 23) and, above, cartouche-of-arms of Jesop ; adjacent, four detached pinnacles evidently from same monument. In nave, reset over N. arcade, (7) of Edward Sly, 1795, and others of his family, 1805-37, marble tablet in form of sarcophagus with urn finial ; reset over S. arcade, (8) of Christian (Helme) Broome, 1720, and others of Broome and Cox families, tablet with pilasters, surmounted by urn and tree, with lozenge-of-arms, by King of Bath, 1812. In nave, reset over tower arch, (9) of Edward Davenant, 1679, vicar, slate tablet with painted Latin inscription, flanked by draped scrolls, on foliate ledge and apron with flower festoon and shield-of-arms of Davenant, above, broken pediment with *putti* and achievement-of-arms of Davenant quartering two other coats, impaling Grove ; (10) of John Tinney, 1728, white marble tablet between Corinthian pilasters, with cherub-head apron, and broken curved pediment with urn and lamp finials. In N. aisle, reset on N. wall, (11) of John Matthews, 1820, and Hester Matthews, 1829, marble tablet by Osmond of Sarum ; (12) of Mary (Goddard) Helyar, 1750, marble tablet with broken pediment and shaped apron, with lozenge-of-arms of Helyar with escutcheon of Goddard. In S. aisle, on S. wall, (13) of Thomas Godwin and Sarah his daughter, both 1814, marble tablet with urn, by Langley of Hinton ; (14) of Mary Read, 1764, marble cartouche with baroque drapery (Plate 18). In N. porch, (15) of John Harris, 1791, and Rachel his wife, 1812, tablet by Phripp of Gillingham ; (16) of Ambrose Heal, 1812, and Rachel (Harris) Heal, 1827, tablet by Phripp. *Floor-slab* : In chancel, on S., of ..muell A..ent, 1702.

Panelling : In chancel, reset in communion table, eleven oak panels with trefoil-headed, cusped and crocketed enrichment, similar to those described under *Seating*. In tower, reset on N. wall, fragments of 17th-century oak panelling with carved frieze. *Piscina* : In chancel, with chamfered two-centred head with trefoil cusping, two stone shelves, and octagonal stone basin with drain-hole, 14th century, restored. *Plate* : includes Elizabethan silver cup and cover-paten (Plate 24), cup with trumpet-shaped stem, knop, and flared bowl with simple incised strapwork, cover-paten inscribed on foot GYLLYNGAM 1574, maker's mark, a disc filled with pellets, no date-letter ; silver cup with baluster stem and plain bowl with date-letter of 1633 ; silver stand-paten with date-letter of 1663 and dedicatory inscription of Robert Thorne ; silver flagon (Plate 25) with date-letter of 1681 and dedicatory inscription of Dorothy Dirdoe, 1678 ; stand-paten with date-letter of 1714 ; silver flagon with date-letter of 1735, dedicatory inscription of Frances Dirdoe, 1733, and lozenge-of-arms of Dirdoe impaling White. *Recess* : In chancel, in N. wall, tomb-recess with chamfered two-centred head and moulded sill, 19th century, probably repeating mediaeval feature. *Royal Arms* : (Frontispiece) of wood, carved in the round and painted on both sides ; probably the ' King's-Arms ' made in 1618 (*S.D.N.Q.*, XV (1914), 25) ; inscribed on base ' painted and gilded by Thos. Matthews, A. Head and I. Read C.W., 1792 ' ; scratched on unicorn ' EI, 1733 ', also 19th-century graffiti.

Seating : of oak, reset in nave and N. and S. aisles (Plate 22), includes twenty-nine square-headed bench-ends with moulded edges ending at splayed stops, carved to represent traceried panelling with foliate spandrels ; also twelve similar, but ogee-headed bench-ends with poppy-head finials representing roses, fleurs-de-lys, leopard mask etc. ; many bench-ends fitted to modern seats, made up with original top rails with roll and hollow-chamfered mouldings ; two seats complete with original panelled backs, each with sixteen trefoil-headed panels with cusped and crocketed enrichment, set in groups of four between traceried stiles ; 16th century, made up with modern work. In N. and S. aisles, panelled pews, formerly with doors, probably 1838. *Sedilia* : In chancel, below S. windows, with three chamfered and trefoiled two-centred heads in chamfered square surround ; recesses blocked, seats missing ; 14th century, restored. *Miscellanea* : (1) bassoon, probably late 18th or early 19th century ; (2) clarinet by Astor Horwood, *c.* 1815 ; (3) organ, 1841, rebuilt 1874 ; (4) remains of pillory with oak board bound in iron, with hinges, probably 18th century.

(2) CARVED STONES, two, built into the N. wall of the late 19th-century vicarage, are probably of the 9th century and presumably from a cross-shaft. The exposed face of the larger fragment (Plate 3) measures 30 ins. by 18 ins. and retains a considerable area of closely woven two-strand interlace ornament. The back and sides of this stone are said also to have carved decoration, but this is no longer seen. The smaller fragment measures 4 ins. by 3 ins. and is much eroded ; it retains vestiges of interlace ornament. (*S.D.N.Q.*, XV (1917), 233.)

SECULAR

GILLINGHAM TOWN, BAY, MADJESTON AND HAM COMMON

(3) BRIDGE (80782652), carrying High Street across the Shreen Water, is of ashlar and has two semicircular arches with a cut-water on the N. side only ; the parapet walls have rounded copings. One stone is inscribed ' County Bridge 1800 '.

(4) FOOTBRIDGE (80602646), spanning the R. Stour, 150 yds. S. of (1), is of ashlar and has three semicircular arches and small triangular cutwaters on the west. Iron railings take the place of parapet walls. The date 1821 is boldly carved on the W. face.
(*Demolished, 1967.*)

(5) BRIDGE (80482649), carrying Wyke Street over the R. Stour, 200 yds. S.W. of (1), is similar to (3). A stone in the parapet wall is inscribed ' County Bridge 1807 '.

(6) LODDEN BRIDGE (81452613), carrying the Shaftesbury road over the R. Lodden, is of squared rubble and has two semicircular arches. It probably is of the late 18th or early 19th century. The parapets are modern.

(7) KINGSCOURT BRIDGE (81772623), on the parish boundary with Motcombe, is of roughly squared rubble and has a single semicircular arch. The parapets are of brickwork, in English bond, with a rounded ashlar coping. The bridge probably is of *c.* 1800.

(8) MADJESTON BRIDGE (80992536), carrying the road from Gillingham to East Stour across the R. Lodden, is similar to (3). A stone above the cutwater on the E. side is inscribed ' R.P. 1801 '.

(9) LOCK-UP (80652651), 70 yds. S. of (1), is a small single-storey building (19½ ft. by 10¾ ft.), of squared rubble with a tiled roof. It probably is of the early 19th century. A narrow doorway in the S. side has a four-centred head under a simple pitched label ; there are no other openings. The interior is lined with brickwork.

(10) FREE SCHOOL, remains of, now incorporated in a shop, stand on the S. side of High Street, some 60 yds. S. of (1). The only notable feature is the late 16th-century ceiling of a ground-floor room, with heavy ogee-moulded and hollow-chamfered oak wall-plates and similarly moulded cross-beams forming a ceiling of four panels. The walls are rendered and no original openings are identifiable. The site is identified as the Free School on the O.S. map of 1884 ; presumably it corresponds with the school mentioned by Hutchins (III, 619).

(11) TOWN MILLS (80792659), 150 yds. E. of (1), have walls of squared and coursed rubble with ashlar quoins ; the roofs are tiled (Plate 47). The W. range is of the 18th century ; adjacent on the E. is an early 19th-century extension, and further N.E. is an 18th-century cottage. Between the cottage and the 19th-century extension, and adjoining both, is a late 19th-century house.

The W. range is of three storeys with dormer-windowed attics. The S. front has four bays of square-headed two-light casement windows with timber lintels and leaded glazing. The W. front has four bays of similar windows and, on the ground floor, a doorway and other casement windows. The N. and E. elevations are similar and respectively of three and of six bays. The southern part of the E. elevation is masked by the E. extension.

The E. extension has a S. front of four bays with segmental-headed two-light casement windows, and doorways on the ground and first floors. A ground-floor opening adjacent to the W. range gives access to a narrow compartment containing the mill-wheel, presumably originally in the open. A stone marking a flood-level of 1768, in the S. front of the 19th-century E. extension, must be reset.

Inside, the W. range has a single large room in each storey. The floors rest on elm beams, chamfered and with splayed stops, housed in the E. and W. walls and supported in the middle on oak columns with Roman-Doric mouldings. The E. range contains no noteworthy features.

The cottage is two-storeyed and has an E. front with casement windows of two and three lights. Inside, on the S., is a large open fireplace.

(12) HOUSE (80752693), some 400 yds. N. of (1), is of two storeys with attics and has rubble walls and a tiled roof. Although masked by modern industrial buildings the range appears to be of mid or late 16th-century origin. The main ground-floor room, now divided, has two large intersecting beams and

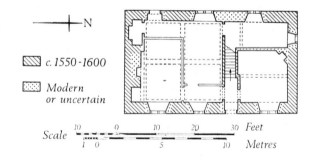

Scale

corresponding wall-plates with elaborate double ovolo mouldings, forming a ceiling of four panels. The open fireplace on the S. is blocked. On the N. of the room is a plank-and-muntin partition ; the modern stairs beside it perhaps take the place of a former through-passage. Presumably the N. rooms were originally service rooms ; the N. fireplace is modern. In the first-floor rooms the ceilings rest on heavy chamfered tie-beams ; the S. chamber has a small fireplace. The original roof is of five bays, with four collar and tie-beam trusses supporting three rows of purlins ; there are mortices for two heights of wind-bracing, now gone.

(13) LIME TREE HOUSE, 50 yds. N.E. of (1) is two-storeyed with attics and has walls of squared rubble with ashlar dressings, and tiled roofs ; it dates from about the middle of the 18th century. The W. front is of five bays, with a central doorway and symmetrically disposed windows with moulded ashlar architraves and plain keystones. The doorway has an eared architrave, a plain frieze and a moulded cornice. The windows have modern casements, but no doubt were originally sashed.

Inside, the plan is of class U. The hallway is spanned by a moulded stone arch with a keystone. The stairs have cut strings with carved spandrels, turned balusters and moulded handrails. One front room has a moulded stone fireplace surround with an eared architrave and a cornice on scrolled brackets.

(14) HARWOOD HOUSE (81032638), 480 yds. E. of (1), is of two storeys with attics and has walls of coursed rubble and of brick, and slated roofs ; it dates probably from the first half of the 17th century. In 1694 the N. gable was partly rebuilt in brickwork, and in the 19th century the house was given new roofs and new windows and the E. front was rendered.

The E. front is symmetrical and of three bays, with a central doorway flanked by casement windows of three lights, corresponding windows on the first floor, and a two-light window over the doorway. The ends of the façade are marked by stucco Doric pilasters, a 19th-century feature often seen in Gillingham. Above first-floor level the gabled N. wall of the E. range is of brick ; at the apex is a chimneystack with a terra-cotta plaque inscribed ' 1694 W.C.'. Inside, the plan is of class T. One room has a lightly chamfered ceiling beam. The stairs have carved spandrels and a late 18th-century balustrade, perhaps brought from elsewhere.

(15) KNAPP HOUSE (80332645), 350 yds. S.W. of (1), is of two storeys with attics ; it has walls of ashlar and of rubble, and tiled roofs. It dates probably from the second half of the 18th century, but it has been much altered. The E. front is ashlar-faced and has sashed windows with moulded architraves in six irregularly spaced bays. The doorway, in the third bay from the S., has moulded jambs and a broken pediment ; in front of the doorway is a modern stone porch. The gabled S. wall of the original range is faced with modern ashlar ; the W. front is largely masked by later additions and the N. end of the range is concealed by a 19th-century extension.

Inside, the original plan is obscured by later modifications ; two of the windows in the E. front are blocked by later chimney-breasts. The stairs formerly had an oval window, now blocked. Some rooms have chamfered beams and moulded cornices, and there are areas of 18th-century panelling.

(16) COTTAGE (80582645), 150 yds. S.W. of (1), is two-storeyed and has coursed rubble walls and a thatched roof ; it dates probably from the 17th century. The gabled W. wall has a large external chimneybreast. Inside, the W. fireplace is partly blocked up, but above, on the first floor, is a fireplace with a chamfered four-centred timber bressummer, and chamfered stone jambs with broach stops. Some chamfered ceiling beams appear to be of the 18th or 19th century.

(17) MADJESTON FARM HOUSE (80692512) has walls of coursed rubble and ashlar, and slated roofs. The three-storeyed S. range and N. wing are of the first half of the 19th century ; a two-storeyed extension of the N. wing appears to be formed from a pair of 18th-century cottages. The ashlar-faced S. front of the main range is symmetrical and of three bays, with large sashed

windows and with a central doorway sheltered by an ashlar porch with Roman-Doric columns.

MONUMENTS (18–57)

Unless otherwise described, the following monuments are of the 18th century and are two-storeyed, or single-storeyed with dormer-windowed attics, and have coursed rubble walls and tiled or slated roofs.

(18) *The Phoenix Hotel*, 50 yds. S. of (1), had originally a half H-shaped plan, but this has been obscured by later additions. The N. front is rendered ; at the centre is a former carriageway with an elliptical arch, now partly blocked. Inside, one bedroom has an 18th-century stone fireplace surround with panelled decorations and an enriched cornice.

(19) *House*, 40 yds. S.W. of the foregoing, on the S. side of The Square, is perhaps of 17th-century origin ; in the 19th century the western part was converted into a shop. The large W. ground-floor room, now divided into two, has heavy chamfered ceiling beams.

(20) *The Red Lion Inn*, 80 yds. S.E. of (1), has a symmetrical N. front of five bays with a central doorway and with large sashed windows in both storeys ; at the eaves is a moulded wooden cornice.

(21) *Houses*, adjoining the foregoing on the E., now comprise two shops and a cottage, but they originally consisted of an 18th-century house with a three-bay N. front and, adjacent on the E., a 17th-century cottage. The cottage contains a heavily chamfered beam.

(22) *House* (81122632), 600 yds. S.E. of (1), has a symmetrical E. front of two bays with a central doorway and with three-light casement windows in each storey. The roof is of mansard form.

(23) *Newbury House* (81142626), ⅜ m. S.E. of (1), is of two storeys and has rendered walls and slated roofs. It was built probably in the first half of the 19th century and has a symmetrical E. front of five bays, with a central doorway flanked by sashed windows and with five corresponding windows on the first floor. To N. and S. are slightly lower wings, perhaps of somewhat later date than the main range.

(24) *House* (81162636), 600 yds. E. of (1), is two-storeyed and has walls of coursed, squared rubble, and tiled roofs (Plate 30) ; it dates from the late 18th or early 19th century. The S. front is symmetrical and of three bays, with a doorway flanked by sashed windows and with uniform windows on the first floor. Each window has a plain pitched label. The ends of the façade are defined by stone pilasters with moulded capitals ; the first floor is marked by a plat-band. The doorway is sheltered by a tent-shaped metal hood supported on wrought-iron uprights with scrolled trellis work. Inside, one room has an original fireplace surround with festoon enrichment.

(25) *The Royal Hotel* (81112640) is of the first half of the 19th century. The S. front is rendered and divided into three bays by shallow pilasters ; the centre bay is gabled. The doorway in the centre bay has a porch with cast-iron columns, probably a later addition.

(26) *House* (81062648) has a S. front of three bays, with a central doorway flanked by three-light casement windows, and with corresponding windows of two and of three lights in the upper storey. It probably is of the 18th century.

(27) *Cottage* (80952648), with coursed rubble walls and a thatched roof, is perhaps of the late 17th century. The W. front is of three bays, with a central doorway flanked by three-light casement windows and with corresponding openings in the upper storey. Inside, the S. room has a large open fireplace, and there are several chamfered ceiling beams with splayed stops.

(28) *House* (80672661), 30 yds. N.E. of (1), has a W. front of five bays, with a central doorway and with casement windows of two and of three lights. Centrally in the upper storey is a bull's-eye window. Inside, several rooms have chamfered beams, and one ground-floor room contains a wooden alcove cupboard with architectural enrichment and shaped shelves.

(29) *House* (80642664), 45 yds. N. of (1), has an E. front of two bays, with a central doorway and with bay windows on each side ; the window on the S. has been made into a shop-window.

(30) *House* (80632665), adjacent to the foregoing, has an E. front of two bays ; it is of the late 18th century.

(31) *House* (80642667), has a symmetrical S. front of three bays, with a round-headed doorway flanked by sashed three-light windows on the ground floor and with three large single-light windows on the first floor. The keystone of the central window is dated 1842.

(32) *Cottage* (80552674), has a S. front of two bays.

(33) *Cottage* (80222676), at Rolls Bridge Farm, has a S. front of two bays with a central doorway. Inside, there are two chamfered beams.

(34) *Cottage* (80542666), has a N. front of two bays.

(35) *Cottage* (80612660), 15 yds. N.W. of (1), has walls partly of brickwork in Flemish bond.

(36) *House* (80612657), 25 yds. W. of (1), has a W. front of ashlar, in two bays, with a central doorway flanked by sashed windows ; it is of the late 18th century.

(37) *House* (80662654), 35 yds. S. of (1), has a S. front of three bays, with a central doorway flanked by sashed windows of three lights, and with corresponding windows on the first floor. The façade is rendered and ornamented with pilasters at the angles.

(38) *Cottage* (80632641), 175 yds. S. of (1), has walls of coursed squared rubble, and a thatched roof.

(39) *House* (80522651), 140 yds. S.W. of (1), incorporates at the rear a service wing which may be of 17th-century origin. The S. front of the 18th-century main range is of four bays, with sashed windows with moulded architraves and projecting keystones in both storeys. The service wing has casement windows of four lights with leaded glazing. Inside, both parts of the house have chamfered beams.

(40) *House* (80462650), 200 yds. S.W. of (1), has a symmetrical S. front of three bays, with a central doorway flanked by three-light casement windows and with corresponding openings in the upper storey. The house is probably of early 18th-century origin.

(41) *House* (80442650), 215 yds. S.W. of (1), is similar to the foregoing. Inside, some intersecting chamfered ceiling beams and wall-plates are exposed.

(42) *Cottage* (81332618), at Lodden Bridge, has walls of rubble with brick dressings, and a thatched roof. The S. front is of two bays with a central doorway.

(43) *Cottages* (81632614), two adjacent, 300 yds. E. of the foregoing, have thatched roofs.

(44) *Cottage* (81682620), 100 yds. N.W. of the foregoing, is of one storey with an attic and has a thatched roof. Inside, the ceilings have chamfered beams and there is a large open fireplace, now blocked.

(45) *Cottage* (81702616), 100 yds. S.W. of (7), has a thatched roof ; it dates probably from the first half of the 18th century. Inside, the main room has a large open fireplace with an unwrought bressummer, and chamfered ceiling beams with splayed stops. Some 17th-century panelling has been brought from elsewhere.

(46) *Higher Ham Farmhouse* (81972551) is probably of the early 18th century. Inside, there are chamfered beams with splayed stops and, at the N. end, a large open fireplace, now blocked.

(47) *Madjeston Farm Cottages* (80722510), 30 yds. E. of (17), are now two tenements but originally were a single farmhouse. The S. front is partly of ashlar with brick dressings and partly of rubble. Inside, one room has a panelled dado and a shell-headed recess with fluted pilasters.

(48) *Cottage* (80642513), 30 yds. W. of (17), was originally two tenements. The building is probably of late 18th-century origin, with modern heightening of the rubble walls in brickwork.

(49) *Cottage* (80452693), ¼ m. N.W. of (1).

(50) *Cottages* (80692686), three adjoining, 300 yds. N. of (1), are of the early 18th century. The rubble walls have ashlar quoins. Inside, some rooms have lightly chamfered beams and blocked open fireplaces.

(51) *Cottage* (80782695), has a symmetrical two-bay N. front with a central doorway ; the first-floor windows have iron frames and leaded glazing.

(52) *Cottages* (80912699), range of three.

(53) *Cottage* (81082694), single-storeyed with a dormer-windowed attic, has an open fireplace at the N. end. One room has a lightly chamfered beam.

(54) *Cottage* (81162703), has a symmetrical S. front of three bays.

(55) *Malthouse Farm* (81272705), house, has walls of ashlar and of rubble, and tiled roofs ; it dates from early in the 18th century. In the S. front, of five bays, the central casement window is modern and evidently replaces a former doorway. Inside, some rooms have lightly chamfered beams.

(56) *Cottage* (81402715), has a thatched roof.

(57) *Cottages* (81412715), two adjoining, with thatched roofs, have recently been combined as a single dwelling.

Monuments of the first half of the 19th century are as follows —In Gillingham town : a *House* (80672653) adjacent to (10) ; a range of four *Houses* (80832649) in High Street ; a pair of *Houses* adjacent to the foregoing on the E. ; another *House* (80882647) in High Street ; a *House* (81122635) 50 yds. S. of (25) ; a *Cottage* 50 yds. N.W. of (25) ; a *Cottage* (80652668) 80 yds. N. of (1) ; a pair of *Cottages* (80542671) 150 yds. N.W. of (1) ; a *House* adjacent to the foregoing on the N.W. ; a *Cottage* (80232678) at Rolls Bridge Farm ; *Church Cottage*, 25 yds. N. of (1), probably dating from the time of the rebuilding of the church in 1838 and having windows and a doorway with four-centred heads and labels ; a pair of *Cottages* adjacent to (35), on the W. ; a range of three *Cottages* 30 yds. W. of (1) ; a pair of *Cottages* 15 yds. S.W. of (1) ; a *House* (80352653) 90 yds. N. of (15) ; a pair of *Cottages* 80 yds. N.W. of the foregoing ; *Lodden Bridge Farmhouse* (81392616) ; *Grosvenor Cottage*

(81592611) ; a *Cottage* (80452696) ; *Portland Cottages* (80682675); a *Range* (80682683) of five cottages.—At Ham Common: a pair of *Cottages* (81742598) 270 yds. S. of (7) ; a pair of *Cottages* 80 yds. N.W. and a *Farmhouse* 50 yds E. of the foregoing ; a pair of *Cottages* (82132537) 250 yds. S.E. of (46) ; a *Cottage* (82192527) 120 yds. S.E. of the foregoing.—At Bay : a *Cottage* (81092695) ; a pair of *Cottages* (81112696) ; a pair of *Cottages* (81162694) ; *Rose Cottage* (81192700), perhaps of *c*. 1800 ; a *Cottage* (81422716).

WYKE, LANGHAM, BUGLEY

(58) WYKE HALL (79212671), house, nearly 1 m. W. of (1), is of two storeys with attics and has rendered walls and tiled roofs. The building has a 17th-century nucleus, but the greater part is of the mid-19th century and probably is dated by a rainwater head of 1853.

The E. front of the original building has four irregularly spaced bays with windows of two, three and four square-headed lights in chamfered stone surrounds with labels. Between the two southern bays is the main doorway, with a late 19th-century stone porch with an embattled parapet and corner pinnacles ; above the porch is a stone carved with the arms of Farquhar, the family which acquired the house early in the 19th century. The 17th-century E. front is extended to N. and S. with additions, of the 19th century and later, incorporating reset 17th-century windows. The 19th-century S. front has mullioned and transomed windows with cinquefoil-headed lights. The N. and W. fronts have no notable features.

Inside, the drawing-room has a 19th-century moulded plaster ceiling in the style of the early 17th century, with the arms of Farquhar ; the late 17th-century stone fireplace surround is decorated with cable mouldings. The dining-room has reset and restored 17th-century panelling with a carved frieze. The windows of the 19th-century hall have fragments of 17th-century heraldic glass, mainly Flemish or German ; one cartouche with arms is dated 1651. Several first-floor rooms have 18th-century pine panelling and one room has 17th-century oak panelling with fluted Ionic pilasters ; the chimneypiece in this room is carved with caryatid figures and strapwork, extensively restored.

A late 18th or early 19th-century *Summerhouse* in the garden has walls of ashlar and brick, and a tiled roof. The S. front is of three bays defined by Doric pilasters ; at the centre is a round-headed doorway with a small pediment ; the side bays have round-headed windows. A date-stone loose in the garden bears the initials T.F., perhaps for Thomas Freke (Hutchins III, 626), and the date 171..

(59) HIGHER LANGHAM HOUSE (77212586), near the W. boundary of the parish, is of two storeys and has walls of rubble with ashlar dressings and is roofed with tiles (Plate 45). The central part of the house was built in 1770 ; a 19th-century wing extends to the E., and a corresponding wing on the W. is of more recent date.

The S. front of the 18th-century range is symmetrical and of three bays. At the centre of the lower storey is a doorway with a rusticated ashlar architrave and a pediment ; on each side are sashed windows with moulded architraves with keystones ; on the first floor are three similar windows. At each end of the S. façade the eaves are supported on brackets in the form of tri-

glyphs. The roof culminates in two large brick chimneystacks, on each of which is a date-stone inscribed 'WB 1770'. The N front has been extensively altered and the E. and W. ends of the original range are masked by the later wings.

Inside, the principal 18th-century rooms have moulded and enriched cornices. The fireplace in the hall has a stone surround with an enriched architrave, fret and leaf ornament on the frieze and an enriched cornice. The stairs have close strings, latticed balustrades and panelled oak dadoes.

A *Barn* some 20 yds. W. of the house has rubble walls and a tiled roof and is probably of the 18th century. The roof has king-post trusses with struts of ogee form.

(60) BAINLY HOUSE (76802744), on the W. boundary of the parish, is of two storeys with a basement and attics. The walls are of coursed rubble with ashlar dressings ; the roof is slate-covered. The house dates from about the middle of the 18th century and has a class-T plan. The S. front (Plate 45) is symmetrical and of three bays. The central bay is of ashlar ; the side bays are of rubble with rusticated ashlar quoins at the corners ; a plain plat-band occurs at first-floor level. At the centre on the gound floor is a round-headed doorway flanked by fluted pilasters which support an open pediment ; on the first floor is a Palladian window with moulded entablatures to the

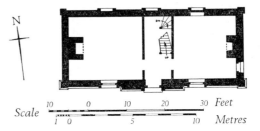

Scale [10 0 10 20 30 Feet] [1 0 5 10 Metres]

flanking lights and with a moulded architrave to the round-headed central light. The lateral bays of the S. front have sashed windows with moulded architraves. The N. elevation has sashed windows uniform with those of the S. front, some of them blind and others now blocked. The gabled E. and W. walls are of rubble with ashlar quoins. In the E. gable is an attic window of two square-headed lights. Each gable culminates in a brick chimneystack. Inside, few original features remain. The curvature of the stairs brings the half-landing at the top of the lower flight to the centre-line of the stair-well ; short flights then run E. and W. to the first-floor rooms. The service rooms are in the basement.

(61) HOUSE (79532660), of two storeys with rendered walls and tiled roofs, dates probably from the second half of the 18th century. The S. front is symmetrical and of three bays, with a central doorway under a porch with stone Tuscan columns. The windows in both storeys are sashed. Inside, the plan is of class U.

(62) HOUSE (79502659), of two storeys with rubble walls and a tiled roof, is of the late 18th century. The S. front is symmetrical and of three bays, with a central doorway and segmental-headed casement windows of two and of three lights. Adjacent on the W. is a slightly lower service range of one bay.

(63) WYKE FARM (79132668), house, nearly 1 m. W. of (1), is two-storeyed and has walls of Flemish-bonded brickwork, and tiled roofs. The original range, with a class-T plan, dates from about 1700 ; rubble-walled extensions on the N., E. and S. are of the 19th century and later. The windows of the three-bay W.

front have segmental brick heads and wrought-iron casements with leaded glazing. Inside, the N. room has a large open fireplace with a cambered oak bressummer; to one side is an oven, to the other a shell-headed wooden recess with shaped shelves. The ground-floor rooms have deeply chamfered beams.

An octagonal *Granary* and dovecote (Plate 31), about 20 paces S. of the house, has walls of Flemish-bonded brickwork and is roofed with slates and lead. The walls rise from timber sill-beams on staddle-stones. The building probably is of the early 19th century.

MONUMENTS (64–74)

Unless otherwise described, the following monuments are of the second half of the 18th century and are two-storeyed, with rubble walls and with tiled or slate-covered roofs.

(64) *Bleet Farm* (79132440), house, has a large open fireplace set against the gabled N. wall.

(65) *Cottages* (79072483), pair.

(66) *Cottage* (78452464).

(67) *Westbrook Farm* (78312546), house.

(68) *The Meads* (78452567), house, has ashlar walls and slate-covered roofs. The E. front is symmetrical and of three bays, with a central doorway, and sashed windows with segmental heads.

(69) *Cottage* (78162627), is roofed with thatch. The E. front is of two bays with a central doorway. Additions on the S. and W. of the original range have brick walls and tiled roofs.

(70) *Cottages* (79272609), pair.

(71) *Cottage* (80102664), with a thatched roof.

(72) *Cottage* (79272717), with a 19th-century extension on the E., has an open fireplace against the gabled W. wall.

(73) *Stock Farm* (78562702), cottage, has a thatched roof. The N. front is of two bays with a central doorway.

(74) *Barn* (77902623), at Lower Langham Farm, has walls of squared and coursed rubble, and tiled roofs; it is of the late 18th century.

Monuments of the first half of the 19th century in Wyke, Langham and Bugley are as follows—Two *Cottages* at Eccliffe (79892543); *Thorngrove House* (79382577), a three-storeyed building of rubble and ashlar, with tiled roofs, dating mainly from the late 19th century; *Springfield* (78662478), of two storeys, with rendered walls and slated roofs and with a symmetrical S. front of three bays, the centre bay gabled; *Westbrook Old Farm* (78312548); *Westbrook Farm Cottage* (78352552), perhaps partly of the late 18th century; *Hay House Farm* (77512593); *Wyke Brewery* (79572661), with walls of coursed rubble with ashlar dressings, and tiled roofs.

MILTON-ON-STOUR AND PEACEMARSH

(75) IVY COTTAGE (79732818), two-storeyed, with rubble walls and thatched roofs, dates from early in the 18th century. Inside, there is an open fireplace with a cambered bressummer and, above, a panel of moulded plasterwork with Tudor rose and pomegranate decoration; the panel dates probably from the late 16th century and is reset (cf. BOURTON (21)).

(76) THE OLD HOUSE (79642819), extensively rebuilt in the first half of the 19th century, retains elements of a late 17th-century building. The 19th-century house is of two storeys, with walls of squared and coursed rubble, and roof-coverings of tile and slate. The E. front has stone windows of two and three transomed lights with plain labels; near the centre is an ashlar porch with a heavy moulded entablature supported on two octagonal stone columns with moulded capitals and with recessed panels on each face of the shafts. The N. front incorporates walls, perhaps of 17th-century origin, with chamfered square-headed stone windows of two and of three lights.

Inside, one ground-floor room and an adjacent passage have heavily moulded ceiling beams of late 16th or early 17th-century origin, probably reset. The fireplace in the same room has a cambered and ovolo-moulded stone lintel carved in low relief with a blank shield flanked by winged horse-headed monsters and foliate scrollwork, probably of the early 17th century; above is a moulded cornice of a somewhat later date, with simple acanthus enrichment. Other rooms contain 17th-century oak panelling.

(77) LOWER BOWRIDGE HILL FARM (81212823), house, of two storeys with coursed rubble walls and tiled roofs, dates probably from the 17th century. The S. front, of two bays with a central doorway, has stone windows of three and of four square-headed lights with chamfered surrounds. The doorway is square-headed and has a moulded surround.

(78) PIERSTON FARM (79462849), house, of two storeys with coursed rubble walls and tiled roofs, is of the late 18th century, with 19th-century additions. The four-bay S. front has an ashlar plat-band at first-floor level. The westernmost bay has a single sashed window in each storey; the other three bays are symmetrical, comprising a five-sided two-storeyed 19th-century porch, with sashed windows of three lights on either side of it. The eaves are decorated with shaped and fretted fascia boards. Adjacent, on the S., is a *Barn* of late 18th-century date.

(79) BOWRIDGE HILL FARM (81412784), house, of two storeys, with coursed rubble walls and thatched roofs, dates from early in the 18th century. The S. front is symmetrical and of three bays, with a central doorway and with three-light sashed windows in the flanking bays and above the doorway. Above the E. gable is an ashlar chimneystack with a date-stone of 1722. A *Barn* some 50 yds. N. of the house has rubble walls and a slate-covered roof; a date-stone inscribed 'John Coombes, 20th Sept. 1844' is set in the E. gable.

MONUMENTS (80–95)

Unless otherwise described, the following monuments in Milton-on-Stour and Peacemarsh are of the late 18th century and of two storeys, with rubble walls and tiled or thatched roofs.

(80) *Ridge Hill Farm* (80623010), house, has the N. front in two parts divided by a vertical joint; to the E. the masonry is of coursed rubble, to the W. it is uncoursed.

(81) *Cottages* (80422986), two adjoining, are single-storeyed with dormer-windowed attics and date from early in the 18th century; they have recently been combined to form a single dwelling. Inside, there are large open fireplaces with chamfered and cambered bressummers against the N. and S. end walls.

(82) *Cottages* (80102871), two adjacent.

(83) *Cottage* (80922801), has a symmetrical S. front of three bays with a central doorway and with uniform sashed windows in both storeys.

(84) *Cottage* (80352792), with a S. front of two bays with a central doorway. Smaller cottages adjoining it on the N. and S. are probably of the 19th century.

(85) *Cottage* (80422763), has a later extension on the W. with brick walls.

(86) *Cottages* (80382757), two adjoining, have each a S. front of two bays with a central doorway. The W. cottage is of the late 17th century and is of one storey with an attic ; that on the E. is two-storeyed.

(87) *Cottages* (80542758), two adjacent, have each a symmetrical S. front of two bays with a central doorway.

(88) *Peacemarsh Farm* (80432752), comprises two adjoining cottages, that on the W. being the earlier.

(89) *House* (80482748), has a symmetrical W. front of two bays with a central doorway.

(90) *Cottage* (80442741), formerly two dwellings, are now united.

(91) *Cottages* (80532734), two adjoining ; the western cottage appears to be slightly later than that on the E.

(92) *Cottages* (80542733), two adjoining.

(93) *House* (80462728) has, on the E. front, a 19th-century porch and flanking bay-windows ; adjacent on the N. is an early 19th-century extension.

(94) *Cottages* (80462721), two adjacent, have now been combined as one dwelling ; the E. front is rendered.

(95) *Cottages* (80362713), three adjacent, wherein the E. tenement, of the late 18th century, is an addition to the other two dwellings. Inside, each tenement has only one room on each floor. The stairs are beside the fireplaces.

Monuments of the first half of the 19th century in Milton-on-Stour and Peacemarsh are as follows—*Woolfields Farm* (79672796), house, originally two cottages ; *Newlands Farm* (79682803), house ; *Cottages* (79642802), pair, with a symmetrical S. front of three bays ; *Dairy House* (79712813), comprising two cottages with dairies adjacent, perhaps of *c.* 1800 ; a *Barn* (79822833) with a date-stone of 1827 in the N. gable ; *Pierston House* (79742847) ; *Cottages* (79912861), two adjacent, now combined ; a *Cottage* (79803048), perhaps of *c.* 1800 ; a *Cottage* (80953000) ; *Cottages* (80952996), two adjacent, that on the W. being perhaps of the late 18th century ; a *Cottage* (82572980) ; *Forest Farm* (82782992), house with a symmetrical S. front of three bays ; *Bowridge Hill Cottage* (81532777) ; a *Cottage* (80692785) ; a *Cottage* (80672787), perhaps of *c.* 1800 ; a *Cottage* (80652793) ; a *Cottage* (80552793) ; *Northmoor Farm* (80432799) ; *Cottages* (80492757), two adjacent, of *c.* 1800 ; *Cottages* (80462742), two adjacent, now combined ; *Peacemarsh Terrace* (80522744), a range of eight uniform tenements ; a *Cottage* (80512740), of *c.* 1800 ; *Houses* (80532725), range of three, with the E. front of ashlar ; *Cottages* (80322713), pair, of *c.* 1800.

MEDIAEVAL AND LATER EARTHWORKS

' KING'S COURT PALACE ', see MOTCOMBE (20), p. 51.

(96) SETTLEMENT REMAINS (771260) of the hamlet of Langham lie some 200 yds. N. of Higher Langham Farm, on the W. side of a small stream ; they cover about 10 acres. The settlement is first recorded in 1156 (Fägersten, 7) and probably is one of the several Gillinghams listed in Domesday ; Eyton (123–4) suggests that it was the estate held by Ulwin (*V.C.H. Dorset*, iii, 110). Since Langham has always been recorded with Gillingham there are no records of population ; O.S. 1811 shows that the remains had already been deserted by that date. The earthworks comprise at least five rectangular closes, up to 100 yds. long and from 20 yds. to 40 yds. wide, bounded by low banks and orientated N.–S. ; low cross-banks divide them into paddocks. Disturbed areas at the southern ends of the closes indicate the sites of houses. The N. parts of the closes are covered with low ridges, up to 7 yds. wide. On the N. the area is bounded by a ditch or hollow-way, 30 ft. wide, beyond which are traces of larger paddocks with low bank boundaries. Further E., on both sides of the stream, traces of banks and disturbed earthworks, now much depleted, may be the sites of former houses ; they continue as far as Lower Langham Farm.

(97) SETTLEMENT REMAINS (800283) of Milton-on-Stour lie 240 yds. S.W. of Milton church and comprise at least four long closes, 50 yds. long and up to 40 yds. wide, bounded by banks 1 ft. high. At the northern ends of the closes are small plots, almost square, with traces of scarped platforms. Excavations by the Gillingham History Society in 1965–6 revealed, in the westernmost plot, two courses of a well-built limestone rubble wall, $1\frac{1}{2}$ ft. thick ; associated pottery was of the 12th and 13th centuries.

(98) CULTIVATION REMAINS are found in several places, but in the absence of documents cannot be associated with particular settlements. Early in the 17th century there appear to have been five open fields at *Gillingham* (P.R.O., LR2/214, f. 1–82). Ridge-and-furrow, perhaps of these fields, was formerly seen N. of the town (806269) and S.W. of the railway station (807255), (R.A.F., V.A.P., CPE/UK 1924 : 2242). Strip lynchets, perhaps the remains of the open fields of *Milton-on-Stour*, are seen on air photographs and on the ground W. of the village (790285–788281) ; they lie along the valley of a small brook (R.A.F., V.A.P., CPE/UK 1924 : 3238). Contour and cross-contour strip lynchets, perhaps the remains of the open fields of *Langham*, occur in three places (776270, 790264, 791254) on the N. and E. sides of Bainly Bottom.

(99) DEER PARK, of some 760 acres, in the S.E. of the parish and extending into Motcombe, was already in existence in 1228 ; its history is well documented from that date until disparkment in 1628. The park is bounded by a bank, 20 ft. to 30 ft. wide and up to 3 ft. high, with shallow ditches on both sides (*Dorset Procs.*, 87 (1965), 223–7).

ROMAN AND PREHISTORIC

(100) ROMAN OCCUPATION DEBRIS (79952620) was found in 1869 and also in 1951 near Common Mead Lane, on an exposed ridge of Kimmeridge Clay, about 300 ft. above sea-level. Stone pitching and loose stones were found, together with 2nd-century samian ware, querns, nails and staples, a bronze spoon, a Constantinian coin, and bones of oxen, sheep, pigs and horses. Pottery noted in 1951 was Romano–British, except for a few fragments probably of Iron Age ware. (Hutchins III, 661–2 ; *Dorset Procs.*, 73 (1951), 112.)

(101) INHUMATION BURIALS (? about 778262), probably a sub-Roman Christian cemetery, were found while quarrying limestone near Langham, on level ground some 350 ft. above sea-level (Hutchins III, 662); the date of discovery is not recorded. At least a hundred extended skeletons were arranged at 2 ft. intervals about 3 ft. below the surface, with heads to the west.

Two brooches and some small sherds of rough pottery were found.

(102) LONGBURY or SLAUGHTER BARROW (78752723), a long barrow, lies N. of Bainly Bottom at an altitude of about 320 ft., on the Corallian Beds; it is orientated E.–W. and measures 130 ft. in length, 40 ft. in width and up to 6½ ft. in height. When opened in 1802 several skeletons, perhaps primary burials, were found on the original ground level; when opened again in 1855 several other skeletons were found, perhaps secondary or intrusive, and fragments of 'some very rude earthen vessel'. A small excavation in 1951–2 gave no significant results. In 1953 part of a secondary or intrusive skeleton was found in the upper part of the mound. (C.T.D., Pt. 3, No. 84; Notes & Queries, 1st series, XII (1855), 364; Hutchins III, 615 (note), 662; Dorset Procs. 73(1951), 113; 76 (1954), 96.)

13 IWERNE MINSTER (8614)

(O.S. 6 ins., ST 81 SE, ST 81 NE, ST 81 NW)

The parish, covering 2,865 acres, occupies a broad strip of land astride the Chalk escarpment. From the Fontmell Brook, which flows through the parish near the N.W. corner, the land rises gently eastwards across Lower Greensand, Gault and Upper Greensand to an altitude of 225 ft. before falling to the headwaters of the R. Iwerne. Further E. two large dry valleys cut deeply into the escarpment, which here is 300 ft. high, rising to more than 600 ft. above sea-level. Beyond

the escarpment the land slopes gently down to a wooded area, part of Cranborne Chase. The parish formerly included the modern parishes of Handley, Hinton St. Mary, Margaret Marsh and East Orchard, all of which were parochial chapelries of Iwerne Minster.

There were two early settlements, Iwerne and Preston, both on the R. Iwerne; a third settlement, Hulle, may also have existed (Dorset Procs., 69 (1947), 45–50). Pegg's Farm on the Fontmell Brook, in existence early in the 14th century, is probably a secondary settlement.

Euneminstre, an old possession of Shaftesbury, was already a large settlement at the time of the Domesday survey, being assessed for 18 hides and having 16 ploughs (V.C.H., Dorset, iii, 82). The name suggests that it was an old minster served by a community of clergy.

ECCLESIASTICAL

(1) THE PARISH CHURCH OF ST. MARY (Plate 49) has walls of flint and rubble with ashlar dressings, of banded flint and ashlar, and of ashlar; the roofs are stone-slated and tiled. The Nave, North Aisle and North Transept are of the mid 12th century; they appear to be parts of an important church, cruciform in its original plan and probably at first without a S. aisle, but with a transept opposite to that which in part survives on the N. The remains of a 12th-century structure in the angle between the nave and the former S. transept prob-

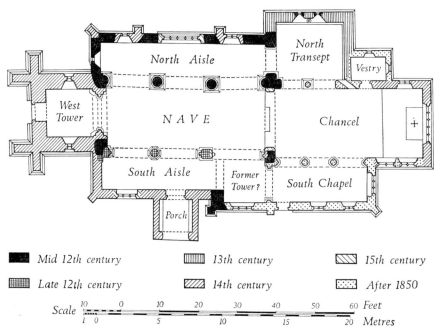

IWERNE MINSTER   *The Parish Church of St. Mary*

North Transept

Vestry

North Aisle

West Tower

NAVE

Chancel

South Aisle

Former Tower?

South Chapel

Porch

■ Mid 12th century　　▥ 13th century　　▨ 15th century

▦ Late 12th century　　▧ 14th century　　▦ After 1850

Scale   10   0   10   20   30   40   50   60 Feet
　　　　 1   0   　 5   　 10   　 15   　 20 Metres

ably represent a former *South Tower*. Late in the 12th century the *South Aisle* was added on the W. of the presumed S. tower and early in the 13th century the N. transept was rebuilt. The present *Chancel* is of the 14th century, as are the *West Tower*, the S. and W. walls of the S. aisle, and the *South Porch*. In the 15th century the chancel arch was widened, and a spire was added to the W. tower. In the 16th century the nave was heightened and provided with clearstorey windows. In 1871 the church was restored by T. H. Wyatt and the N. Vestry was added.

Architectural Description—The E. window of the *Chancel* has a chamfered two-centred head and a two-centred rear-arch, both of the 14th century; the five lights and the curvilinear tracery are of the 19th century. In the N. wall is a 14th-century window of two trefoil-headed lights with a quatrefoil light above; the rear-arch has been rebuilt. Further W. in the N. wall, beyond the 19th-century vestry doorway, a squint from the N. transept is of uncertain date, perhaps modern. The opening to the N. transept (Plate 6) has two two-centred arches, each of two chamfered orders, the inner orders springing from moulded corbels with male and female heads, the outer orders continuous; at the centre the arches rest on an octagonal shaft with a moulded capital and a chamfered square base with broach stops. The arches are of the 14th century and replace an earlier opening, of which there remain the W. respond and the chamfered base of the E. respond, the latter now reused in the central pier. The S. side of the chancel is largely of 1889, but the two S. windows, uniform with that on the N., are restored and reset 14th-century openings. The chancel arch is of 14th-century origin, but altered and widened, probably in the 15th century; it is segmental-pointed, with a wave-moulded inner order springing from restored corbels, and with a continuous outer order chamfered on the W. side and hollow-chamfered on the E. In the gable above the chancel roof a 14th-century window similar to that on the N. of the chancel gives light to the nave.

The *North Transept* has a 19th-century E. window set high enough to clear the vestry roof; it is of three lights, with curvilinear tracery in a two-centred head. In the N. wall are two round-headed lights with wide splays and round-headed rear arches; they are probably of 12th-century origin, reset in the 13th century. The rear-arches spring from a central column with a Purbeck marble shaft, a stone base with hold-water mouldings, and a stone capital with stiff-leaf ornament (Plate 9). Internally, the N. and E. walls have a moulded string-course. The transept is entered from the N. aisle through a round-headed 12th-century archway of two plain orders springing from moulded imposts on chamfered responds.

The *Nave* (Plate 50) has a mid 12th-century N. arcade of three bays, with round arches of two plain orders, and piers and responds with stout cylindrical shafts, scalloped capitals (Plate 9), and moulded bases on high chamfered plinths. Above, the 16th-century clearstorey has two single-light windows with hollow-chamfered four-centred heads, wide splays and chamfered segmental rear-arches. In the S. arcade, the E. bay has an archway of 14th-century origin, with a two-centred head of two chamfered orders, but with the western arc distorted in the widening of the archway, probably in the 15th century. The inner order is continuous on the E. respond while on the W. respond it springs from a shaped corbel; the outer order dies into the E. respond, but continues as a chamfer on the western pier. The two western bays of the S. arcade are of the late 12th century and

have two-centred arches, each of two stop-chamfered orders, springing from chamfered E. and W. responds with attached shafts and moulded capitals, and from a central pier with a cylindrical shaft, a plain bell-shaped capital and a moulded base on an octagonal plinth. Above, the clearstorey has two single-light windows with elliptical heads and segmental rear-arches. A third window has been blocked.

The *North Aisle* has single-stage buttresses with weathered heads and chamfered plinths. In the eastern bay is a late 14th-century window with two trefoiled ogee-headed lights and a two-centred rear-arch. The middle bay has a late 15th-century window of five trefoil-headed lights under a chamfered square head. The western bay has a window with details similar to that of the eastern bay, but of one light. In the W. wall is a small 12th-century window with wide splays and a round rear-arch; the square head of the light is modern.

In the eastern part of the *South Aisle* the S. wall of the presumed South Tower was refaced in the 19th century and the window, of three trefoiled ogee-headed lights with curvilinear tracery in a two-centred head, appears to be of that period; on the other hand the lower part of the S. wall and the entire S.W. buttress, with broad chamfered plinths, are 12th-century work. On the W., the opening to the western part of the aisle is spanned by a half-arch, restored in the 19th century; its apex rests on the spandrel of the eastern arch of the S. arcade. Further W., the S. doorway, with a double roll-moulded two-centred head and continuous jambs, is of the early 14th century; the rear-arch is flat, with shouldered jambs. Adjacent on the W. is a square-headed 15th-century window of three trefoil-headed lights. The S.W. corner of the aisle has a diagonal buttress of two weathered stages.

The *West Tower* is of two stages defined by a weathered string-course; at the top is a corbel-table and an embattled parapet; at the base is a low chamfered plinth. The N.W. and S.W. corners have angle buttresses of four weathered stages; corresponding square-set buttresses rise above the W. walls of the N. and S. aisles. There is no vice. The tower arch is of three chamfered orders with continuous responds ending at broach stops above splayed plinths. In the lower stage the N. and S. walls have original windows of one trefoil-headed light with chamfered surrounds. The W. doorway has a moulded two-centred head with continuous jambs, and a moulded label with returned stops. In the upper part of the lower stage the E. wall of the tower has a doorway to a modern organ-loft; in the W. wall is a single-light window with a trefoil head and a chamfered surround. The upper stage has, in each side, a belfry window of two trefoil-headed lights with a central quatrefoil in a chamfered two-centred head. The octagonal spire has two bands of stonework with cusped panelling; the arrises have roll-mouldings; at the apex is a moulded capstone and an iron weathervane. Rebuilding of the spire in the 19th century has reduced the height and somewhat altered the profile.

The *South Porch* has a two-centred archway with a chamfered inner order dying into the responds, and a continuous chamfer on the outer order and jambs. Above is a plain parapet with a moulded string-course and coping. Inside are plain stone benches.

Fittings—*Bells*: six; 2nd by Abraham Bilbie, inscribed 'Mr Thomas Harvey & Mr John Applin wardens, 1768. My treble voice makes hearts reoice Abram Bilbie founder'; 3rd by John Wallis, inscribed 'Feare The Lorde, IW, 1609'; 4th inscribed in Lombardic letters 'huic ecclesie dedit mercia sit bona sub iesv nomina sona', early 14th century; 5th by John Wallis, inscribed 'Give laud to God, IW, 1618'; 6th by John Wallis, inscribed ' O be joyful in the Lord, IW, 1618 '; 1st modern. *Bracket :* inserted in capital of eastern pier in N. nave arcade, with moulded edges and sunk panel on underside, probably mediaeval. *Chests :* of oak, one with beaded panel and lid, 18th century ; another with moulded panels, decorated stiles, drawer below, 18th century. *Clock :* in belfry, *c.* 1750 with modern variable chiming mechanism. *Communion table :* of oak, with turned legs, beaded stretchers and moulded rails, 17th century. *Font :* octagonal, with slightly tapering sides, each with a quatrefoil, plain octagonal stem and hollow-chamfered base, 15th century. *Glass :* in S. window of chancel, by Willament, 1847. *Graffito :* on stone bench in porch, ' W.D. 1773 '. *Hatchments :* three ; on canvas, in wooden frames, with shields-of-arms of Bower quartering and impaling other coats, 19th century.

Monument and *Floor-slabs. Monument :* In S. aisle, on W. wall, of Robert Fry, 1684, his wife Mary (Cox) and others of their family ; slate inscription panel in foliate stone surround above apron with drapery, skull, wreath and cherub-heads, also with scrolled cheek-pieces, cornice, and finial with cartouche containing arms of Fry (Plate 16). *Floor-slabs :* In nave, near S.E. corner, (1) of [John Ridout, 1764] and his wife Henrietta, 1730. In S. aisle, (2) of [Katherine, wife of] Francis Melmo[uth], 1718, and of Mrs. Bower, 1721 ; (3) of Thomas Bower, 1728, with worn shield-of-arms ; (4) of John Bower, 1711 ; (5) of (undecipherable), with arms of Bower ; (6) of R... Freke, 1655, stone slab with bold lettering.

Niche : In porch, over S. doorway, with roll-moulded and hollow-chamfered two-centred head and continuous jambs, 14th century. *Plate :* includes Elizabethan silver cup by the ' Gillingham ' silversmith (*Dorset* III, liii), with churchwardens' inscription probably of 1782, and cover-paten, probably 18th century ; also set of silver cup, stand-paten and almsdish, with date-marks of 1832 and donor's inscriptions of Rev. Christopher Nevill ; also pewter dish and flagon, late 17th century. *Pulpit :* of oak, with five sides, panelled in two heights (Plate 13), with fluted corner stiles, rails with guilloche and brattished enrichment, and panels with reticulate enrichment, mid 17th century ; cornice and base modern. *Recess :* In N. aisle, in middle bay of N. wall, with chamfered four-centred head, late 15th century, restored. *Royal Arms :* of George III, on canvas in moulded wood frame (Plate 27). *Sundial :* on S.W. buttress of W. tower, scratch-dial, much worn, perhaps 16th century. *Wall :* bounding churchyard on S. and W., of banded flint and ashlar with weathered, roll-moulded coping, and in part with weathered ashlar buttresses ; mediaeval. *Miscellanea :* In vestry, fragment of shaft capital, late 12th century ; glazed slip-tiles, 14th and 15th century.

(2) BAPTIST CHAPEL (86641432), of one storey with rendered walls and tiled roofs, stands nearly 200 yds. S.W. of the church. According to an inscription it was built in 1810 and enlarged in 1860. The main part of the building has a round-headed doorway in the gabled E. wall and, above, a round-headed sashed window. The S. elevation has three windows similar to those described. At the corners of the building and between the windows are plain pilasters with moulded capitals ; similar pilasters occur on the N. wall, but there are no windows. On the W. is an extension with lower walls than the main hall, but with pilasters and windows as described. Inside, a W. gallery with a panelled wooden front rests on two plain iron columns.

SECULAR

(3) WEST LODGE (89411573), on the N. boundary of the parish, is partly of one storey and partly of two,

with cellars, and has brick walls, partly rendered, and slated and tiled roofs. The site is that of one of the ancient lodges of Cranborne Chase (W. Shipp, *Chronicle of Cranborne,* (Blandford 1841), 270), and a map of the Chase dated 1677, copying a map of 1618, shows a house in this position. Nothing seen above ground today, however, is likely to be of so early a date,

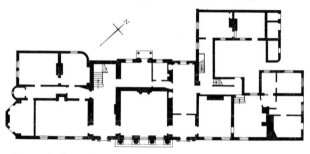

although the cellars may perhaps be of the 17th century. The present building is of the first half of the 18th century, with early 19th-century single-storeyed wings on the S.W. and N.E., the latter incorporating part of a late 18th-century kitchen building.

The S.E. front (Plate 44) is symmetrical and of eleven bays, comprising a five-bay central pavilion of two storeys, flanked by single-storeyed three-bay wings. The three central bays of the façade are emphasised by a portico with stone three-quarter columns of the Tuscan order, supporting a timber entablature and pediment. Between the shafts the lower storey has three large sashed windows and the upper storey has three circular windows ; a lunette window opens in the pediment. The flanking bays of the central pavilion have doorways with pedimented Tuscan surrounds in the lower storey, and sashed windows above. The extremities of the centre pavilion are defined by wooden pilasters, beyond which each single-storeyed wing has three large sashed windows. The last bay of the N.E. wing includes part of the two-storeyed kitchen wing, probably of the late 18th century and perhaps originally a separate building.

The N.W. front of the centre pavilion is of Flemish-bonded brickwork, with wooden cornices and pediment. At the centre is a wooden porch with a pedimental hood supported on Ionic columns and pilasters. The ground and first-floor windows of the three central bays are mullioned and transomed and of two lights, with wooden frames and 18th-century wrought iron casements with leaded glazing. At right-angles to the N.W. façade, the S.W. elevation of the projecting N.W. wing is of two storeys, with mullioned and transomed windows as before ; presumably this is part of an original service building, but there have been many alterations and the original plan cannot be recovered.

Inside, the house was remodelled in the second half of the 19th century and few original features remain. Until quite recently the large central room was higher than at present, the circular windows opening into the upper part of the room, but a floor has now been inserted. The S.W. staircase has cast-iron balusters and newel-posts. In a corridor of the service wing, a plinth projecting from the N.E. wall of the central block shows that this wall was originally external.

The cellars under the N.W. part of the central pavilion have rubble walls and brick vaults.

STABLES, see Sutton Waldron (5).

(4) PEGG'S MILL BRIDGE (84891529), crossing the Fontmell Brook, has a single segmental arch of ashlar and parapets of coursed rubble with rounded ashlar capping. It is of the early 19th century.

(5) PEGG'S FARM (851155), in the N.W. of the parish, comprises a farmhouse, a cottage, a water-mill and a barn. The *House*, two-storeyed with header-bonded brick walls and with tiled roofs with stone-slate verges, is of the 18th century; in the *Salisbury Journal*, 18 July 1774, it is advertised as new-built. The S. front is symmetrical and of three bays, with a central doorway and with wooden casement windows of two and three lights. The gabled E. and W. end walls culminate in brick chimney-stacks.

The *Cottage*, adjoining the house on the N., is two-storeyed, with Flemish-bonded brick walls and with a tiled roof; it is of 18th-century date, but later than the house.

The *Mill*, adjoining the house on the W., has ashlar walls and tiled roofs and dates from *c.* 1800. The mill-wheel is now used to generate electricity.

The *Barn*, some 60 yds. E. of the house, has walls of rubble and of brick, and a thatched roof. The rubble occurs at the base of the walls in the N. part of the building and is probably of the 17th century; the brickwork represents 18th-century rebuilding. At intervals the walls are strengthened with brick buttresses. The roof rests on crude tie-beam trusses, strutted in some places, with rough hammer-beams below.

(6) PRESTON HOUSE (86411396), of two storeys with an attic, has walls of ashlar and of rubble, and a tiled roof. It dates from early in the 17th century, but was considerably altered late in the 19th century. In plan the house was originally L-shaped. The ashlar-faced S. front is symmetrical and of five bays, with a central doorway flanked by Tuscan columns supporting an open pedimental hood, and with uniform casement windows of two lights in both storeys of the lateral bays; above the doorway is a bull's-eye window. A weathered label over each casement window appears to be original, but the openings have been altered and enlarged. The other elevations are of rubble and contain some original casement windows with hollow-chamfered ashlar surrounds and weathered labels. An original doorway, now converted into a window, occurs in the N. wall of a small lean-to projection on the W.; it has a chamfered four-centred head and continuous jambs with moulded stops. Inside, the two ground-floor rooms of the S. range have 18th-century fireplace surrounds of carved wood. A first-floor room has an original stone fireplace surround with a moulded four-centred head and continuous jambs with run-out stops.

(7) 'THE CHANTRY' (86791441), house, 50 yds. S.W. of (1), is of three storeys with attics and has walls of banded flint and ashlar, with chamfered plinths and ashlar dressings, and stone-slated roofs. The house dates from the first half of the 17th century.

The S. front is of three bays, that in the centre projecting and gabled (Plate 52). The central doorway has a moulded square-headed surround with a label. The windows are of two and of three square-headed casement lights with hollow-chamfered stone jambs and mullions, and moulded labels with returned stops. The first-floor window in the W. bay, however, has been enlarged and has sliding sashes, probably of the 18th century. The central brick chimneystack with two diagonally set flues appears to be original; the similar chimneystack on the E.

gable is modern, but it replaces a plain square stack which probably was added in the 18th century. The gabled E. elevation has a blocked doorway at first-floor level and a small attic window in the brick gable. To the N. the ground floor is below ground level, and the lower windows in the two-storeyed elevation are those of the first-floor rooms; the

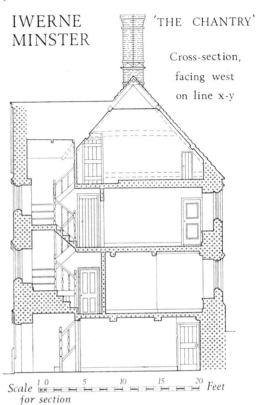

IWERNE MINSTER   'THE CHANTRY'

Cross-section,

facing west

on line x-y

Scale ├─────┼─────┼─────┼─────┤ *Feet*
     1 0   5   10   15   20
for section

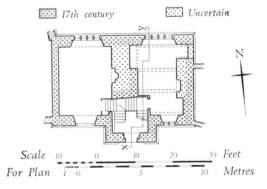

▨ *17th century*   ▨ *Uncertain*

N

Scale   10   0   10   20   30 *Feet*
For Plan 1 0   5   10 *Metres*

elevation is of two bays, with stone windows of four square-headed lights. The W. elevation is masked by the adjoining house (8).

Inside, the centre bay of the S. front contains an original oak staircase with closed strings, turned and enriched newel posts, turned balusters and moulded handrails. The two first-floor rooms (see plan) have 17th-century stone fireplace surrounds, with chamfered four-centred heads and continuous jambs with shaped stops; that on the E., served by an 18th-century chimney, is presumably reset. In the original plan, it is probable that the W. room on the first floor was the hall and that on the E. was the parlour; the lower storey, lit only from the S., presumably contained the service rooms.

(8) BAY HOUSE, adjacent to the foregoing on the W., is of two storeys, with brick walls and tiled roofs; the greater part of the building is of the late 19th century, but it incorporates early features and evidently replaces an earlier house. Projecting at the E. end of the N. front is a stone porch in which the plinth is continuous with that of the N. wall of 'The Chantry'; over the porch is a chamber with timber-framed walls. Projecting northwards at the W. end of the same front is a two-storeyed wing with walls of flint and rubble in the lower storey, and of timber-framework above; the upper storey is jettied and gabled on the N., the gable having cusped bargeboards, probably of c. 1500.

(9) BARN (86751440), with rubble walls and a tiled roof, dates probably from the late 16th or early 17th century. The long N.W. side has ashlar buttresses of two stages with weathered offsets.

(10) BROOKMAN'S FARM (86981434), house, is single-storeyed with attics and has walls of rubble with brick dressings, and thatched roofs; it is of 18th-century origin with 19th-century additions. The S. range is symmetrical and of two bays with a central doorway. There is a large brick chimneybreast with stepped and weathered offsets on the gabled N. wall of the N. wing.

A Barn, some 70 yds. N.W. of the house, with brick walls and formerly with a thatched roof, is of 18th-century origin. A projecting bay with a doorway occurs on the E. side.

(11) THE VICARAGE (86931438), of two storeys with attics, has walls of ashlar and of coursed rubble, and tiled roofs. It was built in 1836. The windows have stone mullions, transoms and labels, and the porch has a chamfered round-headed doorway.

(12) BARN (86711462), at Churchill's Farm, with walls of ashlar, coursed rubble and clunch, and with stone-slated roofs, is of the 17th century. The walls have ashlar buttresses generally of two and of three stages, with chamfered plinths and weathered offsets. The S. end has two-stage diagonal corner buttresses and, at the centre of the gable, a square-set buttress of five stages.

(13) COTTAGE (86571451), of one storey with attics, has walls of brick, rubble and cob, and a thatched roof; it is of 17th-century origin. Inside, two stop-chamfered beams are exposed, and an open fireplace has a chamfered and cambered oak bressummer.

MEDIAEVAL AND LATER EARTHWORKS

(14) CULTIVATION REMAINS. The last fragments of the former open fields of Iwerne Minster, then divided into two fields known as Town and Poly Fields, were enclosed in 1848 (Enclosure Map and Award, D.C.R.O.); they lay respectively N.E. and S. of the village. The strip lynchets on both sides of Brookman's Valley (around 876142) lay within old enclosures. Strip lynchets on the N. side of Preston Hill (868136) are the remains of cultivation associated with the mediaeval settlement of Preston.

ROMAN AND PREHISTORIC

(15) IRON AGE SETTLEMENT and ROMAN VILLA (856137), near Park House Farm Buildings, were excavated in 1897 by General Pitt-Rivers. The site is on Upper Greensand, about 230 ft. above sea-level, on a gentle rise in the low-lying ground at the headwaters of the R. Iwerne; from S. and E. it is overlooked by the higher ground of the escarpment.

The Iron Age settlement is represented by numerous pits. From it came Durotrigian silver coins, a La Tène I bronze brooch, a bronze belt-link, and a bone weaving comb. In early Roman times the settlement was modified by the digging of ditches and sub-rectangular pits; finds of this period included coins from Vespasian to Commodus, brooches, and samian pottery of the 1st and 2nd centuries. No house-site was found, but there were suggestions that the centre of occupation lay N.W. of the excavated area.

During the 3rd century a building, nearly rectangular in plan, 112 ft. by 39 ft., with flint footings 3 ft. wide, occupied the western part of the site. The N.E. end of the building was divided into three rooms, 8 ft. in length and respectively 7 ft., 13 ft. and 8 ft. in width. The entrance was probably on the N.E., where post-holes for a porch were found. The rest of the building, with a pit or post-hole at the centre measuring 8 ft. by 2½ ft. by 6 ft. deep, was partly flint-paved; it has been suggested that it was an aisled barn, although no holes or bases for aisle-posts were noted. Coins ranging in date from Gordian I to Tacitus were found in or near the building.

Lastly, c. A.D. 300, a substantial building was erected on an oblong site levelled into the rising ground on the E., some 25 ft. away from the building described above; it measures 126 ft. by 18 ft. and the walls, of flint rubble, 2¼ ft. to 3½ ft. in thickness, remain standing in places to a height of 6 ft. (Plate 48). The main range is divided into four compartments, and a fifth room, 16 ft. square, projects from the N.W. side. A corridor or out-

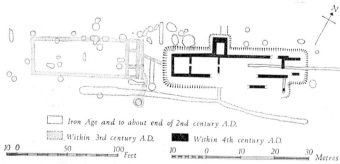

Iron Age and to about end of 2nd century A.D.

Within 3rd century A.D.　　　Within 4th century A.D.

10 0　　　50　　　100 Feet

10　　0　　10　　20　　30 Metres

IWERNE MINSTER. (15) Iron Age Settlement and Roman Villa.

PLATE 49

IWERNE MINSTER CHURCH. From S.E.

12th, 14th and 19th century

PLATE 50

Nave, looking N.W.   Mid 12th century and later

Nave, looking S.W.

IWERNE MINSTER CHURCH.

PLATE 51

Late 12th-century features

Chancel arch reset on N. of chancel.

Doorway reset in W. wall of S. aisle.
PIMPERNE CHURCH.

PLATE 52

IWERNE MINSTER. (7) 'The Chantry', S. front.   Early 17th century

PLATE 53

MOTCOMBE. (3) North End Farm House, from S.W. Early 17th century

KINGTON MAGNA. (7) Lower Farm House, S.E. front. Late 17th century

PLATE 54

Air view, from S.E.

Air view, from W.N.W.

PIMPERNE. (18) Enclosure.

Probably Iron Age

PLATE 55

PIMPERNE. (20–28) Chestnut Farm Barrow Group, from S.

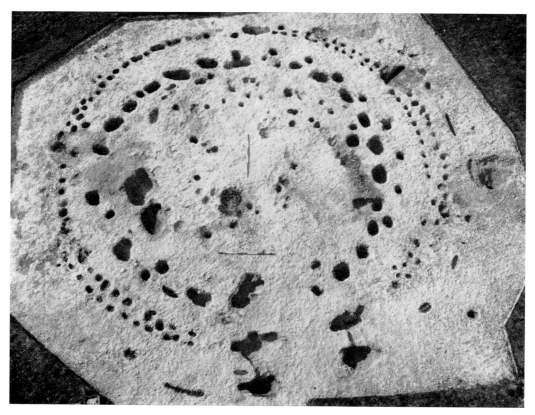

PIMPERNE. (15) Remains of Iron Age house.

(Photo: I. M. Blake)

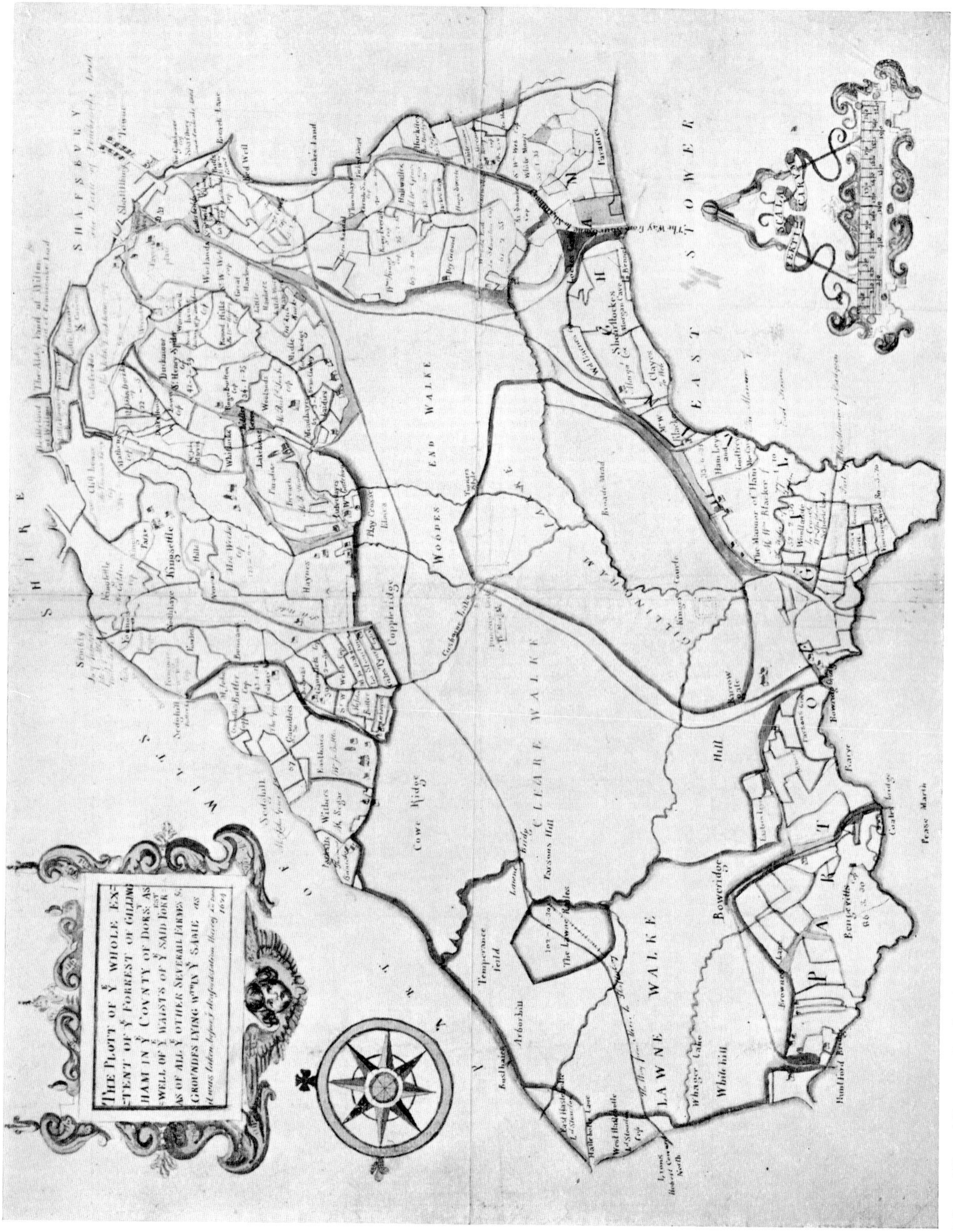

PLATE 56

Map of Royal Forest of Gillingham, 1624.
GILLINGHAM and MOTCOMBE.

Copied 1816 or later
(N. to left; scale in perches)

building lay along the S.E. side. The compartment at the N.E. end, 15 ft. long, may have been a porch. The adjacent room, 64 ft. long, was probably a cattle-shed since a stone-filled drain 2 ft. wide extended down the centre of the range from a point 28 ft. from the S.W. end of the room ; a quern was found *in situ* near the middle of the western part of the room. Next on the S.W. is a room 27 ft. long, roughly paved, and communicating by axial doorways 2 ft. wide with the rooms to N.E. and S.W. The S.W. room is paved with small slabs of Kimmeridge shale and its walls, except on the N.E., are lined with plaster, painted with rectangular panels above a broad dado-line. The fifth room, on the N.W., has doubled walls, the inner of which, only 4 ft. high, probably carried a floor ; this is likely to have been a granary. Coins ranging from Maximian to Decentius and New Forest ware and coarse pottery, found during the excavations, indicate occupation of the building until *c.* A.D. 360. (*Arch. J.*, CIV (1947), 50–62. Finds and models in Farnham Museum, Dorset. Photographs in D.C.M.)

Monuments (16–20), Round Barrows

All the barrows lie on high ground in the E. of the parish, four of them composing a group on Iwerne Hill. A small barrow was destroyed in 1846 during the ploughing of the high downland between Iwerne Hill and West Lodge ; on its floor was an inverted urn covered by a quantity of black ash and surrounded by six cremations in cists cut in the Chalk ; its exact location is not known. (Hutchins III, 555 ; *C.T.D.*, Pt. 2, no. 4 ; *Dorset Procs.*, L (1928), 121 ; Warne, MS. album in D.C.M., 209.)

(16) *Folly Barrow* (88561563), bowl, about 600 ft. above O.D. on Bareden Down, on a southward-facing slope, lies just below the crest of the escarpment. It is in a small wood and is thickly overgrown. Diameter 50 ft., height 5½ ft. ; ditch 9 ft. across and 1 ft. deep.

The *Iwerne Hill Group* comprises four barrows on the crest of the escarpment, more than 600 ft. above O.D. All have been reduced by ploughing ; (17) is in arable land, the others are under grass.

(17) *Bowl* (88941490) ; diam. 70 ft., ht. 1 ft.

(18) *Bowl* (89061493), 140 yds. E.N.E. of (17) ; diam. 45 ft., ht. 1 ft.

(19) *Bowl* (89071499), 60 yds. N. of (18) ; diam. 45 ft., ht. 1 ft.

(20) *Bowl* (89081503), 40 yds. N. of (19) ; diam. 45 ft., ht. 1 ft.

14 KINGTON MAGNA (7623)

(O.S. 6 ins., ST 72 SW, ST 72 SE)

The parish, extending to nearly 2,000 acres, is divided into two parts, Kington and Nyland, by the R. Cale. Kington in the N.E. occupies some two-thirds of the total area, with land on Oxford Clay rising gently from the Cale at about 180 ft. above sea-level, to 300 ft. ; further N.E. the land ascends steeply to 400 ft. on the Corallian Limestone escarpment. The village of Kington Magna stands at the foot of the escarpment, with the parish church prominently sited on the rising ground to the E. ; until the enclosure of the open fields Kington probably was the only settlement in this part of the parish. Enclosure appears to have taken place in the 17th century, and several outlying farms came into existence as a result.

As its name implies, Nyland, in the S.W., is an island of Oxford Clay surrounded by the alluvium and marshland of the Cale and the Bow Brook. The settlement is mentioned in Domesday (*V.C.H., Dorset*, iii, 84, 91), but neither Higher nor Lower Nyland now contains any monument of note.

ECCLESIASTICAL

(1) The Parish Church of All Saints[1] has walls of rubble with ashlar dressings, and tiled roofs. The *West Tower* is of the late 15th century. The *Chancel, Nave, North* and *South Aisles*, and the *South Porch* were rebuilt in 1862, the architect being Charles Turner of Southampton (Faculty, Sarum Dioc. Regy., 1861).

Architectural Description—The massive *West Tower* (Plate 1) is of three main stages, with a moulded plinth, weathered and hollow-chamfered string-courses between the stages, and an embattled parapet with moulded coping. At the N.W. and S.W. corners are diagonal buttresses of four weathered stages, that on the N.W. partly restored and having an additional weathered offset half-way up the second stage ; the tops of the buttresses coincide with the string-course between the second and third tower stages. The N.E. corner has a square-set buttress of five stages, the top stage extending into the top tower stage, or belfry ; this buttress was rebuilt, using old material, in 1862. The S.E. corner has a rectangular vice turret with a weathered stone head. The tower arch, rebuilt in 1862, is two-centred and of two orders, the inner order wave-moulded, the outer order hollow-chamfered ; both orders die into plain chamfered responds. The doorway to the vice turret has a chamfered four-centred head and chamfered jambs. The W. doorway has an ogee-moulded and hollow-chamfered four centred head with continuous jambs and run-out stops, and a moulded label with square stops with foliate centres. The W. window, of 1862, has three ogee-headed lights and curvilinear tracery in a two-centred head ; the jambs are those of an earlier window, of which the head and sill were lower than at present. In the second stage the S. wall of the tower has a small window with a moulded trefoil head. The doorway at the top of the vice has a chamfered four-centred head and chamfered jambs with broach stops. In the top stage the N., S. and W. sides have belfry windows of two trefoil-headed lights, with trefoil tracery lights in two-centred heads under moulded labels with square stops ; a former E. belfry window has been blocked.

Fittings—Bells : five ; treble modern ; 2nd and 3rd by John Wallis, both inscribed ' Love God IW 1608 ' ; 4th inscribed ' I sound to bid the sick repent in hoe of life when breath is spent '

---

[1] Not *The Holy Trinity*, as on O.S. maps.

reading from right to left, also 8461, presumably 1648 ; tenor with ' Sancte Georgi ora pro nobis ' in fine crowned Lombardic letters, second half of the 14th century. *Bell-frame :* with two heavily chamfered beams, mediaeval. *Chest :* In vestry, of oak, with panelled front and sides, and enriched stiles and rails, 17th century. *Communion Table :* In vestry, of oak, with turned legs, moulded stretchers,enriched rails and scrolled brackets, 17th century, top modern.

Monument : In tower, on N. wall, of John Dowding, 1747, and others of his family, round-headed slate tablet on gadrooned stone apron.

Piscina : In S. aisle, reset in S. wall, with trefoil head and label with finial, bowl cut away, 14th century. *Royal Arms :* In tower, painted on wood panel with moulded surround, Stuart arms with cypher C R, 17th century. *Miscellanea :* In nave, standing on floor, fragments of window tracery, 14th century.

(2) METHODIST CHAPEL (76522284), with squared rubble walls and a tiled roof, dates from 1851. The gabled S. front is of three bays, with a central doorway with a two-centred head and shafted jambs, flanked by plain windows with two-centred heads and surmounted by a third such window. In the gable is a stone inscribed ' 1851 Primitive Methodist Chapel, T. Tanner Mason '.

SECULAR

(3) MANOR FARM (76842308), house, of two storeys with attics, with rubble walls with ashlar dressings and with stone-slated and tiled roofs, is of the mid 17th century. The N. front has a chamfered plinth and a weathered and hollow-chamfered first-floor string-course. Inside a modern porch, on the W. of the projecting stair bay, is a doorway with a four-centred head

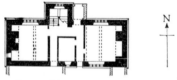

with double ovolo mouldings, continuous jambs and chamfered stops. The stone windows are of two, three and four square-headed lights with recessed and hollow-chamfered surrounds ; the three-light window in the stair bay is at mezzanine level, showing that the stairs are in the original position. The S. elevation is partly hidden by later additions, but plinth, string-course and several stone windows remain exposed. Inside, the original fireplaces are blocked and the stairs have been renewed ; of original fittings only two chamfered beams are visible.

(4) PROSPECT COTTAGE (76772317), of two storeys, with rubble walls and a tiled roof, is of 17th-century origin, but was altered in the 18th century. The S. front is of four bays, with a plain doorway and with sashed windows uniform in each storey ; the flat window-heads have stone voussoirs with projecting keystones. In the S. wall the outline of an earlier gable suggests that the cottage was originally single-storeyed. Adjacent on the W. is a *Barn*, with rubble walls and a tiled roof, also of 17th-century origin.

(5) HOUSE (76612315), of two storeys, with rubble walls and tiled roofs with stone-slated verges, is of the late 17th century. The W. front is symmetrical and of three bays, with a central doorway and wooden three-light casement windows. Inside, a stop-chamfered beam is exposed.

(6) HOUSE (76512297), of two storeys, with rubble walls and stone-slated roofs, is probably of early 17th-century origin, but was much altered in the 18th century. The plan is a half-H, with the main range on the S. and with subsidiary wings projecting N. at the rear ; the narrow yard which formerly lay between the wings was filled in, perhaps in the 18th century. The 18th-century S. front is symmetrical and of five bays, with a central doorway and with sashed windows in both storeys ; one former ground-floor window has become a doorway, and two of the first-floor openings have been blocked. The door is of oak planks, heavily studded and hung on wrought-iron strap-hinges. In the lower storey of the N. elevation, both wings retain stone casement windows of four square-headed lights with sunk-chamfered jambs and heads ; the window in the western wing has a casement-moulded surround. In the upper storey the casement windows have wooden frames and leaded glazing. Inside, some rooms have chamfered ceiling beams with splayed stops.

(7) LOWER FARM (75832265), house, of two and three storeys (Plate 53), has walls of coursed rubble with dressings of lighter coloured ashlar, and is roofed partly with stone-slates and partly with tiles ; it dates from late in the 17th century. The original plan comprises a main E.–W. range, facing S., with a wing projecting from the centre of the N. side ; the wing now is partly enclosed in 19th-century and later extensions. The S. front is symmetrical and of five bays ; at the base is a square plinth and at first-floor level is a weathered and ogee-moulded string-course ; the corners have ashlar quoins. The ground-floor and first-floor windows are uniform, each being of two transomed square-headed lights with recessed and hollow-chamfered jambs, heads and mullions ; some original wrought-iron casements with quadrant stays remain. At the centre is a square-headed ashlar doorway with a moulded and eared architrave flanked by Roman-Doric pilasters ; it is now in a porch, but originally may have been in the plane of the façade. The gabled E. wall of the range has a small blocked window with a moulded square-headed surround ; it is set at mezzanine level and indicates the former position of a small stair beside the chimneybreast. The N. wing has casement windows of three square-headed lights at ground-floor, mezzanine and upper first-floor levels, suggesting that the wing originally contained a second staircase. The gabled W. wall has two blocked bull's-eye windows in the upper storey. Inside, the house has been much altered and the original disposition of rooms is lost ; it may have resembled that of Motcombe (3). The chimney-stacks on the gabled E. and W. walls of the S. range are original, although the fireplaces are blocked. A 17th-century staircase, probably in the N. wing originally, has been moved to the S. range ; it is of oak, with heavily moulded close strings, stout turned balusters, square newel posts, and handrails rounded on top and moulded on one side only.

(8) HOUSE (76542321), of two storeys, with brick walls and a slate-covered roof, is of the late 18th century. The S. front is of four bays, with a doorway and elliptical-headed sashed windows on the ground floor, similar sashed windows in the upper storey and a plain plat-band at first-floor level.

MONUMENTS (9–20)

Unless otherwise described, the following monuments are two-storeyed, with rubble walls and tiled roofs, and are of 18th-century origin.

(9) *Cottages* (76632318), two adjoining, have been much altered from their original form.

(10) *House* (76552316), with a N. front of three bays, has wood-framed casement windows of two and of three lights.

(11) *Cottage* (76442327), with a thatched roof, has a symmetrical S.W. front.

(12) *House* (76472316), with a slated roof, has a symmetrical S. front of three bays, with segmental-headed openings with projecting keystones.

(13) *Cottages* (76402309), two adjoining, have segmental-headed openings, as in the foregoing.

(14) *Cottages* (76482296), range of three.

(15) *House* (76512284), of two storeys with an attic and with a slate-covered roof, is of the late 18th century, but incorporated in it is a *Cottage* of somewhat earlier 18th-century date.

(16) *Cottages* (76282275), four adjoining, comprise two on the W. which have now been combined to make one dwelling; inside is an open fireplace with a wooden newel staircase on the S. The cottages on the E. are of the late 18th or early 19th century.

(17) *Cottages* (76582284), range of three.

(18) *Cottages* (76592300), four adjacent, include two on the E. which may be of late 17th-century origin.

(19) *Cottage* (76852293), with a slate-covered roof, retains two chamfered ceiling beams and an open fireplace with an oven, now blocked up.

(20) *Bye Farm* (75982391), house, with slate-covered roofs, comprises two parallel ranges. The symmetrical E. front is of three bays, with a central doorway and sashed windows.

BOWDEN

(21) LAWRENCE FARM (77372303), house, of two storeys, with walls partly of rubble and partly of brickwork and with a tiled roof, is of the late 17th or early 18th century, with a later 18th-century extension on the N. Inside, there are stop-chamfered beams and two open fireplaces.

(22) BOWDEN FARM (77312359), house, of two storeys with rubble walls and a tiled roof, was built at three periods: the middle part of the range is of the 17th century, the N. part is of the 18th, and the S. part is of the late 19th century.

(23) FOLLY FARM (77282383), house, of two storeys, with rubble walls and a tiled roof, is of 17th-century origin. The original building, in the N.E. part of the range, has low casement windows with heavy timber surrounds and appears formerly to have been single-storeyed. The S.W. part of the range and the upper storey of the N.E. part were added at the end of the 18th or early in the 19th century.

(24) COTTAGE (77292343), of two storeys, with rubble walls and a tile-covered roof, is of the 18th century.

(25) COTTAGE (77312345) has characteristics similar to the foregoing.

(26) COTTAGE (77272355), of two storeys, with rubble walls and a slated roof, is of the first half of the 18th century. The S. front is of two bays with a central doorway.

(27) FOLLY COTTAGE (77392402), similar to (24), contains a large open fireplace on the E.

NYLAND

(28) BRIDGE (75722148), carrying the Shaftesbury–Sherborne road across the R. Cale, is of rubble and ashlar and has four segmental-pointed arches.

On the S. side the arches are of the 17th century and have chamfered ashlar voussoirs with the chamfers dying into plain responds. (In April 1631 repairs to the bridge were ordered at Quarter Sessions.) On the N. side the arches have rubble voussoirs springing from ashlar responds and cut-waters, the latter with pyramidal heads; this side of the bridge appears to have been rebuilt in 1792 (contract, D.C.R.O.). Reset in the N. parapet wall is a stone inscribed 1670, probably recording the completion of repairs ordered at Quarter Sessions in July 1669.

(29) NYLAND MANOR FARM (74782183), house, of two storeys, with rubble walls and slate-covered roofs, dates from *c.* 1800. The E. front is nearly symmetrical and of five bays, with a central doorway flanked by sashed windows of three lights on the ground floor, and single-light sashed windows in the upper storey. Adjacent on the S.E. is a 19th-century *Barn*.

(30) HIGHER FARM (73882217), house, of two storeys with rubble walls and a tiled roof, is of the 17th century; until 1947 the roof was thatched. Set in the S. front is an inscription tablet with 'T.D. 1632' above and 'I.D. 1723' below. The N. elevation retains casement windows of three square-headed lights with chamfered timber surrounds. Inside, some rooms have chamfered beams with splayed stops. One room has an open fireplace with an oven.

(31) COTTAGE (74952181), of two storeys with rubble walls and a slate-covered roof, is of the early 18th century. Inside are some chamfered beams of shallow cross-section and a blocked open fireplace.

(32) COTTAGE (74072190), of two storeys with rubble walls and a slate-covered roof, is of the 18th century. Inside, the N. room has a large open fireplace.

(33) LOWER NYLAND FARM (75332172), house, is of the first half of the 19th century.

MEDIAEVAL AND LATER EARTHWORKS

(34) CULTIVATION REMAINS. Of the open fields of Kington and Nyland little is known; those of Kington must have been enclosed by the end of the 17th century, when the house (7) of Lower Farm was built. Traces of ridge-and-furrow of the fields occur here and there around the village (R.A.F., V.A.P. CPE/UK 2018 : 3168).

15 LANGTON LONG BLANDFORD (8905)

(O.S. 6 ins., ST 80 NE, ST 90 NW)

Langton Long Blandford is a parish of some 1,200 acres, lying on the N. bank of the R. Stour, adjacent to Blandford Forum (*Dorset* III, 16). The land is almost wholly Chalk, rising from about 100 ft. in the S. to 350 ft. above sea-level in the N. A dry tributary valley of the Stour forms the N.W. boundary. Until 1933 the parish included Littleton, now part of Blandford St. Mary (*Dorset* III, 40) ; recent enlargement of Blandford Forum also has deprived Langton of a small area in the W. The village, reduced to the parish church and a few houses, stands on the river terrace of the Stour. Some 700 yds. to the S.E. the stables and other out-buildings of Langton House stand in the park of the former mansion, now demolished.

ECCLESIASTICAL

(1) THE PARISH CHURCH OF ALL SAINTS, in the E. of the village, was rebuilt in 1861 to designs by T. H. Wyatt (Sarum Dioc. Regy.) ; the former church, built *c.* 1740, appears to have incorporated some part of a mediaeval structure (Hutchins I, 284), but nothing of this remains today. Some fittings from the two earlier churches are reset in the present building.

Fittings—Bells : three ; treble inscribed 'W. W. TP. Anno Domini 1674', others modern. *Brasses* : reset in modern slate tablet (2¼ ft. by 2¾ ft.), comprising inscription plate, three figures, two scrolls, and shield-of-arms of Whitewood ; presumably from former floor-slab of John Whitewood, his wife Joan, 1457, and his second wife Alice, 1467 (Plate 14) ; spaces left in inscription for date of John's death not filled in. *Communion Table* : In W. tower, of oak, with turned legs, plain stretchers and plain top, late 17th century. *Credence Table* : of mahogany, with moulded edge, legs with fretted stays, drawer with brass drop-handles, secular, late 18th century.

Monuments and *Floor-slab*. *Monuments* : In chancel, on N. wall, (1) of Louisa (Craufurd) Farquharson, 1839, marble tablet by J. Browne, London. In S. transept, on E. wall, (2) of Anne (Staines) Farquharson, 1837, marble tablet with shaped and carved head, by J. Browne ; (3) of James Farquharson, 1795, marble tablet (Plate 38) with sculptured oval panel above, and shield-of-arms of Farquharson impaling Staines ; on W. wall, (4) of Lieutenant Frederick Thomas Farquharson. 1841, marble wall-monument with representation of a sword, by W. G. Nicholl, London ; (5) of Anne Farquharson, 1834, oval tablet with foliate border ; (6) of Henrietta Anne (Farquharson) Grove, 1821, shaped marble tablet with urn finial and, on apron, shield-of-arms of Grove impaling Farquharson, by Shout, London. In nave, above N. arcade, (7) of Edward Vivian Keane, 1840, circular tablet with wreath surround, by J. Browne ; (8) of Marion Harte, 1845, oval tablet by Marshall of Blandford ; on S. wall, (9) of Sir William Fraser Bt., 1827, tablet by H. Wood, Bristol ; (10) of Keith Fraser, 1826, round marble tablet with wreath and crossed-sword enrichment, by G. Mann, London ; (11) of Elizabeth, Lady Fraser, 1834, tablet by H. Wood ; (12) of Sir James Fraser Bt., 1834, wall-monument with shield-of-arms, by J. Browne. In N. aisle, (13) of William Crosse, 1815, and others of his family, 1792–1851, wall-monument with urn finial, by Kent of Blandford. In churchyard, ten paces W. of tower, (14) of Richard Pultney, 1801, and his wife Elizabeth, 1820, table tomb. *Floor-slab* : see *Brasses*.

Plate : includes Elizabethan silver cup and cover-paten, perhaps by Lawrence Stratford, but maker's mark worn away, with date-letter of 1568 ; original cover-paten with modern repairs and date-letter of 1908 ; also silver flagon and paten, *c.* 1850 or later, and silver-plated cup.

SECULAR

LANGTON HOUSE (90240562), built in 1827–33 to the design of C. R. Cockerell in place of an 18th-century house, was demolished in 1949. An engraving of the 18th-century house (Hutchins I, *opp.* 284) shows a two-storeyed main range with six regularly spaced bays, flanked by projecting two-bay wings, also two-storeyed, but lower than the main range. Between the two central bays of the six-bay front the engraving shows a doorway and a columned porch with a Doric pediment ; this porch is now at Langton Farm (8).

(2) STABLES (90250562) of Langton House, with walls of finely jointed ashlar and with slate-covered roofs (Plate 47), stand some 70 yds. N. of the site of the former house (see above) ; they were built in 1832 and comprise an octagonal courtyard surrounded by two-storeyed ranges. Within the courtyard the ranges have eaves of exceptionally wide spread ; externally the N.W. range extends to fill the N. and W. corners of the otherwise octagonal plan. The former coach-house, in the W. corner, has recently been remodelled to make a dwelling-house. The courtyard is entered at the centre of the S.E. and N.W. ranges through round-headed archways surmounted by plain pediments. Over the N.W. pediment is a clock turret with a cupola and a weathervane, the latter with the date 1832.

(3) KITCHEN WING (90260556) of Langton House, of two storeys with walls and roofs as in (2), stands immediately N.E. of the site of the former house ; it dates from *c.* 1827. The three-bay S.W. front, originally facing a courtyard at the back of the main house, has a pedimented centre bay with a round-headed window in the upper storey.

(4) BREW-HOUSE (90320551), of two storeys, with walls and roofs as in (2), has in the S.E. front an archway surmounted by a turret with a cupola. The S.W. front is masked by an arcaded loggia of three bays, with round-headed arches springing from coupled rectangular piers. The building probably is of *c.* 1830.

(5) SOUTH LODGE (89880592), cottage, of one storey with rendered walls and slate-covered roof, was built *c.* 1830. In the S. front and in the E. and W. sides of the central block the wide eaves are supported on slender Roman-Doric colonnades.

(6) LODGE (90460526), cottage, of one storey with walls and roofs as in the foregoing, is probably of *c.* 1840. The S.W. front is symmetrical and of three bays, with a round-headed doorway and with plain sashed windows.

(7) THE RECTORY (89660587), of two storeys, with rendered walls and slate-covered roofs, is mainly of the early 19th century, but it incorporates a small 18th-century range in the western part. The S.E. front is symmetrical and of three bays, the centre bay defined by pilasters and a small pediment. At the centre is a french window ; in the lower storey the side bays have sashed windows, in the upper storey all three bays have casement windows with glazing-bars arranged to form narrow marginal panes. The N.W. elevation incorporates banded rubble and brickwork of 18th-century date. Inside, the stairs have plain balustrades and an inlaid mahogany handrail. Reset in an internal wall is a 16th-century stone window of two lights with four-centred heads ; it is perhaps from the former church.

(8) LANGTON FARM (89590585), house, of two storeys with attics, has walls of flint, rubble and brick, partly banded and partly rendered, and tile-covered roofs. In the N.W. range, now of ten bays, the six bays on the N.E. are of 17th-century

origin ; early in the 18th century the range was extended on the S.W. by another four bays and a S.E. wing was formed at the S.W. end of the extension. The mid 18th-century stone porch from Langton House (see above) was reset on the N.E. front, presumably c. 1827. Recently the main N.E. range has been rendered and the windows have been provided with modern casements. Inside, the original range contains some exposed beams ; the 18th-century extension has chamfered beams with shaped stops resting on lightly chamfered wall-plates. A staircase with slender Tuscan-column balusters and a moulded handrail occurs in the 18th-century extension.

(9) SCOTLAND COTTAGES (90840614), pair, of two storeys, with brick walls with some flint banding near the ground, and with tiled roofs, are probably of late 18th-century origin. Small brick buttresses in the lower storey suggest that the external walls may originally have been those of a barn. A cottage adjacent on the E. is of c. 1800.

(10) LANGBOURNE HOUSE (90500808), of two storeys, has walls of rubble and brickwork, in part rendered, and tiled roofs. The W. range is of c. 1840 and has a rendered W. front of three bays in which a central doorway with a porch with Tuscan columns is flanked by plain sashed windows ; similar windows occur in the upper storey ; the roof is masked by a parapet above a moulded cornice. To the E. of the 19th-century range, on the S., extends an earlier range, probably of the 18th century, with walls partly of rubble and partly of brickwork. Many of the windows have iron casements with leaded lights, but on the S. side of the E. range the windows of the upper storey are sashed.

ROMAN AND PREHISTORIC

A number of finds indicative of Iron Age and Romano-British settlement are known from the parish, all on the lower slopes of the Stour valley. Roman pottery including samian ware, and brooches have been found, principally near 89710597 ; bronze brooches and a pin in the B.M. (Durden Collection) probably came from this site. An inhumation in a cist N. of Langton House might also be Roman, since samian sherds were found nearby (Hutchins I, 289–90 ; Archaeologia, XXIII (1830), 415–6). 'Human remains and British urns' were found in 1840 at 90790544, and at least four silver Durotrigian coins were found at 90500530 (O.S. records).

MONUMENTS (11–13), ROUND BARROWS

(11) Bowl (91260732), on the parish boundary with Tarrant Monkton, lies on the crest of a N.–S. Chalk ridge, 360 ft. above O.D. Diam. 50 ft., ht. 5 ft.

(12) Bowl (91580658), on Little Down, on the crest of a Chalk ridge, 330 ft. above O.D., was about 45 ft. in diameter, but now is ploughed out. Probably this is 'Down Wood Barrow', opened by Cunnington in 1881 to yield three primary contracted inhumations and three secondary cremations, but no grave goods (Dorset Procs., XXXVII (1916), 46 ; Cunnington MS., no. 42).

(13) Bowl (91790613), in Buzbury Plantation, 350 ft. above O.D., probably is the barrow in which several urns were found in 1840 (Durden Catalogue, 18). Diam. 30 ft., ht. 3 ft.

LINEAR DITCHES around Buzbury Rings ; see TARRANT KEYNESTON (18), (19), p. 104.

'CELTIC' FIELDS ; see p. 118, Group (70).

16 MARGARET MARSH (8218)

(O.S. 6 ins., ST 81 NW, ST 82 SW)

This parish, barely 550 acres in extent, comprises two roughly triangular areas joined at a narrow neck. The land is all Kimmeridge Clay, between 150 ft. and 230 ft. above sea-level ; it drains into a small rivulet which flows S.W. to join the Key Brook on the S.W. boundary. The S.W. triangular area, formerly a parochial chapelry of Iwerne Minster, is probably mentioned in a document of 1310 (Hutchins III, 556). The smaller N.E. triangle, Gore Farm, once part of St. James's parish, Shaftesbury, was recorded in 1282 (Fägersten, 42).

ECCLESIASTICAL

(1) THE PARISH CHURCH OF ST. MARGARET has walls of ashlar and rubble and tile-covered roofs. The Chancel, Nave and South Porch were rebuilt in 1872. The West Tower dates from the 15th century.

Architectural Description—The West Tower is of ashlar and has a moulded plinth, three stages defined by moulded, weathered and hollow-chamfered string-courses, and an embattled parapet with a moulded coping. The corners of the lower stages have diagonal buttresses with weathered offsets at the level of the string-courses ; the top stage has plain corner pilasters, perhaps originally with pinnacles, now gone. An octagonal vice turret occupies the E. part of the N. wall and is staged in correspondence with the main stages ; beside the turret the top string-course has a gargoyle. The tower arch is two-centred and of two chamfered orders with continuous jambs. The doorway to the vice has a chamfered four-centred head and chamfered jambs. The W. doorway has a four-centred head of two chamfered orders under a moulded label, and continuous jambs ; above, the W. window is of three trefoil ogee-headed lights under vertical tracery in a two-centred head. The string-course between the two lower stages of the tower forms a label over the window. In the second stage, the S. wall of the tower has a window of two trefoil-headed lights with vertical tracery in a two-centred head ; the lights are closed by stone slabs with lozenge perforation. The belfry in the third stage has, in each wall, a window uniform with that in the second stage.

Fittings—Chest : of cast-iron, inscribed 'Margaret Marsh register chest, John Scammell, 1813, C.W.'. Font : with round bowl, hollow-chamfered and roll-moulded below, on plain cylindrical shaft, and with base as for a Tuscan column; bowl c. 1300, base 18th century. Glass : reset in W. window, fragments including crown, fleurs-de-lis, and black-letter inscriptions 'Margaret' and '... Yong' qui hanc fenestra' mill'imo qui'ge'tesimo xli' ; 15th and 16th century. Graffiti : on responds of tower arch, initials and dates, 1696 and later.

Monuments : In churchyard, on E. wall of S. porch, (1) of William Bennett, 1756, headstone with shield-of-arms of Bennett. Some 4 yds. S. of chancel, (2) of William Bennett, 1792, headstone similar to the foregoing. Some 10 yds. S. of porch, table-tombs with panelled sides and moulded tops : (3) of William Yetman, 1678, (4) of Lucy Fry, formerly wife of William Yetman, (5) anonymous, probably 18th century

Plate : includes Elizabethan silver cup of similar form to that of Gillingham, but smaller, with maker's mark, four lozenges arranged lozengewise, and italic inscription 'This Plate Belong to Margrit Mash Church'.

SECULAR

(2) CHURCH FARM (82371867), house, with walls of squared rubble and with tiled roofs, is of the 16th century and was originally single-storeyed with an attic, but it was heightened to two storeys, probably in the 18th century. The S. range has

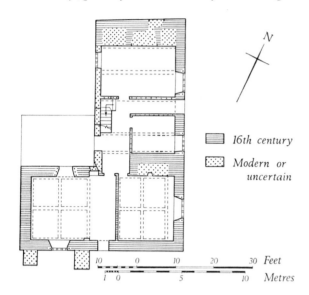

16th century

Modern or uncertain

10   0   10   20   30 *Feet*

1   0   5   10 *Metres*

two rooms with hollow-chamfered intersecting ceiling beams ; originally they were separated by a through-passage, but the W. partition has been removed. The W. room appears always to have been unheated ; the E. room has a blocked open fireplace. The N. range has hollow-chamfered beams with shouldered stops, and the N. room, no doubt the kitchen, has a blocked open fireplace. An oven formerly projected from the N. wall, but the projection has been removed and the cavity has been filled in. It is probable that a staircase formerly occupied one of the spaces beside the N. fireplace, but nothing is seen of it today. The W. wall of the N. range appears to have been rebuilt.

(3) MARSH FARM (82141894), house, of two storeys with an attic, has rubble walls and thatched and tiled roofs. The original range is of the 17th century, and there are 19th-century additions on the W. and S. The three-light first-floor window in the gabled N. wall is original ; other windows are of the 18th century. The exposed parts of the S. and W. walls in the original range have chamfered first-floor string-courses. Inside, a stop-chamfered beam is exposed in the S. room of the original range.

(4) HIGHER FARM (82621902), house, of two storeys with rubble walls and thatched roofs, is of 15th-century origin. Many of the original roof timbers remain *in situ*, masked by the present roof, which is superimposed. From details of the timbers the original plan of the house

can be deduced ; it comprised a two-bay hall, open to the roof, a two-storeyed service bay on the S.W., and another bay on the N.E. In the 16th century the hall was chambered over and an open fireplace and chimney-stack were built in the S.W. bay, leaving the S.W. end of the former hall as a through-passage. To the S.W. of the 16th-century chimneystack the roof has been rebuilt. All windows have been renewed. The N.E. bay has been rearranged and retains no old features ; its widening on the N.W. certainly is not original.

Inside, the inserted 16th-century floor rests on intersecting beams with deep, slightly hollowed chamfers ; the first floor over the kitchen rests on large joists, square in section, perhaps original. The fireplace inserted in the hall has been blocked up ; there is no fireplace in the chamber above. The accompanying drawing shows the original roof members, but omits the present roof ; there are indications that the principals are crucks, but they cannot now be traced below first-floor level. An open truss with arched braces spanned the hall, and a truss corresponding with the N.E. end of the hall was closed with studding. The principals supported two chamfered purlins on each side, with curved windbracing. Above the present first-floor ceilings the roof timbers are encrusted with soot, showing that originally there was an open hearth ; in part of the roof an original wattle lining is attached to the underside of the common rafters.

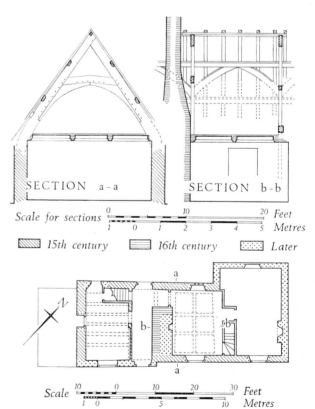

SECTION a-a   SECTION b-b

Scale for sections   0   10   20 *Feet*

1   0   1   2   3   4   5 *Metres*

15th century   16th century   Later

Scale   10   0   10   20   30 *Feet*

1   0   5   10 *Metres*

(5) JOPP'S FARM (82751953), house, with walls of rubble and ashlar and with a thatched roof, is of the early 17th century. The plan, formerly of class F, has been altered by the removal of partitions and the insertion of a staircase. The N., E. and W. elevations have stone windows of three square-headed lights with recessed and hollow-chamfered surrounds; the gabled S. wall retains a small loop with two round-headed openings lighting a newel stair on the W. side of the S. chimney-stack. Inside, the large central fireplace has ashlar jambs and a chamfered timber bressummer; the S. fireplace is similar, but smaller. On the first floor, the S. chimneystack serves a small fireplace with a four-centred head. Several stop-chamfered beams are exposed. Plank-and-muntin partitions, now dismantled, had muntins with moulded edges. A scratching on one of the ashlar window-sills includes the date 1647.

(6) MARGARET MARSH FARM (81931934), house, of two storeys with rubble walls and a modern slated roof, dates from the early 17th century. Inside, the N. ground-floor room has a nine-panel ceiling with chamfered intersecting beams. Several

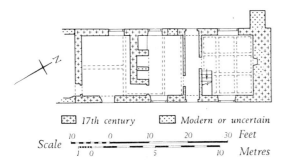

□□ *17th century*   □□ *Modern or uncertain*

Scale 10   0   10   20   30 *Feet*
         1 0   5   10 *Metres*

rooms on the first floor retain original oak panelling. In the N. chamber a modern fireplace surround incorporates 17th-century oak pilasters carved with male and female figures; they spring from strapwork pedestals and support crude Ionic capitals.

(7) GORE FARM (83442056), house, now of two storeys but originally single-storeyed with attics, has squared rubble walls and tiled and slated roofs (Plate 31). It dates from the 16th century and was heightened and enlarged on the S. probably in the 18th century. The continuous footing courses suggest

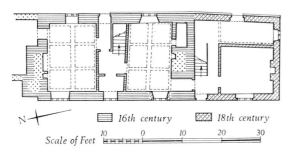

N   ▦ *16th century*   ▧ *18th century*

Scale of Feet 10   0   10   20   30

that the S. bay occupies the site of an original building. Inside, the surviving original range has a plan of class T. The rooms have heavy and elaborately moulded oak main beams and wall-plates, and moulded cross-beams. The open fireplaces are blocked; externally, the N. fireplace has a large chimney-breast with four weathered offsets; the adjacent oven has a lean-to roof.

17 MELBURY ABBAS (8820)

(O.S. 6 ins., ST 81 NE, ST 82 SE, ST 92 SW, ST 91 NW)

The parish, of some 2,700 acres, straddles the Chalk escarpment, occupying the steep S. side of the deep valley of the Melbury Brook, which cuts back into the escarpment for almost 1½ m. The land in the W. part of the area is on Gault and Kimmeridge Clay, falling northwards and westwards from 400 ft. to 250 ft. above sea-level. The central part of the area, between 400 ft. and 700 ft., is on Upper Greensand and Chalk, except where the underlying Gault is exposed at the bottom of the valley; in the S. it rises to 858 ft. on the top of Melbury Hill. The village stands at the foot of the escarpment and has two nuclei, Melbury Abbas and East Melbury. In 1086 it was a moderately large place with a recorded population of 47 (*V.C.H., Dorset*, iii, 82). Contour strip lynchets occur on the N. and on the S.E. of the village. Of the development of the outlying farms in the W. nothing is known.

ECCLESIASTICAL

(1) THE PARISH CHURCH OF ST. THOMAS was entirely rebuilt in 1852 to designs by George Evans of Wimborne (Sarum. Dioc. Regy.).

Fittings—*Monuments*: In N. vestry, reset on W. wall, (1) of Rev. Hugh Grove, 1792, marble tablet with cornice and pediment, with arms of Grove; (2) of Rev. Peter Smith, 1763, and Joanna his wife, 1779, marble tablet with moulded stone surround. In churchyard, 3 paces S.E. of S. transept, (3) of Mary, 1745, and John Hiscock, 1746, headstone. *Plate*: includes silver cup with assay mark of 1806, and paten of 1813 with donor's inscription of 1833.

SECULAR

(2) CROSS BASE (86602038), probably of a 15th-century wayside cross, stands in the garden of Cornhill Cottage. It is of stone, 2½ ft. square and nearly 2 ft. high, and has a mortice 1 ft. square for the foot of the shaft, now gone. Pyramidal stops bring the square to an octagon at the top.

(3) SCHOOL (88152005), of one storey with an attic, has ashlar walls and slated roofs and was built in 1844. The N. front has a doorway with a chamfered four-centred head under a moulded label; above, in a panel, is the crest of Glyn and the date 1844; higher still, above a zone of weathered ashlar, is a bellcote with small buttresses and a weathered stone capping. The windows of the schoolroom and of the schoolmaster's house are square-headed, with chamfered stone surrounds and moulded labels.

(4) EAST MELBURY FARM (88822038), house, of two storeys with an attic, has walls of coursed rubble and of ashlar, and tiled roofs. It is of the 17th century, with 19th-century additions. The original plan was of class T. The W. front of the original range is symmetrical and of three bays, with a central doorway in the lower storey flanked by modern stone windows

of four square-headed lights and with original three-light windows in the upper storey ; these windows have moulded labels with returned stops. The central bay of the W. front has been rebuilt and now has an attic storey with a curvilinear gable. The central doorway has a moulded stone hood on shaped stone brackets, the window above it is of Venetian form and the attic window is round-headed. A 19th-century bay with two-light windows with labels, as before, extends the W. front southwards.

(5) SPRING COTTAGE (88222033), of two storeys, with ashlar and rubble walls and with slated roofs, is of the early part of the 19th century. The S. front is symmetrical and of three bays, with a central doorway, and with square-headed sashed windows in both storeys.

MEDIAEVAL AND LATER EARTHWORKS

(6) CULTIVATION REMAINS. Nothing is known of the open fields of the parish. Contour strip lynchets occur S.W. of Breeze Hill at 890193, and E. of Barfoot farm at 882208 ; the first group is marked on the tithe map of 1838 as 'South Field Launches'.

ROMAN AND PREHISTORIC

'CELTIC' FIELDS, see p. 120, Group (79).

(7) INHUMATION BURIALS, Romano-British, were found in 1846 near Melbury Hill (*Gentleman's Mag.*, new ser., XXVI (1846), 633) ; associated with one burial was a coin of Antoninus Pius.

MONUMENTS (8-15), ROUND BARROWS

(8) *Bowl* (89291884), near the top of the N.-facing scarp of Melbury Down, lies at over 700 ft. above O.D. There are traces of a ditch and the suggestion of an outer bank ; it appears to have been disturbed at the centre. Diam. 54 ft., ht. 3 ft. The barrow may lie within the adjacent 'Celtic' field system.

(9) *Bowl* (89231962), on the S.W. slope of Breeze Hill, lies at over 700 ft. above O.D. ; diam. 27 ft., ht. 1 ft. Traces of a ditch.

(10) *Bowl* (89211982), 200 yds. N. of (9), lies at over 700 ft. above O.D. ; diam. 39 ft., ht. 1 ft. Traces of a ditch.

(11) *Bowl* (89702016), on Breeze Hill, lies just below the 800 ft. contour ; diam. 30 ft., ht. 1 ft. Slight disturbance at centre.

(12) *Bowl* (89892018), 200 yds. E. of (11), lies at over 800 ft. above O.D. ; diam. 30 ft., ht. less than 1 ft.

(13) *Bowl* (89782051), on the level summit of Breeze Hill, is over 800 ft. above O.D. ; diam. 21 ft., ht. less than 1 ft.

(14) *Bowl* (89802055), adjacent to the foregoing on the N.E. and at approximately the same altitude, has been disturbed in the N.W. and S.E. sides ; diam. 42 ft., ht. 1 ft.

(15) *Bowl* (89542091), near the top of Breeze Hill and more than 700 ft. above O.D., lies on the boundary between Dorset and Wiltshire ; diam. 60 ft., ht. 3½ ft.

The 'Ditch' shown on O.S. maps between Compton Down and Melbury Hill (885194-872200) is a disused trackway.

UNDATED

(16) ENCLOSURE (873197), on the summit of Melbury Hill and more than 850 ft. above O.D., commands wide views in every direction. The feature forms an almost perfect circle about 400 ft. in diameter, with a low bank and an internal ditch ; there is no visible entrance. The earthwork appears to be of no great antiquity ; it might be a plantation boundary. There is little doubt that this hill-top was the site of Melbury Beacon, one of a series of fire-beacons in use at the time of the Armada (*Dorset Procs.*, 81 (1959), 103-6).

18 MOTCOMBE (8425)

(O.S. 6 ins., ST 82, all parts).

The parish, with an area of 5,450 acres, comprises much of the former Royal Forest of Gillingham and was part of Gillingham parish until 1883. Near the E. border the Upper Greensand escarpment rises to more than 700 ft. above sea-level ; the rest of the parish lies on Gault and Kimmeridge Clay at altitudes between 250 ft. and 500 ft. The land is drained by small streams flowing W. to the R. Lodden, on the N. and W. boundaries of the parish. The village stands at the confluence of four such streams. Although not named in Domesday the settlement may be one of the several Gillinghams there recorded (see p. 27). Many of the outlying hamlets and farms originated as secondary settlements within the Royal Forest ; Fernbrook, Frog Lane, Kingsettle and Woodsend farms were all in existence by the end of the 13th century (Fägersten 29). On an early 17th-century map, now lost, but known through a 19th-century copy (Plate 56) in D.C.M., secondary settlements such as these are recognisable by their small fields and irregular boundaries ; many of them still exist today. Larger fields with more nearly rectilinear boundaries in the N. and N.W. of the parish result from enclosure after the disafforestation of the Royal Forest in 1624 ; Wolfridge Farm (4) is of this period. In the 19th century under the ownership of the Marquess of Westminster the village was extensively rebuilt and few earlier dwellings survive. The most important Monument in the parish (18) is the earthwork remains of a Royal Hunting Lodge, now reduced to banks and ditches. North End Farm (3), 'Easthaies' on the 17th-century map, has an interesting early 17th-century farmhouse.

ECCLESIASTICAL

(1) THE PARISH CHURCH OF ST. MARY was wholly rebuilt in 1846, in the 'Perpendicular' style (*Builder*, IV (1846), 393) to designs by G. Alexander ; it has ashlar walls and tile-covered roofs. Drawings by J. C. Buckler of the former church are in the B.M. (Add. MS., 36361,

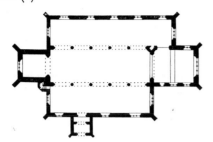

152–5). Fittings from the former church are incorporated in the 19th-century building.

Fittings—*Chest :* of oak, with plank sides, top and bottom bound with four wrought-iron straps with hinges, staples and hasps for four padlocks, and with two horizontal straps forming end-handles, the latter also with hinged hasps attached (one broken) ; *c.* 1500. *Churchyard Cross :* S. of porch, with chamfered square base-block on two steps, and lower part of octagonal shaft with run-out stops, 15th century. *Communion Table :* of oak, with turned legs with leaf enrichment, and fluted rails, late 17th century ; top and feet restored and legs lengthened. *Font :* with round bowl, moulded underneath, cylindrical stem, and round base with ovolo mouldings, 13th century ; font-cover, of oak, with circular board, moulded radial battens and turned central finial, 17th century. *Glass :* in E. window of chancel, grisaille with coloured borders, 1846. *Hatchment :* with arms of Whitaker impaling White of Poole, 1816. *Image : see* Niche.

Monuments and *Floorslabs. Monuments :* In N. aisle, reset on N. wall, (1) of Evelyn Grosvenor, 1839, marble tablet by Marshall of Blandford ; (2) of Elizabeth (Branthwayte) Webbe, 1627, slate tablet in marble surround (Plate 16) with Corinthian columns, broken pediment and shields-of-arms : above, (*i*) Webbe quarterly of seven ; (*ii*) Webbe impaling Branthwayte ; (*iii*) Croke and Haynes quarterly impaling Webbe ; below, (*iv*) Croke and Haynes quarterly with inescutcheon of Webbe. In churchyard, E. of chancel, (3) of Thomas Ta . . ., 160., headstone with wreath and scrollwork ; S. of chancel, (4) of Richard Haimes, table-tomb, 1702 ; S. of S. aisle, (5) of William Broadway, 1763, and others of same family, table-tomb with panelled sides and moulded top. *Floorslabs :* In S. porch, reset over doorway, (1) of William King, 1636. In N. aisle, (2) slab with scrollwork, inscription illegible ; (3) of Henry Whitaker, 1695, and his daughter Jane, 1683 ; (4) of William Whitaker, [1809] ; (5) of William Whitaker, 1726, and others of his family ; (6) of William Whitaker, date illegible. In S. aisle, partly concealed by step, (7) of John Thaine, 1748, and his wife, 1793 ; adjacent on W., (8) of Richard Ewin, 1788, and James Grant, 1789 ; (9) of Arthur Saunders, 1691 ; (10) of Thomas Brick . . ., 1726. In S. aisle, reset on S. wall, (11) of Henry Whitaker, 1696, Purbeck marble slab with achievement-of-arms of Whitaker quartering Mapowder and Cruwys.

Niche : In S. aisle, reset over S. doorway, with cinquefoil ogee head and ribbed soffit, between pinnacles with crude child-head finials, and traceried spandrels, 15th century ; reset in niche, fragment of sculpture (Plate 15), possibly representing St. Catherine, seated, with Emperor Maximian beneath her feet, upper part of main figure missing, 15th century. *Piscina :* In chancel, with chamfered, trefoiled two-centred head, probably mediaeval. *Plate :* includes silver cup with

date-letter of 1631, restored, and stand-paten with date-letter of 1716.

Royal Arms : In S. aisle, on wood panel (Plate 27), Stuart arms with cypher CR, 17th century ; in N. aisle, on canvas, arms and cypher of George III, with churchwardens' inscription, ' James Mayo and Henry Broadway, 1773 '.

SECULAR

(2) SCHOOL (84872524), a few paces W. of (1), is single storeyed and has ashlar walls and tiled roofs (Plate 28) ; a shield over the main doorway bears the date 1839. The windows, generally, are of stone with chamfered surrounds and mullions. A window in the form of a small oriel projects in the gable of the S. wing.

(3) NORTH END FARM (84562751), house (Plate 53), of two storeys with attics, has walls of ashlar and of squared rubble, and stone-slated roofs ; it is of early 17th-century origin and is shown on a map of 1624 (Plate 56) with the name ' Easthaies '. The windows, generally, have square-headed lights with recessed and hollow-chamfered surrounds and mullions ; in the lower storey they are capped by weathered and ovolo-moulded string-courses ; in the upper storey and in the attics they have weathered and hollow-chamfered labels. The chimneystacks are of ashlar, with moulded capping.

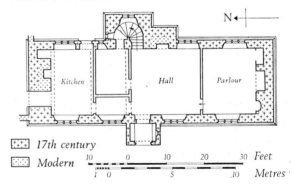

MOTCOMBE   NORTH END FARM HOUSE

The W. front, of ashlar, is symmetrical and of four bays, with chamfered plinths and with a central doorway enclosed in a one-storeyed porch. The porch has an outer archway with a moulded four-centred head, a moulded square outer head, sunk spandrels, continuous jambs and shaped stops. Above the porch arch is an ovolo-moulded, hollow-chamfered and weathered string-course, and over this is a gable with a wave-moulded coping and a square finial. Within the porch, the main doorway is round-headed, with a moulded archivolt, square impost blocks, and moulded jambs ; one impost bears a scratched inscription of 1644. On either side of the porch, the bays of three-light casement windows are paired beneath gables with single three-light attic windows, plain copings and square apex finials. The string-course of the porch continues at a slightly lower level throughout the W. front.

The S. end of the house is of ashlar; it has a gable similar to those of the W. front; the only window, in the gable, is of three lights as described. Symmetrically disposed above the gable are two ashlar chimneystacks. The moulded string-course of the W. front continues across the end wall, approximately at first-floor level. The E. front, of rubble, has three-light casement windows as described; the first-floor string-course lacks an ovolo moulding and has much the same profile as the labels of the upper windows. One bay of the E. front comprises a projecting stair tower with two-light windows at two mezzanine levels, and with a gable with a finial as before; adjacent on the S. is an ashlar chimneystack, rebuilt near the top in brickwork. Reset in the N. side of the stair tower is a small quatrefoil loop, evidently part of the tracery of a 14th-century window. The N. end wall resembles that on the S., having a gable flanked by two chimneystacks, but the lower storeys are masked by an outbuilding, probably of the 19th century.

Inside, the parlour has an open fireplace with a moulded, square-headed surround; the walls have oak panelling with a moulded cornice. In the hall the fireplace has been blocked up and a small modern grate has been substituted. The former open fireplace in the kitchen has been partly blocked, and altered. The steps of the newel staircase are of elm.

(4) Wolfridge Farm (83372767), house, of two storeys, with walls of squared rubble and with tiled roofs, is of the 17th century, but later than the map of c. 1624 (Plate 56); the house has been much altered in recent times, and in part rebuilt. The E. and W. fronts retain stone windows of two and three lights with chamfered surrounds; the former stone mullions have been replaced by woodwork. Projecting from the W. front is a brick chimneystack with weathered offsets, perhaps an 18th-century addition. The chimneystack on the S. gable is of ashlar.

(5) Barn House (85022530), single-storeyed with attics, has rubble walls and thatched roofs; it is of the late 17th or early 18th century and has an L-shaped plan. Inside, there are deeply chamfered ceiling beams with splayed stops, and open fireplaces, now blocked. Adjacent on the S. is a small 18th-century Bakehouse, of two storeys, with rubble walls and tiled roofs.

(6) Cottage (83482332), on Sherborne Causeway near the S. boundary of the parish, is two-storeyed and has rubble walls and a thatched roof. It is of the late 17th century and has a class-S plan. The partition between the ground-floor rooms is of plank-and-muntin construction with roughly chamfered muntins. The date 1691 is incised in plaster over the large open fireplace of the E. room.

(7) Duncliffe Farm (83702317), house, 300 yds. E. of the foregoing, is of two storeys with attics and has walls of brick and rubble, in part rendered; the roofs are partly tiled and partly thatched. The house dates from c. 1700.

(8) House (84632644), originally single-storeyed but now heightened, has brick walls with stone quoins, and thatched roofs; it dates from c. 1700. The W. front is symmetrical and of three bays; reset in it at the level of the first floor is a fragment of 15th-century carved stonework representing an angel bearing a shield; it probably was a vaulting-boss. Inside, one room has a ceiling beam with deep chamfers.

(9) Thane's Farm (86432471), house, is two-storeyed and has walls of coursed rubble, and tiled roofs; it is of the late 18th century, with 19th-century additions on the N. and S. at the W. end of the original range. The S. front of the range

has a central doorway flanked by plain casement windows; above the doorway is an elliptical window with a moulded architrave and keystones; in the upper storey are three casement windows. The N. front of the range has a stone window of four square-headed lights with moulded jambs and mullions. Inside, the original range has chamfered ceiling beams.

(10) Bridewell (84662804), house, single-storeyed with attics, with walls partly of rubble and partly timber-framed and with thatched roofs, is of the late 18th century.

(11) Manor Farm (84192468), house, is two-storeyed with ashlar walls and slated roofs and was built in 1836. The N. front is of three bays, that in the centre having a projecting two-storeyed porch, those on each side having in each storey sashed windows with moulded labels. The S. front has stone-mullioned windows with wooden sashes.

(12) Fernbrook Farm (83672406), house, is two-storeyed and has walls of brickwork with ashlar dressings, and tiled roofs; it was rebuilt in the 'Tudor' style in 1848.

(13) Cottages (85152513), range of four, known as The Old Workhouse, have walls of ashlar and rubble, stone-mullioned windows and stone-slated roofs; they are of the late 17th or early 18th century.

Monuments (14–19)

Unless otherwise described the following monuments are of the second half of the 18th century and of two storeys; the walls are of rubble and the roofs are thatched.

(14) Cottages (84982525–85002528), three, about 100 yds. E. of the church, are approximately uniform, although separated one from another (Plate 29). In each, the S.E. front is of two bays with a central doorway. The front walls are of red brick-work patterned with blue headers; the end walls are of rubble, the stonework extending into the front walls in the form of rough quoins.

(15) Red House Farm (84652620), house, has a symmetrical E. front of three bays, with sashed windows with segmental brick heads and rubble keystones. The roofs are tiled, with stone-slate verges. There are modern extensions on the N. and S. Inside, one room has an open fireplace and bread-oven, now blocked.

(16) White House Farm (84332409), house, has a symmetrical N. front of three bays with a central doorway, and casement windows in both storeys.

(17) Lower Duncliffe Farm (82782352), house, has a slated roof. The N. front is of rubble; the S. elevation is partly of brick, with a rubble plinth.

(18) Kingsettle Farm (86182569), house, with ashlar walls and a stone-slated roof, is now deserted and ruinous.

(19) Cottages, two adjacent (83332334), have been combined as one dwelling. That on the E. has a symmetrical three-bay N. front, with a central doorway, and casement windows with segmental brick heads and rubble keystones. That on the W. is of two bays and has a N. front of squared rubble.

The following small houses and cottages are of the late 18th or first half of the 19th century. Unless otherwise described they are two-storeyed, have rubble walls and are roofed with thatch or tiles : *Cottage* (84972526), with an ashlar-faced E. front ; *Post Office* (85072523), comprising a range of three cottages, now combined ; *Cottages* (85292508), pair, dated 1842, with two-light mullioned windows, and doorways with moulded four-centred heads and continuous jambs ; *Cottage* (85462499) ; *Cottages* (85022544), range of three, of one storey with attics, restored and heightened in brickwork ; *Cottage* (84812502), of one storey with attics, with a rendered N. front ; *Cottage* (85042588) ; *Cottage* (85062595), with a S. front of two bays with a central doorway ; *Cottage* (85152591) ; *Cottage* (84522740) ; *Cottage* (83222338) ; *Cottage* (83352333) ; *Cottage* (83772316) ; *Bittles Green Farm* (85672487), house ; *Larkinglass Farm* (83762767), house, with a three-bay E. front incorporating a carved stone head, perhaps a mediaeval corbel ;

House (83962309), with a symmetrical ashlar front of three bays, probably advertised as new-built in *Salisbury Journal,* 26 Dec. 1814 ; *Woodwater Farm* (82152723), house, now dere-lict.

MEDIAEVAL AND LATER EARTHWORKS

(20) MOAT AND BANKS (818263), known as King's Court Palace, occupy low-lying ground on the western boundary of the parish, at the confluence of the R. Lodden and a small westward-flowing stream, the Fern. The earthworks are the remains of a fortified royal hunting lodge, begun in 1199 and occupied by King

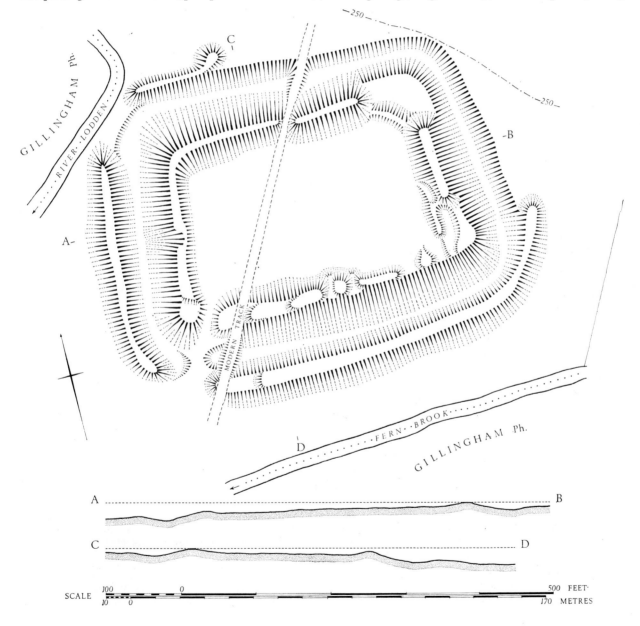

John in 1204 ; the ditch and bank probably date from
c. 1209–11. Extensive alterations were made in 1249–
1250, when the original chapel was rebuilt, a second
chapel was provided, and a new chamber measuring
40 ft. by 22 ft. was made. Buildings ordered by King
Henry III in 1252 and finished in 1255 included a
kitchen, an almonry and a chamber. Repairs were
executed in 1260 and works of that date included a
gateway and a hedge around the courtyard ; in 1269–70
the hedge was replaced by oak palings. Further repairs
are recorded up to 1354. In 1369 King Edward III
ordered the demolition of buildings and the sale of the
materials. (*History of the King's Works*, II, 944–6.)

The remains have been damaged by a modern track and by
drainage ditches and small quarries, but otherwise they are well
preserved ; they comprise a rectangular area, 300 ft. by 170
ft., bounded by a bank some 50 ft. wide and 4 ft. high, with
scarps and platforms cut into it on the S. and S.E. Outside
the bank is a ditch, up to 60 ft. wide and 5 ft. deep, with an
outer bank up to 3 ft. high on the S. and W. The original
entrance was at the S.W. corner of the site, where two rectangular platforms suggest former gate towers. Inside the banks,
the ground is featureless.

DEER PARK. *See* GILLINGHAM (99).

19 PIMPERNE (9009)

(O.S. 6 ins. ST 90 NW, ST 91 SW, ST 80 NE,
ST 81 SE)

The parish, covering some 3,430 acres, extends N.E.
from the R. Stour and lies entirely on Chalk at altitudes
between 170 ft. and 400 ft. ; on the S. it adjoins the
town of Blandford Forum (*Dorset*, III, 16). The north-
eastern third of the parish is occupied by a broad dry
valley which drains S. through Blandford to the Stour ;
the south-western third comprises several small dry
combes. The area of the parish has been increased by
boundary revisions : land in the S.W. comprising the
Domesday settlement of Nutford (*V.C.H., Dorset*, iii,
70) was transferred from Blandford Forum to Pimperne
in 1886 ; land in the S., comprising the manor of
Damory Court, mentioned in 1363, was similarly transferred in 1894. In 1933 small parts of Tarrants Hinton,
Launceston and Monkton were taken into Pimperne,
thus moving the parish boundary away from the village,
through which it formerly passed. The village stands
in the dry valley mentioned above and retains its
mediaeval compactness, largely because the open fields
were not enclosed until 1814 (Award D.C.R.O.).
Newfield Farm in the N. and some cottages in the S.
of the village stand in the area of the former fields.
Excavations in 1960–3 on Pimperne Down yielded important evidence of Iron Age occupation, including a
circular house site.

ECCLESIASTICAL

(1) THE PARISH CHURCH OF ST. PETER, near the
N.W. end of the village, was wholly rebuilt in 1870
(*Dorset Procs.*, XXXIX (1918), 108), except for the *West
Tower* which is of the mid 15th century. Reset in the
present church are the 12th-century chancel arch and
south doorway from the earlier church.

Architectural Description. The former *Chancel Arch* (Plate
51) stands on the N. of the present chancel. It is two-centred
and on the S. side it is of two orders, the inner order plain, the
outer order with roll-moulded chevron decoration on fascia
and intrados ; the N. side is plain. In the outer order the voussoirs are alternately of Greensand and white limestone, the
latter probably from Todber. In the responds, the inner
order has large half-shafts and the outer order has three-quarter
shafts of smaller diameter ; the shafts and their bases, with
hold-water mouldings, are of the 19th century ; the scalloped
capitals (Plate 9) with scroll-work, leaf decoration and bands
of pellets are original ; the hollow-chamfered abaci are restored.
The *Doorway* (Plate 51), now at the W. end of the S. aisle, was
formerly in the S. wall of the nave (Hutchins I, 293). It has a
semicircular outer head of one order with chevron mouldings
similar to those of the chancel arch, and a hood-mould with
lozenge decoration ; below is a tympanum shaped to form a
segmental arch and highly enriched with chevron ornament
and leaf-work (cf. *Dorset* III, xlvii). The responds have three-
quarter shafts with scalloped capitals with leaf enrichment ;
the capitals are original, but shafts, bases and abaci are of the
19th century. Hutchins's engraving (I, 294) shows bases
different from those now seen.

The *West Tower* has a high chamfered and hollow-chamfered
plinth and is in three stages defined by hollow-chamfered
string-courses ; the parapet, gargoyles and pinnacles are of
1870. The western corners have three-stage diagonal buttresses with weathered offsets ; a similar diagonal buttress
occurs on the N. side near the N.E. corner ; in a corresponding
position on the S. side is an octagonal vice turret of 1870. The
tower arch is two-centred and of three hollow-chamfered
orders ; the outer order dies into chamfered responds and the
inner orders spring from angel corbels. The west window has
three trefoil-headed lights with vertical tracery in a two-centred
head under a roll-moulded label with head-stops ; the label
is perhaps earlier than the 15th-century window, and reset.
In the second stage, the S. side of the tower has a window of
two trefoil-headed lights with a quatrefoil tracery light in a
two-centred head under a hollow-chamfered label. In the
third stage, each side of the tower has a belfry window of
two lights with blind trefoil heads and blind vertical tracery in
a two-centred outer head without a label.

Fittings—Bells : five ; 4th inscribed ' William Pitt, George
Selby, R.L. 1703 ' ; tenor recast in 1846 with former inscription ' Glory be to God on high ' in Lombardic letters ; others
1891. *Benefactor's Table* : of wood, with gilt lettering recording
Charity of George Ryves, 1685, below triangular finial with
cartouche painted with arms of Ryves ; 1846. *Brass* : In
vestry, reset on W. wall, panel 1½ ft. square (Plate 14) with
inscription commemorating Dorothy Williams, 1694, with
representation of soul rising from death-bed, engraved by

Edmund Culpeper. *Chair:* of oak, with fretted back and shaped top, 18th century. *Chest:* of oak, heavily bound with iron, with two hasps and staples for lock-bar, and central lock with scroll-sided escutcheon plate, 17th century. *Door:* in W. doorway, of oak, dated 1847. *Font:* of stone (Plate 11) with round bowl enriched with foliate scrollwork and pellet banding on tapering cylindrical stem with moulded base, with masks in spandrels; bowl 12th century, restored in 19th century; stem and base probably 19th century. Font-cover, of stone, tent-shaped, with pierced spandrels and pellet-enriched ribbing; 19th century (Hutchins I, 293).

Monument and *Floorslab. Monument:* In vestry, of Dorothy Williams, 1694, see *Brass. Floorslab:* reset at top of tower vice, Purbeck marble floorslab of William M[artin, 1608 ?], (Hutchins I, 295). *Niche:* In S.E. side of lower stage of S.W. tower buttress, with chamfered four-centred head; mediaeval. *Plate:* includes Elizabethan silver cup by Lawrence Stratford of Dorchester, without inscription or date-letters; in 1849 it was recorded that the church 'possesses no sacramental plate whatever, except a chalice presented by the present curate' (*Ecclesiologist*, X (1849), 255).

(2) CROSS (90420943), some 50 yds. E.N.E. of (1), of Greensand, comprises the lower part of an octagonal shaft set in a square pedestal on a plinth of three steps, square on plan. The lowest step retains traces of moulded nosing, much worn. The cross probably is of the late 15th century.

(3) METHODIST CHAPEL (90450894), with cob walls and until recently with a thatched roof, consists of a simple hall orientated N.–S., with the doorway on the S.; it is of the first half of the 19th century.

SECULAR

(4) THE RECTORY (90440936), of two storeys with attics, with walls of brick banded with flint and with tile-covered roofs, is dated 1712. The N.E. front is symmetrical and of five bays. Reset in the centre bay is part of a 16th-century stone doorway with a moulded four-centred head, continuous jambs and plain stops; the head is original, the rest of the opening is restoration work, presumably of *c.* 1712. Above the head is a square label and on the margin below the label is a damaged black-letter inscription, recorded by Hutchins as '[T.....well alias Weber hanc] porticu'. et capella xpi. superstruxit, anno d'ni MC [CCCCXXX]'; the letters enclosed in brackets have now perished, but the others remain legible. Thomas Weaver was rector of Tarrant Hinton (1514–1536), and his initials are found in the decoration of the Easter Sepulchre in that church (see p. 98); it is possible that these reset fragments were brought from Hinton. Over the doorway and integral with the label is a niche with a canopied head and shafted jambs; carved under the bracket of the niche is a shield-of-arms of Henry VIII, with crown, garter, dragon and greyhound supporters, and a rose and portcullis on the apron (cf. TARRANT GUNVILLE (1), *Glass*). Reset in the upper storey, centrally above the doorway, is a window of three ogee-headed lights with vertical tracery in a square-headed surround; a stone above the window is inscribed 'Nisi Dominus custoderit......' etc., and the date 1712. The two bays on either side of the central bay in the 18th-century N.E. front have false square-headed windows; first-floor level is marked by a plain plat-band. The other elevations of the 18th-century range have similar details. Inside, the main rooms have 19th-century plasterwork, joinery and chimneypieces. The walls flanking the central vestibule are, however, 3 ft. and 2½ ft.

in thickness, suggesting that elements of an older building are incorporated in the 18th-century structure.

(5) NUTFORD FARM (87940799), house, 1¾ m. S.W. of the village, is of two storeys with attics and has brick walls and tile-covered roofs. The building is of the 18th century. In plan the house is L-shaped, with the main range facing E.S.E. and having a wing projecting eastwards from it at the N. end. The E. front of the range is symmetrical and of three bays, with a central doorway and with square-headed casement windows of three lights in both storeys; a plat-band occurs at first-floor level. The E. wing is of one bay. The S. end of the main range and the E. end of the wing are gabled and have rounded brick copings above corbelled brick kneelers; each apex has a brick chimneystack.

Reset in a brick wall separating the garden from the farmyard is a late mediaeval doorway with a moulded four-centred stone head and continuous jambs. The 18th-century gateway into the garden from the road on the S.W. of the house has square brick piers with moulded ashlar caps and ball finials. Between the road and the farmhouse is a detached *Cottage,* perhaps a little later in date than the farmhouse, but with gabled end walls as described above.

(6) MANOR FARM (90400945), house, of two storeys, with walls of banded flint and brickwork, with brick quoins and stone dressings, and with slate-covered roofs, dates from the first half of the 19th century. The S.E. front of the main range is symmetrical and of three bays, with a central doorway, in a projecting porch, with a chamfered and hollow-chamfered square head and continuous jambs. The windows flanking the doorway and in the upper storey are uniform, each having three transomed square-headed lights, with moulded surrounds as in the doorway; the casements have metal glazing-bars arranged to form marginal panes. Extending the main range on the S.W. is an additional bay with details similar to those of the main range. The N.E. and S.W. end walls are gabled, with ashlar copings; the windows, similar to those described, are of two lights and in some cases have no transoms. Extensive farm buildings on the N. and E. are constructed of similar materials and probably are of the same period as the farmhouse.

(7) CHESTNUT FARM (90400939), house, of two storeys with attics, with walls of ashlar and brickwork and with tile-covered roofs, is of late 18th-century origin, but recently has been extensively modernised. Near by, on the N. of the adjacent farmyard, is a late 18th-century *Barn* with walls partly of reused Greensand ashlar and partly of brickwork; the N. and S. walls are strengthened by two-stage brick buttresses with weathered offsets; the N. side has a transeptal exit bay. The barn roof has collared trusses supporting two purlins on each side; curved braces resting on ledges in the brick walls meet each principal at the level of the lower purlins. A range of *Farm Buildings* on the S. of the farmyard, constructed of materials similar to those of the barn, has a date-stone of 1790.

(8) HOUSE (90550918), about 300 yds. S.E. of the church, is of two storeys and has rendered walls and tile-covered roofs. Under the rendering, the S. range has walls of banded brickwork and flint of 18th-century origin. On the N., in continuation of the original range, is a mid 19th-century extension containing the principal rooms. Inside, the original range has some exposed beams, lightly chamfered.

(9) 'THE LAURELS' (90550916), house, a few yards S. of the foregoing, is two-storeyed and has walls of banded brickwork and flint, and a slate-covered roof; it was built in 1802. The E. front is symmetrical and of three bays, with the doorway

under a wooden porch with Roman-Doric columns and entablature ; the windows, all alike, are of three sashed lights with square heads.   A date-stone inscribed C. H. 1802 is set in the S. gable.

(10) COTTAGE (90430947), about 70 yds. N.E. of (1), is two-storeyed and has brick walls and a tiled roof ; it probably is of the early 19th century.   The W. front is symmetrical and of three bays, with a brick plat-band and with two-light casement windows.

(11) COTTAGES (90640929), range of four, now combined, are single-storyed with dormer-windowed attics and have cob walls and thatched roofs ; they are of 18th-century origin.   Inside, some rooms have roughly hewn beams, and several open fire-places with timber bressummers are preserved. (*Partly demolished.*)

(12) COTTAGES (90670930), two adjacent, now combined, are two-storeyed and have rendered walls and tiled roofs ; they date probably from the first half of the 18th century.   Inside, two open fireplaces are preserved, one blocked.   Some 17th-century panelling has been brought from elsewhere.

(13) COTTAGES (90840933), two adjacent, two-storeyed and with brick walls and tiled roofs, are of the late 18th or early 19th century.

Other monuments of the first half of the 19th century are as follows : *Newfield Farm* (90771105), house, with outbuildings and barn ; *Cottages* (90920936), pair, with rendered walls and thatched roofs ; *Cottages* (90930937), two adjacent ; *Cottage* (90910932).   Four *Cottages* in Prior's Lane, with rendered walls and thatched roofs and with class-S plans, stand within the area of the former open fields and therefore date from after 1814.

MEDIAEVAL AND LATER EARTHWORKS

(14) CULTIVATION REMAINS.   Nothing remains of the open fields of Pimperne, enclosed in 1814 (Award and map in D.C.R.O.).   The open fields of Nutford were in existence in 1838 (Tithe Map of Blandford Forum) and the date of their enclosure is unknown ; contour and up-and-down strip lynchets, now largely ploughed down, cover a large area around N.G. 880083 ; in 1838 they were in Nutford Field.

ROMAN AND PREHISTORIC

The parish is notable for several *Enclosures*, all probably of Iron Age origin and comparable with those in the adjacent parishes of Tarrant Hinton (p. 100) and Stourpaine (*Dorset* III, 265).   They have been destroyed almost entirely by cultivation and survive only as crop-marks or soil-marks.

(15) IRON AGE SETTLEMENT (891097), on Pimperne Down, excavated in 1960–3 by I. M. Blake and D. W. Harding, lies about 350 ft. above O.D. on a gentle S.E. slope near the summit of a N.–S. Chalk ridge.[1]   The settlement comprises an oval, univallate enclosure of 11½ acres, bisected by the Pimperne-Stourpaine road and for the greater part visible only on air photographs.   Until recently the N.E. sector survived unploughed and it was there that excavations were largely concentrated. ' Celtic ' fields (Group (73)) adjoin the enclosure on the N.E. and a smaller enclosure (16) lies immediately S. of it.

---

[1] This account of the settlement has been contributed by Mr. D. W. Harding ; the photograph on Plate 55 is by Mr. I. M. Blake.

The excavations indicate early Iron Age occupation, with Second or late First ' A ' culture.   The bank survived to a height of 1 ft. to 1½ ft. in the N.E. sector.   The ditch was initially of shallow ' V ' profile, becoming steeper towards a narrow, flat bottom, and reaching a depth of 5 ft. to 6 ft. below present ground level.

Two entrances to the enclosure were demonstrated.   Excavation of the E. entrance revealed a parallel line of post-holes, 8 ft. apart, which extended a little over 20 ft. into the interior of the camp from the causeway between the ditch terminals.   Recutting of the post-holes indicated that the entrance passageway had been reinforced or rebuilt in a second phase of construction.   The ditch on both sides of the entrance was flat-bottomed, with nearly vertical sides, but on the southern side of the gateway a

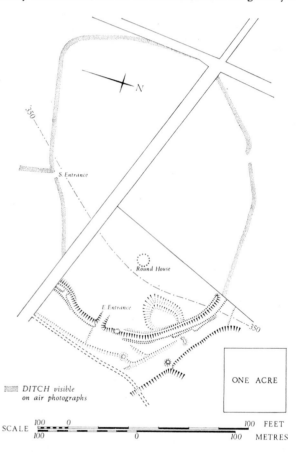

ONE ACRE

DITCH *visible on air photographs*

SCALE

rubbish pit, into which quantities of animal bones had been thrown, had been cut into the ditch after its initial silting.   N. of the entrance the ditch had been refilled shortly after construction, and it had been sealed by a closely-packed flint capping beneath which was found a human femur and the right half of a human skull.

Excavation of the S. entrance revealed three post-holes spanning the entrance causeway, one of them of adequate size for a post to sustain a gate.   The ditch system of the S. entrance was more complex than that on the E.   The main enclosure ditch on the S.W. side of the causeway was intersected by a shallower ditch which led outwards from the camp to a secondary enclosure (16) on the S.E.   This ' antenna ' ditch was not of defensive proportions and more probably served to guide cattle into the camp from the secondary enclosure. At least three major structural phases were represented. Within the butt end of the main enclosure ditch, adjacent to its intersection with the 'antenna' ditch, were found the semi-articulated remains of part of a horse and the skull of an ox, together with two small rectangular chalk lamps. Taken in conjunction with human remains at the E. entrance, there are grounds for supposing that these were deliberate deposits, chosen with regard to the respective functions of each entrance.

The existence of an entrance on the N. side of the camp was indicated in 1963 by magnetometer survey, but no excavations took place in this area.

Inside the settlement the principal discovery was the remains of a circular timber house (Plate 55). It consisted essentially of two concentric circles of post-holes. The inner circle, 32 ft. in diameter, must have been for the main supports of the roof since there was no central post-hole or group of holes. The outer circle, 42 ft. in diameter, was composed of smaller stake-holes cut not more than 9 ins. into the chalk; it probably retained a wall of woven saplings. A larger and less continuous circle of shallow scoops and irregular holes may have held external supports for the walls and roof rafters.

Occupation was clearly in two principal phases, in the second of which the house was completely rebuilt, although the same porched entrance served both phases. A baked clay hearth was located within the house, together with a number of shallow post-holes, the latter probably associated with domestic appliances such as looms or drying racks.

Small finds included a bronze finger-ring, two iron arrow-heads and several fragments of shale bracelets. Pottery included coarse-ware shouldered jars with finger-tip ornament and some haematite-coated bowls. The occupation of the site should most probably be assigned to the 5th century B.C., but insufficient stratified material was available to supply a satisfactory chronology of the structural phases represented.

(16) ENCLOSURE (891095), visible only on air photographs (V 58/RAF/3250 : 0137–8), lies 40 yds. S. of (15) and apparently is linked with it by a shallow ditch. It covers 4 acres and is pear-shaped in plan, measuring 400 ft. by 500 ft. across. There is no certain entrance, but it most probably was on the N.

(17) ENCLOSURE (900094), probably Iron Age, now totally levelled by ploughing, comprises an irregular oval of 20 acres, formerly defined by a single bank and ditch. It lies at just over 250 ft. above O.D. at the S.E. end of a spur overlooking the village and encircles an angle of the Pimperne-Stourpaine road. The site was discovered from air photographs (V 58/RAF/3250 : 0137–8).

(18) ENCLOSURE (916105), probably Iron Age, lies in the extreme E. of the parish on a gentle S.W. slope, near the top of a ridge, about 375 ft. above O.D. It has been levelled by ploughing, but comprises a heart-shaped area of some 10 acres, formerly defined by a bank and ditch, with an inturned entrance on the S.W. side (Plate 54). Within, and concentric with it, lay a roughly oval enclosure of about 5 acres similarly defined and utilising the same entrance. The space between the two enclosures was divided into compartments by three short lengths of bank and ditch (C.U.A.P., WX 15–18). The enclosure appears to have been integrated with 'Celtic' fields (see Group (73)) and possibly with a *Linear Dyke* immediately on the S. (TARRANT HINTON (18)).

'CELTIC' FIELDS, see p. 119, Group (73).

MONUMENTS (19–35), ROUND BARROWS

Remains of at least seventeen barrows are found in the parish, nearly all of them levelled by ploughing. There is no record that any have been excavated.

(19) *Bowl* (88280967), on the edge of France Firs, lies on the boundary with Stourpaine at about 350 ft. above O.D.; diam. 52 ft., ht. 3 ft.

The *Chestnut Farm Group* comprises at least nine barrows, all totally flattened by cultivation, but visible as soil-mark ring-ditches on air photographs (Allen 931, 933, Ashmolean), (Plate 55); they lie at about 225 ft. above O.D. on the N.E. slope of a spur immediately W. of the village. There are possibly traces of other barrows in the group. A linear ditch, seen on the photograph, which makes an angular detour around barrow (24) and cuts into barrow (25), appears to be of comparatively recent origin. References and dimensions are approximate.

(20) *Barrow* (90250930), possibly of two phases, with twin concentric ditches; diam. of mound about 65 ft.

(21) *Barrow* (90270929); diam. about 40 ft.

(22) *Double Barrow* (90290928), within a continuous ditch, measures about 60 ft. by 30 ft.

(23) *Barrow* (90270927), with possible pits inside the ditch;

(24) *Barrow* (90300926); diam. about 55 ft.

(25) *Barrow* (90290923); diam. about 65 ft.

(26) *Barrow* (90330924); diam. about 50 ft.

(27) *Barrow* (90360927); diam. about 65 ft.

(28) *Barrow* (90350917); diam. about 50 ft.

(29) *Barrow* (90450992), at 250 ft. above O.D. on a S.E. slope just N. of the village, is now levelled by ploughing, but is visible as a ring-ditch on air photographs (C.U.A.P., ABX 98); diam. about 45 ft.

(30) *Barrow* (91370870), at over 350 ft. above O.D. on the ridge-top immediately W. of Blandford Camp, is now levelled.

Pimperne East Group comprises five small bowl barrows situated near the E. boundary of the parish, some 250 yds. S.W. of Pimperne Long Barrow (TARRANT HINTON (24)). They lie on a gentle S. slope at 350 ft. above O.D. and are levelled by ploughing. They remain undated; because of their small size it has been suggested that they may be of the Iron Age or Saxon (*Dorset Barrows*, 125).

(31) *Bowl* (91521034).

(32) *Bowl* (91531036).

(33) *Bowl* (91551035).

(34) *Bowl* (91571035).

(35) *Bowl* (91561033).

20 SHAFTESBURY (8622)

(O.S. 6 ins., ST 82 SE)

The modern Borough of Shaftesbury, covering 1,200 acres, includes land in the E. which formerly was part of the parish of Cann, and land in the N.W. which until recently was in Motcombe, itself formerly a division of Gillingham (see above, p. 48). Straddling the Greensand escarpment and varying in altitude from over 700 ft. above sea-level in the E. to less than 400 ft. in the W., the town occupies a prominent position on the summit of a projecting Greensand spur, with precipitous slopes 100 ft. high on all but the N.E. side (Plate 57).

Shaftesbury occupies a strong natural position, and the name suggests that it was from the beginning a fortified settlement. Local tradition, embodied in a stone inscription copied by William of Malmesbury, ascribes the foundation of the town to King Alfred in the year 880—more than a decade before the organisation of the chain of fortresses with which Alfred defended his frontiers against the Danes. A fragment of this inscription, rediscovered in 1902, shows, however, that it was carved during the period c. 975 to 1050; hence the earliest reliable reference to Shaftesbury as a borough is that of the year 926 in Athelstan's

law about currency.[1] Asser reports that Alfred also founded Shaftesbury Abbey for nuns, but nothing remains of the original nunnery; a few pre-conquest carved stones have been found on the site, but the most important appears to come from a cross-shaft. The present church, represented by little more than foundations, dates from late in the 11th century.

The Saxon borough lay on the W. of the abbey, where gardens and scattered houses now flank the street called Bimport. The population at the time of the Domesday survey must have been at least 1,000.[2] In the 12th century a small castle was built at the western extremity of the spur. The present town centre, on the E. of the spur, stems probably from a concentration of buildings outside the gates of the borough and abbey, the broad High Street representing an extramural market place; further growth took place on

---

[1] D. Whitelock, *Eng. Hist. Docs.*, i, 384.
[2] H. C. Darby and R. Welldon Finn (ed.), *Domesday Geography of South-West England*, 121. *V.C.H., Dorset*, iii, 63.

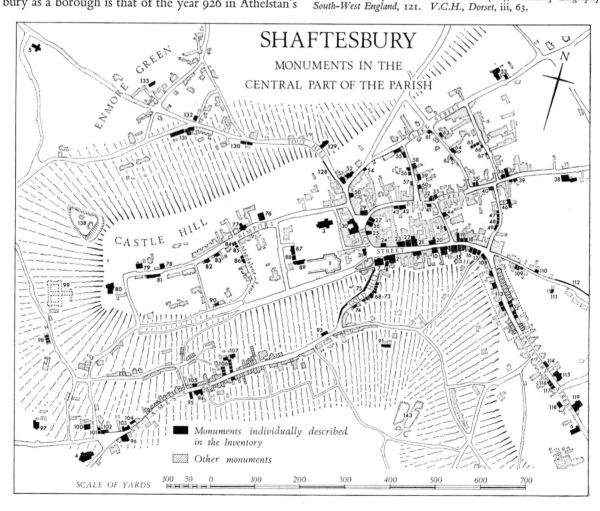

SHAFTESBURY

MONUMENTS IN THE

CENTRAL PART OF THE PARISH

Monuments individually described in the Inventory

Other monuments

SCALE OF YARDS   100 50 0   100   200   300   400   500   600   700

the N. and E. where the ground is fairly level. During the mediaeval period a second nucleus of habitation developed at the foot of the escarpment, on the S.W. around St. James's Church. A map of 1615 (Hutchins III, frontispiece), shows that the town was then beginning to spread S.E. along the Salisbury road, and that the buildings at St. James's were beginning to extend E. along the wall of the abbey park. Further development along the same lines is shown on Upjohn's Map of Shaftesbury, 1799 (Hutchins, 2nd ed., II, opp. 391), and also on the Tithe Map of 1848.

THE INSCRIPTION SEEN BY WILLIAM OF MALMESBURY

In 1902 a fragment of inscribed stone was found on the site of the abbey church.[1] It has since been lost, but a rubbing is preserved in the Shaftesbury Historical Museum (Plate 58). The rubbing shows that the fragment had a maximum measurement of about 5 ins. in each direction and included part of the sinister margin, 1 in. wide, and the ends of three lines of letters; those of the middle line, the only ones fully preserved, were 2 ins. high. The letters, which read as follows,

```
. . . . . I T ·
. . . . N I C
. . A T I O
```

are regular and evenly spaced, with well-marked wedge-shaped serifs. The C is square. In the N the oblique stroke joins the sinister upright well above the base. The O has two crescent strokes crossed at the top, forming a vesica. Letters of this type are used as capitals forming the opening line or phrase of a new entry in a number of late pre-conquest MSS. The forms here used may be noted in these positions in the late 10th-century *Bosworth Psalter* (New Paleographical Society, ser. I, plate 163), in the early 11th-century *Sherborne Pontifical* (ibid., plate 111), and in the late 10th-century *Exeter Book of Old English Poetry* (facsimile, London 1933, ff. 55 b, 65 b, 78 a). In the Shaftesbury inscription the words were separated by triangular stops. The inscription may be assigned to a date between *c.* 975 and *c.* 1050.

The fragment evidently belongs to the inscription seen in the abbey chapter house by William of Malmesbury, whose account of Shaftesbury[2] dates from 1125. His record, not an exact transcript, states that the stone had been brought from the ruins of a very old wall. The inscription may be restored thus—

```
AELFRED·REX·HA
NC·URBEM·FECIT
ANNO · DOMINIC
AE · INCARNATIO
NIS·DCCCLXXX·
REGNI · SUI · VIII
```

In the first line the initial AE was probably ligatured; the uninflected form of the name is normal on coins, with or without ligature (cf. the CNUT REX of the Newminster Register; T. D. Kendrick, *Later Saxon and Viking Art*, plate xviii). The dating as given by William of Malmesbury is inconsistent, since Alfred succeeded Ethelred in April 871 and his eighth year ran from April 878 to April 879.[1]

A formal inscription of this sort would be set up in connection with an important stone building; it may be compared with the inscription commemorating the dedication of the church at Jarrow[2] in 685. A secular stone building in Shaftesbury at the time in question (*c.* 975-1050) is unlikely to have been anything but the town wall, and the most probable position for the inscription would be in association with a tunnel gateway such as has recently been found at Cadbury[3] dating from *c.* 1010. Asser does indeed speak of the E. gate of Shaftesbury at an earlier period,[4] but the grant of Bradford on Avon to the nuns, as a refuge from the barbarians[5] in 1001, may imply that Shaftesbury was not fortified at that time. Domesday Book records that 80 houses out of the 257 in existence twenty years earlier, then lay waste[6] and in 1125 William of Malmesbury calls Shaftesbury a village (*vicus*) which had formerly been a town (*urbs*).[7] The combined evidence suggests that the stone defences of Shaftesbury date from the first half of the 11th century, and that the 11th-century inscription records the tradition of the foundation of the town, but not necessarily the building of the defences, by King Alfred. That the foundation took place early in the reign is borne out by Alfred's charter to the Abbey.[8] Although this is spurious or at best interpolated in the form handed down to us, the inclusion among the witnesses of Eahlfrith, Bishop of Winchester, implies the existence of an original charter bearing that prelate's name. Since Eahlfrith had been succeeded by Tunbeohrt by 877 that charter must have been granted between 871 and 877. The text of the charter, as preserved, records the presentation to the abbey of Alfred's daughter Aethelgeofu, who took the veil on account of ill health. In 877 Aethelgeofu was an infant; she was Alfred's third child and can scarcely have been born before 871. The date 887 for the foundation, given by Symeon of Durham,[9] is no more than conjecture; he repeats Asser's text verbatim and dates the passage more closely than is justified by the source.

ECCLESIASTICAL

(1) THE ABBEY CHURCH OF ST. MARY AND ST. EDWARD (86182290), now reduced to little more than its foundations, lies on the E. of the area formerly occupied by Alfred's borough. Shaftesbury Abbey was the wealthiest Benedictine nunnery in England; its foundation is generally ascribed to King Alfred, whose daughter Aethelgeofu is the first recorded abbess:

---

[1] E. Doran Webb, *Excavations on the site of the Abbey Church*, third report, 1904, p. 4.

[2] *Willelmi Malmesbiriensis monachi gesta pontificum Anglorum*, 86, (Rolls Ser., lii, 186); Scefftonia est vicus modo, quondam urbs locus in praerupto montium situs. Vetustatis inditium dat lapis in capitulo sanctimonialium insculptus ita, a vetustissimi muri ruinis illuc translatus : ' Anno Dominicae incarnationis Elfredus rex fecit hanc urbem DCCC octogesimo, regni sui VIIIvo '.

[1] *English Historical Review* (1898), xiii, 71–7.
[2] E. A. Fisher, *The Greater Anglo-Saxon Churches*, p. 76, plate 16.
[3] *Ant. J.*, xlix (1969), 39.
[4] *De rebus gestis regis Aelfredi*, 98.
[5] Dugdale, *Monasticon Anglicanum* II (London, 1819), 480 : ' quatenus adversus barbarorum insidias ipsa religiosa congregatio . . . impenetrabile optineat confugium '.
[6] *V.C.H.*, Dorset iii, 63.
[7] See note 2.
[8] A. J. Robertson, *Anglo-Saxon Charters*, 24–5, 284–6 ; Sawyer, 357.
[9] *Symeonis monachi Dunelmensis historia Regum*, 101 (Rolls Ser. lxxv. ii, 119).

Monasterium juxta orientalem portam Sceftesburg, habitationi sanctimonialium habile, idem praefatus rex aedificari imperavit ; in quo propriam filiam suam Aethelgeofu, devotam Deo virginem, abbatissam constituit.[1] The 15th-century cartulary (B. M., Harley, 61)[2] includes a number of older charters, some of them apparently genuine and referring to lands later held by the abbey. The oldest, datable between 670 and 676, is a grant to Abbot Bectun of thirty households at Fontmell ;[3] the grant was successfully disputed by the neighbouring minster of Tisbury,[4] but the property was held by Shaftesbury in 1066. Similar grants to individuals, entered in the cartulary, were attributed to Egbert (802–39),[5] Ethelbald (855–860),[6] Ethelbert (860–865/6)[7] and Ethelred I (865/6–871).[8] The charters of Ethelbald, Ethelbert and Ethelred may explain Leland's record,[9] that these princes were co-founders of the abbey with Alfred, their younger brother. The entry of these charters, especially that concerning Abbot Bectun, suggests that a minster church already existed at Shaftesbury in the 7th century, the property of which descended to the abbey. This minster may have sustained the charge of a nunnery (cf. *Trans. R. Hist. Soc.*, 4th ser., xxiii, 51–2).

Asser's record of the foundation of the abbey occurs at a point in the MS. which indicates the year 887, and was so understood by Symeon of Durham (see above), but the passage is clearly recapitulation and its position in the narrative is not to be relied upon in this way. As shown above, the foundation charter appears to date from the years 871–7. Aethelgeofu came to the abbey in her childhood, and her abbacy is likely to date from the end of the 9th century at the earliest.

The 10th century saw many munificent gifts to the abbey. The most highly venerated relic came in 979 when the body of King Edward was brought there from Wareham minster, where it lay for a year after the king had been murdered at Corfe.[10] The original dedication in honour of the Virgin was subsequently augmented to include the name of St. Edward. In the late 11th-century church St. Edward's tomb was on the N. side of the chancel ; the empty grave, lined with dressed ashlar, was opened in 1861.[11] William of Malmesbury, writing *c.* 1125, records that portions of the relics had been removed to Leominster and Abing-

don, and that the remains of the body at Shaftesbury had long perished, although a lung, still preserved, could be seen miraculously pulsating : *miraculo sane ostentatur pulmo, toto dudum consumpto corpore, adhuc integra viriditate palpitans.*[1] There cannot be much doubt that William saw the squat glass jar which was rediscovered, probably in 1901–3, ' under a heart-shaped white marble slab in front of the high altar ' ;[2] probably it was set in this place early in the 14th century as a focus for the devotion of the community when the relics were translated to a newly built chapel on the N. (see below).

Of the pre-conquest church no remains have been identified, although carved stones preserved on the site include some that can be dated to the 10th or early 11th century. A few architectural fragments imply that the church was of stone, but they provide no information as to its form.

Excavations on the site of the church (Plate 60) have disclosed the remains of a late 11th-century cruciform building. The eastern arm of three bays had a central apse and was flanked by chapels with smaller apses, the latter square externally. Square transepts with eastern apses extended N. and S. On the W. was an aisled nave of at least seven bays. A drawing of *c.* 1553 (Plate 58) showing the church in a ruinous state soon after the Dissolution,[3] depicts the nave arcades with large cylindrical columns ; these are unlikely to date from before 1100 and must represent the completion of the church early in the 12th century. On the other hand, many fine architectural details of late 11th-century date, preserved on the site, indicate that the eastern part of the church was complete by 1100 ; presumably this work included the eastern bay of the nave, where the footings of the first pier next to the crossing, on the N. side, remain ; the pier was rectangular with attached shafts, the chamfered base of one shaft remaining *in situ*. No doubt the eastern parts of the church were built under the rule of Abbess Eulalia who succeeded in 1074 ; her name and that of Prioress Agnes appear in the bede rolls of Matilda of Caen (1113), and of Vitalis the founder of the Order of Savigni (1122).[4]

Early in the 14th century a chapel with a crypt beneath it was built in the angle between the N. chapel and the N. transept, eliminating the transeptal apse. Entrance to the crypt was by a canted flight of stairs,

---

[1] Asser, *De rebus gestis Aelfredi*, cap. 98 ; ed. Stevenson, p. 85.
[2] Dugdale *Mon.* II (1819), 474–6.
[3] Ibid., no. 27 ; *Cart. Sax.*, ed. Birch, 107 ; Sawyer 1164.
[4] Birch, 186 ; Sawyer, 1256.
[5] Dugdale, no. 24 ; Birch, 410 ; Sawyer, 237.
[6] Dugdale, no. 25 ; Birch, 500 ; Sawyer, 326.
[7] Dugdale, no. 23 ; Birch, 499 ; Sawyer, 329.
[8] Dugdale, nos. 26, 28 ; Birch, 525, 526 ; Sawyer, 334, 342.
[9] *Collectanea*, ed. Hearne, 1774, I, 67.
[10] *Anglo-Saxon Chronicle* (ed. D. Whitelock), *s.a.* 978–9 ; text D(E).
[11] *W.A.M.* vii (1862), 274.

[1] *Willelmi Malmesbiriensis monachi gesta pontificum Anglorum*, II, 86 (Rolls ser., lii, 188).
[2] D. B. Harden, *Ant. J.* xxxiv (1954), 188–194. At the time of discovery it was suggested that the jar contained the heart of King Canute, who died in Shaftesbury in 1035 ; but Canute's body was carried to Winchester for burial in the Old Minster and there is no evidence to support the theory of a heart burial.
[3] Wilton House Muniment Room : *Survey of the Lands of William, 1st Earl of Pembroke*, roll 3, memb. xxxviii. (Roxburghe Club, 1909.)
[4] *Arch. J.*, (1950) CVI, Suppl. 40-55.

winding down through the S. part of the E. wall of the transept, no doubt in order to leave the central part of the E. wall free for a dignified entry to the upper chapel. A roughly made leaden casket was unearthed in 1931 from a position which would correspond with the threshold of this entry; it contained the fractured bones of a young man, plausibly identified with the relics of St. Edward, perhaps reburied here in haste at the Dissolution. The upper chapel may thus be identified as that of St. Edward; presumably it contained a shrine to which the relics were translated in the 14th century, a more convenient position for the devotions of pilgrims than the earlier tomb on the N. of the chancel.

In the 14th century a large chapel, probably a Lady Chapel, was added on the S. side of the eastern arm, replacing the 11th-century S. chapel and causing the destruction of the S. transept apse. It was of four bays, heavily vaulted and buttressed. At this period a number of monastic churches received the addition of chapels for the celebration of the Mass of the Blessed Virgin. For convenience of access by the laity they were usually situated on the side of the church remote from the cloister, but at Shaftesbury this position was already occupied by the chapel of St. Edward.

The liturgical arrangement of the 11th-century church is likely to have had the choir with the nuns' stalls in the eastern bay of the nave, and extending into the crossing and eastern arm. On the W. the return stalls backed against the pulpitum, the foundations of which traverse the nave between the first pair of piers; there were screens under the arches behind the stalls. The rood-screen, perhaps of wood, stood between the second pair of nave piers, with the rood altar against the W. face; the screen continued across the aisles in masonry, dividing the nuns' church from the western part of the nave, used by the laity. The arrangements probably evolved gradually; a solid screen of the kind indicated by the footings in the aisles is not likely to date from much before 1200.

The remains of the pulpitum and of the screens crossing the aisles show that these features were demolished to a level below that of the nave floor. Such radical destruction implies the deliberate dismantling of the rood and pulpitum while the church was still in use. Many monastic and other churches retain evidence of liturgical rearrangement in the 14th and 15th centuries, and Shaftesbury Abbey probably supplies another example. The remains of foundations, perhaps part of a late pulpitum, occur on the E. of the crossing, and an altar has been added against the W. face of the S.E. crossing pier. The removal of the choir with its stalls into the eastern arm of a church was often carried out in late mediaeval times in order to free the nave for large congregational services, especially sermons. The rearrangement is often associated with eastward extension of a church, but of this there is no sign at Shaftesbury; the boundary of the excavations, however, coincides with the E. part of the 11th-century apse foundations, and it is possible that a later presbytery, extending further E., remains to be discovered.

The rearrangements suggested above may have been connected with the addition of the 14th-century Lady Chapel; the two need not be contemporary, although the removal eastwards of the choir would have made the Lady Chapel more accessible. The change can hardly have been made before 1326, when the community numbered more than 120 and was ordered to admit no more members until the total had been reduced.[1] Precise figures are not again available until the 15th and 16th centuries, when the numbers of nuns vary between 36 and 55.[2] The reduction in numbers probably took place in the earlier part of the interval and the rearrangement, with its smaller choir, may have been effected by the middle of the 14th century. Perhaps a closer date is afforded by an ordinance of 1364 transferring the chaplaincy of the rood altar in the abbey church to the adjacent church of Holy Trinity, where the incumbent of the chaplaincy became a parochial chaplain.[3] This event probably marked the extinction of parish rights in the nave of the abbey church.

The chapter house, with a fine tiled pavement of the late 13th century, was separated from the S. transept by a narrow passage. The cloister lay S. of the nave, in the usual position; only a small part has been excavated. The W. walk with the western processional doorway lay opposite the seventh bay of the nave, suggesting that the nave extended at least one bay further west. Twin western towers are indicated on the 13th-century abbey seal, and perhaps on the Wilton sketch of 1553, and heavy foundations uncovered at the W. extremity of the excavated area probably bear out these indications.

At the Dissolution, on 23 March 1539, the abbey was surrendered by the abbess, Elizabeth Zouche, to the King's Commissioner, Sir John Tregonwell (Hutchins III, 30–2). In 1544 much of the abbey property was bought by Sir Thomas Arundel and in 1553, after Arundel's attainder, it was sold to the Earl of Pembroke, whose descendants still possess Sir Thomas Arundel's terrier. The sketch in the terrier (Plate 58) proves that the abbey church was already in ruins by the middle of the 16th century; in course of time it disappeared altogether and gardens and houses took its place. In

---

[1] *Reg. Rogeri Mortival*, ii (Cant. and York Soc., cxxviii), 162–6.
[2] *V.C.H., Dorset* ii, 77.
[3] Cal. Pat. Rolls, 1364–7, pp. 402–3.

1816 Charles Bowles started excavations on the site; at a depth of 6 ft. he found a tiled floor decorated with griffins, lions, dragons etc., and Purbeck marble monuments (*Gentleman's Magazine*, LXXXVII (1817), 209). Researches of a more systematic nature in 1861 resulted in the clearing of the eastern arm of the church and of part of the crypt of St. Edward's chapel on the N. (Edward Kyte, *W.A.M.*, VII (1862), 272–7; Hutchins III, 32–5); the trenches were filled in again in 1862. In 1902–5 Edward Doran Webb cleared the eastern part of the church (*Excavations on the site of the Abbey Church . . . Shaftesbury*, 1902, 1903, 1904, printed in Shaftesbury by T. Pinney); the glass jar in which St. Edward's lung may have been preserved appears to have come to light during this period. After 1905 Webb's trenches were neglected for many years and much damage was done by frost. In 1930–2 further work was undertaken by J. Wilson-Claridge, who cleared most of the nave; at this time the relics, supposedly of St. Edward, came to light in the N. transept (*Report of Excavations . . . 1930–1*, Crypt House Press, n.d.).

Architectural Description—In the *Chancel* the eastern extremity of the apse is covered by a modern wall. The northern quadrant of the apse is represented by the core of the curved wall; the southern quadrant, entirely perished, has been restored in recent years. The platform which fills the apse is of mediaeval origin but trenches have been cut on N. and S. in an attempt to expose the apse footings. The two W. steps are modern restorations; the third step retains part of an original chamfered offset. Between the apse and the crossing, the chancel probably was of three bays. Immediately W. of the apse the N. wall of the chancel contains a recess lined with diagonally dressed ashlar, carefully coursed; the recess goes down nearly 2 ft. below floor-level, and about 1 ft. above floor-level the N., E. and W. sides have offsets 3 ins. wide; this was evidently an important tomb and originally may well have contained the body of St. Edward. Adjacent on the W. is the threshold and part of the rebated W. jamb of a doorway in a narrow passage cut through the wall between the chancel and the N. chapel; this feature is of doubtful origin. On the W. of the doorway the lowest course of the original ashlar wall face is preserved; set upon it are three stones of a heavy string-course, 10 ins. thick, chamfered above and below; they appear to be part of a pilaster between the two eastern bays of the chancel, but are not necessarily *in situ*. The second bay seems to have had a wide, shallow recess in the N. wall, and in the sill of the recess are three dowel-holes, possibly for the base of a grill. An opening to the N. chapel in the third bay of the chancel is probably not original. On the S. side of the chancel, the heavy chamfered string-course noted on the N. is repeated; to the E. of this feature the S. wall has been razed; to the W. the wall contains a tomb. Further W., beyond a narrow opening to the S. chapel, a semicircular foundation projects on the N. side of the S.E. pier of the crossing; it is not bonded into the main structure and its purpose is uncertain. If the hypothesis advanced above be true, that the choir was moved eastwards in the 14th century, the projection could perhaps represent part of a 14th-century pulpitum.

Many fragments of the chancel pavement remain *in situ*, consisting of terracotta tiles about 5¼ ins. square, with shields-of-arms and various emblems in white slip; the earlier of them date, probably, from the second half of the 13th century. In two places straight margins indicate the position of choir stalls. The chancel floor slopes gently upwards, being about 1½ ft. higher at the E. than at the W. end.

The *North Chapel* was of three bays with an apse on the E. The lowest ashlar course of the internal apse wall-face survives *in situ*; on the chord of the apse a step 6 ins. high is rebated on top for tiles. A few chamfered ashlar blocks in the E. face of the E. wall are part of the plinth. In the N. wall, incorporated in the E. wall of the adjacent 14th-century chapel, is an original chamfered plinth-stone and the base of an 11th-century pilaster buttress. Inside, the N. wall of the chapel retains the base of the respond between the first and second bays; when excavated in 1902 this respond had an attached half-round shaft, 1 ft. 4¾ ins. in diameter, with a moulded base, but these features have gone. The division between the second and the third bay is marked by a step 6 ins. high, but the wall responds have gone; another step leads down to the N. transept. Slight irregularities in the S. wall of the chapel indicate the position of former responds between the bays and at the opening of the apse.

The *South Chapel*, originally uniform in plan with that on the N., was enlarged to E. and S. and given a rectangular E. end in the 14th century. The 11th-century chapel is represented by the footings of its S.E. corner, preserved below the floor-level of the later building and now exposed. In the 14th-century chapel a large block of ashlar at the S.E. corner retains the mouldings of the chamfered vaulting ribs, which evidently sprang at floor-level. This chapel was of four bays; a projecting stone near the middle of the N. wall may be part of the base of one of the responds; straight-joints close to it, on the W., possibly indicate the position of a respond in the original chapel. In the footings of the S. wall of the chapel a projection near the E. end is perhaps the substructure of a shrine. Externally, the three eastern buttresses of the 14th-century S. wall are represented by footings, extensively restored; in the fourth buttress two courses of 14th-century ashlar are preserved and the wall between the third and fourth buttresses retains a chamfered plinth.

The *North Transept* has, on the E., the opening to a stair which winds down to the crypt of St. Edward's chapel (*see below*). Adjacent, on the N., is a rectangular recess in the floor, where the lead box containing bones, believed by many to be the relics of St. Edward, was discovered in 1931. In the southern part of the W. wall, one course of the outer wall-face remains *in situ* and returns at the angle with the N. aisle; it is of squared ashlar and stands nearly 1½ ft. high. The *Crypt* of St. Edward's chapel has walls of squared and coursed rubble with ashlar dressings, in part restored. The *tas-de-charge* of the two-bay cross-vault remain *in situ*. The doorway to the stair on the W. has rebated jambs.

In the *South Transept* the footings of the inner face of the E. wall are preserved as far N. as the S. side of the S. chapel; the footings of the S. and W. walls also remain, but the superstructure has entirely gone. At the time of excavation traces of a doorway were noted at the S.E. corner, possibly giving access to a stair to the dormitory.

The *Crossing* is defined by four massive rectangular piers rising some 2 ft. above the level of the former pavements, but deprived of almost all facing stones. Masonry extending W. from the S.E. pier is probably the base of an altar and its foot-pace. The masonry footing of a semicircular feature built against the N. face of the same pier has been mentioned above.

The *Nave* has been excavated as far W. as the boundary of the adjoining property, revealing six bays and part of a seventh. On the N., the eastern pier retains the chamfered plinth of an attached shaft, indicating that this pier was cruciform in plan.

Further W. the positions of the former piers are occupied by mounds of rubble, presumably lying on original foundations. The drawing of *c.* 1553 in the Wilton Terrier (Plate 58) shows the piers as cylindrical, and unattached ashlar facing stones found on the site, from a convex cylinder about 4 ft. in diameter, indicate the probable size of the former piers. Foundations spanning the nave nearly in line with the easternmost piers are doubtless the substructure of the former pulpitum. A rectangle of rough stones on the axis of the nave, in the third bay, is presumably the footing of a platform for the altar in front of the rood-screen.

Of the *North Aisle* there remain the footings of the N. wall, a few stones of the lowest course of the outer wall-face at the E. end, and part of the core of the wall over a length of some 40 ft. The foundations of a wall or screen separate the two eastern bays from those on the W. The tiled pavement of the aisle lies some 6 ins. higher than that of the nave.

In the *South Aisle* the two eastern bays are divided from those on the W. by the footings of a cross-wall, as in the N. aisle; a similar feature occurs at the sixth pier. Two openings in the foundations of the S. wall are not original, but that on the W. probably indicates the place of an original doorway from the W. walk of the cloister. The foundations of two buttresses which project into the N. walk of the cloister are later additions.

In the *Cloister*, the foundations of part of the N. and W. walks have been exposed. The foundations of two buttresses near the N.W. corner of the garth wall appear to be late repairs, but a buttress which stands 16 ft. S. of the N.W. corner includes original masonry; beside it, on the N., the wall retains a chamfered plinth. Some fragments of tiled paving remain in the W. and N. walks.

The foundations of the N. wall of the *Chapter House* are seen some 5 ft. S. of the S. wall of the transept. Adjacent on the S. are some remains of the chapter-house tiled floor. Further S. the foundations of the conventual buildings probably exist, concealed beneath a public road.

Fittings, etc.—*Carved stone fragments* (Plates 3, 59), found during the excavations and kept in a museum on the site, include the following: Of pre-conquest date—(1) perhaps part of a cross-shaft, with single-strand interlace ornament and, on adjacent side, ‘anglian’ beast-head; (2) small fragment with two-strand interlace; (3) fragment with palmette ornament, subsequently reused and with billet ornament superimposed; (4) grave slabs, four, with crudely carved crosses. Of the late 11th century—

(5) volutes, 16 in number, of various sizes, some retaining pigment; (6) base of attached shaft (diam. 5½ ins.), of Purbeck marble, with cable moulding and palmettes (see drawing); (7) large capital with volute and leaf ornament; (8) volute capital for shaft 13 ins. in diam., and some 20 fragments of similar capitals; (9) sculptured corbel from corbel-table; (10) bases for shafts about 10 ins. diam. Of the 12th century—(11) part of twisted stone shaft, 6 ins. diam; (12) part of spiral-fluted shaft, 1¼ ft. diam.; (13) voussoirs with chevron, dog-tooth and pellet decoration; (14) string-course with billet decoration; (15) double capital for coupled shafts of about 7 ins. diam., perhaps from cloisters; (16) leaf capitals for shafts about 3 ins. and 5 ins. in diam.; (17) two large corbels with grotesque masks. Of the 13th century—(18) two bases with hold-water mouldings for shafts about 5 ins. diam.; (19) stiff-leaf capital 1 ft. high for triple shaft. Of the 14th century—(20) vaulting boss with shield charged with two crossed swords. Of the 15th century—(21) vaulting bosses, 8 in number, with foliate and heraldic decoration.

Coffins and *Coffin-lids*: fragments, from six burials, 11th century, 13th century and of unknown mediaeval date.

Cross: of stone, brought in 1931 from another part of Shaftesbury (Wilson-Claridge, *op. cit.*, p. 8) and reset on stepped base at centre of main apse; inlet in stonework, four original alabaster carvings, much worn, the best preserved representing seated figure, robed and crowned; late 14th or early 15th century.

Glass: many fragments, mainly with grisaille decoration, 14th and 15th century.

Monuments and *Floorslabs. Monuments*: Fragments of broken effigies include—(1) Purbeck marble mail-clad head of man, 12th-century; (2) fragments of mail-clad stone effigy, 12th century; (3) part of Purbeck marble female effigy, 13th century; (4) part of stone effigy of youth, 14th century; (5) part of stone effigy in priest's vestments, 14th century; (6), (7), parts of two stone female effigies, 15th century; (8), (9), (10), parts of three stone figures, 15th century. *Floorslabs*: (1) of Alexander Cater, late mediaeval; (2) of Thomas Scales, 1532, with incised black-letter inscription in square border.

Tiles: of the later 13th and 14th century remain *in situ* in several parts of the church (see plan). Others, better preserved, have been removed to the museum and include those illustrated on pp. xviii, xxiii.

(2) THE PARISH CHURCH OF ST. PETER, near the centre of the town, has walls of Greensand ashlar and rubble and is roofed partly with lead and partly with modern materials. In the *West Tower*, 14th-century N. and S. arches indicate a building of that date; the rest of the tower, the *Nave*, the *North Aisle* and the *West Porch* are of the late 15th century; the *South Aisle* was rebuilt and enlarged in the 16th century. There is no chancel.

Architectural Description—The E. wall of the *Nave* has a chamfered plinth, a chamfered string-course below the sill of the E. window, and a gabled parapet of shallow inclination with a moulded coping and a hollow-chamfered string-course. The restored E. window (Plate 7) has five cinquefoil-headed lights with vertical tracery in a two-centred head. The N. and S. arcades have uniform two-centred arches with wave-moulded inner orders and hollow-chamfered outer orders; they spring from piers with four attached shafts alternating with vertical hollow-chamfers, with capitals with hollow-chamfered abaci and roll-mouldings, and with moulded bases, much mutilated. Above each arcade are four irregularly spaced clearstorey windows; those on the N. are of two square-headed lights with chamfered surrounds; in the S. clearstorey the windows are of two and three lights with trefoil two-centred heads in casement-moulded square-headed surrounds. The clearstorey walls have parapets with string-courses and copings continuous with those of the E. gable.

The *North Aisle* has an E. window of two trefoil-headed lights with vertical tracery in a moulded four-centred head with continuous jambs; over it, a moulded and hollow-chamfered parapet string-course is inclined in correspondence with the low-pitched roof. Above, a horizontal parapet, embattled and enriched as on the N. wall (see below), dies into the sloping string-course. The N. wall has four windows with moulded two-centred heads, continuous jambs and moulded labels ; each opening is divided into two lights by a mullion which runs straight from sill to apex. The N. doorway has a two-centred head of two chamfered orders with continuous jambs and a moulded label ; the wall is thinner near the doorway than elsewhere, but an internal corbel-table above the doorway carries the masonry out to its normal thickness. The N. wall has an elaborate embattled parapet with a hollow-chamfered string-course and a frieze of blind quatrefoils with bosses carved with heraldic devices including Tudor roses, portcullises, suns and crescents, crossed sheaves of arrows, and embowed dolphins ; over these is an upper frieze of pierced panels with cusped diagonal and vertical tracery, and merlons with trefoil-headed panels and continuous chamfered and roll-moulded coping. At intervals along the parapet, pinnacles with panelled, trefoil-headed sides and gable-headed finials rise from gargoyles on the string-course. High up in the W. wall of the N. aisle is a small window of two square-headed lights ; above, the embattled parapet continues horizontally (Plate 62).

In the *South Aisle* the masonry of the E. wall appears to be in two parts, that on the S. resulting from the 16th-century widen-

ing of the aisle. An E. doorway with a chamfered four-centred head, below floor-level in the early part of the aisle, presumably gave access to a crypt in the 15th-century structure ; it is now blocked. The 16th-century E. window is of four segmental-headed lights in a chamfered square-headed surround. Above, the plain wallhead is raised slightly at the centre, following the shallow slope of the double-pitched lead roof. The S. wall has windows of two chamfered square-headed lights flanking a buttress of two weathered stages ; further W. is a reset 15th-century window of three cinquefoil-headed lights in a chamfered square-headed surround. The W. wall has a window similar to that on the E., its lower part masked by the upper storey of an adjacent house (8). The *Crypt* below the S. aisle is of the 16th century. The S. wall has square-headed windows, and a blocked square-headed doorway ; at the W. end is a fireplace with a deep cambered bressummer and a chimneybreast with weathered offsets ; it is disused and a modern window opens in the S. wall. The W. wall contains a blocked doorway which formerly opened into the house (8).

The *West Tower* is of three stages. At the base is a moulded plinth ; the stages are defined by hollow-chamfered string-courses ; at the top is an embattled parapet with a moulded

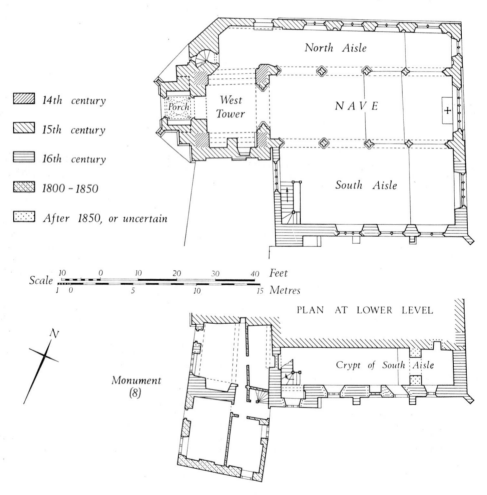

SHAFTESBURY   *The Parish Church of St. Peter*

14th century

15th century

16th century

1800 – 1850

After 1850, or uncertain

North Aisle

West Tower

Porch

NAVE

South Aisle

Scale   10   0   10   20   30   40   Feet
          1   0   5   10   15   Metres

N

Monument (8)

PLAN AT LOWER LEVEL

Crypt of South Aisle

coping and a parapet string-course with corner gargoyles. The top stage has corner pilasters which continue through the parapet and end in crocketed finials. The lower stages have weathered diagonal buttresses on the N.E. and S.E. corners and square-set three-stage buttresses to N. and S. on the W. side; the S. side has three square-set buttresses irregularly spaced, that on the W. being a raking buttress of uncertain date built on the lower part of a mediæval buttress. The polygonal vice turret on the N.W. corner of the tower continues through all stages and ends in a pyramidal stone capping, level with the parapet finials. The E. tower arch is two-centred and of three orders, the inner order wave-moulded, the others hollow-chamfered; the responds have attached shafts flanked by hollow-chamfers and wave mouldings, with moulded polygonal bases and capitals similar to those of the nave piers, but enriched with angels (now headless) bearing scrolls. The 14th-century N. and S. tower arches are two-centred and of two chamfered orders dying into plain responds. The S. arch is closed by a wall on the S. and is reinforced by a pier of rough masonry at the centre; adjacent to the pier is a blocked window with a chamfered two-centred head. The W. doorway has a moulded four-centred head and continuous jambs; above, the W. window has two 18th-century transomed square-headed lights, inserted in a 15th-century opening with a four-centred head and a moulded label. The second stage has small square-headed openings on the N. and E. Each face of the third stage has a belfry window of two trefoil-headed lights with a trefoil tracery light in a two-centred head with a moulded label.

Straight-joints show that the *West Porch* is later than the tower, albeit probably of the 15th century; it has a moulded plinth and a parapet with a hollow-chamfered string-course and a moulded coping; the string-course has foliate bosses. The diagonal western buttresses are of two weathered stages and above them are plain corner pinnacles, formerly with finials, now gone. The porch archway has a casement-moulded four-centred head with continuous responds and a label with square stops.

The *Roof* of the nave (Plate 66) is of 16th-century origin. It is divided into seven bays by heavily moulded main beams with raised centres; shafted timber wall-posts rising from moulded stone corbels support three of the beams and have curved braces with foliate spandrels. Similarly moulded ridge-beams and wall-plates intersect the main beams. On each side of the ridge each bay is divided into four panels by intersecting beams of lighter cross-section than the main beams; the panels are filled with plain boarding. In 1965 the roof was rebuilt in concrete, with the moulded 16th-century timbers suspended beneath it. The roof of the N. aisle is similar to that of the nave, but smaller in scale, having eight bays in its length; in 1969 it was in process of restoration.

The W. porch has a stone lierne *Vault* (Plate 10) with moulded ribs springing from angel corbels (two gone); the rib junctions have bosses carved with foliage, flowers, a blank shield and, at the centre, a large rose. Stone-panelled wall-arches extend the vault laterally to N. and S.

Fittings—*Bells*: six; treble by Thomas Purdue, inscribed 'A wonder great my eye I fix where was but 3 you may see six, 1684, T.P.'; 2nd inscribed 'When I doe ring prepare to pray, RA, TB, 1670'; 3rd inscribed 'Wm. Cockey Bell Founder 1738'; 4th inscribed '1738 Mr Henry Saunders & Mr Richard Wilkins Ch. Wds.'; 5th inscribed 'While thus we join in chearful sound may love and loyalty abound. H. Oram, C. Warden. R. Wells Aldbourne fecit MDCCLXXVI'; tenor by Thomas Purdue, inscribed 'When you hear me for to tole then pray to God to save the soul, anno domini 1672, TH, RW.

CW. TP'. *Brass* and *Indents*: In N. aisle, stone floorslab with central plate (17 by 3¾ ins.) with worn black-letter inscription of Stephen Payne (Hutchins III, 46), 1508 or 1514, and indents for four shields. *Communion Rails*: In eastern bay of N. and S. nave arcades, with stout turned oak balusters and moulded rails, late 17th century; defining two eastern bays of nave, with profiled flat balusters and moulded rails, 17th century, made up with modern work. *Communion Tables*: In S. aisle, of oak, with plain stretchers, heavy turned legs enriched with acanthus carving, and enriched rails with escutcheon dated 1631. Near N. doorway, of oak, with tapering octagonal legs with claw feet, arcuated rails, scrolled diagonal stretchers with turned finial at intersection, and beaded edge to top board, *c.* 1700. *Font*: (Plate 12) with octagonal bowl with two trefoil-headed sunk panels on each face and moulded underside, similarly panelled octagonal stem and plain octagonal base, 15th century; ovolo-moulded plinth, perhaps 17th century. Font cover, of wood, low eight-sided dome with moulded rim and ribs, 18th century. *Glass*: Five small panels reset in E. window of nave; (1) in a roundel with indecipherable inscription, shield-of-arms of Fitzjames impaling Newburgh (Sir John Fitzjames of Lewston, d. 1539, married Alice Newburgh of E. Lulworth); (2) former tracery light depicting Virgin and Child, *c.* 1500; (3) former tracery light with shield of Five Wounds, 15th century; (4) shield-of-arms of Eliot quartering another coat; (5) emblem of Trinity. *Graffiti*: on communion table in S. aisle, W.K., H.R.E.; on lead roof of tower, Jn. Reynolds, 1779.

Monument and *Floorslabs*. *Monument*: In N. aisle, of Robert Woolridge, 1777, oval tablet with cherub and foliage. *Floorslabs*: In nave, (1) of Walter Barnes, 1776, and his wives Elizabeth, 1729, Frances, 1757, and Mary, 1767, stone slab with shield-of-arms now indecipherable; (2) of Elizabeth Barnes, 1729, stone slab with inscription in architectural framework. In N. aisle, (3) of Stephen Payne, see *Brass and Indents*.

Niches: In N. aisle, in E. wall, with soffit carved to represent vaulting, formerly with canopy, pinnacles and corbel; in N.E. angle, with trefoil ogee head, carved enrichment at springing of soffit, shelf cut back; in N. wall, three ogee-headed niches, one with cinquefoil cusping, others trefoiled; externally, in N. wall of N. aisle, with crocketed ogee head and shafted jambs; over arch of W. porch, with canopied cinquefoil head and shafted jambs with crocketed finials; all 15th century.

Panelling: In nave, on E. wall, of oak, with moulded and shaped cornices and fielded panels surrounding tables of Creed, Decalogue etc., 18th century; in S. aisle, reset fragments with chip-carving and fielded panels, 17th and 18th century. *Plate*: includes undated Elizabethan silver cup by 'Gillingham' maker; silver paten inscribed 1714; silver stand-paten inscribed 'ex dono Thomae Hackny 1714'; large pewter flagon inscribed 'Shaston St. Peter's 1770', with no marks; (some of these items may belong to Holy Trinity Church, proper attribution being impossible since the union of the two benefices). *Poorbox*: of oak, with foliate carving and inscription 'Remember the poore', and with three locks, probably 17th century. *Pulpit*: of oak, polygonal, with fielded panels and moulded cornice, 18th century, base gone.

Rainwater Head: on S. wall of nave, of lead, inscribed I.M., R.W., 1674, with contemporary down-pipe. *Royal Arms*: see (3). *Seating*: incorporates twenty-three reused oak bench-ends with traceried decoration, 15th century; also one oak bench with beaded decoration, 17th century. *Stoup*: in W. porch, with bowl cut off, 15th century. *Tables of Creed and Decalogue etc.*: In nave, on panelled E. wall, with shaped and gilded frames, one panel with Creed, one with Lord's Prayer, two with Decalogue, 18th century.

SHAFTESBURY   *The Church of the Holy Trinity*

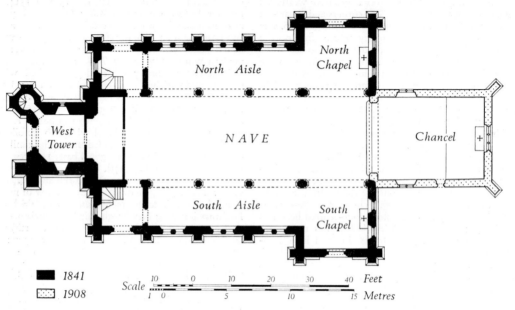

North Aisle

North Chapel

West Tower

NAVE

Chancel

South Aisle

South Chapel

■ 1841
⬚ 1908

Scale 10 0 10 20 30 40 Feet
1 0 5 10 15 Metres

(3) The Parish Church of The Holy Trinity, some 80 yds. N. of the abbey site, has ashlar walls and slate-covered roofs. The *Nave, Aisles, North* and *South Chapels,* and *West Tower* were rebuilt in 1840–2, to designs in the 'Early English' style by Gilbert Scott (Plate 63). The *Chancel,* by Doran Webb, was added in 1908. The mediaeval church appears in a sketch in the Wilton terrier of *c.* 1553 (Plate 58).

Fittings—*Bells :* treble, 2nd and 3rd by Mears, 1844 ; 4th by John Wallis, inscribed 'Praise the Lord I.W., 1597' ; 5th by William Purdue, inscribed 'God is all my hope, 1641, WP ', with 'John Buckton, John Masters 'in smaller letters, the words of the two inscriptions alternating ; tenor by Mears, 1844. *Churchyard Cross :* S.W. of tower, with moulded square base on two steps, and tapering chamfered shaft with run-out stops ; probably 15th century, cross-head modern. *Glass :* reset in N. window of N. Chapel, shield-of-arms of Whitaker, with rectangular inscription panel 'Good men need not marble wee dare trust to glass the memory of William Whitaker Esq. who died the 3rd of October, 1646 '.

Monuments and *Floorslabs. Monuments :* In N. chapel, (1) of Maria Buckland, 1822, marble wall tablet with shield-of-arms, by Hiscock of Blandford. In S. chapel, (2) of Abraham Gapper, 1733, marble and stone cartouche with scrollwork surround (Plate 18) ; (3) of Elizabeth Atchison, 1766, and her mother Honor, 1769, wall-monument with scrolled cheek-pieces, shaped cornice and gadrooned apron ; (4) of John Bennett, 1676, metal plate in oval stone cartouche with heavily enriched and gilded surround, and shield-of-arms of Bennett and Ashlock quarterly, impaling Hall (Plate 18). In N. aisle, (5) of Christopher Erle, 1817, and his wife Margaret (Bowles), 1807, tablet with shield-of-arms of Erle impaling Bowles, by T. King of Bath ; (6) of John Mill, 1821, sarcophagus-shaped marble tablet with shield-of-arms of Mill, by Osmund of Sarum. In S. aisle, (7) of Henry

Edwards, 1803, and Mary (Ernly) his wife, 1796, marble tablet surmounted by urn, with shield-of-arms, by Waddilove, London. erected 1805 ; (8) of Matilda Mill, 1833, wall-monument with kneeling figure beside urn, and shield-of-arms of Mill impaling another coat, by Osmund, Sarum ; (9) of William Collins, 1810, marble tablet by T. King of Bath. Reset in S. porch, (10) stone effigy of priest with hands together in prayer (Plate 15), late 13th century (*W.A.M.*, VII (1862), 261) ; adjacent, tablet recording discovery of effigy in 1817. In churchyard, some 50 paces S. of tower, (11) of Margaret Swyer, 1745, her husband Robert, 1767, and others of same family, table-tomb (Plate 19) with balusters at corners and moulded top slab with dentil enrichment ; also, dispersed in churchyard, several 17th-century headstones. *Floorslabs :* In N. chapel, adjacent to N. wall, (1) of William Bowles, 1717, slate slab with shield-of-arms. In N. porch, (2) of Arundell B[ennett, 1682]. In S. porch, (3) of George Howe, 1666, with shield-of-arms of Howe.

Plate : the plate listed in St. Peter's church (2) may include items which belong to this church, proper attribution being no longer possible ; items which belong certainly to Holy Trinity are—silver cup inscribed 'This chalice belongeth to the holy trinity of Shaston, 1670 ', with stand-paten designed to act as cover, foot hanging inside cup ; silver stand-paten with date-letter of 1709, donor's inscription of Humphrey Bishop, and shield-of-arms of Bishop ; silver flagon with date-letter, donor's inscription and arms as on foregoing.

Royal Arms : formerly in (2), painted on canvas, with cypher GR and inscription 'Ed. Buckland and Willm. Everett Ch. wardens, M. Wilmot fecit, 1780 ' (Plate 27). *Miscellanea :* reset in ringing chamber of W. tower, 17th-century wood panelling with moulded stiles and rails.

(4) The Church of St. James, at the foot of Castle Hill, in the S.W. part of the town, was rebuilt in 1866 to designs by T. H. Wyatt. Reset on the wall of the N. aisle is a 15th-century stone parapet from the former

PLATE 57

SHAFTESBURY. Air view from W.

PLATE 58

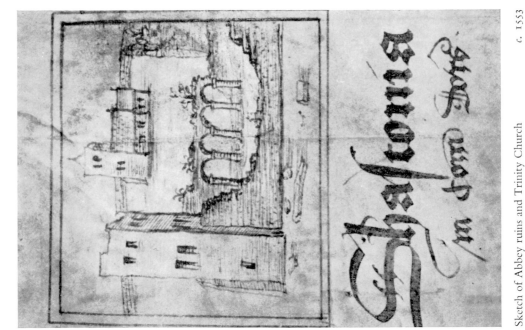

Sketch of Abbey ruins and Trinity Church   c. 1553

Rubbing of fragment of inscription, now lost.   c. 1075–c. 1150

SHAFTESBURY. Historical documents.

PLATE 59

(16) Capital.   12th century

(3) Palmette, with billet superimposed.   Pre-conquest; 11th century

(7) Parts of large capital.   Late 11th century

(15) Double capital.   12th century

(9) Corbel.   Late 11th century

SHAFTESBURY ABBEY. Carved stone fragments recovered during excavations.

PLATE 60

SHAFTESBURY. Site of Abbey Church, from N.W.

PLATE 61

SHAFTESBURY. (7) Town Hall, from S.W.

PLATE 62

SILTON CHURCH. From W.   Early 16th century

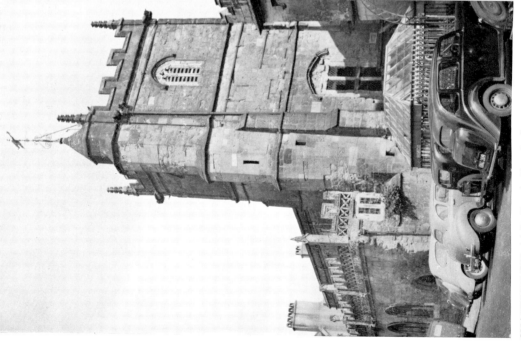

SHAFTESBURY. (2) St. Peter's Church, from N.W.   15th century

PLATE 63

1847

SUTTON WALDRON CHURCH. From N.W.

1841

SHAFTESBURY. (3) Holy Trinity Church, from N.W.

PLATE 64

SHAFTESBURY. (68–75) Gold Hill.

Late 14th and 18th century

church; it is embattled, with a continuous moulded coping and with a trefoil-headed panel on each merlon; below the crenellation is a continuous frieze of quatrefoils. The S. aisle wall has a similar reset parapet, but not embattled. The E. window of the S. aisle is of three trefoil ogee-headed lights under quatrefoil tracery in a two-centred head; an old drawing kept in the church shows that this is the restored 14th-century E. window of the former chancel. The W. windows of the S. aisle and of the N. aisle are similar to that on the E., but of two lights; they also are of the 14th century and presumably come from the former church.

Fittings—Bells: six; 2nd by John Wallis, inscribed 'I.W. 1597 Praise God'; 3rd inscribed 'Sancte Jacobe ora pro nobis' in Lombardic lettering, 14th-century; 4th by John Danton, inscribed 'NC, EC, ID, O give thanks unto God, 1629'; others 1875–6. *Chest*: of cast-iron, embossed 'St. James's Shaston Register Chest Stn. Burden 1813 C.W.'

Monuments and *Floorslabs. Monuments*: In S. aisle, (1) of Thomas Naish, 1784, and his wife Lydia (Collier), 1823, marble tablet with arms, by Hiscock of Blandford. In W. tower, (2) of Robert Jolliffe, 1731, and Anna (Matthew) Jolliffe, 1732, stone tablet with rounded top. *Floorslabs*: In nave, on N.E., of Thomas Nicholls, 1793, slate slab divided into two pieces. In W. tower, several worn Purbeck marble and slate slabs, 17th and 18th century.

Plate: includes Elizabethan silver cup and cover, without marks, but of similar design to those of the anonymous 'Gillingham' silversmith; also 18th-century pewter paten and three pewter almsdishes. *Royal Arms*: In W. tower, of painted and gilt woodwork, with Stuart arms carved in high relief, late 17th century (Plate 27).

(5) THE CHURCH OF ST. JOHN, Enmore Green, has ashlar walls and slated roofs. It was built in 1843, in the Romanesque style to the design of G. Alexander, and comprises *Chancel, North* and *South Transepts, Nave* and *Central Tower* (Plate 5).

SHAFTESBURY   *St. John's Church*

ENMORE GREEN

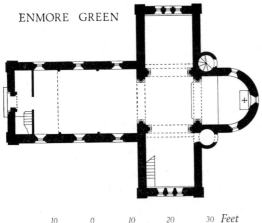

Scale

| 10 | 0 | 10 | 20 | 30 | Feet |
| 1 | 0 | | 5 | | 10 | Metres |

Fittings—Font: with stone bowl with vertical sides, moulded above and below, square on plan with chamfered corners, with decoration of two roughly outlined and apparently unfinished poppy-heads to each side, on square pedestal, 15th century. *Font-cover*, of oak, with flat boards with moulded border; at centre, oak boss in form of square aedicule with ogee-headed 'window' in each side, and pyramidal roof, probably 15th century. *Galleries*: in nave and transepts, with timber parapets enriched with Romanesque arcading, 1843. *Glass*: in three chancel windows, each window with two shields-of-arms, 1843.

(6) THE PARISH CHURCH OF ST. RUMBOLD, although situated in the borough of Shaftesbury, is the parish church of the adjoining village of Cann (see p. 9). It has ashlar walls and a slate-covered roof and comprises a combined *Chancel* and *Nave*, a *West Tower* and a small *South Porch*; these date from 1840. A *Vestry* and *Organ Chamber* were added on the N. of the chancel in 1909.

SHAFTESBURY   *St. Rumbold's Church*

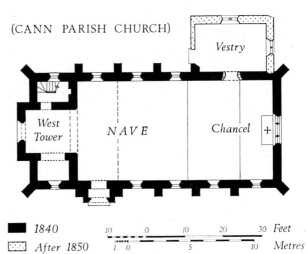

| ■ | 1840 |
| :::: | After 1850 |

| 10 | 0 | 10 | 20 | 30 | Feet |
| 1 | 0 | | 5 | | 10 | Metres |

Architectural Description—The E. window is of three graded lancet lights under a two-centred label. The N. and S. walls are approximately uniform and of six bays defined by plain two-stage buttresses; each bay has a lancet window with a label. The W. tower is without stages; at the top is a hollow-chamfered string-course and an embattled parapet. The W. doorway has a two-centred head; above it are three storeys of lancet windows, the topmost lancet being in the belfry; similar belfry windows occur in the N., S. and E. walls. The S. porch has a doorway similar to that of the W. tower; above the doorhead is a hollow-chamfered string-course and a plain parapet. Inside, the W. bay of the nave has a gallery; the roof has tie-beam trusses with curved braces springing from shaped stone corbels.

Fittings—Font: (Plate 11) of stone, with circular bowl scribed with arcs for unfinished or painted decoration, shaft with reeded capital with flower and leaf enrichment in alternate scallops, and ovolo-moulded base with spur spandrels, *c.* 1200. *Inscription*: incised on side of font bowl, in a border, 'Iohn Monde Church worden 1664'. *Monuments*: In nave, (1) of

Matthew Bowles, 1768, segmental-headed inscription-tablet with arms of Bowles, in architectural surround, with skull on apron, and urn finial above ; (2) of Henrietta Bowles, 1795, and two infants, marble tablet surmounted by urn, with arms. In churchyard, S. of nave, (3) of Margaret Erle, 1807, Charles Bowles, 1837 and Sara Burlton, 1843, urn with scroll-work, on stone pedestal.

Plate : includes silver stand-paten with inscription of 1712, but no date-letter. *Royal Arms :* painted on wooden panel, arms of Queen Anne, with cypher AR.

(6A) CONGREGATIONAL CHAPEL, in Muston's Lane, was built in 1858. Fittings—*Font :* of stone, with gadrooned and fluted bowl, cylindrical stem with moulded octagonal capping, and moulded octagonal base (Plate 12), 17th century, said to have been found during the demolition of (99). *Plate :* includes two two-handled cups with assay-marks of 1751.

FRIENDS' MEETING HOUSE, see (107).

SECULAR

HIGH STREET

(7) THE TOWN HALL stands on the W. of St. Peter's church (2), on the S. side of High Street. Because of the sharply falling ground it is of two storeys on the N. and of three on the S. ; the walls are of ashlar and the roofs are slate-covered (Plate 61). The building dates from 1826 (*Salisbury Journal*, 5 Aug.) and the clock-tower on the N. front was added in 1879 ; the N. porch probably is contemporary with the tower.

In the S. front the second floor is marked by a hollow-chamfered string-course, and the parapet rises above a string-course of bolder profile ; these features are continuous on the E. and N. fronts. Until recently the N. and S. fronts had crenellated parapets, and a stone shield at the centre of the S. front bore the date 1827 ; the corresponding part of the N. front is masked by the clock-tower. The two lower storeys of the S. front and the lower storey on the N. were originally open arcades of five bays, with chamfered, elliptical-headed archways, presumably providing accommodation for covered markets. The openings have now been filled in, and on the first floor are fitted with windows of ' Gothic ' pattern. In the top storey, the N. and S. fronts have each five bays of square-headed three-light windows with lozenge glazing, moulded wood surrounds, chamfered jambs and heads, and moulded stone labels. Inside, the mayor's seat in the council chamber has a wooden hood with enriched mouldings, resting on scrolled brackets.

Civic Plate etc. Two maces, similar to one another and 1½ ft. in length, are of iron, silver and gilt (Plate 26). They have flanges and knob finials of iron, plain silver shafts with central knops and raised bands with cable decoration, and plain bowl-shaped silver heads with cable decoration on the rims, and pierced and gilded brattishing ; set within the brattishing of each mace-head is a silver-gilt arms-plate with heraldic engraving. One has the shield-of-arms of James I with the initials I.R. and the date 1604 ; the other, probably earlier, is tierced in pale and engraved rather crudely with arms : (*i*) per fess France and England, (*ii*) Shaftesbury Abbey, (*iii*) a lion rampant beside a tree, in chief a bird.

A silver seal ⅞ ins. in diameter has the tree-and-bird device on a shield, flanked by the letters B S, with the date 1570 above. Another silver seal, nearly 1½ ins. in diameter, has the arms of the town under the date 1570, enclosed in a roped border on which is inscribed SIGILLVM OFFICII MAIORATVS BVRGI SHASTON.

An emblem known as ' The Byzant ' (probably a corruption of besom) is of carved wood, gilded, and about 4 ft. high (Plate 21). It probably is of the 18th century and appears to represent a palm tree surmounted by a crown with a pineapple finial. The byzant was borne in annual procession to Enmore Green, where, until 1830, ceremonies were enacted confirming Shaftesbury's right to water from that place (Hutchins III, 44).

(8) HOUSE, perhaps originally the clergy-house of St. Peter's Church (2), but subsequently an inn and now in private occupation, is two-storeyed and has rendered walls and tiled roofs (for plan, see p. 62). The N. bay is of the 16th century ; the S. bay is a 19th-century addition. The W. front retains an iron inn-sign bracket with sun and moon emblems, probably from the arms of Bowles. The dwelling formerly extended below the S. aisle of the church, occupying part at least of the crypt, in which a fireplace has been noted (above, p. 62).

(9) HOUSE AND SHOP, No. 29, formerly an inn, dates from *c.* 1850. Reset in one N. gable is a carved stone, perhaps a vaulting boss, of the 14th century, with the arms of Shaftesbury Abbey.

(10) HOUSE AND SHOP, No. 39, of two storeys and a basement, has walls partly of ashlar and partly rendered, and slated roofs. The basement and ground floor are of the early 18th century ; the upper storey is of the 19th century. Inside, the 18th-century part of the building has stop-chamfered beams, and one ground-floor room contains some 18th-century pine panelling.

(11) HOUSE AND SHOP, No. 43, is two-storeyed with attics and basements, and has walls of ashlar, partly rendered, and slated roofs ; it is of the 18th century, with 19th-century alterations. The N. front is modern, but on the S., facing into a court, the S. and E. fronts are of ashlar with stone mullioned windows. Inside, a ground-floor room has 18th-century pine panelling in two heights, with fielded panels and beaded styles and rails, and a shell-headed niche with flanking pilasters, shaped shelves and glazed doors. A first-floor room has an open fireplace with a cambered timber bressummer resting on moulded stone corbels.

(12) HOUSE, No. 45, of three storeys in addition to attics and basements, dates from late in the 18th century. The N. front, of two bays, is ashlar-faced with rusticated quoins and has a modillion cornice above the second storey. The original ground-floor windows have gone, but the first and second storeys retain sashed windows with moulded architraves and fluted keystones. The S. front is tile-hung. Inside, the stairs have open strings with scrolled spandrels, turned balusters and moulded mahogany handrails ; a cupboard on one of the landings has jambs with fluted pilasters, and a moulded cornice with dentil enrichment.

(13) HOUSE AND SHOP, No. 49, is three-storeyed and has rendered walls and tiled roofs. The building is perhaps of late 18th-century origin, but was altered externally in the 19th century.

(14) HOUSE, No. 53, is of three storeys and a basement, and has rendered walls and slated roofs. It is of 18th-century origin, but the N. front and the whole top storey are of the late 19th century ; the ground floor is now a shop. Inside, the S. room on the ground floor and another room on the first floor have 18th-century panelling. The open-string stairs are of oak and

have scrolled spandrels, vase-and-column balusters, moulded handrails and panelled dados.

(15) HOUSE AND SHOP, No. 55, two-storeyed, with rendered walls and tiled roofs, dates from the late 17th or early 18th century. The three-bay N. front retains some original casement windows with iron frames and leaded glazing. Inside, there are stop-chamfered beams and an open fireplace.

(16) HOUSE AND SHOPS, Nos. 59, 61, are of two storeys with basements and attics and have rubble walls, partly rendered, and tiled roofs; they are of 17th-century origin, but were much altered in the 19th century. Inside, the basement has several stop-chamfered beams.

(17) HOUSE AND SHOP, No. 63, of two storeys with an attic, has walls of ashlar, rubble and brick and a slated roof; it dates from the 17th century. The ashlar-faced N. front is of two bays with a central doorway; in the western bay it retains 18th-century sashed windows in each storey; the other openings have later fittings. The gabled E. wall is of rubble chequered with ashlar blocks. On the S. wall the level of the first floor is marked by a hollow-chamfered string-course and above this the building is tile-hung. Inside, the ground-floor rooms have chamfered beams; the W. room has an open fireplace, now blocked, and, on the S. of the fireplace, a wooden newel staircase.

(18) HOUSE AND SHOP, No. 52, two-storeyed with rendered walls and tiled roofs, is of the early 17th century. In the N. wall, at the back, is a stone window of three square-headed lights with moulded heads, mullions and jambs. Inside, several rooms have heavily moulded beams in which the mouldings are returned at intervals, to continue on intersecting beams, now gone.

(19) HOUSES AND SHOPS, Nos. 48 and 50, two adjacent, are two-storeyed and have walls of rubble and of timber-framework, in part rendered, and tile-covered roofs; they are of 17th-century origin, but were refronted in the 19th century. Inside, a common through-passage has walls partly of timber-framework with brick infilling; one ground-floor room has a stop-chamfered beam.

(20) THE CROWN INN, No. 42, was extensively rebuilt in 1862, but it retains part of an earlier structure, possibly mediaeval in origin. Where seen in a yard at the back, the E. wall is of rubble in the lower storey and of timber-framework with brick infilling above. Inside, one room has a 16th-century stone fireplace surround with a hollow-chamfered and cambered head; it is decorated with trefoil-headed panels and quatrefoils, each quatrefoil enclosing a blank shield.

(21) HOUSE AND SHOP, No. 38, is two storeyed with attics and has rendered walls and slated roofs; it dates from c. 1800. The S. front is of three bays, with Doric pilasters in both storeys. On the ground floor, the shop-front occupies two bays; the shop door and flanking windows have glazing with round-headed arcading. On the first floor each bay has a large round-headed sashed window.

(22) HOUSE AND SHOP, No. 36, is three-storeyed with brick walls and slated roofs; it dates from c. 1850. Behind the main range is a two-storeyed cottage with rendered walls, probably of the late 18th century.

(23) HOUSE, No. 34, now a bank, is of three storeys with ashlar walls and slate-covered roofs; it dates from c. 1800. The S. front is symmetrical and of three bays; the lower storey has been rebuilt in recent years, but the two upper storeys are original; the centre bay projects in a shallow bow. Above the first-floor windows an ashlar plat-band is enriched with roundels and fluting; above the second-floor windows is a moulded

cornice; at the top is a plain parapet. All the windows are sashed; those of the first floor are of three lights, the central window being square-headed while those of the flanking bays are of Venetian form; on the second floor the central window is uniform with that below it, but the flanking windows are square-headed and of one light. Inside, the staircase has open strings, scrolled spandrels, plain balusters and moulded mahogany handrails.

(24) HOUSE AND SHOP, No. 24, appears externally to be of the late 19th century but it retains, inside, two intersecting beams with chamfered edges, probably of the 18th century.

(25) HOUSE AND SHOP, No. 14, is three-storeyed with brick walls and slated roofs. It is of the late 18th century and has a W. front of three bays, defined in the upper storeys by four Tuscan pilasters, each with an isolated architrave and a triglyph frieze; above is a continuous cornice with an open pediment at the centre. The sashed windows are square-headed, except for the middle window of the third storey which has a round head.

(26) HOUSE AND SHOP, No. 10, is three-storeyed and has brick walls and slated roofs; it dates from c. 1820. The W. front is symmetrical and of three bays.

(27) HOUSE AND SHOP, No. 8, is three-storeyed and has brick walls with ashlar dressings and a slated roof; it dates from c. 1820. In the W. front, of two bays, the shop-window and doorway have elliptical heads; the upper storeys have square-headed sashed windows. Reset below the sill of the shop window is a fragment of stonework, perhaps of the 14th century, with eleven trefoil-headed recesses.

(28) CORRIDOR, in No. 6, with walls of squared rubble and with a barrel-vaulted roof, extends eastwards, underground, from the cellar of a modern shop and ends at a 16th-century stone archway with a chamfered four-centred head.

(29) HOUSE AND SHOP, of two storeys with rendered walls and a slated roof, dates from the mid 19th century. The S. front is of five bays, the three bays on the W. comprising the shop-front.

(30) THE GROSVENOR HOTEL, three-storeyed, with rendered walls and slated roofs, dates from c. 1800. The E. front is symmetrical and of five bays, with the three bays in the centre projecting in the two upper storeys and supported on six Tuscan columns. The middle bay of the projection stands slightly in advance of the other two and has a pediment; in the second storey all three bays have large sashed windows.

(31) HOUSES AND SHOPS, No. 13, are of two and of three storeys and have timber-framed walls, in part rendered, and tiled roofs. The two-storeyed southern part of the range is of 17th-century origin, much altered and with a few reset 18th-century features. The three-storeyed building on the N. is of the 19th century.

BELL STREET AND LANES ADJACENT ON S. AND E.

(32) COTTAGE, No. 16 Bell Street, is of two storeys with rendered walls and a thatched roof; it dates from the 18th century.

(33) COTTAGES, Nos. 18 and 20, are of two storeys with attics and have walls of rubble and of brickwork, and thatched roofs; they are of 17th-century origin with 18th-century alterations. In the S. front the lower storey is of rubble and the upper storey is of red brickwork with blue-brick patterns; between the storeys is a slate-roofed pentice. Inside, one cottage has a chamfered beam with splayed stops.

(34) FRAGMENT of moulded stone, reset in a wall 130 feet E. of (33), appears to be part of a 15th-century door-jamb.

(35) COTTAGES, 44 and 46 Bell Street, are of two storeys with attics and have walls of rubble, and thatched roofs ; they are of 18th-century origin. In each tenement the lower storey has a three-light casement window in a timber frame ; the upper and attic storeys have two-light windows.

(36) HOUSE, on N. side of Barton Hill, is two-storeyed, with walls of rough ashlar and with tiled roofs ; it is of the 17th century. The S. front, rebuilt in the 18th century, is symmetrical and of three bays. Inside, one room has a large stop-chamfered beam and another room has moulded wall-plates and some 17th-century panelling.

(37) HOUSE, adjacent to the foregoing on the E., is two-storeyed and has rubble walls, in part rendered and in part tile-hung, and tiled and stone-slated roofs. The main range, facing the street, is of the 18th century ; a range adjacent on the N. is of 17th-century origin. The two-bay S. front has a reset 17th-century doorway with a chamfered four-centred head. The W. wall of the 17th-century range retains a stone window of three lights with chamfered surrounds. Inside, the ground-floor room of the S. range has moulded timber wall-plates and a chamfered beam with splayed stops ; the adjoining room in the N. range has a similar beam, and hollow-chamfered wall-plates. The close-string staircase incorporates heavy 17th-century balustrades with square newel-posts, moulded handrails and ball finials ; part of the balustrade is formed with planks profiled to represent balusters. Some rooms have nail-studded doors hung on wrought iron strap-hinges. A first-floor room has a bolection-moulded fireplace surround.

(38) BARTON HILL HOUSE is mainly of the late 19th century. The *Stables* on the E., perhaps of the first half of the 19th century, have rubble walls with ashlar dressings, and tiled roofs. The S. front of the stable range was originally symmetrical and of five bays, having a rusticated and elliptical-headed carriage entrance at the centre, and plain round-headed doorways on either side ; above the carriage entrance is a bull's-eye window and a pediment.

Reset in the S. wall of the stables and of the adjacent house are two vaulting-bosses similar to those described in monuments (9) and (46) ; in one the carving is obliterated, the other represents a flying bird. Inside, some rooms have marquetry fittings, reputedly from Fonthill Abbey.

The garden contains many fragments of mediaeval carved stonework brought from (1). At the S. end of the garden is an *Ice House* with brick walls and a barrel-vaulted roof ; it probably is of the late 18th or early 19th century.

(39) COTTAGES, two adjacent, on the S. side of Barton Hill, are two-storeyed and have rubble walls and tiled roofs ; they are of the 18th century.

(40) HOUSE, on the corner of Bell Street and Angel Lane, is two-storeyed with attics and has rubble walls and slated roofs ; it probably is of 17th-century origin, but has been much altered. The N. front is symmetrical and of three bays, with a central doorway flanked by three-light casement windows and with three two-light casement windows in the upper storey. Inside, several rooms have large beams with chamfered arrises and splayed stops. The staircase has square newel-posts with chamfered arrises ; part of it is enclosed by plank-and-muntin partitions. Several rooms have 17th-century panelling.

(41) HOUSE, No. 29 Bell Street, is two-storeyed, with rubble walls and a tiled roof ; it is of the 18th century.

(42) HOUSE, No. 19 Bell Street, is of two storeys with a basement and attics, and has walls of squared rubble and a tile-covered roof ; it dates from c. 1800. The N. front is of four bays, with a plain doorway, sashed windows, a plat-band at first-floor level and a small moulded cornice under the eaves. Reset below the cornice at the N.E. corner of the house is a 12th-century capital with acanthus leaves and angle volutes.

(43) HOUSE, adjacent to (42) on the W., is two-storeyed and has rubble walls with ashlar dressings, and slated roofs ; it is of the 17th century. The three-bay N. front has a chamfered plinth ; the ground-floor openings are modern, but in the upper storey are three stone windows of two and of three chamfered square-headed lights, with iron casements and leaded glazing. Inside, several rooms have beams with wide chamfers and shaped stops ; one stop has pierced enrichment. The roof incorporates a chamfered arch-brace.

(44) HOUSE, No. 5 Muston's Lane, is two-storeyed, with rubble walls and tiled roofs ; it is mainly of the 18th century but incorporates earlier walls. The W. front is of two bays with a central doorway. The E. elevation incorporates a 15th or 16th-century wall in which is a small doorway with a chamfered two-centred head. Inside, one room has a large chamfered beam ; another has a plank-and-muntin partition.

(45) COTTAGE, 25 yds. S. of the foregoing, is two-storeyed with brick walls and a tiled roof and dates probably from c. 1850. The E. front is symmetrical and of two bays with a central doorway.

(46) HOUSE, in Angel Lane, has ashlar walls and tiled roofs and dates from c. 1840. The W. front is symmetrical and of three bays, with a central doorway and sashed windows. Reset in the W. front are nine carved stones, probably vaulting bosses, two of them perhaps of the 12th century, the others of the 14th century. The former are decorated with crosses with leopard masks in the angles. Of the latter, one has a bearded human face, one has a shield with a letter on it, perhaps T, one has a shield-of-arms probably of Damory ; one has a shield-of-arms probably of Hawnes of Sturminster Newton, the others have shields-of-arms too mutilated for identification (see also (9) and (38)).

A pair of *Cottages*, adjacent on the W., is of the mid 19th century.

(47) COTTAGES, range of three, 30 yds. S.W. of (46), are two-storeyed and have rubble walls and thatched roofs ; they date from c. 1700.

(48) COTTAGES, two adjacent, on the S. of (47), have rubble walls and slated roofs ; they are of the 18th century.

(49) COTTAGE, adjacent to (48) on the S., has rubble walls and tiled, slated and stone-slated roofs ; it is of the 18th century. Inside, there are some lightly chamfered beams.

BLEKE STREET AND LANES ADJACENT ON S. AND E.

(50) THE ROSE AND CROWN INN, of two storeys with ashlar walls and tiled roofs, probably is of the 18th century. The W. front is symmetrical and of three bays, with a central doorway and sashed windows. Inside, some rooms have reset 17th and 18th-century panelling.

(51) THE SHIP INN, of two storeys with attics, with ashlar walls and tiled roofs, dates from the 17th century. The walls have chamfered plinths ; the casement windows are square-headed and of two and three lights with recessed, chamfered surrounds and weathered labels. The chimneystack on the

gabled S.W. wall has weathered offsets. An extension which fills the re-entrant of the L-shaped plan probably is of the 18th century ; it has details similar to those described, but the first floor is marked externally by a modillion cornice. An extension on the N.W. is of the late 18th or early 19th century. Inside, the building has been extensively altered, but a 17th-century oak staircase is preserved ; it has moulded close strings, a moulded handrail, profiled balusters formed of planks, and square newel-posts with shaped and ball-headed finials.

(52) HOUSE, adjacent to (51), is two-storeyed with ashlar walls and slated roofs. The S.E. range is of 18th-century origin, but it has been remodelled and greatly altered.

(53) 'BELLE VUE', a house of two storeys with attics, has rendered walls and slated roofs and dates from about the middle of the 19th century. Adjacent on the S.E. is a contemporary stable building with brick walls, windows with pointed heads, other openings square-headed, and oval ventilators under the eaves. Reset in the rubble wall of the stable yard are two late 12th-century respond capitals with volute decoration.

(54) THE KING'S ARMS INN, two-storeyed with rubble walls and slated roofs, is of the early 19th century.

(55) HOUSE, now a school, on the corner of Bleke Street and Parson's Pool, is of three storeys, with walls of brick and of ashlar and with slated and tile-covered roofs ; it dates from the 18th century. The main building, on Bleke Street, appears originally to have been of brick and two-storeyed, but in the second half of the 19th century the N. front was refaced in rubble and ashlar ; the third storey was added at the same time. The brick S. front is symmetrical and of five bays, with a square-headed central doorway and with tall sashed windows in the two lower storeys. The plinth is of squared rubble and the level of the first floor is indicated by a projecting brick plat-band. Inside, some rooms have 18th-century panelling and moulded wooden cornices ; a few doors retain brass rim-locks.

Adjacent on the E., an extension to the school, of two storeys with an attic, with square rubble walls and with a tiled roof, dates probably from the early 19th century. The W. front was originally symmetrical and of five bays, with segmental-headed casement windows of two and of three lights and with a segmental-headed central doorway ; this doorway has now been converted into a window.

(56) COTTAGES, two adjacent, are of two storeys with attics and have rubble walls, in part tile-hung, and tiled roofs ; they appear to be of the late 17th or early 18th century.

(57) COTTAGES, two adjacent, are of two storeys and have rough ashlar walls and tiled roofs ; they are of the 18th century.

(58) HOUSE, of two storeys with an attic, has squared rubble walls and slated roofs ; it dates probably from the latter part of the 18th century. Inside, one room has a fireplace surround with simple *carton pierre* enrichment.

(59) HOUSE, of two storeys with attics and basement, has rough ashlar walls and tiled roofs. It is mainly of the late 18th century, but it appears to retain elements of an earlier building, perhaps of the 17th century ; these include a reset weathered and hollow-chamfered string-course, and basement windows with chamfered stone surrounds.

(60) HOUSE, of two storeys with rendered walls above an ashlar plinth, and with rusticated ashlar quoins, is of the early 19th century. The symmetrical three-bay W. front has sashed windows and a central doorway.

(61) HOUSE, of two storeys with squared rubble walls and tiled and stone-slated roofs, is of the 18th century.

(62) COTTAGE, of two storeys with rubble walls and a thatched roof, is of the 18th century.

(63) COTTAGE, of one storey with an attic, has walls of rubble and brick, and thatched roofs ; it is of the 18th century.

(64) COTTAGE AND SHOP, of two storeys with rubble walls, partly rendered, and with slated roofs, is perhaps of the 17th century ; it has been extensively modernised and the only early feature to remain visible is a large rubble chimneybreast.

(65) COTTAGES, range of three, are of two storeys and have rubble walls and thatched and tiled roofs. The two tenements on the W. are of the 18th century, that on the E. is of the early 19th century.

(66) COTTAGE, of one storey with an attic, has rubble walls and a thatched roof ; it probably is of the 18th century.

(67) HOUSE, of two storeys, with walls of rubble and brickwork and with slated roofs, is of the early 18th century.

GOLD HILL

Gold Hill is a steep lane connecting High Street with St. James's Street (Plate 64). On the W. it is flanked by a high stone wall (75), and on the E. by a number of cottages. Unless otherwise described the cottages are of the 18th century and are two-storeyed, with rubble walls and tiled roofs ; the plans generally are of class S.

(68) COTTAGE, No. 8, has a wide ledge in the W. wall at the level of the first floor, suggesting that it was originally single-storeyed ; the roof is partly stone-slated.

(69) COTTAGES, two adjacent, Nos. 9 and 10, are similar to (68), but the W. fronts have recently been rebuilt.

(70) COTTAGE. No. 11 is contemporary with the two foregoing monuments, but larger, having a class-T plan.

(71) COTTAGE, No. 12, is probably of the early 18th century. The W. doorway has a cambered stone head with a chamfer which continues on the jambs.

(72) COTTAGE, No. 13, is probably of the 17th century since the front wall is continuous with that of (73).

(73) HOUSE, now two cottages, Nos. 14 and 15, has a thatched roof, but the S. gable has been heightened in brickwork and shows that the roof-pitch was formerly less steep ; the original roof-covering may have been of tiles or of stone-slates. Inside, some rooms have deeply chamfered beams and it is reported that one room has a fireplace with an 'arched' stone surround, now hidden. The building may be of 17th-century origin.

(74) COTTAGE, No. 17, is probably of the late 17th century, but much altered. The original building, with a class-S plan, was extended on the N. and S. in the 19th century ; the W. front has been rebuilt in brickwork.

(75) STONE WALL, bounding Gold Hill on the W., is largely of ashlar (Plate 64). Although repaired and rebuilt in several places, much of it dates from the late 14th or early 15th century and it probably formed part of the boundary of the Abbey land. It is about 130 yds. in length and, where the height is

greatest, some 35 ft. from ground to coping. The part which stands nearest the bottom of Gold Hill has been rebuilt, but original material appears to have been reused. Towards the top of the hill the original masonry is preserved, with buttresses of two and of three weathered stages, with chamfered plinths and hollow-chamfered drip-moulds ; the buttresses are set at intervals of about 12 ft. ; supplementing them are later buttresses with inclined faces, probably of the 19th century. Between the original buttresses the bays of the wall have weathered plinths and string-courses, stepped in correspondence with the hill. About half-way up the hill there is a blocked round-headed doorway. Near the top of the hill the wall is strengthened by an additional thickness of finely-jointed masonry which brings the wall-face almost to the same plane as the buttresses.

CASTLE HILL

CASTLE, see Monument (138).

(76) CASTLE HILL HOUSE, of two storeys with attics and cellars, has walls of coursed rubble, and tiled roofs (Plate 28) ; it dates from the end of the 18th century. The E. front is symmetrical and of three bays ; at the centre on the ground floor is a square-headed doorway with a segmental hood enriched with dentils, and scrolled brackets ; on each side are Palladian windows with Tuscan pilasters, dentil cornices and moulded archivolts. The first floor has three sashed windows with plain architraves and keystones ; above is a moulded cornice and a plain parapet. Inside, the house has been extensively altered for conversion to a hospital, but a plain 18th-century staircase with a moulded mahogany handrail survives. The plan is of class U.

(77) OX HOUSE, of two storeys with attics and cellars, has walls of ashlar and of rubble, and tiled roofs ; it is of the late 16th or early 17th century and still retains some original features although recently modernised ; the plan is of class T, with a wing at the rear.

The S. front, symmetrical and of three bays, has a chamfered plinth and a weathered and hollow-chamfered first-floor

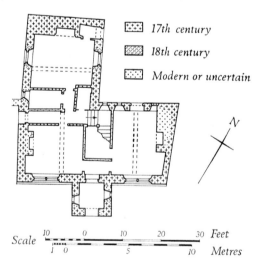

17th century

18th century

Modern or uncertain

N

Scale
10   0   10   20   30 Feet
1   0   5   10 Metres

string-course. The porch at the centre is two-storeyed, but the upper storey is probably secondary ; the string-course does not continue on the walls of the porch. The windows of the S. front are uniform in both storeys ; each now consists of two sashed lights separated by a hollow-chamfered mullion, but it is evident that originally there were four casement lights in each window. The first-floor windows have weathered labels with plain stops. The porch has modern openings in both storeys ; a blocked doorway in the E. side may have been the original entrance. The E. and W. walls of the S. range are gabled and at the apex of each gable is an ashlar chimneystack with a moulded coping. Rubble in the lower part of each E. and W. wall, as opposed to ashlar in the upper part, suggests that originally there were contiguous single-storeyed houses. The N. elevation of the range has stone casement windows with hollow-chamfered surrounds, and a doorway with a moulded four-centred head with continuous jambs. In the E. and W. walls of the N. wing are sashed windows of the late 18th century ; adjacent to that on the E. is an original doorway with a moulded four-centred head and continuous jambs. The gabled N. wall of the wing has a two-light stone window on the first floor ; in the gable is a similar attic window.

Inside, the doorway within the porch is uniform with that of the N. wing ; it has an original door of nail-studded oak planks, divided vertically into two parts, hinged together, and with ornate original wrought-iron fittings. The small inner vestibule has a plank-and-muntin partition with chamfered and beaded muntins ; similar partitions separate the staircase from the E. and W. rooms. The kitchen, on the E., has a ceiling beam with ovolo mouldings and a blocked open fireplace with a moulded timber bressummer with a raised centre. The W. room has a similar ceiling beam, resting, at the N. end, on a chamfered and beaded oak post. The oak stairs have closed strings, chamfered and beaded newel-posts with turned finials, turned balusters and moulded handrails. The parlour in the N. wing has a ceiling beam similar to those in the S. range. The stone fireplace surround has a moulded four-centred head and continuous jambs ; above is a plain fascia and a moulded stone cornice. The room is lined with early 17th-century oak panelling in five heights, with plain panels, beaded styles and rails, a frieze of carved panels alternating with brackets, and a moulded cornice. On either side of the stone fireplace are fluted oak pilasters with Ionic capitals ; the overmantel has panels carved with arabesques alternating with coupled half-columns ; at the top of the overmantel is a frieze continuous with that of the wall panelling, but more richly carved.

On the first floor, the partitions generally are of plank-and-muntin construction, chamfered and beaded. The E. chamber has a fireplace with a moulded square-headed stone surround. The chamber in the N. wing has a stone fireplace surround and oak panelling on the walls, both nearly uniform with those of the parlour below. The plaster ceiling has moulded margins and foliate enrichments.

The cellar of the N. wing contains a fireplace. A shallow sinking in the floor may be the blocked opening to a cistern.

(Extensively altered, 1965.)

(78) HOUSE, of two storeys, with ashlar walls and slated roofs, is of the mid 19th century. The E. front is symmetrical and of three bays, with a central doorway and with uniform sashed windows in both storeys.

(79) HOUSES, two adjacent, are two-storeyed and have ashlar walls and tiled roofs ; they are of the early 19th century. The W. house contains some reset 17th-century oak panelling.

(80) ST. JOHN'S COTTAGE, house, of two storeys with ashlar walls and tiled roofs, dates from the first half of the 19th century; it is said to contain material salvaged from Fonthill. The porch in the E. front has a reset doorway of *c.* 1800 with a moulded four-centred head and continuous jambs, also two recesses with surrounds similar to that of the doorway, trefoil-headed stone-panelled reveals, and a moulded stone cornice. A ground-floor room has a reset marble fireplace surround with a wooden overmantel of heavily moulded panelling under a pediment on which is carved the date 1600; the walls have reset 17th-century panelling, in one place inscribed 'ID 1620'. Another room has a stone fireplace surround of *c.* 1800 with cinquefoil-headed stone-panelled enrichment.

(81) 'EDWARDSTOWE', house, of two storeys with rubble walls and tiled roofs, comprises a three-roomed class-F house of *c.* 1500 together with two 18th-century cottages, one at each end of the original range, all combined as one dwelling. The N. front of the original range has modern square-headed casement windows in each storey; on the ground floor one of these windows replaces a former doorway; in the upper storey are two original stone windows of three square-headed lights

it has plain square-headed openings with slightly projecting keystones, and an oval datestone over the central doorway.

(84) COTTAGE, of two storeys, with rubble walls and thatched roofs, is of the late 18th century. Reset in the E. quoin of the N. front is an early 12th-century fragment comprising two small shafts with cushion capitals and moulded bases.

(85) COTTAGES, two adjacent, on the corner of Bimport and Magdalene Lane, are of two storeys with rubble walls and slated roofs; they are of the late 18th or early 19th century.

(86) COTTAGES, pair, of two storeys with rendered fronts and tiled roofs, are of the early 19th century.

(87) PRIMARY SCHOOL, single-storeyed, with squared rubble walls and a slated roof, dates from about the middle of the 19th century.

(88) SCHOOL, immediately S. of the foregoing, is largely of the early 19th century, but appears to incorporate fragmentary mediaeval walls. On the E. is a late 14th or early 15th-century window of one light with an ogee head with trefoil cusping, now blocked. A large stone in the gable above the doorway is carved with the badge of the Grosvenor family, a garb.

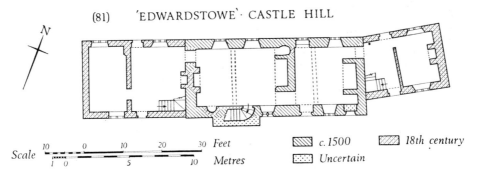

(81) 'EDWARDSTOWE'· CASTLE HILL

N

Scale 　10　　0　　10　　20　　30　*Feet*
　　　　1　0　　　　5　　　　10　*Metres*

▨ *c. 1500*　　▨ *18th century*
▨ *Uncertain*

and one of two lights; the other openings have modern casements. The S. front retains two original doorways with chamfered four-centred heads and continuous jambs; that on the E. is blocked. Near the middle of the S. front is a stone window of two square-headed lights, recently restored; adjacent is a projection of uncertain date containing the stairs. Inside, the original class-F plan has been modified by the removal of the partition between the two western ground-floor rooms, and of that on the E. of the through-passage; their position is indicated by beams with mortices for former muntins. The chimneybreast of the central fireplace has a chamfered wooden bressummer with a raised centre and chamfered stone jambs. The house contains some reset plank-and-muntin partitions and also an 18th-century shell-headed niche with shaped shelves. In the range of *c.* 1500 the original roof is partly preserved; it has cambered tie-beam trusses, two rows of stout purlins, and curved windbraces. The 18th-century cottages have no notable features.

(82) COTTAGES, two adjacent, are two-storeyed and have rubble walls and tiled roofs. They are of the late 18th or early 19th century.

(83) COTTAGE, of two storeys, with squared rubble walls and tiled roofs, appears to be of the late 17th century. In the S. front, partly hidden by later buildings, are casement windows of two and of three square-headed lights with hollow-chamfered stone surrounds. The N. front was rebuilt in 1750;

(89) ABBEY HOUSE, of two storeys with attics and cellars, has walls of ashlar and squared rubble, and slate-covered roofs. It incorporates elements of an early 17th-century building, but in its present state appears to be largely of the 18th century and later. The N. front, originally the entrance front, is of five bays and was formerly symmetrical, with a central doorway and with large sashed windows in both storeys; some of the windows have now been blocked and the former doorway has become a window. The level of the first floor is marked by a plat-band and the top of the façade has a modillion cornice and a parapet. The former E. elevation is masked by a two-storeyed 19th-century extension, polygonal in plan. The S. elevation has a large projecting bay containing the stairs; the lower part probably is of the early 17th century. Further W. is a small 17th-century basement window.

Inside, the W. room of the main range has a modelled plaster ceiling of uncertain date, with four segmental panels surrounding a circular centre panel. The segmental panels are enriched with fruit, flowers and leaves growing out of sinuous tendrils, in the style of the 17th century; the centre panel has an 18th-century flavour. The E. room has an open fireplace with a moulded square-headed stone surround. The staircase is of the early 18th century and has cut strings, scroll spandrels, vase-and-column balusters and column-shaped newel-posts. The plaster ceiling of the staircase hall has a rich cornice with dentil and egg-and-dart mouldings.

Built into the walls of the house and garden are numerous

carved stones, some probably from the nearby abbey church (1) and others from mediaeval tombs ; noteworthy is a late 13th-century stone coffin-lid with a moulded and hollow-chamfered margin, and a raised cross composed of intersecting circles.

(90) COTTAGE, of two storeys with attics, has rubble walls and thatched roofs ; it probably is of the 18th century and has a symmetrical S. front of two bays with a central doorway. The plan is of class S, with service rooms added on the N.

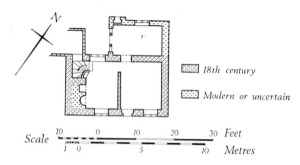

Scale 10 0 10 20 30 Feet
1 0 5 10 Metres

☒ 18th century

▦ Modern or uncertain

ST. JAMES'S AND ALCESTER

(91) LAYTON HOUSE, of two storeys with cellars, has squared rubble walls and tiled roofs. The house was built c. 1800 and was enlarged and much altered in the second half of the 19th century ; the plan of the original building probably was of class T. The S. front of the main block was symmetrical and of three bays, with large sashed windows on the ground floor and with slightly smaller windows above ; several of these openings have since been modified. A service wing extends to the E., its S. front set back from that of the main range. A late 19th-century range stands on the N. of the original building and masks the original N. front.

(92) HOLYROOD FARM (86372226), house, of two storeys with attics, has ashlar walls and slate-covered roofs ; it is of the second half of the 17th century. The symmetrical E. front has a plain plinth and a weathered and hollow-chamfered first-floor string-course. The windows in both storeys are of two

SHAFTESBURY

HOLYROOD FARM HOUSE

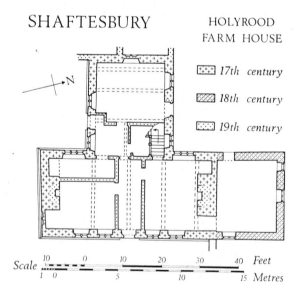

▦ 17th century

☒ 18th century

▦ 19th century

Scale 10 0 10 20 30 40 Feet
1 0 5 10 15 Metres

square-headed lights with recessed and chamfered stone surrounds and chamfered mullions. The central doorway has a chamfered head with a raised centre, and chamfered jambs. The gabled S. wall of the E. range has a string-course continuous with that of the E. front and a similar string-course at attic level ; two-light windows occur in all three storeys. In the W. wing and on the W. side of the E. range the string-courses continue, and the windows and doorways are as before. A single-storeyed addition at the N. end of the E. range is of the 18th century.

Inside, all partitions are of the 19th century, the chamfered ceiling beams have been reset and the original ground plan is lost ; it is likely to have been a variant of class T. The original staircase survives, though not certainly in situ ; it has moulded close strings, turned balusters, square newel-posts with ball finials, and heavy moulded handrails ; the stairwell is lined with oak panelling with beaded rails and stiles.

About 30 yds. N. of the farmhouse is a 19th-century outbuilding with brick walls with ashlar dressings and with a slated roof. The doorways in the E. side have elliptical heads.

(93) HOUSE, of two storeys with attics and cellars, has squared rubble walls and slate-covered roofs ; it dates from early in the 19th century. The S. front is nearly symmetrical and of three bays, with a central doorway flanked by casement windows of two and of three lights, three corresponding windows in the upper storey, and basement windows of two lights. The long timber lintel and vertical joints in the stonework show that the three-light ground-floor window on the E. of the doorway was originally of five or six lights.

(94) HOUSE, with rubble walls with some ashlar dressings and tiled roofs, is of 17th-century origin, but has been much altered. The western third of the range, now used as a garage and store-room, has walls of chequered ashlar and rubble. In the eastern two-thirds the masonry appears to have been rebuilt, but the S. elevation contains two original stone windows with chamfered stone surrounds ; a similar window of one light occurs in the upper storey of the gabled W. wall. Inside, the eastern part of the house contains, on the W., a ground-floor room with a deeply chamfered beam and corresponding wall-plates. The western part has been gutted, but visible on the W. wall are the outlines of a large open fireplace and an adjacent staircase, both removed. A stone doorway with a chamfered four-centred head and continuous jambs, communicating with the adjacent room in the eastern part of the house, is blocked with rough rubble masonry. Adjacent to the house on the W. is a pair of 18th-century gate piers with ball finials.

(95) BARN, with rubble walls and tiled roofs, is of 18th-century origin.

(96) HOUSE, of two storeys, with rendered walls with ashlar quoins and dressings and with slate-covered roofs, dates from c. 1800. The N. front is symmetrical and of three bays, with a central doorway in a rusticated ashlar surround ; above the doorway is a sashed window of three lights and on either side, in both storeys, are single sashed windows with plain ashlar architraves and simple keystones. The doorway has an ogee-shaped iron porch.

(97) HOUSE, of two storeys, with ashlar walls and tiled roofs, dates from the first half of the 19th century. The S. front is symmetrical and of three bays.

(98) COTTAGES, range of three, are two-storeyed and have rubble walls and tiled roofs ; they date from the first half of the 19th century.

(99) Poor Law Institution, of two storeys with ashlar walls and slated roofs, was built in 1838 (*Architectural Magazine*, Dec. 1838, 622). (*Recently demolished.*)

(100) St. James's Old Rectory, of two storeys and attics, with walls of ashlar and rubble and with tiled and slate-covered roofs, is probably of 18th-century origin, but it has been extensively altered. In the main S. range the three-bay S. front is of ashlar, with a plat-band at first-floor level; in the lower storey the former central opening has been walled up and those of the lateral bays have been enlarged to make french windows; in the upper storey each bay retains a sashed window. A subsidiary W. range with rubble walls was perhaps originally a separate house, earlier than the S. range. Service rooms on the N., occupying the angle formed by the W. and S. ranges, are of the late 19th century. Inside, the house has been extensively remodelled. In the S. range, which originally had a class-T plan, the former entrance passage and staircase have been abolished and the two principal rooms have been correspondingly enlarged, a vestibule and staircase being built on the N. and the main entrance being transferred to the E. Plasterwork and joinery throughout the house appear to be of *c.* 1840, presumably the date of alteration of the plan.

(101) Houses, two adjacent, formerly a school, are two-storeyed and have ashlar walls and tiled roofs; they date from *c.* 1850. Doorways and window openings have weathered. labels with returned stops; the gables have shaped kneelers.

(102) House, of two storeys, with walls of squared rubble and with roof-covering of corrugated iron, is of early 17th-century origin. The S. front has four bays; in each storey the western bay comprises a projecting stone window of five square-headed lights with hollow-chamfered surrounds under a weathered label; the adjacent bay has a square-headed doorway with a chamfered surround and shaped stops; the two eastern bays have ground-floor windows of four and of three lights, and first-floor windows of two lights, all similar in detail to the projecting window on the W. The gabled E. wall has been heightened and formerly was steeper than at

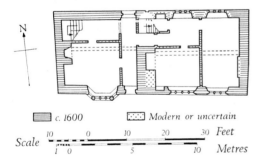

c. 1600 Modern or uncertain

Scale 10 0 10 20 30 Feet
1 0 5 10 Metres

present; the chimneystack at the apex is modern. The N elevation has two modern windows in the lower storey and a small original loop with a two-centred head, now blocked; it is probable that the loop formerly gave light to a stair. In the upper storey are two three-light stone windows. The W. wall is masked by the adjacent house. Inside, the plan appears to be a variant of class F; instead of service rooms on the side of the through-passage opposite to the central living room, we have here a parlour. The service rooms were probably on the E. of the centre room, where there now is an original plank-and-muntin partition with two doorways (one blocked).

(103) House, of two storeys, with walls of ashlar and coursed rubble and with slate-covered roofs, is of 17th-century origin, but much altered. The S. front is approximately symmetrical and of three bays, with a central doorway and with sashed windows in both storeys of the lateral bays; there is no window above the doorway, but a mezzanine window occurs between the doorway and the windows on the E. The E. gable has a stone window of two square-headed lights. The N. wall has a large chimneystack in the eastern part. Near the N.E. corner is a doorway with a moulded four-centred head and continuous jambs; further to the W. in the N. wall are square-headed casement windows with hollow-chamfered surrounds. Inside, the house has been modernised, but the roof retains some original timbers.

(104) House, of two storeys with attics, with rubble and ashlar walls and with tiled roofs, dates from late in the 18th century; an extension on the E. is of the 19th century. The symmetrical three-bay S. front has a central doorway under a flat hood on shaped brackets, and sashed windows in both storeys.

(105) House, two-storeyed, with ashlar walls and tiled roofs dates from the 18th century. The S. front has a plat-band at first-floor level and a moulded ashlar cornice at the eaves. The façade is symmetrical and of three bays. In the lower storey a square-headed doorway is flanked by plain sashed windows; in the upper storey a small elliptical central bull's-eye window is flanked by two sashed windows and by two blind lights, making five features altogether, as against three in the lower storey.

(106) Old Pump Court comprises a group of cottages, of the late 18th and early 19th century, arranged in a quadrangle on the N. side of St. James's street. All the tenements are two-storeyed, with rubble walls and thatched or tiled roofs. At the centre of the courtyard, a small stone aedicule with a chamfered plinth and a pyramidal capstone contains a hand operated water-pump.

(107) Friends' Meeting House, now disused, is of the mid 18th century; it has ashlar walls and formerly had stone-slated roofs, but is now roofless. The S. front is symmetrical and of three bays, with a square-headed central doorway and, on either side, square-headed sashed windows under semicircular relieving arches; above the doorway is a round-headed window.

In addition to the monuments described above, St. James's Street and the lanes adjacent to it on the N. and W. contain seventy-four late 18th or early 19th-century houses and cottages, of two storeys or of one storey with an attic, with walls of coursed rubble and with roof-coverings of thatch, tile or slate (Plate 29). The plans of the cottages generally are of class S; locations are shown on the town plan on p. 56. Typical of the group is No. 72 St. James's Street, on the S. side of the street, facing the E. range of (106); it has a symmetrical N. front of three bays, with a central doorway flanked by three-light casement windows, and corresponding two-light windows in the upper storey.

EAST SHAFTESBURY

(108) Cottage, at the N.W. end of Salisbury Street, is of two storeys with cellar and attics; it has brick and rubble walls and tiled and stone-slated roofs. It dates probably from the 17th century but has been much altered from its original state. The N.E. front and the N.W. gable are of the 19th

century ; the gabled S.E. wall is of rubble and perhaps includes some original material ; the S.W. elevation has been refaced in brickwork and tiles. Inside, some rooms have intersecting ceiling beams, now cased. The cellar has a stone window of two square-headed lights with chamfered and hollow-chamfered surrounds.

(109) Cottages, three adjacent, Nos. 5, 7 and 9 Coppice Street, are two-storeyed and have rubble walls and slated and thatched roofs ; they are of c. 1800.

(110) Cottage, 30 yds. E. of the foregoing, is two-storeyed, with rubble walls and a thatched roof ; it is of the second half of the 18th century.

(111) Cottage, No. 15 Coppice Street, is two-storeyed, with ashlar walls and a tiled roof ; it is of the 18th century.

(112) Wall, on the N. of Coppice Street, about 100 yds. long and 5 ft. high, is of ashlar and squared rubble. Incised on one stone is a cross and the inscription ' Parish Boundary 1772 '.

(113) Cottages, eight, of mid and late 18th-century date, are located in the N.W. part of Salisbury Street in the positions shown on the town plan (p. 56). They are two-storeyed, with brick, rubble and rendered walls and with tiled or slated roofs. Also in the N.W. part of Salisbury Street and shown on the same plan are eighteen dwellings of the first half of the 19th century ; of them, one group forms a range of ten dwellings, another a range of four, and another a range of three.

(114) House, of two storeys with an attic, has rendered walls and slate-covered roofs and appears to be of the second half of the 18th century ; it was partly refronted in the 19th century and has casement windows with moulded labels.

(115) Almshouses, founded in 1655, have been rebuilt and in their present form appear to be of the first half of the 19th century. Reset in the central gable is a stone tablet with a shield-of arms of Spiller of Laleham and an inscription now largely indecipherable ; it probably is of 1805 (Hutchins III, 44).

(116) Cottage, No. 53 Salisbury Street, is two-storeyed, with rubble walls heightened in brickwork, and with a tiled roof. The date 1791 roughly carved above the doorway is probably the date of erection.

(117) Cottages, two adjacent, immediately S.E. of the foregoing, are two-storeyed, with rubble walls and slated roofs and are probably of the 18th century.

(118) Cann Rectory, of two storeys, with walls of squared rubble and ashlar and with slate-covered roofs, is of the 18th century, with later additions on the S.E. The N.E. front is of four bays, with sashed windows with moulded architraves and plain keystones. The second window from the E. was originally the doorway and has a rusticated architrave and pediment. The N.W. elevation has a gable with a plain coping on shaped kneelers. The S.W. elevation is rendered. Inside, some rooms have fielded panelling. The stables on the S.E. of the house are probably contemporary.

(119) Cann Cottage, three-storeyed, with rendered walls and slated roofs, is probably of c. 1800.

(120) The Mount (86892266), of two storeys, with ashlar walls and slated roofs, is of the first half of the 19th century.

(121) Cornley Villa (86972261), of two storeys, with rendered walls and slated roofs, is mainly of the late 19th century, but it incorporates an older building, possibly of 17th-century origin. Inside, a circular staircase has timber treads radiating from an octagonal newel-post.

(122) School (87032259), with ashlar walls and slated roofs, was built in 1845. It has large windows with mullioned and transomed square-headed lights and, at the centre of the S.W. front, a doorway, now blocked, with a two-centred head. The inscription 'National School 1845' is painted above the doorway.

(123) Belmont House (87142261), now an hotel, is of two storeys with attics and has ashlar walls and slated roofs ; it dates from the late 18th or early 19th century. The S. front is symmetrical and of three bays, with a first-floor plat-band and a moulded cornice. The middle bay projects slightly and continues in the attic storey, being capped with a low gable. The central doorway has a round head, jambs with composite capitals, pilasters and free-standing columns with similar capitals, and a barrel-vaulted porch. The side bays of the lower storey have late 19th-century three-sided bow windows. In the second storey the side bays have plain sashed windows and the middle bay has a large segmental-headed window. The E. and W. elevations have each three bays of plain sashed windows. The building was extended to the N. late in the 19th century and the interior has been entirely remodelled.

(124) The Half Moon Inn (87192248), of two storeys, with rubble walls and tiled roofs, is probably of 18th-century origin, but it has been modernised and much altered.

(125) Toll House (87222250), standing in the fork of the roads to Salisbury and Melbury Abbas, is of two storeys, with ashlar walls and slated roofs, and dates from about the middle of the 19th century. The windows generally have square-headed lights with chamfered stone surrounds and moulded labels. Projecting from the N. and S. elevations are small bow windows.

Enmore Green

(126) Pensbury House (23558634), on the northern outskirts of the town, is of two storeys with attics and has ashlar walls and slated mansard roofs ; the S. part of the house dates from the middle of the 18th century ; The N. range is of the 19th century.

In the 18th-century range the W. front is symmetrical and of five bays, the central bay being accentuated by a pedimented projection ; the first floor is marked by a plat-band and above the second storey is a cornice and parapet. The round-headed doorway at the centre of the W. front has a stone surround with architrave, pilasters, entablature and pediment of the Roman-Doric order. The sashed windows in both storeys have moulded stone architraves. The plat-band and cornice continue on the S. elevation ; reset in the parapet is a date-stone of 1654. The E. elevation is asymmetrical ; near the centre it has a pedimented projecting bay, with a square-headed doorway with a moulded architrave under an open pediment which rests on scrolled consoles, all of stone. Above and to the N. are sashed windows similar to those of the W. front ; the plat-band, cornice and parapet continue, as before.

Inside, the drawing room has an 18th-century fireplace surround with scrolled cheek-pieces, an eared and enriched architrave, a richly carved frieze with acanthus scrollwork and flower festoons, and an enriched cornice. Some rooms have plain 18th-century panelling.

(127) Drinking Fountain (85952340), near the junction of the roads from Gillingham and Sherborne, comprises an ashlar wall with a stone recess with a four-centred head, and a cast-iron spout and trough ; it is dated 1844.

(128) WALL, flanking Tout Hill, includes ashlar and squared rubble masonry of mediaeval origin. For part of its length the wall on the S. side of the road has a chamfered and roll-moulded plinth, stepped to follow the slope of the ground. The rebuilding of another part of this wall is recorded in an inscription dated 1817. A much eroded 12th-century capital has been reset in the wall on the N. side of the road.

(129) HOUSE, of two storeys, has walls of rubble and brickwork, in part rendered, and tiled roofs. The mid 19th-century N.W. range is added to an earlier building, probably of the 18th century. At the N.E. end of the earlier range is a large projecting chimneybreast with several weathered set-backs.

(130) COTTAGES, two adjacent, are two-storeyed, with ashlar walls and tiled and thatched roofs ; they are of the early 19th century.

(131) THE FOUNTAIN INN, of two storeys with squared rubble walls and tiled roofs, comprises a small 18th-century house and a larger addition of 1816 on the E. (*Salisbury Journal*, 23 Dec.). The addition has a symmetrical N. front of two bays with a central doorway, and sashed windows in both storeys. The earlier house also has a symmetrical two-bay N. front with a central doorway, but the windows are casements. Adjacent on the W. is a long stable range. Inside, one room of the W. house has a shell-headed niche.

(132) HOUSE, of two storeys with ashlar walls and tiled roofs, is probably of *c.* 1800.

(133) COTTAGE, of one storey with attics, has walls of rubble and brickwork, in part rendered, and a thatched roof ; the plan is of class J. It is of the late 17th century.

(134) COTTAGES (85302322), range of four, of two storeys with rubble walls and tiled roofs, are of the early 19th century.

(135) COTTAGES (85032332), pair, of two storeys with ashlar walls and slated roofs, are of the early 19th century.

(136) COTTAGES (85812335), two adjacent, of two storeys with rubble walls and thatched and tiled roofs, are of the early 19th century.

(137) HOUSE (86412367), of two storeys with ashlar walls and a thatched roof, is of late 17th-century origin. The S. front is symmetrical and of three bays, with a central doorway flanked by three-light casement windows, and corresponding two-light windows in the upper storey. A moulded string-course traverses the S. front a little below first-floor level. In the 18th century the building was divided into two tenements, and two doorways were made in place of the original entrance. Recently the house has been remodelled as a single dwelling.

MEDIAEVAL AND LATER EARTHWORKS

THE SAXON BOROUGH has no positively identifiable remains. Asser's record that the Abbey was established ‘juxta orientalem portam Sceftesbury’ (*De rebus gestis Alfredi*, 98, 2) indicates that the borough lay westwards from the abbey church, and military considerations confirm such a location, for it is there that the steep-sided Greensand spur would be most easily defended. Seven hundred hides (Birch, 1335—the oldest text omits the entry) point to a wall 960 yards long (Robertson, *A–S. Charters*, 246–9). The borough probably occupied the end of the spur with a rampart across the neck, perhaps on the line of Magdalene Lane. A slight but continuous rise in the level of the ground immediately N.E. of this lane may be a vestige of the rampart. Camden records ‘a tradition that an old citie stood upon the place which is called the castle greene’ (*Britannia*, 215).

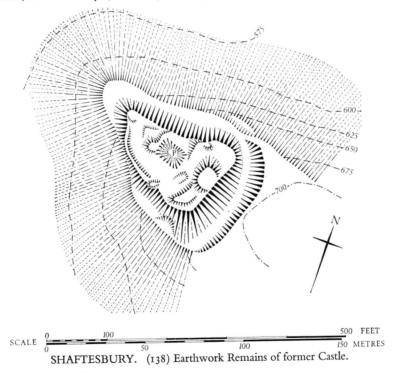

SCALE
0 ... 100 ... 500 FEET
0 ... 50 ... 100 ... 150 METRES

SHAFTESBURY. (138) Earthwork Remains of former Castle.

(138) DITCH AND PLATFORM (856228), remains of a former castle on the N.W. extremity of the Greensand promontory, occupy a small triangular spur a little below the 700 ft. contour. To the E. the ground rises to the plateau of the presumed borough ; elsewhere it drops precipitously (plan, p. 75).

In 1947–9 the site was systematically examined by trenching (*Dorset Procs.*, 71 (1949), 54–7). Fragments of three tripod pitchers of the 12th or 13th century, a small bronze chain, and a 'cut' halfpenny of Stephen's reign were found ; a paved floor of the early 18th century came to light, but no trace of any other structure. The slender evidence available suggests that the castle was a temporary fortification dating from the period of the 12th-century civil war.

The site is overgrown and disturbed by former excavations ; several old trenches still lie open ; near the middle is a rectangular pond (P) about 10 ft. deep. A crescent-shaped ditch up to 65 ft. wide and 15 ft. deep separates the spur from the higher ground on the E. Earthworks within the area include a low bank on the S.W., a roughly rectangular mound about 1½ ft. high on the E., and some roughly rectangular platforms of varying size ; the triangular area is artificially scarped above the natural slopes of the spur.

(139) BUILDING FOUNDATIONS (85752281), discovered in 1947 (*Dorset Procs.*, 71 (1949), 54–7), lie about 150 yds. E. of the castle (138). They comprise fragmentary footings, 2 ft. wide and some 9 ins. high, of poor stone buildings ; the best preserved of these were circular and some 13 ft. in diameter. Associated pottery was of the 13th century.

(140) SITE OF ST. JOHN'S CHURCH, some 200 yds. S.E. of (80) is an uneven area of ground in the S. part of a disused churchyard, at one time a burial ground for St. James's church, and still containing a few 18th and 19th-century monuments. St. John's parish was united with St. James's in 1446 and the church may already have been disused at that date. Hutchins (1st ed., II, 32) records marks of the foundations of a little church and chancel, visible in his time, but today there are no traces of a building.

(141) BARTON MANOR HOUSE (86752316), site, was excavated in 1951 (*Dorset Procs.*, 76 (1954), 67). The floors of two yards with associated drains were revealed ; they were of 18th-century date, but 12th and 13th-century pottery, floor-tiles and glazed ridge-tiles indicated mediaeval occupation. The manor house appears to have been the centre of a mediaeval estate which extended N. and N.W. In the 16th century the estate had gardens, paddocks, a house, a barn, an ox shed and a pinfold, in all covering 2 acres (*Survey of Lands of William, Earl of Pembroke*, ed. C. R. Stratton, Roxburghe Club, 1909, II, 502).

(142) OCCUPATION SITE (869225), with 13th and 14th-century pottery, was discovered in 1949 on the S. side of Hawkesdean Lane (*Dorset Procs.*, 71 (1949), 60).

(143) ABBEY PONDS (864226). Near the head of a wide valley, 320 yds. S.E. of (1), are the remains of fishponds belonging to the nunnery ; they are now dry, but in the middle of the 16th century they were *repleta cum piscibus vocatus carpes et tenches* (Stratton, *op. cit.*, 504). The earthworks comprise two depressions, roughly rectangular and 2 ft. to 3½ ft. deep, lying side by side ; immediately N. of the E. depression and joined to it by a narrow channel is a third depression, smaller and roughly square. Mediaeval and later pottery and other objects, found immediately W. of the depressions, are preserved in the Shaftesbury Museum (*Dorset Procs.*, 71 (1949), 67).

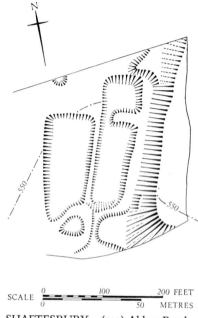

SCALE

SHAFTESBURY. (143) Abbey Ponds.

ROMAN

Coins of Commodus, Diocletian, and Constantine are reported from Barton Hill (868231) ; 'Roman pottery' found with mediaeval sherds S.S.E. of Layton House (864227) could be connected with this site (Hutchins III, 80 ; *Dorset Procs.*, LXXI (1949), 67). It is claimed that 'architectural remains of the Doric order' were found here (*W.A.M.*, VII (1862), 252).

21 SILTON (7829)

(O.S. 6 ins., ST 72 NE, ST 73 SE)

Silton covers some 1,225 acres near the N.W. extremity of the county and is divided into two parts by the R. Stour, which here flows S.E. in a broad valley. To the N.E. of the river the land is Kimmeridge Clay, about 300 ft. above sea-level ; to the S.W. the parish lies on the dip-slope of the Corallian Limestone escarpment, with somewhat broken country at altitudes between 300 ft. and 450 ft. The original settlement, mentioned in Domesday (*V.C.H., Dorset*, iii, 92), lay near the church on a low ridge between the Stour and a small tributary brook on the S.W. Feltham Farm, some ¾ m. to the N.W., existed in 1327 and was probably a secondary settlement. At present, habitation is principally in the N. and N.W. of the parish, where there are scattered cottages of the late 18th and early 19th century ; many of these dwellings were built on waste land which remained unenclosed until 1862 (Enclosure Award and Map ; O.S., 1811). This extension of settlement was probably associated with the 18th and 19th-century textile industry (see BOURTON, p. 3).

ECCLESIASTICAL

(1) THE PARISH CHURCH OF ST. NICHOLAS (Plate 62) stands near the centre of the parish. The walls are of rubble with ashlar dressings, and in places wholly ashlar-faced; the roofs are tiled. The S. arcade of the *Nave* is of the late 12th century; the *Chancel* was largely rebuilt in the 15th century; the *North Chapel*, the *West Tower*, the *South Aisle* and the *South Porch* are of the early 16th century. For a description and sketch of the church in 1820, see T. D. Powell, Topographical Collections (B.M. Add. MS. 17459), f. 121.

light window with vertical tracery. The S. wall of the chancel has, on the E., a restored 15th-century window of two cinquefoil-headed lights with vertical tracery in a two-centred casement-moulded surround. Beneath the window sill is a weathered string-course and below this the S. wall, more than 3 ft. thick, is probably of the 12th century. Further W., the S. wall of the chancel contains a restored archway, uniform and continuous with the nave arcade; the arch, two-centred and of two chamfered orders, springs from a 19th-century moulded corbel inserted in the E. respond. Piercing this respond is a rough squint to the S. aisle, with a chamfered four-centred head and continuous jambs. The chancel arch, of 1869, is two-centred and of two-chamfered orders, the inner order springing from fluted corbels.

The *North Chapel* has ashlar walls with moulded and hollow-chamfered plinths and embattled parapets with hollow-chamfered string-courses and continuous moulded coping; the string-courses have grotesque lion gargoyles at the N.W., N.E. and S.E. corners. The buttresses are of two weathered stages. Above

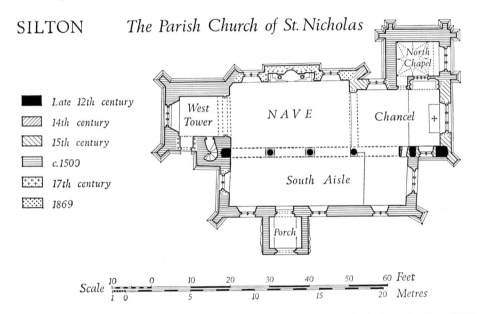

SILTON   *The Parish Church of St. Nicholas*

■ Late 12th century
▨ 14th century
▨ 15th century
▤ c.1500
⊞ 17th century
▨ 1869

West Tower
NAVE
Chancel
South Aisle
North Chapel
Porch

Scale   10 0 10 20 30 40 50 60 *Feet*
         1 0   5   10   15   20 *Metres*

The church was restored in 1869. The N. chapel and the 17th-century monument of Sir Hugh Wyndham are the most noteworthy features.

Architectural Description—The E. wall of the *Chancel* has a chamfered plinth and, at the S.E. corner, a buttress of two stages with weathered offsets. The E. window, of 1869, comprises three cinquefoil-headed lights with vertical tracery in a two-centred head. The archway to the N. chapel has a four-centred head and continuous responds decorated with stone panelling comprising moulded ribs and trefoil-headed panels set in pairs; the responds have chamfered plinths continuous with the plinth at the foot of a pierced stone screen which closes the opening. The screen was originally of six lights, but the two eastern lights have been blocked; each remaining light has a cinquefoil ogee head under open quatrefoil spandrels; the archway above the screen, no doubt originally open, has been walled up. The doorway to the N. chapel has a moulded four-centred head with continuous jambs and a chamfered four-centred rear-arch. Further W., the N. wall of the chancel has a 19th-century two-

the parapet and set back from the E. and W. wall-faces are ashlar gables with weathered copings and cross-weathered apex stones. The E. window is of three cinquefoil-headed lights under a four-centred, casement-moulded head with continuous jambs; the moulded label has square stops. The chapel has a stone fan vault in which the ribs spring from corbels carved to represent angels bearing shields. Each fan has two heights of trefoil-headed stone panelling with ogee-moulded ribbing; at the centre of the vault is a circular panel containing four roundels with quatrefoil cusping; the intervening spandrels are also cusped. To the E. the vaulting continues in the form of a four-centred arch with a ribbed and panelled soffit.

The *Nave* (Plate 6) has, at the centre of the N. wall, a recess built in 1869 to accommodate monument (1), previously in the chancel. On each side of the recess is a window with two ogee-headed lights with vertical tracery in a two-centred head. A diagonal buttress of two weathered stages at the N.E. corner of the nave appears to be of 14th-century origin. The S. side of the nave has a late 12th-century three-bay arcade, continuous with the arch on the S. of the chancel; the piers have moulded bases, cylindrical drums, fluted capitals (Plate 9) and moulded abaci.

The *South Aisle* has S.E. and S.W. buttresses of two weathered stages. The gabled E. wall contains a three-light window with a casement-moulded two-centred head and continuous jambs; the tracery is of 1869. In the gable is a fragment of mediaeval carving, perhaps a former apex stone. The S. wall has three restored windows, each of two ogee-headed lights with vertical tracery in a casement-moulded two-centred head with continuous jambs. The S. doorway has a roll-moulded and casement-moulded four-centred head with continuous jambs and run-out stops; the roll-moulding ends in miniature bases; the rear-arch is four-centred and chamfered. The W. wall has a 19th-century two-light window with a four-centred head.

The *West Tower* is of two stages, with a moulded plinth and a weathered and hollow-chamfered string-course; above is an embattled parapet with a moulded string-course with corner gargoyles and small angle pinnacles; the pinnacles are perhaps of the 17th century. The N.E., N.W. and S.W. corners have buttresses of four weathered stages; the S.E. corner has a stair turret with a weathered head just above the base of the upper stage. The tower arch is two-centred and of two chamfered orders, the outer order continuing on the responds, the inner order resting on half-round shafts with moulded bases and capitals; carved on each capital is a shield with the arms of Carent, with a crescent for difference. High up in the N. side of the lower stage is a small square-headed window. In the W. side of the lower stage is a restored three-light window with a casement-moulded two-centred head and continuous jambs. The doorway to the stair has a chamfered four-centred head and continuous jambs; adjacent on the W. is an external doorway of similar form, perhaps of the 17th century. In the top stage each face of the tower has a belfry window of two trefoil-headed lights, with a quatrefoil in a two-centred head under a moulded label; the lights are closed by perforated stone slabs.

The *South Porch* has a moulded four-centred arch with continuous jambs and a moulded square surround with a label with head stops; the spandrels have carved leaf decoration (Plate 10). Inside, on either side, are stone benches with chamfered tops.

The *Roofs* of the nave, S. aisle and S. porch are of the early 16th century, with restoration and painted enrichment of 1869. They are of wagon type, but the plaster infilling between the ribs has been removed. The principal transverse and longitudinal members are moulded and each intersection is covered by a heavy leaf boss; the wall-plates are hollow-chamfered and enriched at intervals with leaf bosses and shields. In the porch the wall-plates incorporate small attached capitals. The moulded transverse members divide the nave roof into four bays, the aisle roof into six bays, and the porch roof into two bays. The roof of the chancel is a 19th-century replica of the nave roof.

Fittings—*Bells:* five; 1st modern; 2nd inscribed 'The gift of Judge Wyndham 1657 I.L.'; 3rd inscribed 'Dominus W. Bidyck I.G. rector duo fecerunt' in Lombardic letters, probably early 15th century (John Gardener, rector 1412–33); 4th inscribed 'Anno Domini 1633 I.L.', with royal arms; 5th inscribed 'John Ellis, John Burputt C.W. Anno Domini 1702, T.K. B.F.'. *Brass:* In chancel, on screen to N. chapel, plate (9¾ ins. by 8 ins.), with inscription of Sir Hugh Wyndham, 1684, in italic lettering (Plate 14). *Chair:* of oak, modern assembly of carved 16th-century woodwork brought from elsewhere. *Chest:* for registers, of cast-iron, dated 1813. *Communion Table:* In N. chapel, of oak, with turned baluster legs and scrolled side rails, other rails plain; 17th century. *Door:* In S. doorway, with oak planks in two layers, iron strap-hinges, studs, escutcheon-plate and latch ; c. 1600.

Monuments: In nave, reset on N. wall, (1) of Sir Hugh Wyndham, Kt., Justice of the Court of Common Pleas, 1684 (Plate 65); white and grey marble monument, probably earliest known work by Nost (*Oxford History of English Art*, VIII, 250), erected in 1692, with statue of judge on gadrooned pedestal within round-headed niche, on either side mourning women (Plate 20) bearing skull and hourglass; group of figures flanked by composite columns with spiral shafts supporting segmental marble canopy and, above, three cartouches-of-arms—at centre, Wyndham impaling Woodhouse, on E., Wyndham impaling Fleming, on W., Wyndham impaling Minn; whole composition on panelled plinth with wreath, palms, scales and sword, and centre panel with epitaph. In S. aisle, on N. wall, (2) of Isaac Maggs and others of same family 1774 to 1818, white marble tablet by Osmund of Sarum; on S. wall, (3) of Dorothy (Morin) Kingeswell, 1638, stone tablet (Plate 23) with billet-moulded surround under moulded cornice, with shield-of-arms of Kingeswell impaling Morin; (4) of Samuel Davis, 1833, marble tablet in stone surround with Gothic enrichment, by Chapman of Frome; (5) of Silas Benjafield, 1843, marble tablet by Osmund of Sarum. In tower, on N. wall, (6) of John White, 1809 and others of same family, marble tablet by Osmund of Sarum. In churchyard, immediately E. of S. porch, (7) of Edward Punn, 1639, table-tomb with heavy moulded top; 2 paces from S.E. angle of S. aisle, (8) of William Boulting and others of his family, 1764–89, rectangular stone pedestal with weathered head; adjacent, (9) of Augustine Browne, 1618, table-tomb.

Piscinae: In chancel, on S. wall, with chamfered ogee-headed recess with trefoil cusping, 15th century; in N. chapel on S. wall, with chamfered four-centred recess, shelf at half height, and corbelled polygonal basin, c. 1500; in S. aisle, on S. wall, with hollow-chamfered ogee-headed recess with trefoil cusping, 15th century. *Plate:* includes silver cup of 1744 or 1746, stand-paten of same date, and stand-paten of 1722; also silver-plated flagon of c. 1800. *Sedile:* In chancel, below S. window, with hollow-chamfered and ogee-moulded square-headed surround, seat missing, much restored, 15th century. *Sundial:* on S. side of tower, rectangular stone plate with incised Roman numerals and wrought-iron gnomon, 1790. *Tables of Creed, etc.:* In chancel, on E. wall, two Purbeck marble panels with Creed and Paternoster in incised and gilded lettering, late 17th or early 18th century (Plate 23).

SECULAR

(2) BRIDGE (78093042), across the R. Stour, has a single segmental arch of squared rubble, and a rubble parapet; it probably is of the mid 19th century.

(3) BRIDGE (78772945), across the R. Stour, has two semicircular ashlar arches and brick parapet walls. An inscription in the N. parapet records that the bridge was built in 1820.

(4) THE RECTORY (78132939), 120 yds. W. of (1), is two-storeyed and has walls of ashlar and rubble, and slated roofs. The principal range is of the 18th century and there are 19th-century additions at the rear. At the centre of the S.E. front is a projecting two-storeyed gabled bay with a round-headed doorway on the ground floor, a sashed window above and a small casement window in the attic. In the lateral bays of the S.W. front the fenestration is asymmetrical and in part masked, but it is probable that the façade originally was symmetrical and of three bays. Inside, several rooms have 18th-century ceiling beams of shallow cross-section; one room has an 18th-century fireplace surround, with stone jambs with moulded panelling and a panelled and shouldered lintel shaped at the centre to represent a fluted keystone.

(5) THE ROOKERY (78703038), house, of two storeys with rubble walls and tiled roofs, appears to be of the 18th century. In the three-bay S. front the ground-floor openings are modern; the upper storey has original casement windows of three lights with two-centred heads under square labels with returned stops. Inside, the plan is of class T. The W. room has a cornice with cable and egg-and-dart mouldings; the room has been enlarged westwards in a modern addition. The E. ground-floor room has a late 18th-century chimneypiece with *carton-pierre* enrichment.

(6) MANOR FARM (78252925), house and outbuildings, is two-storeyed and has walls of ashlar and of rubble, and slated and tiled roofs. The present farmhouse is of the 19th century; it has a symmetrical S. front of ashlar, in three bays with a central doorway and with sashed windows. Adjacent on the E. is an 18th-century cottage with a rubble S. front of two bays. Further E. is a 17th-century building, presumably the former farmhouse, now used as a dairy; it has walls of coursed rubble and a centrally placed ashlar chimneystack with moulded capping.

A *Barn* with rubble walls and tiled roofs, some 30 yds. S. of the farmhouse, is probably of the 17th century. The plan is a rectangle, with doorway bays projecting N. and S. The roof has tie-beam trusses with braced collar-beams. Adjacent on the E. and S. are 18th-century farm buildings; the stables on the S. contain oak stalls with shaped finials to the partition posts.

(7) BAGMORE FARM (78613016), house, is two-storeyed and has rubble walls and tiled roofs; it dates from *c.* 1700 and is said to have been used for cloth-weaving during the 18th century. Inside, one room contains an open fireplace with a deeply chamfered and cambered oak bressummer; another room has deeply chamfered ceiling beams.

(8) WATERLOO MILL (78782948), of two storeys with lofts and substructures, presumably dates from *c.* 1815; it has walls of rubble with squared rubble quoins, and some brickwork, and is roofed with slates (Plate 31). The gabled W. wall flanks the R. Stour and contains a circular opening for the former mill-wheel shaft. A stable and carthouse adjoins the mill on the E. A contemporary *Cottage*, some 20 yds. N.E. of the mill, is two-storeyed and has rubble walls and a thatched roof. The S.E. front is of two bays with a central doorway.

(9) COTTAGE (78283059), with rubble walls and a thatched roof, was formerly two dwellings. The N. tenement is single-storeyed with an attic and dates from late in the 17th century; that on the S. is two-storeyed and was added in the 18th century. Inside, the N. room has an open fireplace with a deeply chamfered bressummer.

(10) COTTAGES (78373062), two adjacent and at rightangles to one another, are two-storeyed and have rubble walls; they are roofed partly with thatch and partly with iron. The N. tenement is of the late 17th century and was originally single-storeyed; the W. tenement was added in the 18th century. On the first floor in the S. front is a stone window of two square-headed lights.

Monuments of the late 18th and early 19th century include the following dwellings; unless described otherwise they are two-storeyed and have rubble walls, occasionally rendered, and roof-coverings of thatch, tile or iron: *Feltham Farm* (77423005), house, with a symmetrical S. front of three bays; *Card's Farm* (77953063), two adjoining cottages, now combined; *Cottages* (78533017), two adjacent, now combined; *Cottages* (78493020), two adjacent, now combined; *Cottage* (78083053); *Cottage* (78073057), originally single-storeyed, but heightened with brickwork; *Cottage* (78103008), with an approximately symmetrical W. front of three bays; *Cottages* (78023028), two adjacent; *Cottages* (78023022), two adjacent; *Cottages* (78043061), pair, now combined; *Cottages* (78193100), range of four, set in pairs, with a chimneystack at each end of the range and with a double chimneystack at the centre; *Cottage* (78413052), originally single-storeyed, but now heightened in brickwork.

22 STOUR PROVOST (7921)

(O.S. 6 ins., ST 72 SE, ST 82 SW, ST 81 NW)

Stour Provost is a parish of 2,815 acres, extending E. from the R. Stour which forms its western boundary. The W. part of the area is on Corallian Limestone between 200 ft. and 300 ft. above sea-level, sloping gently down to the Stour. The rest of the parish, mainly on Kimmeridge Clay at about the same altitude, is undulating and well-wooded and is drained by small streams flowing S. and S.E. At the N.E. corner of the parish the land rises steeply to 690 ft. on the wooded Greensand outlier, Duncliffe Hill.

The village stands compactly on the bank of the Stour, and the still existing pattern of long narrow fields shows that the former open fields lay around it, on the Limestone, to N., E. and S. Further E., on the Clay, at Woodville and beyond, a scatter of farms and cottages reflects gradual encroachment on the former waste, a slow and ill-documented process which must have started at least as early as the 13th century (P.R.O., E32/11, m.3). The pattern of the present boundaries suggests that originally there were at least four such areas of encroachment, separated from each other by waste, each comprising a small group of farms surrounded by irregularly shaped fields; although the earliest remaining building (15) is of 17th-century date, occupation is certainly very much older. Later, probably in the 18th century, the remaining waste was enclosed in rectilinear fields. In the late 18th and early 19th century many small cottages were built on the broad verges of the lanes, notably at Stour Row.

ECCLESIASTICAL

(1) THE PARISH CHURCH OF ST. MICHAEL stands near the centre of the village. It has walls of rubble, squared rubble and ashlar; the roofs are covered with stone-slates and, in part, with Welsh slates. The *Nave* and chancel arch are of the early 14th century; a small lancet window in the nave which appears to be more in the style of the 13th century could be a late survival, or perhaps is from an older building. The *South Tower* is of the 15th century with 17th-century rebuilding of the upper part, and 19th-century repairs. The N. arcade of the nave and the *North Aisle* are of the early 16th century. The *Chancel* and the *South Porch* are of the first half of the 19th century.

Architectural Description—The *Chancel* has an E. window of three lights with reset 18th-century tracery in a four-centred head; the lights have two-centred heads and the tracery lights have trefoil heads. The rear arch is outlined by a roll moulding and the jambs have attached shafts with moulded caps and bases. In the N. wall is a window of two trefoil-headed lights with a central quatrefoil above; the jambs and mullion are shafted externally and internally; a painted inscription implies that the opening dates from 1845. The S. wall has two lancet windows with shafted and hollow-chamfered jambs and detached rear arch shafts; the shafts have moulded caps and bases and moulded collars at half height. Two stone steps with moulded nosing in front of the communion rail are mediaeval, but reset. The chancel arch is two-centred and of two chamfered orders springing from hollow-chamfered imposts; the responds are three-sided and appear to have been partly recut; at the base are shaped and run-out stops. Weathered stonework seen externally, N.E. of the N. respond, is probably part of a rood stair turret.

square-set, strengthens the N.W. corner of the nave and provides abutment for the 16th-century arcade; there is evidence that the buttress is part of a former angle-buttress and the reason for its contrast with the diagonal S.W. buttress is obscure. The 19th-century W. window incorporates reused 14th-century material; the head is segmental-pointed and ovolo-moulded, with continuous jambs; the opening is of three gradated lights with plain two-centred heads, the centre light being slightly wider than those on each side.

In the *North Aisle*, diagonal buttresses of two weathered stages stand at the N.E. and N.W. corners and two similar buttresses are set square against the N. wall; all walls have hollow-chamfered plinths, that on the N. being stepped to follow the slope of the ground. The lean-to roof joins the N. slope of the nave roof, but is of lower pitch. The E. window has three plain gradated two-centred lights under a four-centred casement-moulded head with continuous jambs; the lights and a label above are of the 19th century, but the surround and the moulded

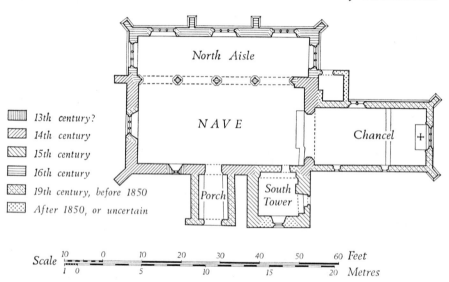

STOUR PROVOST   *The Parish Church of St. Michael*

13th century?
14th century
15th century
16th century
19th century, before 1850
After 1850, or uncertain

North Aisle

NAVE

Chancel

Porch

South Tower

Scale 10 0 10 20 30 40 50 60 *Feet*
1 0 5 10 15 20 *Metres*

The *Nave* has, on the N., a four-bay arcade with uniform two-centred arches of 16th-century date. Each arch has two orders, the inner order wave-moulded and the outer order hollow-chamfered. The piers and responds have attached shafts alternating with hollow chamfers, with plain conical capitals and hollow-chamfered bases. The shafted E. respond appears to be formed partly from reused 14th-century stonework with thin courses; the adjacent masonry is probably part of the original N. wall. On the S. side of the nave is the tower arch (see below); adjacent, on the W. and above the porch roof, is a 19th-century window of two pointed lights with a plain spandrel light. The 14th-century S. doorway has a moulded two-centred head with continuous jambs, partly recut, but terminating on the E. in small base mouldings and a crude broach stop; above is a moulded label with returned stops. To the W. of the doorway is a lancet window of 13th-century form, with a chamfered surround, a moulded label, deep internal splays and a segmental rear arch. The W. wall has been extensively rebuilt, but it is probably of 14th-century origin. At the S. corner is a diagonally-set buttress of two weathered stages. A similar buttress, but

rear arch with continuous jambs are of the 16th century. The three windows of the N. wall are uniform and of three lights; the 19th-century tracery is uniform with that of the E. window and here the surrounds also are of the 19th century although they incorporate 16th-century material; beneath the central window is a blocked N. doorway. The W. window of the N. aisle is similar to that on the E.

The *South Tower*, of ashlar and coursed rubble, has two stages separated by a weathered and hollow-chamfered string-course. The lower stage, including the string-course, is of the 15th century; the upper stage is of the 17th century, but it incorporates reused 15th-century material. The S. wall was restored in 1854. In the lower stage, the E. wall has a doorway with a chamfered segmental-pointed head and continuous jambs; inside, it has a wide two-centred rear arch. Adjacent, on the N., is the crease of the roof of a former chancel which appears to have been wider than the present structure. In the N. side of the tower is an archway to the nave, now blocked, with a chamfered two-centred head and continuous jambs; in the blocking is a small doorway with a two-centred head, of uncertain date. The S. wall has a

19th-century window of one light with a two-centred head; above is a square-headed 15th-century window with a moulded surround. The W. wall has no openings in the lower stage. The upper stage of the tower has slender corner pilasters; those on the N.E. and N.W. are divided at half height by moulded strings, the others are plain. In the E. and N. sides are 19th-century belfry windows of one trefoil-headed light; in the S. side is a reset 15th-century window of two trefoil-headed lights with vertical tracery in a casement-moulded two-centred head; in the W. side the belfry window has tracery similar to that on the S., but the surround is of the 17th century and without casement mouldings. At the top is an embattled parapet, with a hollow-chamfered string-course with 15th-century gargoyles to S.E. and S.W., and corner pinnacles with crocketed finials.

The 19th-century *South Porch* incorporates some mediaeval material. It has an archway with a chamfered two-centred head and continuous jambs. At the S.W. corner is a square-set weathered buttress. Inside, stone wall-seats are reset on the E. and W. sides.

The *Roof* of the chancel (Plate 66) incorporates 16th-century material, probably from the N. aisle. The raised central area has moulded wall-plates and intersecting beams, forming four bays, each bay being divided into twelve coffers; the coffers have fretted panels similar to those of the nave roof at Marnhull (*Dorset* III, 151). The surrounding zone of coffering and the coved wall-plates are of the 19th century, but the fretted panels are original.

Fittings—*Bells*: four; treble by John Wallis, inscribed 'Love the Lord, IW, 1602'; 2nd inscribed 'Regina celi letare' in black-letter, probably 15th-century; 3rd inscribed 'Ave Maris Stella Dei Mater Alma' in crowned Lombardic letters, 15th century; 4th, with inscription of 1683, recast 1902. Bell-frame, modern, incorporating older members, perhaps 16th or 17th century. *Brass*: In nave pavement, near chancel steps, plate (9½ ins. square) with inscription of James White, 1694. *Chests*: of oak, one with tapering ends, shaped feet and three locks, 17th-century; another with panelled front and sides, 18th century. *Communion Rails*: with Tuscan-column posts and turned balusters, late 18th century; moulded rail and sill modern. *Communion Table*: of oak, with crude cabriole legs, enriched rails, scrolled brackets and moulded top; late 17th century. *Door*: In S. doorway, of six panels with beaded borders, c. 1800. *Font*: of Purbeck stone, with octagonal bowl with two trefoil-headed panels to each face, and octagonal shaft with one trefoil-headed panel to each face and roll-moulded and chamfered capping above, on chamfered octagonal plinth; 15th century. *Glass*: In N. window of chancel, with two panels of scriptural subjects, 1845.

Monument and *Floor-slabs*. Monument: In churchyard, 5 paces S. of tower, of Richard Snooke, 1606, Joan his wife, 1607, and William Snooke, 1672, stone table-tomb with moulded top and plinth. *Floor-slabs*: In chancel, (1) of Humphry Newberry, rector, 1712; (2) of William Wray, rector, 1780.

Plate: Silver cup with conical bowl gadrooned at base, knopped stem and gadrooned foot, no marks, probably 17th century; silver stand-paten and flagon, both of 1844; silver alms-dish with donor's inscription of Susannah Newbary, 1728. *Royal Arms*: In nave, above chancel arch, lozenge-shaped panel with painted arms, date 1707 and initials A.R.; on surround, Psalm 72, v. 1. in black-letter.

(2) CONGREGATIONAL CHAPEL (81952107), at Stour Row, now a parish hall, has walls of squared rubble with ashlar dressings, and slate-covered roofs; it was built in 1843. The gabled S. front has a doorway with a chamfered two-centred head and continuous jambs, and a moulded label with returned stops. In the gable

above the doorway is a roundel with a quatrefoil panel. Flanking the doorway are two lancet windows with labels as before. The E. and W. walls have each three lancet windows without labels; the N. wall has no openings.

SECULAR

STOUR PROVOST VILLAGE

(3) THE RECTORY (79302168), 165 yds. N.W. of (1), is two-storeyed, with rubble walls and slated roofs. The main range was built c. 1825, but the service range on the N.E. may be a little earlier. The windows are square-headed, with large sliding sashes; the roofs are of low pitch with wide eaves. Inside, the principal rooms have moulded ceiling cornices. The staircase has a scrolled spandrel to each step, plain balusters and a mahogany handrail.

(4) CHURCH HOUSE (79352157), some 50 yds. W. of the church, is of two storeys with attics and has walls of rubble with ashlar dressings; the roofs are covered with modern tiles. The house is of the early 17th century with modern additions and restoration.

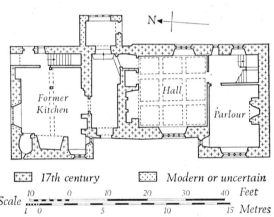

STOUR PROVOST   CHURCH HOUSE

The W. front is of four bays; the two middle bays have a N.–S. roof and the projecting end bays are gabled. The middle bays and the southern bay have a continuous weathered string-course at first-floor level. The northern bay has a small square-headed loop, probably to light a former stair; a similar loop at first-floor level has been blocked, but is seen internally. Adjacent is a large original chimneybreast, to the S. of which, on each floor, is a modern casement window. The second bay contains the front doorway, with a moulded four-centred head and continuous jambs with run-out stops; above, on the first floor, is an original square-headed stone window of three lights with hollow-chamfered surrounds. The third bay has a four-light window on the ground floor and a three-light window above, both with details as described. The southern bay has a four-light ground-floor window, as described, a window of three lights on the first floor and one of two lights in the gable; the first-floor and the gable windows have moulded labels. The S. elevation is gabled, with a chimneystack on the apex; on the first floor, immediately W. of the chimneybreast, is a stone window of one square-headed light. The E. elevation has a three-light stone window with a label in the lower storey of the third bay, a similar two-light window in the southern bay and, between them, a square-headed loop; the other E. openings are modern. The N. front has no noteworthy features.

The front doorway opens into a through-passage, to the S. of which is a hall with deeply chamfered ceiling beams intersecting to form nine panels; the open fireplace on the N. has a cambered and chamfered timber bressummer and chamfered stone jambs; on the S. side of the room is a reset plank-and-muntin partition with moulded muntins and top rail. The parlour has 17th-century oak panelling, perhaps reset. The kitchen on the N. of the through-passage, now used as a dining-room, has a large open fireplace with a timber bressummer; beside it is a circular recess, probably for a former newel stair. On the first floor, the S. chamber has a fireplace of c. 1600 with a stone surround with a hollow-chamfered and ovolo-moulded four-centred head, continuous jambs and pedestal stops. The chamber over the hall has a stone fireplace with a chamfered four-centred head.

(5) DIAMOND FARM (79272147), house, 165 yds. S.W. of the church, is of two storeys with attics and has walls of rubble with ashlar dressings; the roofs are covered with modern tiles. The house is probably of the late 17th century, with modern additions on the W.

The original S. front is of six bays; that on the W. is wider than the others, but the five eastern bays are more or less symmetrical in themselves, comprising a central doorway with two three-light windows on each side of it on the ground floor and, on the first-floor, three similar windows; the first-floor openings do not, however, correspond with those below. All windows are square-headed, with chamfered and hollow-chamfered stone surrounds; immediately over the ground-floor openings is a continuous weathered and hollow-chamfered string-course; the doorway has a four-centred ovolo-moulded head with continuous jambs and an 18th-century timber hood on shaped brackets. The N. elevation has a doorway similar to that on the S.; to the E. is a modern stone three-light window; to the W. is an original window of four lights, as before, with a moulded label with returned stops. The first floor has three original windows of two and of three lights. The gabled E. wall has a large chimneybreast; on the S. side the projection rests on a moulded corbel.

Inside, the original ground-floor plan is preserved. The through-passage is flanked by plank-and-muntin partitions in which the top rails and the edges of each muntin are moulded. The parlour on the E. has a fireplace with a moulded ashlar surround in which the deep, slightly cambered head is formed of three large stones; the mouldings are rounded at the shoulders and continue on the jambs. The hall on the W. of the through-passage has moulded beams, which intersect to form four panels; the fireplace has a moulded timber bressummer and moulded stone jambs, the moulding being continuous and rounded at the corners. On the first floor, two chambers have stone fireplace surrounds with

moulded four-centred heads and continuous jambs. In the attics are two fireplace surrounds of similar form; that on the E. bears the initials and date IH 1707, roughly carved.

(6) MANOR FARM (79432147), house, of two storeys with rubble walls and slate-covered roofs, is of 17th-century origin, but it was largely rebuilt in the 18th century, and an extension on the W. is of the 19th century. The gabled E. wall of the S. range is original and has a chamfered plinth and a projecting chimney-breast; the rest of the building is later. Inside, the original E. fireplace is blocked by an 18th-century chimney-piece.

(7) MILL HOUSE (79102149), of two storeys, has ashlar walls and slated roofs. The N.W. front is symmetrical, with a central doorway and with square-headed sashed windows in both storeys. The adjacent Mill has rubble walls and tiled roofs; to the E. is a two-storeyed Cottage and to the W. is a range of farm buildings, of materials similar to the mill. All these buildings are of the early 19th century.

(8) COTTAGES (79312156), two adjacent, now combined, are of one storey with attics and have rubble walls and thatched roofs; they date from the 17th century. Inside, two rooms have large open fireplaces with timber bressummers and ovens. There are several chamfered ceiling beams.

(9) COTTAGE (79242143), of one storey with an attic, has rubble walls and a thatched roof; it is of 17th-century origin with a 19th-century addition on the W. Inside, the two rooms of the class-T

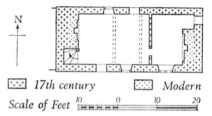

[::::] 17th century   [:::] Modern

Scale of Feet 10   0   10   20

plan are divided by an original plank-and-muntin partition. Both open fireplaces are blocked and modern grates have been inserted. On the S. of the W. fireplace is a winding stair.

MONUMENTS (10–14)

Unless otherwise described the following are two-storeyed 18th-century cottages, with rubble walls and thatched roofs.

(10) Cottage (79342155), originally single-storeyed, is now heightened and has a tiled roof.

(11) Cottage (79502148), now two tenements, has 19th-century and modern additions on the W.

(12) Cottage (79342145) has a blocked open fireplace.

(13) Cottage (79332148) has a 19th-century extension on the N.

(14) Cottage (79332150), formerly the Royal Oak Inn, is of early 18th-century origin. The gabled N. and S. end walls contain large open fireplaces, and several rooms have deeply chamfered beams.

Monuments of the late 18th and early 19th century in Stour Provost village include twelve Cottages, generally two-storeyed and with rubble walls and thatched roofs, located as follows—79342152, 79382152 and 79382151, about 50 yds. S. and S.W. of the church; 79352150, 79352148 and 79362146, about 80 yds. S.W. of the church; 79352144, about 140 yds. S.W. of the church; the Post Office, 79332151, about 80 yds. W. of the church; 79242160, about 170 yds. W. of the church; 79262144, about 200 yds. W. of the church; 79352168 and 79352170, about 150 yds. N. of the church.

WOODVILLE

(15) GREAT HOUSE FARM (81852066), house, with rubble walls and thatched roofs, comprises an early 17th-century cottage of one storey with an attic, and an 18th-century range added on the S., the resulting plan being T-shaped with the earlier range in the upright of the T. All elevations are asymmetrical, with plain casement windows and doorways. Inside, a ground-floor room of the early range has moulded beams and wall-plates intersecting to form a ceiling of four panels.

MONUMENTS (16–24)

The following farmhouses and isolated cottages, dating from the 17th century, are dispersed around Woodville in the central part of the parish, from ½ m. to 1¼ m. E. of the parish church. Unless described otherwise they are two-storeyed and have rubble walls and thatched roofs.

(16) *Lyde Hill Farm* (80582168), house, with tiled roofs has the original range adapted to form the service wing at the W. end of a 19th-century house. The latter has a symmetrical N. front of three bays, with a central doorway and uniform square-headed sashed windows; the original range has casement windows. Inside are several chamfered beams.

(17) *Cottage* (80362143), with a tiled roof, was partly rebuilt in the 18th century.

(18) *Shade House Farm* (80502116), house, with slate-covered roofs, was rebuilt in 1842 as recorded in an inscription on the N. front; the E., S. and W. elevations, however, retain 17th-century stone windows of two, three and four square-headed lights, some of them with moulded labels. Inside, some rooms retain stop-chamfered beams, perhaps reset. A first-floor room has a stone fireplace surround with an ovolo-moulded four-centred head.

(19) *Yeatman's Farm* (81312108), house, has the S. front in two bays with a central doorway; a date stone in the western bay is inscribed 'P. G. Tucker, 1805' and probably records the rebuilding of this part of the S. wall. The eastern bay retains a moulded string-course at first-floor level. Inside, the plan is of class T, having a central through-passage with a heated room on each side of it; that on the E. has a large open fireplace with an oven adjacent, also moulded wall-plates and moulded beams forming a ceiling of four panels. A small closet is made of 17th-century panelling with guilloche enrichment.

(20) *Cottage* (81462097), comprises only one room and an attic. Inside, there is an open fireplace, now blocked, with an oven on one side and a stone vice on the other. The N. wall contains a round-headed alcove.

(21) *Cottage* (80802062), single-storeyed with attics, has early 18th-century additions on the E.; a fragment of hollow-chamfered string-course in the 18th-century part is presumably reset. Inside, the original part of the cottage has stop-chamfered ceiling beams.

(22) *Sweet's Farm* (81222068), house, formerly of one storey with dormer-windowed attics, but now of two storeys, retains several casement windows of three square-headed lights with hollow-chamfered stone surrounds and moulded labels. Inside, one room has deep-chamfered beams intersecting to form a four-panel ceiling, and an open fireplace; another room has a stop-chamfered beam.

(23) *Good's Farm* (81272069), house, with a tiled roof, was heightened and provided with new windows in the 19th century. Inside, a room at the N. end of the range has an open fireplace and a four-panel ceiling with deep-chamfered beams.

(24) *Cottages* (80392227), two adjacent, with tiled roofs, were originally single-storeyed with attics. Inside, the E. cottage retains chamfered ceiling beams and an open fireplace.

MONUMENTS (25–28)

The following 18th-century buildings occur in the same area as the foregoing group. They all are two-storeyed and have rubble walls.

(25) *Vanner's Farm* (80392258), house, with tiled roofs, was built in 1798, as attested by a date-stone in the S. gable.

(26) *Cottage* (80502225), with a thatched roof.

(27) *Cottage* (80342147), with a thatched roof, is of the late 18th century; it contains an open fireplace and a chamfered beam.

(28) *Wadmill Farm* (81681979), with a tiled roof, is of *c.* 1800. The S. front is symmetrical, with a central doorway flanked by three-light casement windows, corresponding windows in the upper storey, and a window of one light over the doorway.

Monuments of the 19th century in Woodville include the *School* and *Schoolmaster's House* (80782163), with ashlar walls and tiled roofs, erected in 1850, a *Cottage* (80842215) with rubble walls and a thatched roof, and a *Cottage* (80502163) with rubble walls, a tiled roof and a symmetrical S. front of three bays.

STOUR ROW

Five 17th or early 18th-century farmhouses are situated near the eastern boundary of the parish.

(29) JOLLIFFE'S FARM (83172182), house, of two storeys with rubble walls and slated roofs, is of the late 17th century and retains many original features. The plan is of class T. In the lower storey the E. front has windows of two and of four square-headed lights with

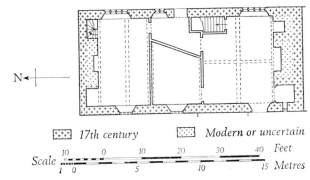

N◄

⫶⫶⫶⫶ *17th century*   ⫶⫶⫶⫶ *Modern or uncertain*

Scale 10 0 10 20 30 40 *Feet*
       0   5   10   15 *Metres*

ovolo-moulded stone surrounds; above them, a continuous weathered string-course descends to a lower level between each opening, as a label, and similarly follows the outline of the door-head. A stone window, set at mezzanine level on the S. of the doorway, lights the stairs and shows that these remain in their original position. The first-floor windows have moulded wooden surrounds. On the gabled N. wall the string-course continues, but it stops at the N.W. corner. The W. front has casement windows with chamfered wooden surrounds. The S. wall is masked by later buildings.

Inside, the hall on the S. has a large open fireplace, now partly filled in, with the remains of an oven on the E. and a small larder on the W.; the ceiling has deeply chamfered beams with moulded stops intersecting to form four panels; the S. wall-plate is chamfered and stopped in correspondence with the N.–S. beam. The middle room, perhaps a buttery, is divided from the N. room by an original plank-and-muntin partition with a moulded head; on the S. a small section of plank-and-muntin work encloses the main staircase. The stairs are modern, but a section of original balustrading remains at the first-floor landing; it has square newel posts with turned, ball-headed finials, stout turned balusters and moulded top and bottom rails. In the parlour on the N., the ceiling has a deeply chamfered beam with splay stops; adjacent to the blocked fireplace is a small newel staircase. The upper storey retains original plank-and-muntin partitions.

(30) HILL FARM (82562140), house, of two storeys with rubble walls and slate-covered roofs, is of the 18th century. The S.E. front is symmetrical and of three bays; at the centre is a square-headed doorway and, on the first floor, a small bull's-eye window; flanking these, each storey has large sashed windows. The plan is of class T.

(31) YEW TREE FARM (82742126), house, of two storeys with rubble walls and tile-covered roofs, is of the early 18th century. It has casement windows of two and three lights with wooden surrounds and leaded glazing. Inside, some rooms have stop-chamfered beams.

(32) WOODVILLE FARM (82792100), house, of two storeys with rubble walls and tiled roofs, is of the early 18th century.

(33) RUDDOCK'S FARM (82822055), house, of two storeys with rubble walls and tiled roofs, is of the early 18th century and resembles (31) in its general characteristics.

Monuments of the 19th century in Stour Row include the following, all with rubble walls and with thatched or slate-covered roofs: Cottage (81852108), originally two tenements; Cottage (81912107); Cottages (81982108), two adjacent; Cottage (82002108); Inn (82032107), with a symmetrical N. front of three bays; Cottage (82082112); Cottage (82132113); Cottages (82152115), two adjacent, possibly of the late 18th century; Cottage (82222114); Cottage (82332119); Cottages (82422125), pair; Cottage (82582142), with a symmetrical ashlar-faced S. front; Cottage (82832157); Cottage (83042166); Cottage (83172173), formerly two tenements, possibly of the late 18th century; Cottage (83302184); Thomas's Farm (83412184), house, built c. 1850 with materials from an earlier building; Cottage (82282094); Cottage (81812147); Cottage (81812162).

MEDIAEVAL AND LATER EARTHWORKS

(34) CULTIVATION REMAINS. Nothing is known of the open fields of the parish. Some traces of 7-yard ridge-and-furrow occur N.W. of the village, and fields which extend S.E. of the village seem from their shape to comprise enclosed furlongs. It is probable that the mediaeval open fields lay only in the western third of the parish.

ROMAN

(35) POTTERY of the late Romano–British period was found in 1950 at 81482107, in an area of Kimmeridge Clay, about 200 ft. above O.D. (Dorset Procs., 72 (1950), 78).

23 SUTTON WALDRON (8615)

(O.S. 6 ins., ST 81 NE, ST 81 NW)

The parish consists of a narrow strip of land, some 1,300 acres in extent, straddling the Chalk escarpment. The W. part, on Kimmeridge Clay, Lower Greensand and Gault Clay, lies between 180 ft. and 300 ft. above sea-level and is drained by the southward flowing Fontmell Brook. Eastwards the ground rises gently at first on Upper Greensand, and then steeply on the Chalk, to the crest of the escarpment at 650 ft.; beyond the crest it slopes down gently to about 400 ft. The village stands at the foot of the escarpment, on the Upper Greensand.

ECCLESIASTICAL

(1) THE PARISH CHURCH OF ST. BARTHOLOMEW (Plate 63), in the S. of the village, was built in 1847 to the design of George Alexander and has walls of flint and squared rubble with ashlar dressings, and tiled roofs; the W. tower is partly rendered and partly of ashlar; the spire is of ashlar. A drawing of the former church, preserved in the D.C.R.O., shows a chancel, a nave and a low west tower.

Architectural Description—The Chancel windows have two-centred heads with curvilinear tracery above trefoil-headed lights, except the central E. light which is cinquefoil-headed; the two-centred and moulded rear-arches spring from shafted jambs; the windows have moulded labels internally and externally, with foliate stops. The archway to the vestry has a two-centred head of two chamfered orders and a label with foliate stops. A squint from the S. aisle opens in the back of a sedile. The chancel arch is two-centred and of three moulded orders, continuous on the responds, with the inner order ending on octagonal bases; above are E. and W. moulded labels with foliate stops.

The Vestry has square-headed windows with moulded labels and trefoil ogee-headed lights; that on the N. has quatrefoil tracery. In the N. gable is a trefoil loop. The apex of the gable has a polygonal traceried pinnacle with a crocketed finial.

The Nave has N. windows similar to the S. window of the chancel, with curvilinear tracery of differing design; internally, moulded labels continue as a string-course. The S. arcade has two-centred arches of three moulded orders, with labels as on the chancel arch; the octagonal piers have moulded caps and bases.

In the *South Aisle* the windows are as in the nave. The S. doorway has a moulded two-centred head with continuous jambs, and a chamfered segmental rear-arch of three orders.

The *West Tower* is of three stages, with a moulded plinth and weathered and moulded string-courses; on the W. side the two lower stages are merged in one. Each corner has a diagonal buttress, those on the E. occurring above the level of the nave roof, those on the W. having four weathered stages; at the top, each buttress has a gargoyle and a pinnacle with a crocketed finial; the pinnacles support flying buttresses to the spire, with trefoil-headed tracery in the spandrels. The octagonal spire, with roll-moulded arrises, rises from a base in the form of an embattled parapet; each face of the spire is pierced by quatrefoil loops at two levels; the apex has a metal shaft with a weathervane. The tower arch is two-centred and of three moulded orders, as in the chancel arch. The W. window has four ogee-headed lights set in pairs on each side of a stout centre mullion, and geometrical tracery in a two-centred head. The rear-arch is similar to those in the chancel. A length of moulded string-course with

turned legs; 17th century. *Font:* of stone, octagonal, with moulded bowl and stem; cover, of oak, pyramidal, with pierced sides and crocketed angles. *Glass:* In chancel windows, by Hudson & Powell (*Builder*, 27 Nov. 1847, 565). *Lectern:* of stone, with trefoil-headed arcading and moulded coping. *Niche:* In chancel, on N., with trefoil ogee head; in nave, on N., with cinquefoil two-centred head and shafted jambs. *Painting:* on nave arcade and chancel arch; stencilled decoration. *Plate:* includes Elizabethan silver cup by the anonymous 'Gillingham' silversmith (*see* p. xxxiv) with later inscription 'JA, CW, 82'; cover-paten with inscription of 1793; also chalice, paten and flagon, dated 1847. *Pulpit:* of stone, with carved panels and moulded top. *Sedilia:* with cinquefoil two-centred arches, on shafted responds and shafts with moulded caps and bases; square label with ball-flower stops. *Tiles:* on floor of chancel and nave, with geometrical patterns. *Miscellaneous:* In belfry, reset in E. wall, mediaeval carving with heart, hands and entrails, probably monument of a heart-burial; heart subsequently cut to represent grotesque face.

SUTTON WALDRON

The Parish Church of St. Bartholomew · 1847

two head-stops below the window-sill is perhaps of 14th-century origin. Above is a small window with a trefoil-headed light. The vice has a chamfered ogee-headed doorway and two trefoil-headed loops; it is capped with weathered stonework at the foot of the upper stage. In the upper stage each side of the tower has a belfry window of two trefoil ogee-headed lights with curvilinear tracery in a two-centred head with a moulded label.

The *South Porch* has an archway of two-moulded orders with continuous jambs and moulded labels outside and inside; the inside label has reset 14th-century head-stops.

The *Roofs* in the chancel, nave and S. aisle have arch-braced principals resting on stone corbels; in the chancel the roof is painted.

Fittings (of 1847, unless otherwise stated)—*Bells:* two, by Mears. *Chest:* of oak, with plain lid, panelled sides and front richly carved (Plate 22), mid 17th century. *Coffin-stools:* two, with beaded tops, turned legs and plain stretchers, 17th century. *Communion Rails:* of stone, with moulded top and bottom members and with trefoil tracery; gate similar, of wood. *Communion Table:* in vestry, with plain top, moulded rails and

SECULAR

(2) SUTTON WALDRON HOUSE (86291595), of two storeys, with rendered walls and low-pitched slate-covered roofs, is of the first half of the 19th century.

(3) ALMSHOUSES (86201600), range of eight, have brick walls and tiled roofs and were built in 1830. The range is symmetrical, comprising four two-storeyed dwellings in the middle and two single-storeyed dwellings at each end. The doorways have segmental-pointed heads; the windows have plain wooden casements, those of the two-storeyed houses having ornamental labels. The sides of the chimneystacks have round-headed recesses.

(4) COTTAGE (86441591), single-storeyed with an attic, has rubble walls with flint banding and brick quoins, and a thatched roof; it is of the 17th century. Inside, there are several chamfered beams and an open fireplace with a chamfered bressummer. The plan is of class J.

(5) STABLES (89281565), belonging to West Lodge (see IWERNE MINSTER (3)), are of one and of two storeys with lofts and have

brick walls and tiled roofs; they are of the early 19th century with modern additions and alterations.

MEDIAEVAL AND LATER EARTHWORKS

(6) CULTIVATION REMAINS. A map of the parish of *c.* 1776 (copy in D.C.R.O.) shows the remains of the open fields on the E. of the village; they were named North, Whiteway, East and Ledge Fields. Contour strip lynchets, formerly in Ledge Field, remain on the S.E. slope of Combe Bottom (874158). Traces of strip fields on the W. of the parish church (858157) are in an area enclosed before *c.* 1770 (Map of Sutton Waldron Farm, D.C.R.O.; *Dorset Procs.*, 64 (1942), 75–83).

UNDATED

(7) ENCLOSURE (876161), on the steep S.E. declivity of Combe Bottom, about 500 ft. above sea-level, is nearly square and has sides 35 yds. long, each with a low bank and a shallow internal ditch. No entrance is visible. The interior is featureless, apart from disturbance, probably recent, at the lower, W. end, which appears partly to have destroyed a platform cut into the slope. The earthwork is called 'Satan's Square'; in the 18th century it was called 'The Devil's Trencher and Spoon' (Map by I. Taylor, 1765–7, photo-copy in D.C.R.O.).

24 TARRANT CRAWFORD (9203)

(O.S. 6 ins., ST 90 SW)

This parish, 543 acres in extent and roughly square in outline, occupies the valley of the R. Tarrant at its confluence with the R. Stour, the latter forming the S.W. boundary. The land is entirely Chalk, between 80 ft. and 200 ft. above sea-level. Early settlement is likely to have been near the parish church, in the N. of the parish, but no trace of it is found today; the present village, some ½ m. to the S., includes part of a late mediaeval wayside cross and evidence of deserted house-sites and closes. The distance between church and village suggests intentional removal of the settlement at some time, perhaps in connection with the development of the mediaeval abbey, or with the disposal of its property at the Dissolution.

Tarrant Crawford Abbey originated at the end of the 12th century (*V.C.H., Dorset*, ii, 87–90) as a small community of nuns; by 1233 the convent had adopted the Cistercian rule. In 1237 Bishop Poore of Salisbury was buried there and in the following year Henry III's sister, Queen Joan of Scotland, also was buried there; by the end of the 13th century Tarrant was one of the richest Cistercian nunneries in England.[1] There is little doubt that there was a convent church in addition to the small parish church which survives, and that the tombs of the Bishop and of the Queen were in it, but nothing is visible today; it was built between 1240 and 1246 (*Cal. Lib. Rolls*, Hen. III, iii (1245–51), 62, 69). Most of the abbey buildings appear to have been demolished at the Dissolution; a few late mediaeval buildings which stand some 200 yds. to 300 yds. W. and S.W. of the parish church (Plate 34), include farm buildings and part of a dwelling of uncertain use (3–5). A disturbed area of scarps and banks (8) could be the site of the abbey church.

ECCLESIASTICAL

(1) THE PARISH CHURCH OF ST. MARY, in the N. of the parish, has walls of flint and of rubble, in part rendered, with dressings of Greensand and of Heathstone ashlar; the roof covering is of tile and stoneslate. The *Chancel* is of 12th-century origin, with windows enlarged in the 13th century (Plate 68). The *Nave* is of the 13th century and its walls retain 14th-century painted decorations, including scenes from the life of St. Margaret of Antioch (Plates 67–9). The absence of windows in much of the S. wall suggests that a building formerly adjoined the nave on this side, perhaps part of the former nunnery. The *North Porch* is of the second half of the 15th century. The *West Tower* appears to be of the 16th century, perhaps *c.* 1508 (Hutchins III, 122), and the nave roof is of about the same period.

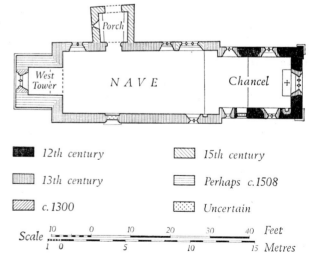

TARRANT CRAWFORD
The Parish Church of St. Mary

- ■ *12th century*
- ▥ *13th century*
- ▨ *c. 1300*
- ▤ *15th century*
- □ *Perhaps c.1508*
- ▦ *Uncertain*

Scale [10 0 10 20 30 40 Feet / 1 0 5 10 15 Metres]

---

[1] The theory that the celebrated *Ancrene Riwle* was originally written by Bishop Poore early in the 13th century for the convent at Tarrant Crawford is discredited (Chambers, *Review of English Studies*, I (1925), 13–14). It is stated in a late manuscript (Magdalen College, Oxford, MS. 67, f. 1 : *c.* 1400) that a Latin version of the Rule was written by Simon of Ghent, Bishop of Salisbury (d. 1315) ' sororibus suis anachoritis apud Tarente '. This implies that there were anchoresses at Tarrant *c.* 1300, either distinct from or identical with the Cistercian community. If the anchoresses inhabited a separate house it may have adjoined the existing church or, perhaps more probably, the convent church. Excavation on the site (8) might clarify this point.

Architectural Description—In the *Chancel* the remains of a 12th-century pilaster buttress are found at the N.E. corner. The E. window is of the 13th century and comprises three gradated, trefoil-headed lights in a chamfered two-centred head, with a chamfered segmental-pointed rear arch. Above springing-level of the window head the E. wall has been rebuilt and is thinner than below. The N. wall of the chancel has two uniform 13th-century windows, each with two trefoil-headed lights; that on the E. is set at a higher level than the other. The eastern window of the S. wall is uniform with those on the N. Further W. in the S. wall is a blocked doorway of 12th-century origin, rebuilt externally and provided with a two-centred head; at the base of the W. jamb is an original moulded impost block, inverted; the rear arch is semicircular. Adjacent is a 13th-century window of one trefoil-headed light. There is no chancel arch.

The *Nave* has, near the E. end of the N. wall, a late 15th-century window of three trefoil-headed lights in a square-headed surround; adjacent is a 13th-century two-light window uniform with those of the chancel. The N. doorway has a chamfered two-centred head and continuous jambs; adjacent on the W. is a late 15th or early 16th-century window of two trefoil-headed lights with a square label. Near the E. end of the S. wall is a two-light 13th-century window, uniform with those described. The late 13th-century S. doorway, now blocked, has a chamfered two-centred head and continuous jambs with run-out stops; the rear arch is a flat stone lintel, shaped on the upper surface and evidently reused since a scratch-dial occurs on the N. face.

The *West Tower* is of two stages, with a chamfered plinth, a weathered string-course and an embattled parapet. The tower arch is two-centred and of one chamfered order dying into plain responds. The W. window is of *c.* 1300 and reset; it has two trefoil-headed lights and a plain central tracery light in a two-centred head. In the upper stage of the tower a quatrefoil loop occurs in the E. wall; a similar loop is in the lower part of the N. wall and above it is a belfry window of two trefoil-headed lights in a square-headed surround, with a label with square stops. Similar belfry windows occur in the S. and W. sides.

The *North Porch* has an archway with a two-centred head of two chamfered orders dying into plain responds. In the W. wall is a chamfered square-headed loop.

The *Roof* of the nave is of arch-braced trussed rafters, with chamfered wall-plates, and chamfered longitudinal members forming a wagon roof; the former plaster ceiling has been removed and the rafters are exposed.

Fittings—Bells: three; 1st inscribed 'regina celi letare' in black-letter, mediaeval; 2nd with 'God be our guyd IW 1589'; 3rd with 'sancte Petre' in Lombardic letters, mediaeval, probably from Salisbury foundry. *Bracket:* in nave, on S. wall, plain, hollow-chamfered underneath. *Brass and Indent. Brass:* (6¼ ins. by 3 ins.) discovered near church in 1862, with black-letter inscription of Joh(ann)es Karrant, late 15th century. *Indent:* (19 ins. wide) in Purbeck marble floor-slab, upper part hidden by chancel step. *Chest:* of cast iron, with panelled decoration, inscribed 'WH, Bramshaw Foundry, 1813'. *Coffin-lids:* Reset (*Dorset Procs.*, 39 (1918), 109) in chancel, on N., (1) of Purbeck marble, with double hollow-chamfered border and foliate cross in relief, 13th century; on S., (2) similar to foregoing, but upper surface eroded and cross gone; further W., (3) of Purbeck marble with lightly incised base and stem of cross, upper part missing, early 14th century. In nave, near E. end, (4) of Purbeck marble, much worn, mediaeval; reset as S. window-sill, (5) similar to (3), 14th century. In churchyard, N. of church, reused as headstone, (6) of lime-stone, with incised cross, perhaps 14th century. *Coffin-stools:* three, of oak with turned legs, 17th century. *Communion rails:*

of oak, with turned balusters and moulded capping, late 17th century. *Font:* comprising plain square bowl of Purbeck stone, with holes for lock, on tapered and hollow-chamfered Greensand capping to square Greensand pedestal with chamfered angles, 16th-century, plinth modern. *Font-cover:* of oak, pyramidal, with panelled sides, 16th century; finial and base modern. *Glass:* in N.E. nave window, crowns and foliage, 15th century; one quarry with glazier's inscription of 1806.

Paintings: In chancel, in E. reveal of N.E. window, fragments of drapery, a hand, ashlar ruling; on S., ashlar ruling and cinquefoils in red, *c.* 1300. In nave, on N. wall, at E. end, part of robed figure in red on yellow, with red margin, early 14th century; E. of N. doorway, panel containing three figures with a balance, in yellow, red and black, 14th century; over N. doorway, part of roundel, formerly enclosing text, 17th century; W. of N. doorway, in lozengy border, two figures, one nimbed and with book, on chequered pavement, in black, white and red, 15th century. In nave, on S. wall at E. end, Annunciation (Plate 67) in yellow and red with incised outline, first half of 14th century. On S. wall, in upper zone, extending from S. window to W. wall, below scroll frieze, twelve panels (Plate 69) depicting acts of St. Margaret of Antioch, in black, yellow, blue and red, with incised outlines, first half of 14th century; in lower zone, between window and S. doorway, allegory of Three Living and Three Dead, first half of 14th century (Plate 68); on W. of doorway, fragmentary panels, probably 14th century, overpainted with Crucifixion in red, black, yellow and blue, *c.* 1400.

Piscinae: two; one in chancel, on S., with basin formed from 12th-century cushion capital; another in nave, on S., with chamfered square-headed recess and round basin; mediaeval. *Plate:* includes pewter chalice and paten, without marks, probably 19th century; also pewter almsdish, 19th century. *Pulpit:* of oak, hexagonal, with panelled sides, beaded stiles and rails, guilloche frieze and moulded capping, 17th century. *Seating:* incorporates reset elements of 17th-century panelled oak box-pews; other panels reset as dado in chancel. *Sundial:* on rear arch of S. doorway, scratch-dial, 13th century or earlier. *Tiles:* reset in chancel pavement, four quarries with slip decoration, one with shield-of-arms of Clare, Earl of Gloucester, others with conventional beasts, 13th or 14th century. *Miscellanea:* reset in E. jamb of N. doorway, moulded loop-head, probably pre-conquest. Reset on N. door, two iron strap-hinges with fleur-de-lis finials, 13th century; shaped lock scutcheon, 16th century.

(2) WAYSIDE CROSS (92310271), in the village about ½ m. S. of the church, comprises a square stone plinth and the lower part of a stone shaft, both probably of the 15th century. The upper part of the shaft and two steps at the base are modern.

SECULAR

(3) TARRANT ABBEY HOUSE (92060330), 300 yds. S.W. of the church, is of two storeys with walls partly of rubble, partly timber-framed and partly of brick, and with tile-covered roofs (Plate 34, bottom r.). The short transverse range orientated N.W.–S.E. is of mediaeval origin, the stone lower storey being perhaps of the early 15th century while the timber-framed upper storey may be of later 15th-century date. The N.E. range is of the 16th century, with the walls refaced in brickwork about the middle of the 18th century. The S.W. wing is of the late 18th century.

In the early range the lower storey is of rubble and flint, with original ashlar dressings and with some repairs in brickwork. Low down in the S.E. elevation is a small stone window of two plain square-headed lights, now blocked; the gabled upper storey is of late 15th-century timber framework with 17th-century brick nogging. The N.E. side of the early range, where not masked by the N.E. wing, is in both storeys of similar construction to the S.E. front; a stone window similar to that described occurs near the re-entrant angle with the N.E. wing; adjacent, on the S.E., the chamfered jamb of a mediaeval doorway forms one side of a modern window. Inside the early range the first floor rests on stop-chamfered beams. The roof of the early range is of nine bays, with arch-braced collar-beams to the trusses and with curved wind-braces. The 16th-century N.E. wing has ceiling beams with stopped chamfers.

(4) BARN (92160344), 120 yds. W. of the church. In the lower part the walls are of rubble and flint with ashlar dressings and are of the 15th century; the upper part, in brick, is of 1759. The gabled W. wall has a chamfered plinth and two weathered buttresses, mediaeval below and of the 18th century above. The N. wall has 18th-century brick buttresses. The roof is of eight bays, with 'sling-brace' trusses (see *Dorset* II, lxvii). The E. gable has a date-stone of 1759.

(5) RANGE OF FARM BUILDINGS (92110339), 50 yds. W. of (4), is single-storeyed and has rubble walls with ashlar dressings, and tiled roofs; it is of the late 15th century. The E. and W. sides have ashlar buttresses of one to four weathered stages. The original roof is of six bays, with plain hammerbeam trusses with chamfered curved braces and with slightly cambered collar-beams at two levels; the wall-posts are shaped and chamfered. There are three purlins on each side, with curved wind-bracing between the two lower purlins.

(6) COTTAGE (92270263), 100 yds. S.W. of (2), is of two storeys, with cob walls and a thatched roof. It probably is of the early 19th century, and has a class-S plan.

MEDIAEVAL AND LATER EARTHWORKS

(7) BANK AND DITCH, presumably bounding the abbey precinct, occurs in several places and appears to have enclosed a roughly rectangular area of some 7½ acres (Plate 34). On the S.E., extending about 150 yds. S.W. from 92180338, a double bank 2 ft. to 3 ft. high has a ditch 3 ft. deep on the N.W. side. The S.W. boundary is marked by a bank 3 ft. high with a slight inner ditch, immediately S.W. of (3); formerly this part of the bank was over 200 yds. long, but only 80 yds. remain at the N.W. end. On the N.W. the precinct probably was bounded by the Tarrant. The N.E. boundary is no longer defined.

(8) SCARPS AND BANKS (92030338), much disturbed in unrecorded 19th-century excavations, lie on the W. of (5) and cover an area some 200 ft. by 50 ft., roughly L-shaped in plan; the longer side is orientated E.–W. Mounds which appear to contain masonry from the walls of a substantial building stand up to 3 ft. high. It is reported locally that mediaeval floor-tiles have been found on the site, but none could be produced for examination.

(9) SETTLEMENT REMAINS (921026), with traces of deserted house-sites and closes, occur in a field on the W. of Crawford Farm. They are visible on air photographs (R.A.F. CPE/UK 1934: 4201–2), and several buildings are shown in this position on O.S. 1811.

(10) CULTIVATION REMAINS. A three-field system appears to have been in existence in 1542 (Hutchins III, 118), but nothing is known of the date of enclosure. Remains of contour strip lynchets (922027) with very low risers occur on a gentle S.W. slope, adjacent to (9).

ROMAN AND PREHISTORIC

It is reported that Roman pottery and tiles have been found under the church floor (92300347); a Roman bronze brooch now in the British Museum possibly comes from this site (*Dorset Procs.*, 39 (1918), 109).

'CELTIC' FIELDS, see p. 118, Group (69).

25 TARRANT GUNVILLE (9212)

(O.S. 6 ins., ST 81 SE, ST 91 SW, ST 91 NW)

Tarrant Gunville, covering 3,469 acres, is the most northerly of the parishes which take their name from the R. Tarrant; it lies on Chalk, the land sloping down from 500 ft. above sea-level in the N.W. to 240 ft. in the S.E. (Plate 73); it is drained by the Tarrant. In the N. and N.E. much of the land is still forested with coppices of Cranborne Chase. Two Iron Age enclosures and traces of extensive 'Celtic' fields are found. There were two mediaeval settlements, Stubhampton in the centre of the Parish and Gunville in the S.E. Tarrant Gunville contains the parish church and Eastbury House, a surviving fragment of one ot Vanbrugh's great mansions; the contours of extensive gardens designed by Bridgeman can still be traced. A number of houses and cottages in Gunville, with walls of ashlar and flint, presumably are built with materials salvaged from the mansion after its demolition in 1782.

ECCLESIASTICAL

(1) THE PARISH CHURCH OF ST. MARY stands in the S.W. of the village. Wall arcading discovered during the 19th century and reset in the N. aisle, above the eastern bay of the nave arcade, indicates a former church of *c.* 1100. The western part of the *North and South Aisles*, the *South Porch* and the tower arch are of late 14th-century origin. The *Tower* was completed by the early 15th century, but the top stage appears to have been partly rebuilt in the 16th century. In 1843 the *Chancel* and *Nave* were rebuilt, the aisles were reroofed and the *North Vestry* was added (*Ecclesiologist*, III (1843), 58, 96; XI (1850), 207; XII (1851), 122–5).

Architectural Description—The 19th-century *Chancel* has an E. window of three trefoil-headed lights with vertical tracery

PLATE 65

SILTON CHURCH. Monument (1) of Sir Hugh Wyndham, 1684.   Erected, 1692

PLATE 66

STOUR PROVOST CHURCH. Chancel roof.   16th century

SHAFTESBURY. (2) St. Peter's Church, nave roof.   16th century

PLATE 67

TARRANT CRAWFORD CHURCH. Wall-painting of Annunciation. 14th century

PLATE 68

Interior, looking E.   13th century and later

S. wall of nave, lower zone: Allegory of Three Living and Three Dead.   14th century

TARRANT CRAWFORD CHURCH.

PLATE 69

Four panels on E.

Four centre panels.

Four panels on W.

TARRANT CRAWFORD CHURCH. S. wall of nave, upper zone: Acts of St. Margaret.   14th century

PLATE 70

Surviving wing, formerly stables, exterior from S.E.

Bridge and gateway at entrance to park.
TARRANT GUNVILLE. (2) Eastbury.

1717–38

PLATE 71

The house in course of demolition; watercolour, Society of Antiquaries' collection.   *c.* 1780

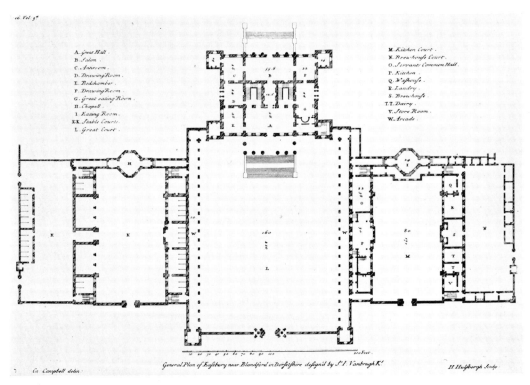

Plan, from *Vitruvius Britannicus*.
TARRANT GUNVILLE. (2) Eastbury.   1717–38

PLATE 72

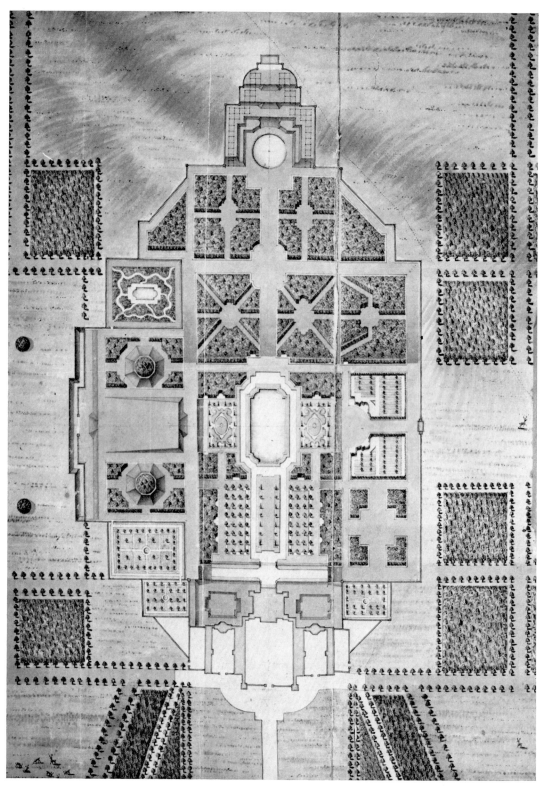

Bridgeman's plan of gardens; watercolour, Bodleian Library.   *c.* 1717
TARRANT GUNVILLE. (2) Eastbury.

in a two-centred head; the N. and S. walls have windows with single trefoil-headed lights. The chancel arch is two-centred and of two chamfered orders springing from responds with attached shafts.

Above the chancel arch the *Nave* has two small E. windows, each of one cinquefoil-headed light in a square-headed surround. The N. and S. arcades are of 1843 and have two-centred arches of two chamfered orders rising from cylindrical piers with moulded capitals. On each side the first, third and fifth bays have square-headed clearstorey windows of two cinquefoil-headed lights.

The *North Aisle* has an E. window of 1843 with two trefoil-headed lights with a central quatrefoil in a two-centred head. In the N. wall the vestry doorway has a chamfered two-centred head. Further W. are two square-headed windows each of two

quatrefoil tracery light, under a two-centred head with a moulded label with square stops with leaf centres, and with a chamfered segmental-pointed rear-arch.

The *West Tower* is of three stages, with a battered, weathered and moulded plinth, weathered and moulded string-courses, and an embattled parapet with a moulded coping. In the two lower stages the N.W. and S.W. corners have diagonal buttresses with weathered offsets. The third stage, altered in the 16th century, has corner pilasters which continue in the parapet, passing through the parapet string-course; a badly decayed gargoyle masks the intersection of each pilaster and the string-course. Crocketed finials which formerly capped the pilasters are now inside the belfry. In the lower stage the 14th-century tower arch, two-centred and of two chamfered orders, springs from three-sided responds with moulded capitals, shaped stops and

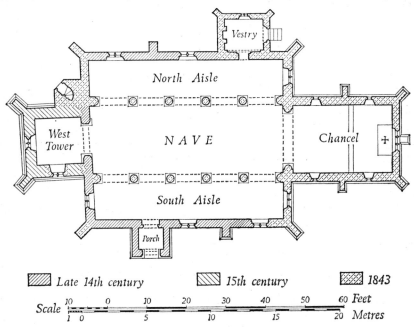

TARRANT GUNVILLE *The Parish Church of St. Mary*

Vestry

North Aisle

West Tower

N A V E

Chancel

South Aisle

Porch

Late 14th century   15th century   1843

Scale   10   0   10   20   30   40   50   60 *Feet*
         1   0   5   10   15   20 *Metres*

trefoil ogee-headed lights; the heads are of 1843, but the lower part of each opening is of the 14th century. Reset in the S. wall of the aisle, between the nave arcade and the aisle roof, are two and a half bays of interlaced round-headed wall arcading, with plain pilasters, moulded imposts and plain archivolts (Plate 8). Hutchins (III, 459) records that the arcading was discovered 'in a like position' when the old building was demolished; it probably decorated the outer face of the N. wall of the original chancel. In the *Vestry* the E. doorway, with a chamfered two-centred head, chamfered jambs and a relieving arch of small voussoirs, incorporates reset mediaeval material; the N. window is similar to the E. window of the N. aisle, but smaller.

The *South Aisle* has E. and S. windows similar to the windows of the N. aisle. The 14th-century S. doorway has a chamfered two-centred head and continuous jambs; the surface of the masonry has been reworked and the chamfered segmental-pointed rear-arch is rendered. In the W. wall of the aisle is a late 14th-century window of two trefoil ogee-headed lights and a

rectangular chamfered plinths. The stair turret, of 1843, has a reset mediaeval two-centred door-head with a weathered label. The W. window in the lower stage of the tower is of the 15th century and has two trefoil-headed lights under a quatrefoil tracery light in a casement-moulded two-centred head; the S. window, uniform with that on the W., but without casement mouldings, is of 1843. In the second stage the tower has a small 15th-century S. window of one light with a chamfered two-centred head; the hollow-chamfered inner surround is later. In the third stage the E. side of the tower retains the creasing of a former nave roof, higher than the present roof. The N. side has a belfry window of two trefoil-headed lights with a central quatrefoil in a casement-moulded two-centred head; the central mullion has gone. The W. side has a similar window, complete. The S. belfry window has two square-headed lights from which the mullion has gone, under blind tracery in a two-centred head.

The *South Porch*, partly rebuilt in 1843, retains a 14th-century archway with a two-centred head of two chamfered orders, the inner order dying into the responds and the outer order continuous, with broach stops. The S. gable has chamfered kneelers and a plain coping.

Fittings—*Bells:* three; 1st inscribed 'Iohn Tvrner, Thomas Sannders, Chvrchwarde: Clement Tosier cast me in yer of 1714, NS'; 2nd by John Wallace, inscribed 'In God reioyce ever, IW 1623'; 3rd by Thomas Mears, 1843. *Brass* and *Indent:* In S. aisle, reset below E. window of S. wall, portion of brass plate with black-letter inscription; 15th century. Reset in tower vice, broken floor-slab with indent 7 ins. by 1½ ins. *Chair:* with turned legs, uprights and stretchers, shaped front stretcher, shaped and fretted back cresting, cane back-panel; 17th century. *Coffin-stools:* pair, with turned legs, plain stretchers and beaded tops; late 17th century. *Glass:* In nave, reset in N. window above chancel arch, panel with shield-of-arms of King Henry VIII impaling those of Queen Katharine Howard, in garter, with crown above and rose and portcullis badges below, and with initials HR and KH; reset in corresponding S. window, similar panel with King Henry's arms impaling those of Queen Katharine Parr, with initials KP, other details as before; 16th century. In S. aisle, reset in W. window, small shield-of-arms of Keynell impaling another coat, probably 18th century. In N. window of vestry, black-letter inscription 'IW restoravit 1845', with foliate ornament. In W. window of tower, two panels with grisaille, foliate borders and black-letter inscription 'Ex dono THW et TB, 1845'. *Graffiti:* on N. respond of tower arch, scratched names from 1768.

Monuments: In S. aisle, on S. wall, (1) of Thomas Wedgwood, 1805, marble tablet by Kent of Blandford. In tower, on N. wall, (2) of Richard and Abigail Swayne, 1725, segmental-headed marble monument with cherub-head frieze, pilasters and segmental cornice. Externally, reset in S. wall of chancel, (3) of [Thomas Daccomb], stone tablet with inscription in incised Roman capitals 'HERE LITHE S.T.D. PARSON: ALL FOWRE BE BVT ONE, EARTHE FLESCH, WORME AND BONE: X : MCCCCCLXVII' (Plate 23). Above, on separate tablet, shield-of-arms of Daccomb of Stepleton.

Niche: Above porch arch, with cinquefoil two-centred head, 14th century. *Plate:* includes Elizabethan cup by the 'Gillingham' silversmith, of usual pattern; two cups with assay marks of 1809, one inscribed 'Tarrant Gunville near Blandford Dorset', the other with 'Given to the Parish of Gunville by Francis Simpson Rector 1810'; stand-paten without assay marks, perhaps 17th century; stand-paten with mark of 1723 and inscription 'Gunvil 1727'; spoon with round bowl and tapering handle, square in section, with finial in form of beast holding shield, perhaps 16th century, foreign. *Royal Arms:* above tower arch, painted metal panel with arms of Victoria in foliate border; above, scroll with inscription 'Fear God Honour the King', 1843. *Scratch Dial:* on S. wall of porch, with black-letter numerals and stump of iron gnomon, early 16th century.

SECULAR

(2) EASTBURY HOUSE (93211270), of two and of three storeys, with walls mainly of Greensand ashlar and with slate-covered roofs (Plate 70), is a surviving fragment of the splendid mansion designed by Vanbrugh for George Dodington and his nephew George Bubb, afterwards Lord Melcombe, and erected between 1717 and 1738. On Lord Melcombe's death in 1762 the house passed to Lord Temple who, unable to find either a buyer or a tenant for what then was considered an

eyesore, demolished the greater part, between c. 1775 and 1782 (Plate 71).

For descriptions and illustrations of the former house, see Colen Campbell, *Vitruvius Britannicus*, III, pls. 15–19 ; Bishop Pococke, *Travels through England*, II, 138–40 (Camden Soc., xliv, 1889) ; Hutchins III, 454–8 ; Oswald, 149–153 ; Laurence Whistler, *Country Life*, 1948, 1386–9. Campbell's plan is reproduced on Plate 71.

The present house is formed from part of two parallel ranges, formerly stables, which stood on the N. of Vanbrugh's forecourt. Early in the 19th century the house was aquired by J. J. Farquharson, whose descendants still own it. From 1800 to 1805 it was occupied by Thomas Wedgwood, a son of the great potter.

Other surviving elements of Vanbrugh's work include the arch on the W. of the former stable court (Plate 80), the main gateway of the park (Plate 70), the cellar under the octagonal 'Eating Room' on the E. of the former kitchen court, and earthwork remains of the former gardens.

Architectural Description—The S. range of the house comprises the nine central bays of Vanbrugh's stable range, together with the corresponding forecourt arcade. The S. front is symmetrical, with the three middle bays in the form of a three-storeyed tower, flanked by two-storeyed wings. The lower storey, with round-headed sashed windows, is fronted by the nine uniform round-headed arches of the arcade, with moulded archivolts springing from plain imposts on rectangular ashlar piers. The loggia behind the arcade has plain cross-vaulting. In the second storey the tower has three tall round-headed sashed windows, and each wing has three small bull's-eye lights below a plain entablature with a moulded cornice. In the third storey the tower has small segmental-headed sashed windows; above is a bold modillion cornice and a parapet with a plain coping. An 18th-century painting in the house (*Country Life, loc. cit.*, fig. 2) shows that the tower parapet originally had acorn finials; these now stand on the ground in front of the building.

The E. elevation has, in the lower storey, a large three-light sashed window with Ionic pilasters and entablature of Bath stone, probably formed c. 1800 when the eastern bays of the original range were removed. The upper storey has two small square-headed windows. The gable, with a blind roundel and a chimneystack finial, appears to be the E. gable of the original stable range, moved to a new position. The W. elevation is similar to that on the E., but with two round-headed windows in the lower storey; again the gable and finial are likely to have originated at the W. end of the former stable range. The N. elevation of Vanbrugh's stable range is partly masked by 19th-century additions, but the western part is exposed. In the lower storey, corresponding with the three western bays of the S. front, are two round-headed recesses with plain archivolts springing from pilasters with plain imposts; each recess contains a round-headed window, now walled up. Further E. the lower storey is masked, but the first and second storeys have details as described in the S. front; the central bay, however, is set forward from the lateral bays to emphasize the former entrance to the stables.

The two-storeyed N. range comprises the eastern half of Vanbrugh's second stable range. The walls are of coursed Greensand ashlar, with plain plinths and cornices similar to those of the

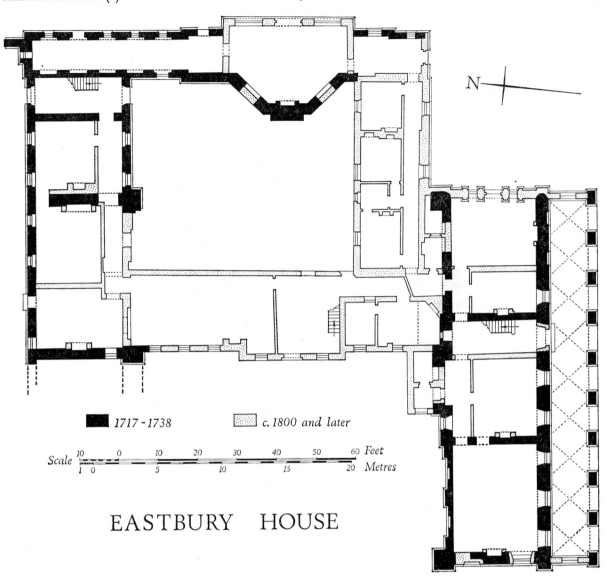

■ *1717 - 1738*   ▨ *c. 1800 and later*

Scale   10   0   10   20   30   40   50   60 *Feet*
        1   0   5   10   15   20 *Metres*

EASTBURY HOUSE

S. range. The range now is of seven bays, with tall round-headed windows in the lower storey and with segmental-headed windows above. The gabled N. wall has a simple open pediment formed by the return of the cornice, and a round-headed first-floor window. The S. wall, of rubble, was originally an internal partition. The piers at the S.E. and S.W. angles retain the imposts for the archway which connected the two stable courts in Vanbrugh's design.

The E. range is single-storeyed and remains externally much as built, except that the octagonal chapel has been reduced in height from two storeys to one, and a straight wall with three large round-headed arches has taken the place of the three eastern sides. The original form of the chapel is seen in the painting mentioned above. In the E. elevation, immediately N. and S. of the former chapel, are single-storeyed bays with original round-headed openings. Further N. and S. are original galleries with elliptical bull's-eye windows; the southern gallery is now reduced to a single bay.

Inside, the rooms are of *c.* 1800. The ground-floor drawing-room at the W. end of the S. range has a richly carved fireplace surround and other carved woodwork of 18th-century date, brought from elsewhere. The doorways have carved pulvinated friezes and broken pediments enclosing shell finials. The adjoining room has a reset chimneypiece with a pedimented over-mantel with Ionic pilasters, and panelled walls enriched with swags of drapery and flower pendants. The rooms on the E. also have reset enrichments similar to those described. The stairs up to the first floor in the S. range are modern; above, they are of *c.* 1800 and have open strings, turned balusters, square newels and heavy moulded handrails; the step spandrels have plain scrolls; the dado has fielded panelling, and moulded capping corresponding with the handrail. The staircase in the N. range,

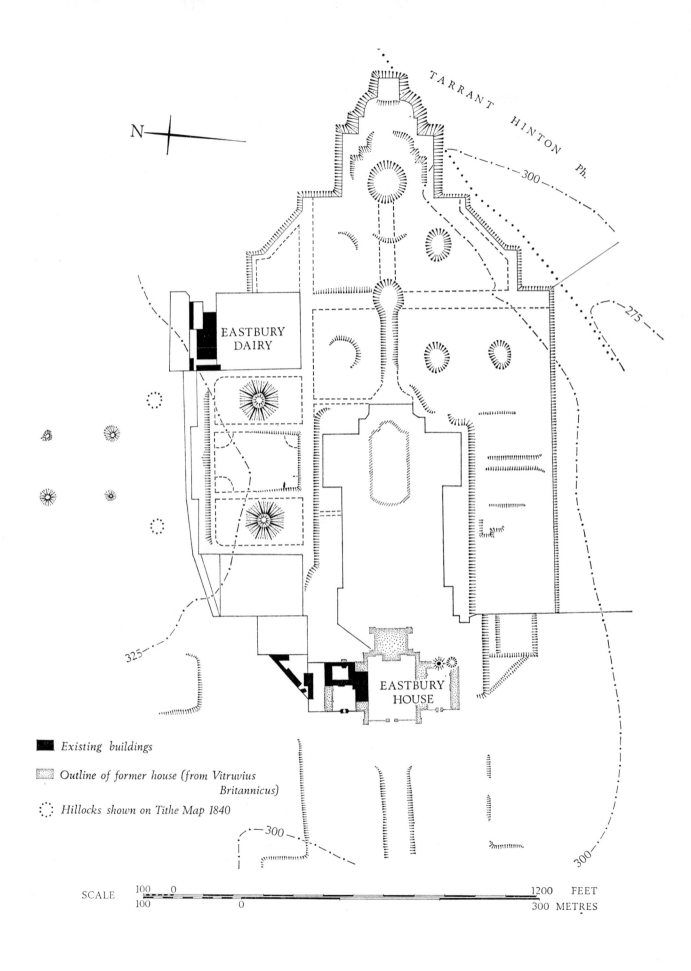

N

TARRANT HINTON Ph.

300

275

EASTBURY DAIRY

325

EASTBURY HOUSE

■ Existing buildings

▦ Outline of former house (from Vitruvius
Britannicus)

⋯ Hillocks shown on Tithe Map 1840

300

300

SCALE

100   0   1200   FEET

100   0   300 METRES

with close strings, turned balusters and heavy moulded handrails carried across plain newel-posts, is an original feature of Vanbrugh's stable range.

The third and northernmost *Stable Range* of the three parallel ranges, shown on Campbell's plan (Plate 71) but not on Bridgeman's garden plan (Plate 72), appears to have been added in the second half of the 18th century. It is single-storeyed and has gabled E. and W. ends and a S. front of ashlar, with plain round-headed windows. The N. wall, of brick, is probably part of Bridgeman's garden wall, adapted when the range was built. Immediately on the E. of the range the brick wall is pierced by an elliptical-headed ashlar archway.

Below ground, some 80 yds. S. of the present house is a half-ruined octagonal *Cellar*, nearly 24 ft. in diameter, with walls and shallow domical vault in English-bonded brickwork. Adjacent on the N. is a small rectangular chamber with a cross-vault, and further N. is a corridor with a barrel-vaulted roof. These are the substructures of the range on the S. of Vanbrugh's house, corresponding with the Chapel range on the N.; the octagonal building is described on Campbell's plan as the 'Eating Room'.

The original *Archway* on the W. of Vanbrugh's stable court (Plate 80) is of Greensand ashlar and comprises a single round-headed arch, with a slightly projecting archivolt, above massive piers with plain plinths and string-courses. Above is an entablature with an arcaded corbel-table and a plain coping. Buttresses flanking the arch are surmounted by stone scrolls, decorated with acanthus foliage in contrast with the austere plainness of the other masonry. By a freak of nature two saplings lodged in the parapet have grown to a considerable size.

The *Gateway* to the main approach, about 500 yds. W. of the former house, has original rusticated piers with ball finials, flanked by plain ashlar screen walls with smaller ball finials at each end (Plate 70). On the E. side, facing into the park, each screen wall has a round-headed niche. On the W., set forward from the gateway, detached piers, smaller than those first described, are said to be of recent construction. At the approach to the gateway the road passes over the R. Tarrant on an original round-arched bridge with heavy rusticated voussoirs.

Another *Gateway* to the park, 800 yds. S. of the former house, on the parish boundary with Tarrant Hinton, has ashlar piers with vermiculate rustication surmounted by pedimented finials with swags of drapery on the friezes; below the friezes are plat-bands with Greek-key enrichment.

The *Gardens* on the E. of the house, designed by Charles Bridgeman, were laid out while the house was under construction. They were one of Bridgeman's early works and serve to illustrate the combination of formal 17th-century garden layout with the 18th-century concept of romantic parkland, the park becoming a background for the garden. Several of Bridgeman's drawings, basically alike, but with minor variations, are preserved in the Bodleian Library (Gough Maps, vi, ff. 93, 94); the central part of one drawing is reproduced on Plate 72. The general outline of the gardens, preserved in the form of earthworks (plan opposite), composed an approximately oval shape some 500 yds. by 300 yds., with the house set axially at the W. end. A ha-ha formed much of the perimeter and within it the gardens were laid out in the old formal style. A long vista, extending eastwards from the great saloon at the centre of the E. front of the house, traversed a parterre, a canal, a glade and a round pool, and terminated in a terraced amphitheatre at the top of which was a portico, called the Great Temple. On each side of the vista, near the house, were formal flower beds, groves and lawns; beyond, to the E., rectangular groves were intersected by grassy walks. A cross-axis centred on the canal extended northwards across a terraced lawn between two octagonal

mounds crowned with trees; to E. and W. were walled gardens. On the S. the cross-axis passed through an area with flower beds, flanked to E. and W. by rectangular groves of trees; further W. lay another walled garden.

The formal gardens were surrounded by an extensive park, broken up by groves into rectangular and triangular areas. On the N. the two octagonal mounds of the N.–S. cross-axis were echoed by fourteen small tree-covered hillocks, set out in two parallel lines across the park.

The garden was abandoned in 1782 and the area appears without regular form on O.S., 1811. Some of the trees were 'removed hither some miles off after fifty years growth and weighed three tons' (Hutchins III, 456). The park was altered in the 19th century, and some of the square groves were incorporated with belts of trees, forming a triangle with Gunville House (3) at the apex; probably at about the same time houses on either side of the main gate were removed. The W. half of the central garden, including the lawns and the canal, was destroyed before 1840; the Tithe Map of that year shows the area as arable. The E. part of the garden remained, abandoned but intact, until it was ploughed up in 1958.

In spite of the destruction much of the layout remains; the adaptation of the original design to the sloping ground necessitated considerable earthworks, and these are still seen, even in the ploughed areas. The W. part of the central vista and its associated lawns, canal and groves was separated from the areas on the N. and S. by scarps 6 ft. to 8 ft. high, which still remain; the glades at the E. end also remain as slight depressions in the modern fields. In the same area part of the central vista survives as a broad sunk way, 50 ft. wide and 3 ft. deep. The canal appears as a soil-mark on air photographs (R.A.F., V.A.P., 58/3250 : 0133–4), probably because it is lined with masonry. The circular pond and the amphitheatre at the E. end have now entirely gone, but traces of the general layout and of the enclosing ha-ha are seen on air photographs taken before the ploughing (R.A.F., V.A.P. CPE/UK 1974 : 4150–1 and CPE/UK 1944 : 4315–6). On the S. side of the garden the ha-ha remains intact, and slight traces of one of the groves together with a sunk way which was one of the grassy walks continue to exist in an overgrown wood. The walled garden in the S.W. corner, immediately S. of the S. wing of the former house, remains as a sunk rectangular area 1 ft. deep.

On the N., the brick perimeter walls of the three gardens remain. The terraced lawn at the centre of this side of the garden remains, as do the octagonal mounds; the latter are about 140 ft. in diameter and 20 ft. high, and retain their octagonal pyramidal form, with small rounded mounds on top. Beyond, in the park, eleven of the fourteen hillocks still exist, some 50 ft. in diameter and 4 ft. high. The two southernmost hillocks were destroyed in the present century and one of the others had already been destroyed before 1840; of the remaining hillocks, two have been reduced by modern ploughing.

Elsewhere in the park the sites of former groves are marked by square or triangular enclosures, bounded by low banks up to 1 ft. high and 8 ft. wide. The road approaching the house from the W. lies in the bottom of an artificial valley, 130 ft. wide and 3 ft. to 5 ft. deep.

GUNVILLE

(3) GUNVILLE HOUSE (92491261), of three storeys, with walls partly of ashlar and partly rendered, and with slate-covered roofs, is of the late 18th century; in 1798 it was advertised as 'newly erected' (*Salisbury Journal*, 19 March). The house appears to have been built by

the Chapman family in place of an old manor house which formerly belonged to the Swaynes. Some of the materials may well have been taken from Eastbury on its demolition in 1782. In 1799 the house was occupied by Josiah Wedgwood II, a year before his brother Thomas moved into the remains of Eastbury.

The rendered N. front, symmetrical and of five bays, has on the ground floor a central doorway under a porch with Ionic columns and a flat entablature, flanked by square-headed sashed windows and, in the outer bays, Palladian windows with Tuscan columns; the two upper storeys have plain square-headed sashed windows; the roof is masked by an ashlar parapet above a moulded cornice. The ashlar S. front is a severely plain composition of seven bays, with a central doorway in the lower storey and plain square-headed sashed windows elsewhere. A two-storeyed service wing on the E. of the main block has the windows of the S. front so arranged that the wing appears to be single-storeyed. A corresponding wing on the W., containing a ball-room, was built c. 1880 and has recently been demolished.

Inside, the principal rooms have dadoes and fireplace surrounds in the 'Adam' style with *carton-pierre* enrichment; the room at the centre of the S. front has doorcases, frieze and ceiling cornice richly decorated in the same manner. A small marble chimney-piece was supplied by Flaxman in 1800 (B.M. Add. MS. 37884, BB, 14). Until recently the S.W. room had a wooden dado painted with bacchanalian scenes; these panels, perhaps of 18th-century origin, are said to have been brought from Holland in the second half of the 19th century.

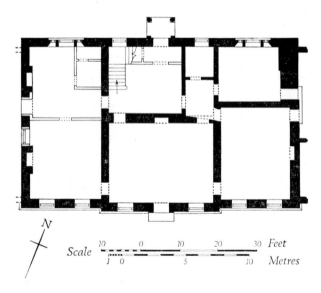

Scale

The *Stables*, 50 yds. N. of the house, are two-storeyed and have brick walls and slated roofs with lead ridges; they are of the late 18th century and have a half-H plan. In the gardens are seven heraldic stone lions, sejant and bearing shields-of-arms; three shields are blank, one has the arms of Dodington, the others are not decipherable; presumably these ornaments were brought from Eastbury and are of the first half of the 18th century. A cast lead pump-head has the initials J.W. for Josiah Wedgwood, and the date 1801.

(4) THE OLD RECTORY (92621271), of three storeys with cellars, has walls of banded flint and ashlar, and tile-covered roofs (Plate 74); it was built for Francis Simpson, rector 1797–1827, probably early in his incumbency (letter from Simpson, B.M. Add. MS. 37909, f. 138). The N., E. and S. fronts are each symmetrical and of three bays, with tall windows in the two principal storeys and with square windows in the third storey, all sashed. The W. elevation has only the staircase windows.

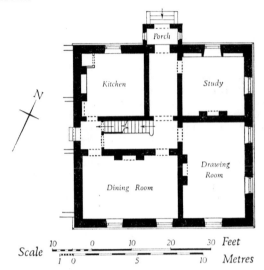

Scale

Inside, the stairs up to first-floor level are of stone, with moulded nosing and plain timber balustrades; above the first floor they are of wood, with Tuscan column newel-posts. The principal ground-floor rooms have moulded plaster cornices and marble fireplace-surrounds. The study has original bookcases.

(5) BUSSEY STOOL FARM (92821476), house, partly of two storeys and partly single-storeyed with attics, has walls partly of brick and partly of flint and rubble with random blocks of ashlar, and ashlar quoins; the roofs are tiled. The original 17th-century range was single-storeyed and had a class-I plan.[1] Early in the 18th century a two-storeyed brick-built wing was added on the W. side of the range, at the N. end, and soon afterwards the N. end of the 17th-century range was refaced in brickwork and increased in height to correspond with the wing, thus creating a two-storeyed N. elevation of four bays, with square-headed casement windows, simple brick pilasters, and a brick dentil eaves cornice. Inside, the ground-floor rooms of the 17th-century range have stop-chamfered ceiling beams; several rooms in the attic have doors with 17th-century moulded panelling, one of them hung on original wrought-iron hinges. The first-floor room of the 18th-century wing has fielded panelling in two heights, and a fireplace surround and overmantel with bolection-moulded wood panelling.

(6) MARLBOROUGH FARM (92431308), house, of two storeys, with walls of banded flint and ashlar, is of the late 18th century; the roofs were formerly thatched, but are now asbestos-covered. The S.W. front is symmetrical and of three bays, with a central doorway under a hood with shaped timber brackets, and with square-headed casement windows in both storeys of the side bays; above the doorway is a blind recess. Inside, the plan is of

---

[1] *Dorset* III, lviii.

class I. Each main ground-floor room has an exposed chamfered ceiling beam.

(7) CHINA COTTAGE (92581297), of two storeys, with walls partly of brickwork and partly of flint and ashlar, and with thatched roofs, is probably of the late 18th century. The building appears to have originated as two tenements. Inside, an open fireplace has a chamfered oak bressummer.

(8) HOUSE (92601282), of two storeys, with walls of banded flint and brickwork and with a slate-covered roof, is of the early 19th century. The S.W. front is symmetrical and of three bays with segmental-headed two-light casement windows and a central doorway. Inside, the plan is of class T. The parlour has an original chimneypiece with a moulded mantelshelf; flanking it are cupboards with shaped shelves.

(9) HOME FARM (91721210), formerly 'Glebe Farm', is a two-storeyed farmhouse with cob walls and a tiled roof. The house is of the late 19th century, but it is constructed within the walls and under the roof of a small barn of c. 1800.

MONUMENTS (10–18)

Unless otherwise described, the following 18th-century dwellings are of two storeys and have cob walls and thatched roofs; the ground-plans are of class S.

(10) *Cottage* (92591278), probably of the early 18th century, is single-storeyed with an attic. Inside, two chamfered beams are exposed. Adjacent on the S. is a 19th-century smithy.

(11) *Cottage* (92551278), with walls of flint and ashlar and with slate-covered roofs, is of the early 19th century. Adjoining cottages on the N.W. and S.E. are of somewhat later date.

(12) *Cottage* (92521284), with a high plinth of flint with ashlar quoins at the base of the cob, has a symmetrical N.E. front of three bays.

(13) *Cottage* (92471285), with the lower storey of flint and ashlar, and the upper storey of cob, dates probably from early in the 18th century. The two original rooms have been combined and another room has been added on the N.W. Inside, some chamfered beams are exposed.

(14) *Cottage* (92521291), with walls of rubble with brick quoins, is of late 18th or early 19th-century origin. The original dwelling has been enlarged by the addition of an adjoining tenement, with one room in each storey.

(15) *Westbury* (92441293), farmhouse, was originally two class-S cottages. One cottage is of the mid 18th century and has cob walls; at right-angles on the W. is a late 18th-century cottage with walls of chequered flint and ashlar, probably derived from Eastbury. Additions on the E., of flint with brick quoins, are of the 19th century.

(16) *Cottage* (92421300).

(17) *Cottages* (92201330), two adjacent, now combined to form one dwelling, have each a class-S plan. The S. tenement is the older of the two, but its upper storey was rebuilt in the 19th century. The N. tenement is of ashlar and rubble, probably taken from Eastbury.

(18) *Cottage* (92071341), of one storey with an attic, has cob walls heightened in brickwork, and tiled roofs; it comprises two small class-S tenements.   (*N. tenement demolished, 1968.*)

Four early 19th-century cottages in Gunville are two-storeyed, with cob walls and thatched or modern slated roofs; all but one

have class-S plans: *Park Cottage* (92751254); *Cottage* (92501288), with a class-J plan; *Cottage* (92381310); *Cottage* (92181332).

STUBHAMPTON

(19) COTTAGES (91431418), two adjacent, now combined, are single-storeyed and have cob walls and thatched roofs. Both dwellings are of the 18th century, that on the S.W. being the earlier; in each the plan is of class S. Inside, there are exposed beams and two open fireplaces.

(20) STUBHAMPTON FARM (91751378), house, of two storeys, with flint and rubble walls, ashlar and brick quoins, and slate-covered roofs, is of the late 18th century. The S.W. front is symmetrical and of three bays, with a central doorway and with segmental-headed three-light casement windows. Inside, the plan is of class T. A stable building on the N. of the house is probably contemporary.

(21) FARMHOUSE (91841366), of two storeys, with banded brick and flint walls and slate-covered roofs, is of the early 19th century. The plan is of class T.

MONUMENTS (22–27)

The following monuments are of the late 18th or of the first half of the 19th century; they are two-storeyed with tiled roofs, and all have class-S plans, either paired or single. In each case the range is set at right-angles to the road.

(22) *Cottage* (91401409), with walls of brick, flint and cob.

(23) *Cottage* (91481405), with cob walls, has been extended on the N.E.

(24) *Cottages* (91691383), pair, have walls of banded brick-work and flint in the lower storey, and of cob above.

(25) *Cottage* (91841362), has walls as described in (24).

(26) *House* (91851359), formerly a pair of cottages, has walls wholly of brickwork banded with flint.

(27) *Cottages* (91861356), pair, are uniform with (24).

MEDIAEVAL AND LATER EARTHWORKS

For earthwork remains at EASTBURY, see (2).

(28) SETTLEMENT REMAINS (927126), near the principal gateway to Eastbury, occur on both sides of the Tarrant brook. Houses were still standing early in the 19th century (O.S., 1811), but at least four of them had gone by 1840 (Tithe Map) and the others were removed later in the 19th century. The remains comprise ten or more long closes, bounded by low banks set at right-angles to the brook. Disturbed areas at the lower ends of the closes indicate former buildings.

(29) CULTIVATION REMAINS. Nothing is known of the mediaeval fields of Stubhampton or Gunville. Indistinct traces of contour strip lynchets N.W. of Gunville (920133) probably represent the fields of that settlement. More extensive traces of contour strip lynchets on the S.W. of Stubhampton (917136) have recently been ploughed down. 'Celtic' fields on Stubhampton Down (see p. 120, Group (76)) were reploughed to form strip cultivation in mediaeval times, or perhaps later.

(30) HARBIN'S PARK (9013), a Deer Park of 115 acres recorded in 1279, lies in the W. of the parish and extends across the E. declivity of a dry valley. More or less rectangular in plan, it is bounded by banks up to 16 ft. in width and 5 ft. in height, with inner ditches 15 ft. wide (*Dorset Procs.*, 86 (1965), 170–2).

(31) PILLOW MOUND (90741422), an unploughed 'island surrounded by arable on the steep S. slope of Earl's Hill, lies parallel with the contours and is 85 ft. long and 16 ft. wide. A shallow ditch 7 ft. wide lies along the up-hill side, and a terrace 9 ft. wide, probably the remains of a ditch, lies along the down-hill side of the mound. From above the mound stands 1 ft. high; from below it is 4 ft. high. (*Wessex from the Air*, 20.)

ROMAN AND PREHISTORIC

ROMAN ROAD from Badbury Rings to Bath, traversing the E. side of the parish, see *Dorset* V.

'CELTIC' FIELDS, see pp. 119, 120; Groups (73), (76).

(32) IRON AGE HILL-FORT (930156), at Bussey Stool Park, 450 ft. above sea-level, occupies a level site at the S. end of a Chalk spur. It is an oval, univallate enclosure of 5½ acres, with entrances on the N.W. and S.E. The earthwork is planted with trees and much of it, especially the defences, is barely accessible

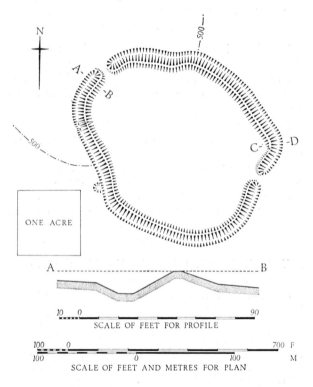

ONE ACRE

SCALE OF FEET FOR PROFILE

SCALE OF FEET AND METRES FOR PLAN

on account of the thick undergrowth. Where well-preserved the bank is 34 ft. across and 6 ft. high; the ditch is 28 ft. across and 5 ft. deep. The entrances are about 15 ft. wide, flanked by the out-turned ends of the banks. On the N. of the S.E. entrance some 80 ft. of the bank has been removed. (Sumner, *Cranborne Chase*, 31.)

(33) ENCLOSURE (93051523), probably of the Iron Age, lies on a gentle S. slope at the head of a shallow combe, some 250 yds. S. of (32). It is sub-rectangular in plan, with an internal area of 1¼ acres; the entrance, on the S., faces down the combe. The enclosure was levelled *c.* 1911 and today appears only as a soil-mark or crop-mark, but before levelling it had a bank and ditch up to 45 ft. wide, with the bank standing some 4 ft. high above

the interior. Burnt flints have been found on the site, but nothing else. (Sumner, *op. cit.*, 31; *Dorset Procs.*, 82 (1960), 84.)

(34) ENCLOSURE (934140), probably of the Iron Age, on Main Down, some 390 ft. above sea-level, lies on the nearly flat top of a N.–S. Chalk ridge, just E. of the Roman Road. In plan it is kidney-shaped, measuring some 600 ft. by 450 ft. and covering about 4 acres. Although flattened by cultivation it is still seen on air photographs (N.M.R., ST 9313/2–6; 9314/1–3).

(35) ENCLOSURE ? (91651425), on Dungrove Hill, at about 390 ft. above O.D. and on a S.W. slope at the end of a spur, is visible only on air photographs (N.M.R., ST 9114/1–2). The feature is roughly circular and about 200 ft. in diameter. A narrow funnelled entrance leads into it on the S.E.

(36) BOWL BARROW (90831438), in Earl's Hill Coppice, lies on the E. slope of a spur, over 400 ft. above O.D.; diam. 30 ft., ht. 2 ft.

(37) BOWL BARROW (91091488), on the shoulder of a spur overlooking Stubhampton Bottom, is 450 ft. above O.D.; diam. 40 ft., ht. less than 1 ft.

26 TARRANT HINTON

(O.S. 6 ins., ST 90 NW, ST 91 SW, ST 91 SE)

Tarrant Hinton, a parish of some 2,300 acres, occupies the Tarrant valley immediately S. of Gunville (Plate 73). The land, entirely Chalk, falls from about 400 ft. above sea-level in the S.W. to about 220 ft. at the Tarrant, and then rises to a little over 300 ft. before falling once more to the Crichel Brook, which crosses the narrow N.E. extremity of the parish.

The open fields, together with some downland, were finally enclosed in 1827 (Map and Award, D.C.R.O.). Until 1933 the parish included the mediaeval settlement of Hyde, now part of PIMPERNE (p. 52). Hinton village, the original mediaeval settlement, consists of farmhouses and cottages, mostly grouped between the church and the point where the road from Blandford Forum to Salisbury crosses the Tarrant. The church is the most noteworthy monument. Notable monuments outside the village include Pimperne Long Barrow (24) and two Iron Age settlement sites (18), (19).

ECCLESIASTICAL

(1) THE PARISH CHURCH OF ST. MARY stands in the N. of the village. The walls are partly of ashlar and partly of squared Greensand rubble with flint banding and ashlar dressings; the roofs are lead-covered (Plates 4, 75). The font and some carved stone fragments reset in the S. wall of the aisle indicate a 12th-century church; the earliest part of the present building, how-ever, is the 14th-century *Nave* and its S. arcade. The *Chancel Arch* and the *West Tower* are of the 15th century. Later in the 15th century the nave roof was raised and a clearstorey was inserted, the *South Aisle* was rebuilt, and the *South Porch* was built. In the first half of the

PLATE 73

THE TARRANT VALLEY. Air view, looking N.W. In foreground, Tarrant Hinton; centre, Tarrant Gunville; background, crest of Chalk escarpment with Blackmoor Vale beyond.

D.IV—N

PLATE 74

TARRANT HINTON. (4) The Old Rectory. *c.* 1850

TARRANT GUNVILLE. (4) The Old Rectory. *c.* 1800

PLATE 75

TARRANT HINTON CHURCH. Tower, from S.W.   15th century

PLATE 76

TARRANT HINTON CHURCH. Easter Sepulchre.   Probably *c.* 1536

PLATE 77

TARRANT HINTON CHURCH. Easter Sepulchre, details.   Probably *c.* 1536

PLATE 78

TARRANT LAUNCESTON. (14) Track, ditches and enclosures, N.E. of Romano–British settlement, from S.W.

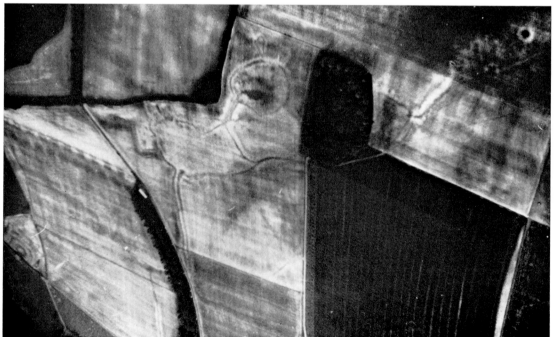

TARRANT HINTON. (19) Iron Age and Romano–British settlement on Tarrant Hinton Down, from S.E.

PLATE 79

TARRANT KEYNESTON. (16) Buzbury Rings, Iron Age and Romano–British settlement site.

TARRANT HINTON. (18) Iron Age and Romano–British settlement S. of Hinton Bushes.

PLATE 80

TARRANT GUNVILLE. (2) Eastbury. Archway to stable court, from W.

1717–38

16th century the *North Chapel* was added, together with an *Easter Sepulchre* on the N. of the chancel. At an unknown date, perhaps early in the 19th century, the easternmost bay of the N. chapel was removed and the present E. wall was built. In 1874 the church was reroofed and the chancel was largely rebuilt under the direction of Benjamin Ferrey.—The S. doorway is of 1892.

The *Easter Sepulchre* (Plates 76, 77) is one of the most important monuments in North Dorset. The initials of Thomas Weaver, rector 1514–36, are incorporated in the design. Hutchins (I, 316) assigns it to the year 1515, but gives no authority; stylistically it appears to be somewhat later, perhaps of *c.* 1536.

Architectural Description—The E. and S. walls of the *Chancel* are of 1874 (Sarum Dioc. Regy.). In the N. wall is the arched recess of the 16th-century Easter Sepulchre (see *Fittings*). Two plinths. Above each arch is a late 15th-century clearstorey window of two cinquefoil-headed lights, with blind spandrels externally in a chamfered square-headed surround; the rear-arches are segmental and of two chamfered orders dying into splayed jambs.

The 16th-century *North Chapel* appears originally to have had an additional bay on the E., removed at an uncertain date when the present E. wall was built. The N. wall has a chamfered and wave-moulded plinth, and two-stage buttresses with weathered and wave-moulded offsets; the eastern buttress is partly of brick. Although now considerably lower, the present E. bay appears formerly to have been of equal height with the W. bay of the chapel. The N. window in the E. bay is of three lights with uncusped four-centred heads below intersecting tracery in a shallow four-centred outer head; internally the mullions and tracery have ogee mouldings; the opening has deep casement-mouldings inside and outside, and an external label with square stops; this window may have been taller originally than now. In the W. bay of the chapel the N. wall is two-storeyed, each

TARRANT HINTON   *The Parish Church of St. Mary*

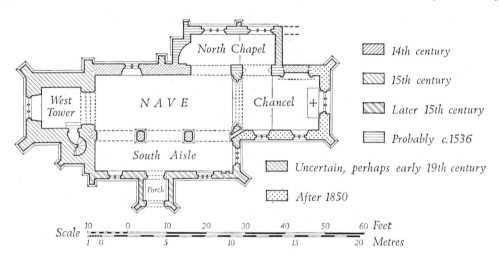

14th century

15th century

Later 15th century

Probably c.1536

Uncertain, perhaps early 19th century

After 1850

Scale   10   0   10   20   30   40   50   60 *Feet*

1   0   5   10   15   20 *Metres*

small windows with two-centred heads appear to be of the 19th century and to take the place of blind panels in the original design. The recess has a four-centred head with double ogee mouldings and continuous jambs. Adjacent on the W., the archway to the N. chapel has mouldings uniform with those of the recess, ending in pyramidal stops. The 15th-century chancel arch is of two hollow-chamfered orders above responds with attached shafts and hollow chamfers; the pseudo-14th-century moulded capitals are probably of 1874. The S. respond is pierced by a small square-headed squint from the S. aisle.

The N. wall of the *Nave* has a chamfered and wave-moulded plinth which continues inside the N. chapel; the square-set central buttress, of two stages with moulded weathering, is a 15th-century addition. The archway to the N. chapel is uniform with that on the N. of the chancel, but higher; incorporated with the W. respond is part of the jamb and head of an original N. window. Further W., the existing N. window is of two uncusped pointed lights, with a central tracery light in a two-centred outer head with a moulded label. On the S. the nave arcade has three plain two-centred arches with chamfers which continue on the piers and responds and end in carved stops above chamfered

D. VI—O

storey having a low window of three lights with four-centred heads in a square-headed casement-moulded surround; the upper storey evidently corresponded with a gallery, now gone, but attested by blocked holes for the floor beams; the rounded recess on the W. presumably contained a wooden stair. A plan of 1874 (Sarum Dioc. Regy.) shows that the two bays of the chapel were at that time separated by a wall, but this is unlikely to have been an original feature and the former gallery probably overlooked the eastern bay of the chapel as well as the nave.

The *South Aisle* has a chamfered and moulded plinth, a diagonal S.E. buttress of two weathered stages, and a corresponding square-set buttress on the S.W. The roof is masked by an embattled parapet with a hollow-chamfered string-course and continuous moulded coping. The E. window is of three cinque-foil-headed lights, with vertical tracery in a two-centred head under a moulded label with square stops with leaf centres; mullions, jambs and tracery have hollow-chamfers and ogee mouldings inside and outside; the rear-arch is chamfered. The eastern window of the S. wall is similar to that in the E. wall; the label has head-stops. The two-light western window is square-headed and without tracery; here the label-stops are shield-shaped .

The *West Tower* (Plate 75) has three stages, with a chamfered and moulded plinth, weathered string-courses between the stages, and an embattled parapet similar to that of the S. aisle. In the two lower stages the N.E. and S.E. corners have square-set three-stage buttresses, and the N.W. and S.W. corners have diagonal buttresses of four stages; the top stage has corner pilasters which continue in the parapet and support gargoyles where they intersect the parapet string-course. The vice turret has a small single-stage buttress, and a weathered stone roof below the second stage of the tower. The tower arch is two-centred and of two chamfered orders, the outer order continuous and the inner order dying into the responds. Above the tower arch and below the present nave roof are the remains of the creasing-course of a low-pitched roof, dating from before the construction of the clearstorey. The lower and upper doorways in the stair turret have chamfered two-centred heads and continuous jambs; four plain loops light the stairs. The W. window is of three cinquefoil-headed lights with vertical tracery in a two-centred head under a moulded label with square stops, and with a chamfered two-centred rear-arch. The ringing chamber floor rests on four stop-chamfered beams. In the second stage there is a square-headed N. window. In the top stage each side of the belfry has a window of two trefoil-headed lights with a central quatrefoil in a two-centred head under a moulded label with square stops.

The *South Porch* has plinth and parapet continuous with those of the S. aisle; the S.E. and S.W. corners have small two-stage buttresses. The porch archway has a rounded head with a moulded arris under a moulded label with square stops with leaf centres.

Fittings—*Bells:* three; 1st with black-letter inscription 'Sunt mea spes hij tres xpe. maria joh'es', mediaeval; 2nd by Robert Austen (*Dorset Procs.*, 60 (1938), 119), inscribed 'At thy departure I shall sound and ring to bring thee into ground' above band of scrollwork, roses and thistles, and '1640 WI.RH'; 3rd by T. Mears, 1831. *Brackets:* two, on responds of archway from chancel to N. chapel, octagonal, with mouldings corresponding with those on Easter Sepulchre (see below) and with deeply carved foliate enrichment on under side; W. bracket retains dowel hole of supporting shaft, now gone; *c.* 1536. *Communion Rails:* (Plate 21) with moulded and foliated rails shouldered at N. and S. ends, enriched turned and twisted balusters, and end-posts carved with cherub heads and flower pendants; made *c.* 1665 for Pembroke College Chapel, Cambridge; transferred *c.* 1880 (see R.C.H.M., *Cambridge City*, 153).

The *Easter Sepulchre* (Plates 76, 77) comprises a recess with a moulded four-centred head and continuous jambs flanked by half-columns which carry an entablature. Part of the four-centred head is visible on the N. face of the wall, showing that the recess was originally an opening through the wall and implying that the N. chapel formerly comprised a third bay on the E. The spandrels on the S. face of the four-centred head are embellished with scroll-like ribbons and medallions; the E. medallion contains three figures, probably the three Marys, one bearing a vase, the others defaced; the W. medallion contains an angel bust. The columns have pedestals with cherub heads; the shafts are fluted in the lower half and in the upper part are enriched with arabesques; the capitals are composite, with tall acanthus leaves and reversed volutes, a possible prototype of the reversed volutes of the 18th-century Blandford architects (*Dorset* III, BLANDFORD FORUM (45), (47); Oswald, 32–5). Carved in relief on the frieze of the entablature is the inscription VENITE ET VIDETE LOCV[M] VBI POSIT[US] ER[AT] D[OMI]N[U]S, flanked by cherub-head panels and, at each end, by the mono-

grams TW and TT, for Thomas Weaver, alias Trotteswell (see PIMPERNE (4)), rector 1514–36. Over the entablature is a recess with a four-centred head with double ogee mouldings, continuous on the jambs and running out in plain chamfers. The splayed sides of the recess contain semicircular niches with four-centred heads with carved spandrels. The rear wall of the recess has three panels, the two lateral panels now with windows, the central panel blind. On the wall flanking the recess are two kneeling angels, in high relief, their knees on small moulded corbels. On the W. of the sepulchre the archway to the N. chapel has mouldings of the same profile as the upper recess; the brackets (*q.v.*) which project from the responds have details corresponding with those of the entablature above the lower recess.

Font: (Plate 11) of Purbeck marble, with square bowl with five round-headed sunken panels on each side, on cylindrical centre shaft and four small corner shafts, and chamfered square base, 12th century; font-cover of oak, with flat round board and six scroll-shaped supports to centre post, 17th century. *Lectern:* (Plate 13) of wrought-iron and brass, 1909.

Monument and *Floorslabs: Monument:* In S. aisle, of Ann King, 1822, marble tablet by Simmonds of Blandford. *Floorslabs:* In nave, at E. end, (1) of Richard Fowler, 1697; (2) of [Mrs. Holden], 1744.

Niches: In S. aisle, reset at E. end of S. wall, with chamfered pointed head and continuous jambs, perhaps originally a window, 13th century; in S. porch, reset above doorway, with chamfered four-centred head, continuous jambs and shaped stops, 15th or 16th century.

Plate: includes silver cup with assay marks of 1820, paten of [1716], alms-bowl of 1804, and flagon of 1840. *Piscina:* in S. aisle, adjacent to niche, with reused double-chamfered round head, perhaps from a 12th-century window, and rectangular bowl with drain, probably 15th century. *Pulpit:* of oak, hexagonal, with two heights of fielded panelling, and moulded cornice and base, 18th century. *Royal Arms:* painted on board in moulded frame, 1802. *Seating:* in tower, oak bench with plain arm-rests and back, upright members with knob finials, 17th century. *Stoup:* in S. aisle, beside S. doorway, with projecting bowl cut off, in recess with chamfered two-centred head. *Wall:* bounding churchyard on S. and W., of rubble and ashlar, with chamfered plinth, weathered and roll-moulded coping, and weathered buttress, 15th century. *Miscellanea:* In S. aisle, on sill of E. window, part of Purbeck marble slab carved in relief with cross patonce, perhaps from small 13th-century coffin-slab; reset above S. doorway, carved fragments of column shaft and of chevron mouldings, 12th century.

SECULAR

(2) BRIDGE (93701114), across the Tarrant, with a single brick arch, and brick parapets with stone coping, has a date stone of 1836.

(3) OLD TURNPIKE (94741148), cottage, of one storey, with rendered walls and a slate-covered roof, is of *c.* 1840; the N.W. front has a three-sided bay with casement windows with traceried cast-iron glazing bars.

(4) THE OLD RECTORY (93621103), of two storeys with attics, has walls of red brick patterned with blue headers, ashlar dressings, and tiled roofs. The house was designed by Benjamin Ferrey in the 'Tudor' style and dates probably from *c.* 1850. The S. front (Plate 74) is of three bays, with ground-floor windows of four mullioned and transomed square-headed lights with iron casements with geometrical glazing, first-floor windows of three untransomed lights, and gabled dormer windows of two lights.

A weathered first-floor string-course is turned up, as a label, above the windows of the lower storey; the first-floor windows have separate labels. The gabled E. and W. walls of the S. range have ashlar coping above shaped kneelers, projecting chimney-stacks with weathered offsets and, at the apex, coupled diagonally-set brick flues. The main doorway, in the N.E. wing, has a moulded four-centred head with pierced spandrels in a square-headed surround, and continuous moulded jambs. Inside, the principal rooms have stone fireplace surrounds with moulded four-centred heads.

Reset over an opening in the wall of a courtyard on the N. is a 16th-century four-centred stone door-head, with ogee and hollow-chamfered mouldings, and carved spandrels. One spandrel has a crowned shield-of-arms charged with three coronets, and scrollwork with lettering EST: the other spandrel has similar scrollwork with VIRGO entwined in foliage. The inscription of Thomas Trotteswell/Weaver, recorded by Hutchins (I, 318), has gone.

(5) COTTAGE (93441080), of one storey with an attic, with cob walls and a thatched roof, dates from about the middle of the 18th century and originally had a class-S plan. Early in the 19th century a two-storeyed bay was added on the N. (*Demolished*, 1965.)

(6) 'CROSSWAYS' (93831091), house, of two storeys, has walls partly of brickwork and flint, partly rendered and perhaps of cob, and a thatched roof. The N. end of the E. range retains two pairs of crucks and is probably of 16th-century origin. In the 17th century a bay was added on the S., with a large open fireplace, now blocked. The range was extended further to the S. in the 18th century; at the same time a fireplace was inserted in the original part of the building, a service wing was built on the W., and the E. front was remodelled and made nearly symmetrical.

(7) SOUTH FARM (93811100), house, of two storeys, with walls partly of banded brick and flint, partly of brick and partly of cob, and with tiled roofs, is of the late 18th century. The S.W. front is symmetrical and of three bays, with segmental-headed windows of two and of three lights, and with a central doorway under a hip-roofed porch. The plan is of class T, with a large central vestibule.

(8) POST OFFICE (93761108), of two storeys, with cob walls and a thatched roof, is of the late 18th century.

(9) COTTAGE (93731112), single-storeyed with an attic, with walls of flint and rubble in the lower part and of cob above, and with a thatched roof, is of 17th-century origin. Inside, the attic floor rests on a stop-chamfered beam. Extensions on the S.W. and S.E. are of the 19th century.

(10) HOUSE (93691112), formerly a *School*, of one storey with attics, has walls of flint and ashlar, and tiled roofs. It was built in 1849 in the 'Tudor' style, and has recently been extended on the S.

(11) COTTAGE (93641112), of two storeys, with brick, flint and cob walls, and with a thatched roof, is of the late 18th century. The plan is of class T.

(12) COTTAGE (93621112), of one storey with an attic, with cob walls and a thatched roof, may be of the 18th century, perhaps incorporating parts of an earlier building.

(13) COTTAGE (93601113), of one storey with an attic, has cob walls and a thatched roof; it probably is of the early 18th century, but has been greatly altered internally. A 17th-century chamfered beam is from elsewhere.

(14) COTTAGE (93691115), of one storey with an attic, has cob walls and a thatched roof; it dates from *c.* 1800 and originally had a class-S plan.

(15) COTTAGE (93711112), probably of *c.* 1830.

(16) NEW BARN (93631156), about 400 yds. N. of the church, with walls of weather-boarded studding above high flint and brick plinths, is of the early 18th century. The roof-trusses have tie-beams and braced collar-beams and support two purlins on each side; the roof covering is modern. A *Granary* adjacent on the N.W. has timber walls on staddle-stones. A *Stable* range on the S.E. of the farmyard has flint and brick walls and a tiled roof and probably is of the 18th century.

ROMAN AND PREHISTORIC

(17) ROMAN SETTLEMENT (926119), including a villa, lies N.W. of Barton Hill Dairy on a site overlooking the Tarrant, on the S. and E. slopes of a Chalk spur between 300 ft. and 360 ft. above sea-level. Excavations in 1845 revealed 'extensive remains of foundations, and walls with stucco and coloured facings, extending over an area of nearly twenty acres'. On the N. side of the field, 'at some distance from the spot where the principal remains of foundations were discovered', two rooms about $5\frac{1}{2}$ ft. square flanked a narrow corridor; their floors were variously described as paved with red and white tesserae arranged in parallel rows, or as stuccoed. The walls, of flint and greensand 3 ft. thick, were plastered internally and were painted with 'ribbon-work, arches, foliage etc.'. A well 30 ft. deep contained the base and part of the shaft of a large column 'of a classic character and resembling the Ionic'. Finds included flue and roofing tiles, tesserae, samian and coarse pottery, amphorae, circular pipes (presumably of earthenware), querns, bronze brooches, shale rings, and coins of Constantine and Constantius. Some of these finds, and also fragments of mosaic with guilloche, angular and curved patterns in red, white and two shades of grey, are in D.C.M.; other finds are in the B.M. It has been suggested that the site is *Anicetis* of the Ravenna Cosmography (*J.B.A.A.*, 3rd ser. XVII (1954), 77–8).

The two primary accounts of the excavations of 1845, both by W. Shipp, differ in detail (Hutchins I, 318–19; *Brit. Archaeol. Ass.* (Winchester Congress, 1846), 179–82). Two Durotrigian silver coins in the Pitt-Rivers collection, described as from Tarrant Gunville, may come from this site (S. Frere, ed., *Problems of the Iron Age in Southern Britain* (1960), 240).

Limited test excavations in 1968 and 1969 tended to confirm the 19th-century accounts, yielding evidence of flint walls, generally 2 ft. thick, over a wide area. Two plain tesselated pavements, severely damaged by ploughing, and much decorated wall plaster also came to light. Nearly 50 coins were found, ranging from Lucius Verus to Valentinian, but chiefly of the 3rd and 4th centuries.

(18) IRON AGE AND ROMANO-BRITISH SETTLEMENT (920110), S. of Hinton Bushes, now almost entirely levelled by ploughing, lies between 300 ft. and 380 ft. above sea-level on the gentle S. and E. slopes of a Chalk ridge. It comprises two oval enclosures (Plate 79), linked by a ditch and associated with a series of irregular angular enclosures defined by banks and ditches; it also is associated with 'Celtic' fields (Group 73) immediately on the W., which appear to connect the settlement with the neighbouring enclosure, PIMPERNE (18).

The northern oval, a fragment of which survives in Hinton Bushes, is 600 ft. by 450 ft. in diameter and some 5 acres in area. Formerly it was defined on the S. and E. by a low bank between ditches, and on the N. and W. by a ditch between banks. Slight hollows have been observed in the interior, but no certain entrance is identifiable. A ditch runs southwards from the oval and then curves to link it with the E. side of the southern oval, some 200 yds. away. The latter, 850 ft. by 500 ft. in diameter, is 8 acres in area and appears to have been entered on the E. It was formerly defined by a bank between ditches on the S. and E., and by a bank with an external ditch on the N. and W. Numerous hollows and irregularities inside the oval indicated occupation.

The site is almost certainly of more than one structural phase; finds, chiefly from the southern oval, indicate a lengthy period of occupation. The finds include Iron Age 'A' and 'C' pottery, samian ware, flanged bowls and New Forest ware, parts of two stone mortars, part of a rotary quern, a roof tile, iron nails, and a point, perhaps from a goad. (Sumner, *Cranborne Chase*, 41–2 and pl. xx; *Dorset Procs.*, 82 (1960), 84.)

A boundary dyke, now levelled by ploughing, extends S.W. from the southern oval for some 800 yds., curving around the southern end of Pimperne Long Barrow and extending into Pimperne parish. It consists of a ditch, formerly flanked on each side by low banks. (Sumner, *Cranborne Chase*, 75–6 and pl. xlvi.)

(19) IRON AGE AND ROMANO-BRITISH SETTLEMENT (945126), on Tarrant Hinton Down in the N. of the parish, lies on the S.E. slope of a Chalk ridge, between 260 ft. and 340 ft. above sea-level; it has been levelled by cultivation. Air photographs (Plate 78; N.M.R., ST 9412/5–7), and finds, indicate that the main area of occupation is a strip of land, some 500 ft. by 200 ft., adjoining the parish boundary with Chettle. Immediately S. of this area is an approximately rectangular enclosure, 550 ft. by 250 ft., from the N.E. corner of which a narrow, parallel-sided way leads to a smaller oval enclosure, 320 ft. by 250 ft. It is probable that a third enclosure adjoins these on the S.E., and lengths of boundary dyke extend away from the settlement to the S.W. (apparently linking it with the Roman road), and to the S.E. Pottery from the site is chiefly of late Iron Age or early Romano-British type, and later occupation is represented by 3rd and 4th-century flanged bowls and New Forest ware. (Sumner, *Cranborne Chase*, 42 and pl. xxi; *Dorset Procs.*, 82 (1960), 84.)

(20) ENCLOSURE (91651175), at Hinton Bushes, probably of Iron Age or Romano-British date, lies at 390 ft. above O.D. near the crest of a spur which slopes E. to the Tarrant valley. Now levelled by cultivation, the ditch surrounding the enclosure is visible on air photographs (C.U.A.P., WX 59–61) as a roughly circular crop-mark, about 400 ft. in diameter and enclosing an area of 3 acres. On the S., a second ditch runs for a short distance outside the main ditch, which it joins on the S.W.

(21) ENCLOSURE (925102), on South Tarrant Hinton Down, probably of Iron Age or Romano-British date, lies at 270 ft. above O.D. on the S. slope of a Chalk spur. Although ploughed flat, the enclosure is seen on air photographs (C.U.A.P., XZ 22, 25; 58/RAF/3250 : 0135–6) as a pear-shaped crop-mark, about 650 ft. by 400 ft., 5 acres in area.

(22) DYKE (96401328–96071285), in the extreme N.E. of the parish, is now totally flattened by ploughing. It extends from N.E. to S.W. for some 600 yds. and then turns abruptly and runs N.W. for 135 yds. to 95971294. The earthwork appears on air photographs (C.U.A.P., ANC 26, 28) as a soil-mark comprising twin ditches, with a medial and possibly with flanking banks.

(23) LONG BARROW (92270935), at Telegraph Clump, lies across the parish boundary with Tarrant Launceston and forms part of the Telegraph Clump barrow group (see below, (27–34)). The barrow is aligned W.N.W.–E.S.E. along the summit of a Chalk ridge, at an altitude of 400 ft. The mound, damaged by

a modern brick structure, is 315 ft. long, up to 75 ft across and 10 ft. high; between it and the irregular and disturbed side ditches are the remains of a berm.

(24) PIMPERNE LONG BARROW (91751050), one of the finest surviving burial mounds in Wessex, lies along the boundary with Pimperne on the summit of a Chalk ridge, at an altitude of 370 ft. above O.D. Aligned from N.N.W. to S.S.E., the mound is parallel-sided, 330 ft. long, 65 ft. wide and up to 9 ft. high. On the E. it is flanked by a berm up to 10 ft. wide and by a ditch 40 ft. across, and up to 4 ft. deep. On the W. side there are traces of a narrow berm at the N. and S. ends, and of a ditch narrower and shallower than that on the E. (Sumner, *Cranborne Chase* 75–6 and pl. xlvi.)

(25) LONG BARROW (96451317), near Thickthorn Farm in the extreme E. of the parish, lies 280 ft. above O.D. on the almost flat summit of a Chalk ridge. The oval mound, which has been heavily ploughed, measures 110 ft. by 70 ft. and is 3 ft. high. It is aligned S.S.E.–N.N.W. There are traces of a ditch, which seems to have encircled the mound (C.U.A.P., ANC 26, 28).

[DYKE (94851191–95481185) on Tarrant Hinton Down continues into the adjacent parish. See *Dorset V*, s.v. LONG CRICHEL.]

'CELTIC' FIELDS, see p. 119, Groups (72–4).

MONUMENTS (26–53), ROUND BARROWS

In addition to five undated mounds (54), some twenty-eight round barrows occur in the parish, most of them levelled or damaged by cultivation. A few were dug into in the 19th century, and among these are two which cannot be precisely located. One of them, 'near Pimperne Long Barrow', was small and contained at the centre an extended, probably intrusive inhumation with the head to the W.; in a cist in the Chalk near its feet lay another inhumation, probably primary (*C.T.D.*, Pt. 2, no. 24). The other unlocated barrow, 'about ¼ mile E. of Pimperne Long Barrow', contained an extended inhumation, probably primary, with 'fragments of a rude urn' at its side, covered by a cairn of flints. Above the cairn was a pot containing a hoard of Constantinian coins (*C.T.D.*, Pt. 3, no. 99; Hutchins I, 318–9).

(26) *Barrow* (91870906), has been destroyed in the construction of Blandford military camp.

Telegraph Clump Group comprises eight barrows (27–34), together with Long Barrow (23), all over 360 ft. above O.D., on and near the summit of a Chalk ridge. Barrows (29–32) lie close together in a line immediately W. of (23); the others are more scattered. It is possible that some of these barrows, together with neighbouring barrows in Tarrant Launceston, were opened in the 19th century. W. Shipp opened a barrow 'near the Telegraph' which contained a human leg-bone beneath a large cairn (*C.T.D.*, Pt. 2, no. 5). J. H. Austen opened two barrows in the same area; in one he found a primary cremation in a cist, in the other he found nothing (*Ibid.*, nos. 25 and 26). In 1840 Austen opened another barrow 'near Race Course', which contained a primary crouched interment with a long-necked beaker (*Ibid.*, no. 23 and Pl. VII, no. 1).

(27) *Bowl* (91950935), destroyed since 1939 by the military camp.

(28) *Bowl* (92010931), damaged by a modern road; diam. 30 ft., ht. under 1 ft.

(29) *Bowl* (92120935), now much disturbed; diam. 20 ft., ht. 1 ft.

(30) *Bowl* (92160937), severely damaged by digging; diam. about 40 ft., ht. 2 ft.

(31) *Bowl* (92190936), disturbed and spread; diam. 70 ft., ht. 1 ft., with traces of a ditch about 10 ft. wide.

(32) *Bowl* (92210935), immediately S.E. of (31); diam. 21 ft. by 15 ft., ht. less than 1 ft., surrounding ditch 3 ft. across.

(33) *Bowl* (92260945), now much ploughed; diam. 65 ft., ht. less than 1 ft.

(34) *Bowl* (92150950), under arable; diam. 45 ft., ht. less than 1 ft.

(35) *Bowl* (91901028), within arable, S.S.E. of (24); diam. 40 ft., ht. 3 ft.

Four barrows (36–39) lie between 360 ft. and 380 ft. above O.D., on the S.E. slopes of a Chalk ridge at the S. end of Hinton Bushes; (36–38) are in woodland, (39) has been levelled by cultivation.

(36) *Bowl* (91651135); diam. 30 ft., ht. 3 ft.

(37) *Bowl* (91681132); diam. 60 ft., ht. 3½ ft., with a well-marked ditch 10 ft. across, and an outer bank best preserved on the W. side.

(38) *Bowl* (91791129), damaged in the centre; diam. 55 ft., ht. 3 ft.

(39) *Bowl* (91811130); former diam. 45 ft., ht. 3 ft.

Four round barrows on Barton Hill (40–43), now totally flattened by cultivation, are visible as soil-marks on air photographs (N.M.R. ST 9113/1; V 58/RAF/3250 : 0134); they lie at over 300 ft. above O.D. on the summit of a spur overlooking the Tarrant valley.

(40) *Barrow* (92901150); diam. about 45 ft.

(41) *Double Barrow* (92931150); diam. of each segment about 50 ft.

(42) *Barrow* (92991152); diam. about 50 ft.

(43) *Barrow* (93031154); diam. about 55 ft.

(44) *Barrow* (94341081), now levelled by ploughing, but visible as a soil-mark on an air photograph (N.M.R. ST 9410/1), lies at over 250 ft. above O.D. on a gentle W. slope, E. of Manor Farm; diam. about 140 ft.

(45) *Bowl* (95571194), adjacent to the boundary with Tarrant Launceston, lies on a N.E. slope at 240 ft. above O.D.; diam. 22 ft., ht. 1 ft.

Tarrant Hinton Down Group comprises five barrows (46–50), all now flattened by cultivation. They lie at 260 ft. above O.D. on the gentle N. slope of Tarrant Hinton Down.

(46) *Bowl* (94931213); former diam. 48 ft., ht. under 1 ft.

(47) *Bowl* (94951214); former diam. 55 ft., ht. 2 ft.

(48) *Bowl* (94971216); former diam. 40 ft., ht. 1 ft.

(49) *Bowl* (94961216); former diam. 33 ft., ht. 1 ft.

(50) *Bowl* (94941216); former diam. 21 ft., ht. under 1 ft.

Three barrows lie at about 240 ft. above O.D. on the S.E. slope of the Chalk ridge of Thickthorn Down. Now levelled by ploughing, they are visible as soil-marks on air photographs (C.U.A.P., ANC 26, 28).

(51) *Barrow* (96131286), immediately S. of Dyke (22); diameter about 55 ft. A second, smaller barrow appears to adjoin it on the N.E.

(52) *Barrow* (96131299); diam. about 48 ft.

(53) *Barrow* (96151300), immediately adjacent to (52); diam. about 40 ft.

UNDATED

(54) MOUNDS (917106). Five very small barrows or mounds, now levelled by ploughing, formerly lay N.N.W. of (24). Their position, almost on the parish boundary with Pimperne, and their small size suggest that these earthworks may be of pagan Saxon origin.

27 TARRANT KEYNESTON

(O.S. 6 ins., ST 90 SW, ST 90 NW)

The parish, extending to 1,347 acres, lies on the N.W. bank of the Tarrant and the N.E. bank of the Stour, immediately N. of Tarrant Crawford. The land is entirely Chalk, falling from an altitude of 300 ft. at Buzbury Rings (16) in the N., to about 100 ft. at the river in the S. The village extends along the N. side of the Tarrant. The open fields, of which no traces remain, were enclosed by Act of Parliament in 1814.

ECCLESIASTICAL

(1) THE PARISH CHURCH OF ALL SAINTS stands at the S.W. end of the village. The walls are of coursed rubble and flint with ashlar dressings, and the roofs are tiled. The *West Tower* dates from the 15th century ; *Chancel, Nave, North Vestry, Aisles* and *Porch* were rebuilt in 1852 to designs by T. H. Wyatt.

Architectural Description—A pseudo-14th-century N. window in the N. vestry is of three ovolo-moulded lights, the centre light trefoil-headed, the others cinquefoiled, with curvilinear tracery in a two-centred head; it probably is of 18th-century origin, reset in the 19th century.

The *West Tower* (7¾ ft. by 8½ ft.) is of two stages, with a chamfered plinth, weathered string-courses and an embattled parapet with a moulded coping. In the lower stage the N.W. and S.W. corners have diagonal buttresses of two weathered stages. The tower arch, rendered, is two-centred and of two chamfered orders which die into plain responds. The restored W. window has two trefoil-headed lights under a quatrefoil in a two-centred head with a label. Low down in the upper stage is a S. window of one rebated round-headed light; above, each face of the tower has a belfry window of two trefoil-headed lights in a square-headed surround.

Fittings—Bells: four; 4th with MARIA in crowned Lombardic letters alternating with fleur-de-lis stops, 15th century; also with incised initials W.F., R.F., 1716; others modern. *Communion Table:* with moulded top rails, shaped brackets, turned legs and plain stretchers, 17th century; top modern. *Plate:* include

Elizabethan silver cup with assay mark of 1570, and paten of 1831; also two pewter almsdishes. *Monument:* In churchyard, immediately S. of tower, table-tomb (Plate 19) above brick-vaulted tomb chamber of the Bastard family (cf. *Dorset* III, 21, *monuments* (10), (24)), with inscriptions of Thomas Bastard, joiner and architect, 1731, William his son, John Barfoot, 1777, John Bastard, mason and architect of St. Marylebone, 1778, Mary Bastard, 1791, Mary (Bastard) Barfoot, 1804, Mary Barfoot, 1828.

SECULAR

(2) BRIDGE (93310455), with three elliptical arches, carrying the road from Blandford Forum to Wimborne Minster across the Tarrant, is partly of rubble and partly of brick, with ashlar coping to the parapets; it probably is of *c.* 1800.

(3) KEYNESTON LODGE (92840434), of two storeys with attics, has rendered cob walls and tiled roofs. The service range on the E. was formerly a small independent house of *c.* 1700; the main range is of the late 18th century, with early 19th-century additions on the N. A lead rain-water head is dated 1793. The S. front, of seven bays, has plain sashed windows regularly spaced in the upper storey; in the lower storey the three middle bays retain their original form, with tall sashed windows and a round-headed doorway, but the four end bays are masked by projecting flat-roofed extensions with three-light windows. Inside, the lower flight of the stairs was remodelled in the 19th century and has plain balustrades; above, the original stairs have column-shaped balusters of *c.* 1793.

(4) KEYNESTON MILL (91450350), with brick walls and slate-covered roofs, dates from the mid 19th century. It was worked as a water-powered flour mill until 1925, but now is disused. A two-storeyed cottage and house, adjacent on the N.E., have square-headed sashed windows. A 19th-century ashlar bridge over the mill-leat appears to incorporate elements of earlier sluices.

(5) HOUSE (93170457), of two storeys, with brick walls and a tiled roof, is of the late 18th or early 19th century. The S.E. front is approximately symmetrical and of three bays, with a central doorway and with segmental-headed sashed windows.

MONUMENTS (6–13)

Unless described otherwise, the following cottages have cob walls and thatched roofs and are of the early 18th century.

(6) *Cottages* (93050478), two adjacent, are two-storeyed and have recently been combined as a single dwelling; that on the W. has a tiled roof. The E. tenement originally had a class-I plan. Some rooms have exposed chamfered beams.

(7) *Cottage* (93100476), single-storeyed with attics, originally with a class-S plan, retains an exposed chamfered beam. Extensions on the W. appear formerly to have constituted a second dwelling, but both tenements are now combined.

(8) *Cottage* (93260462), of two storeys, originally with a class-S plan, retains a stop-chamfered beam in the living room, and a plank-and-muntin partition between the ground-floor rooms. The stairs have a newel post with a shaped head. A single-storeyed extension on the N.W. is perhaps of the late 18th century.

(9) *Cottage* (93210460), single-storeyed with attics, has a modern iron roof.

(10) *Cottage* (93170453), single-storeyed with attics, retains two stop-chamfered beams and an original casement window with a moulded timber surround. A barn, adjacent on the S.W., probably is contemporary with the dwelling.

(11) *Cottages* (93100448), two adjoining, now combined as one dwelling, are single-storeyed with attics and retain chamfered and stop-chamfered beams, and an open fireplace with a stop-chamfered bressummer.

(12) *Cottage* (92900433), originally single-storeyed, has been heightened to two storeys and has a tiled roof; it dates from the second half of the 17th century and has a class-S plan. The ground-floor rooms retain three original square-headed casement windows with ovolo-moulded timber surrounds. The beams are deeply chamfered and that in the living room has carved stops. The cross partition is original plank-and-muntin work, and the partition dividing the western compartment into two small rooms is probably also original.

(13) *Cottage* (92620413), of one storey with attics, is of the late 18th or early 19th century.

(14) BARN (92560403), of rubble, flint and brick, with ashlar quoins, chamfered plinths, and two-stage buttresses partly of stone and partly of brick, appears to be mainly of the late 16th or early 17th century. The walls incorporate earlier masonry in the S.W. side, and have many later repairs and alterations.

(15) BARN (92590405), with weather-boarded timber walls above brick plinths and with a thatched roof, is of the 18th century. The roof trusses have braced tie-beams, and collar-beams with queen struts.

ROMAN AND PREHISTORIC

(16) BUZBURY RINGS (919059), an enclosed Iron Age and Romano-British settlement in the extreme N.W. of the parish, lies at the head of a gully on the E. slope of a broad N.–S. Chalk ridge, between 300 ft. and 360 ft. above sea-level (Plate 79). The remains are much damaged by the modern road from Blandford Forum to Wimborne Minster, which cuts across the site from N.W.–S.E., and by numerous tracks. Part of a golf-course occupies the N.E. third of the site, and much of the rest has been damaged or destroyed by ploughing. Several linear ditches or tracks run up to or pass close by the site ; some of them are integrated with 'Celtic' fields which extend S., S.W. and E. (see p. 118, Group (70)).

The settlement has an inner and an outer enclosure. The inner enclosure, roughly hexagonal in shape and about 400 ft. in diameter, covers a little under 3 acres; it is bounded by a single bank 30 ft. wide and 4 ft. high; the N.E. part has been obliterated by the road. Close to the road a large number of breaks in the bank have probably been caused by later tracks, except for two in the S.E., one or both of which may be original. Within the enclosure, which appears to have been the main area of occupation, a number of roughly circular depressions, between 20 ft. and 30 ft. in diameter and much mutilated by modern ploughing, are probably hut sites; air photographs (N.M.R.) indicate many pits.

The outer enclosure is kidney-shaped and covers about 10 acres. On the N. and W. it is bounded by a single bank, 20 ft.

N

BUZBURY PLANTATION

B
A
D
F C
E

SCALE 100 0 1000 FEET
100 0 200 METRES

ONE ACRE

A········B   C········D

SCALE OF FEET 10 0 70 FOR PROFILES

E········F

TARRANT KEYNESTON. (16) Buzbury Rings.

wide and up to 3 ft. high. There now is virtually no sign of the outer ditch, but excavation revealed that it was V-shaped, 10 ft. wide and 5 ft. deep. An inner ditch, just visible along the W. side, was of similar depth, but only 7 ft. wide. The S. half of the outer enclosure is bounded by double banks with a medial ditch; where best preserved the banks are 24 ft. wide and stand 4 ft. above the bottom of the ditch, which is 10 ft. across. Numerous breaks in these banks appear to be caused by later tracks. In the S.E., immediately W. of the modern road, the double banks are replaced by a single, more massive bank, 6 ft. high and set somewhat outside the general line of the outer banks. Three oval depressions cut into the inner face of the single bank are possibly hut circles. About 50 ft. to the N.W., immediately outside the bank of the inner enclosure, three U-shaped scoops may also be hut circles. In the S.W. quadrant of the outer enclosure the inner bank swings back from the outer bank and curves around on a line parallel with and 80 ft. away from the bank of the inner enclosure.

Numerous objects and much occupation debris have been found at various times, almost all in the inner enclosure. They include Iron Age sherds and Roman pottery, mainly of the 2nd century but also of the 3rd and 4th centuries, with large quantities of ox and sheep bones, struck flints, and much wattle-marked daub, presumably from huts. Excavation through the outer enclosure bank on the W. yielded no datable material.

The earthworks and finds indicate a small rural settlement, continuously occupied from the Iron Age to the end of the Roman period. The form of the earthworks suggests more than one stage of construction. (*Wessex from the Air*, 64–5, Pl. v; *Dorset Procs.*, 78 (1956), 91; *Ibid.* 80 (1958), 107–8; *Ibid.* 86 (1964), 112–14. Finds in D.C.M.)

MONUMENTS (17–21)

Five Linear Ditches lie in the vicinity of Buzbury Rings and extend into the adjacent parishes of Langton Long Blandford, Tarrant Monkton and Tarrant Rawston. Their full extent is no longer clearly visible on the ground, but it can be traced on air photographs (R.A.F. CPE/UK 1893 : 3067–8). Together with Buzbury Rings, ‘Celtic’ fields of Group (70), and later tracks, they comprise a complex of earthworks which recent destruction by cultivation makes difficult to interpret satisfactorily (Map in end-pocket).

(17) *Linear Earthwork*, 400 yds. long, curving around the S. and W. sides of Buzbury Rings, is almost certainly contemporary with some phase of the settlement; it has been almost entirely destroyed by ploughing. On the S., where it adjoined the Rings and was best preserved, it comprised a ditch 30 ft. across and 2 ft. deep, with widely spread banks up to 75 ft. across and no more than 1 ft. high on either side. At the S.E. end (91930579) the outer bank divided to form an oval enclosure 70 ft. by 55 ft., with a gap, not certainly an entrance, in the N. side. At the N.W. end (91680600), where it diverges furthest from the Rings, the earthwork meets (18), but it is not certainly contemporary with it.

(18) *Linear Dyke* (921064), traceable for 1,000 yds. from the N. side of Rawston Down, Tarrant Rawston, continues past the N.W. corner of Buzbury Rings and along the parish boundary between Langton Long Blandford and Tarrant Keyneston. Where best preserved, on the golf-course, it comprises a ditch 10 ft. to 15 ft. wide and 3 ft. deep, with low banks on either side.

West of the Blandford–Wimborne road, along the edge of Buzbury Plantation, a bank exists only on the N. side, and the ditch has for long been occupied by a track; in this section the dyke deviates slightly to avoid a round barrow (Langton Long Blandford (13)). S.W. of Buzbury Plantation the line of the dyke continues as a slightly hollowed terrace above ‘Celtic’ fields, which have been almost entirely destroyed by cultivation.

(19) *Linear Dyke*, traceable for some 2,000 yds., extends from Luton Down in Tarrant Monkton, on the N. (921071), to a point 800 yds. S.W. of Buzbury Rings, in Langton Long Blandford (912055); its S. half is roughly parallel with (18). Where best preserved, N.E. of the Blandford–Wimborne road, the dyke consists of a ditch 25 ft. across and 3 ft. deep, flanked by low spread banks. S.W. of Buzbury Plantation it is marked only by a scarp on the hillside, bounded on both sides by contemporary or later ‘Celtic’ fields.

(20) *Linear Earthwork*, some 600 yds. long, runs S.W. from Buzbury Rings along the crest of a broad spur and obliquely down its S. side to 91490532. It now is much ploughed, but formerly, where best preserved, it comprised a ditch 35 ft. wide and 2 ft. deep, with traces of low banks on either side. Near Buzbury Rings the earthwork divides into two branches which appear to cut (17) and which are probably due to its use as a track. Air photographs (N.M.R., ST 9106/4, ST 9205/2) suggest that it is contemporary with or earlier than ‘Celtic’ fields in the area, but the remains are too much damaged for the relationship to be certain.

(21) *Dyke*, now largely destroyed by ploughing, but formerly of similar dimensions to (20), runs N.E. from near the N.E. side of Buzbury Rings (92030600) into a re-entrant valley. Most of the dyke lies in Tarrant Rawston. Air photographs indicate that after proceeding 200 yds. the dyke divides to follow each side of the re-entrant valley, one branch continuing N.E. for 500 yds., the other curving E. for some 300 yds. as a scarp, apparently integrated with ‘Celtic’ fields.

MONUMENTS (22–26), ROUND BARROWS

Five barrows survive in the N.W. of the parish, on the S. and S.E. of Buzbury Rings (16). There are records of three other barrows ‘on Keyneston Down’, excavated in 1846, but these almost certainly lay in Tarrant Launceston or Tarrant Monkton, for they appear to have been not more than 300 yds. from the Romano-British settlement on Blandford Race Down. One of these three barrows yielded a primary cremation with fragments of ‘a coarse urn’ in a cist, and a secondary cremation of a child in a two-handled vase, together with a piece of dark thick glass; a fragment of samian ware found at the side of the barrow, where the ground appeared to have been anciently disturbed, suggests that the secondary burial was Romano-British (*C.T.D.*, Pt. 2, No. 6; Pt. 3, note on p. 76). A barrow near by yielded ‘fragments of British Pottery’ with ashes and charcoal, in a cist 8 ft. deep and 3 ft. in diameter (*C.T.D.*, Pt. 2, No. 7). The third barrow yielded three cremations, probably primary, two cremations in upright urns, probably secondary, and one other, probably secondary, in an inverted urn; all were in separate cists, two of which were connected by a circular hole (*C.T.D.*, Pt. 2, No. 8). A further barrow, perhaps in Tarrant Keyneston or Tarrant Rawston, was opened by J. H. Austen in 1840 and yielded a bowl-shaped urn with two lugs pierced perpendicularly (*C.T.D.*, Pt. 2, No. 30).

A globular urn (Calkin's type II) from a barrow on Keyneston Down is in the Durden Collection at the B.M. (*B.A.P.*, ii, 401; *Durden Catalogue*, 18, Nos. 22, 23; *Ant. J.*, XIII (1933), 447; *Arch. J.*, CXIX (1962), 57).

(22) *Bowl* (91510566), 500 yds. S.W. of Buzbury Rings, near the S. end of a N.–S. Chalk ridge, lies 330 ft. above O.D. Diam. 70 ft., ht. 3 ft.

(23) *Bowl* (92280525), within and near the W. side of Ashley Wood, lies 310 ft. above O.D. Diam. 28 ft., ht. 3 ft.

(24) *Bowl* (92300527), 25 yds. N.E. of (23). Diam. 20 ft., ht. 2 ft.

(25) *Bowl* (92650551), N.E. of Ashley Wood on a gentle E. slope, lies about 280 ft above O.D. Diam. 30 ft., ht. 3 ft.

(26) *Bowl* (92660552), immediately N.E. of (25). Diam. 20 ft., ht. 2 ft.

28 TARRANT LAUNCESTON (9409)

(O.S. 6 ins., ST 90 NW, ST 90 NE, ST 91 SW, ST 91 SE)

The parish, with an area of about 1,500 acres entirely on Chalk, extends from side to side of the Tarrant valley at altitudes between 180 ft. and 390 ft. above sea-level. Until late in the 19th century Tarrant Launceston and Tarrant Monkton, adjacent on the S., were regarded as one parish, although each formerly had its own place of worship. The village now consists of farms and cottages scattered along the banks of the Tarrant, but fragmentary earthwork remains indicate more extensive settlement in the past. In 1086, when the settlement belonged to Trinity Abbey, Caen, the recorded population was 24 (*V.C.H., Dorset* iii, 83). In 1327 the same number of taxpayers was recorded, indicating a relatively large and constant population. A muster-roll of 1542 (*L. & P. Hen. VIII*, xvii, 496) records 10 able-bodied men, a large quota by Dorset standards, perhaps indicating a total population of 60 or 70, or 14 to 17 households. This suggests some decline in population, and there certainly had been further decline by the 17th century, for the Hearth Tax Assessment of 1662 lists only 9 householders (Meekings, 67). In the 18th century, however, the population increased, and in 1801 it was 67 (*V.C.H., Dorset*, ii, 266).

The interest of an important area of Iron Age and Romano-British settlement, on Race Down in the W. of the parish, has been greatly reduced by modern construction.

ECCLESIASTICAL

CHAPEL-OF-EASE, demolished in 1762 (Hutchins, 1st ed., II, 213), see (2), (12).

SECULAR

(1) HIGHER DAIRY (93990979), a two-storeyed farmhouse with walls of flint and squared rubble and with a thatched roof, is of 17th-century origin. The class-T plan has been somewhat altered, but both ground-floor rooms retain chamfered beams with shaped stops. A fireplace bressummer has the incised inscription '1669 RW' in a roundel.

(2) BRIDGE (94020981), of stone, crossing the Tarrant with two small approximately semicircular arches, incorporated large chamfered voussoirs which probably were taken from the neighbouring chapel on its demolition in 1762. It carried a former trackway to Higher Dairy, now disused. (*Demolished.*)

(3) COTTAGES (94160993), three adjacent, with walls of banded flint and rubble, banded flint and brick, and with thatched roofs, are single-storeyed with dormer-windowed attics; they probably are of the 17th century and may originally have been a single house. Some rooms retain stop-chamfered beams.

(4) COTTAGE (94240969), with cob walls and a thatched roof, is single-storeyed with a dormer-windowed attic and has a plan of class S, with additions on the N. The original building is probably of the 18th century.

(5) LAUNCESTON FARM (94320950), house, of two storeys, with walls partly of rubble and flint and partly of brick, and with slate-covered roofs, probably is of 17th-century origin. The E. range, with a symmetrical brick façade with square-headed sashed windows of one and of two lights, was added early in the 19th century.

(6) COTTAGE (94420945), of two storeys, with walls of cob and brick and with a thatched roof, is of the late 18th century. Inside, the class-S plan has been modified by the insertion of a fireplace in the room which formerly was unheated, and by the addition of a third room on the E.

(7) COTTAGES (94410941), two adjacent, of one storey with attics, have walls of rubble, brick and flint, and tiled roofs. They are of 17th-century origin, much altered.

(8) COTTAGE (94480920), of one storey with attics, has walls of cob and brick, and a thatched roof. It dates from the 17th century although a stone window of three square-headed lights is a recent insertion. Inside, some stop-chamfered beams are exposed, and an open fireplace has a chamfered and cambered bressummer. The attic chambers have original plank-and-muntin partitions.

(9) COTTAGES (94480911), range of three, of one storey with attics, have walls of flint, rubble, and banded flint and brick, and thatched roofs. The range is of the 17th century, but the two S. tenements were restored and to some extent rebuilt in the 18th century.

(10) COTTAGE (94340900), of one storey with attics, has cob walls and a thatched roof; it probably is of 17th-century origin, with 18th-century restoration. Inside, the plan is of class J. Some large stop-chamfered beams are exposed, and a doorway has a heavy oak frame with a chamfered segmental head.

(11) COTTAGE (94270898), of one storey with attics, has cob walls and a thatched roof. It probably is of the late 17th century. The plan is of class S.

MEDIAEVAL AND LATER EARTHWORKS

(12) PLATFORM (93090982), the site of the former Chapel (Tithe Map, 1840), measures 55 ft. by 36 ft. and is orientated N.E.–S.W. A low bank about 25 yds. long, some 20 yds. S.E. of the platform, marks one side of the chapel-yard. Part of the earthwork has been obliterated by chalk digging.

(13) SETTLEMENT REMAINS (939098–940096) occur on both sides of the Tarrant, in and around the village; although damaged by quarrying and drainage ditches, they cover about 6 acres on the W. bank of the Tarrant. At least 5 closes are found, 30 yds. wide and 30 yds. to 60 yds. long, bounded by low banks and scarps, with traces of building platforms up to 40 ft. by 25 ft. cut into the slope of the valley. Low banks and mounds of uncertain origin occur on the floodplain to the E. Other closes and a hollow-way on the E. bank of the Tarrant have now gone (R.A.F., V.A.P., CPE/UK 1939 : 2152).

ROMAN AND PREHISTORIC

(14) ROMANO-BRITISH SETTLEMENT (925092), on Blandford Down, lies on the gentle E. slope of a Chalk ridge between 325 ft. and 375 ft. above O.D. The site, severely damaged during the present century by a military camp, comprises a nucleated occupation area of about eight acres characterised by low earthworks, now much disturbed, among which a number of sunken platforms are probably the sites of former buildings. The area of occupation lies within a larger area, about 500 yds. in diameter, defined by shallow ditches, low banks and scarps. At least four contemporary tracks in the form of shallow hollow-ways, 25 ft. to 50 ft. across, run into this area. Outside the settlement on the N.E., air photographs (C.U.A.P., AMO 2–4, AQY 87; N.M.R., ST 9309/1–4) show a small subrectangular enclosure (93000947), about 250 ft. by 150 ft., associated with linear ditches and possibly with other enclosures (Plate 78); it lies on the N. side of a track which extends E.N.E. from the settlement for at least 1,000 yds., as far as 937097. 'Celtic' fields (Group 72) extend S.W. of the settlement, but nowhere do they join it. (Sumner, Cranborne Chase, 74 and pl. xlv.)

(15) ENCLOSURE (948095), probably Iron Age or Romano-British, lies 500 yds. E. of Launceston Farm on the S.W. slope of a Chalk spur, between 250 ft. and 275 ft. above O.D., overlooking the Tarrant valley. The site, revealed by a soil-mark on air photographs (C.U.A.P., ANC 75, AQY 90), is an almost circular enclosure, about 500 ft. in diameter, defined by a narrow ditch. There are traces of an entrance on the N. side, and of a ditch running N.W. in a curve for some 500 ft. from just E. of the entrance. Faint traces of a ditched feature are found inside the enclosure, and there is evidence of a smaller angular enclosure attached to the exterior on the S.E.

(16) LINEAR DYKES, on Launceston Down in the extreme N.E. of the parish, lie between 200 ft. and 350 ft. above O.D. on the summit and on the E. slopes of the Chalk ridge between the Tarrant and the Crichel brooks. The dykes have been almost totally levelled by cultivation since 1947.

A dyke beginning in Tarrant Hinton parish (94811126) runs approximately W.S.W.–E.N.E. in a sinuous course for just over one mile across Launceston Down; it is lost in Long Crichel parish at 96251150. The dyke formerly consisted of a ditch with a low bank along its N. side and measured about 35 ft. across overall. At a sharp change of direction near the middle of its course (95611123) the earthwork bifurcates, a short length which extends almost due W. for 100 yds. suggesting two phases of construction. At the W. end the dyke appears to cross an earlier dyke which follows the parish boundary with Tarrant Hinton.

The earlier dyke consists of a ditch with traces of a bank on the S. side, measuring about 35 ft. across overall; it extends across the ridge-top, from 95031115 in the N.E. at least as far as 94661094, a distance of nearly 350 yds.; possibly it continued further S.W. It is also possible that a third dyke extended S.W., from a junction with the first mentioned dyke at 94851120, towards the W. end of the second dyke, but this last named earthwork could be no more than a bank formed by trackways. (Sumner, Cranborne Chase, 35–7, pl. xvi A.)

(17) LONG BARROW (92950885), on Blandford Race Down, lies at over 350 ft. above O.D. on a gentle E. slope, just off the crest of a Chalk ridge. Orientated S.E.–N.W., the mound is parallel-sided, 115 ft. long by 48 ft. wide, and up to 6 ft. high. It may be the one opened in 1840 by J. H. Austen, who found an extended inhumation, probably intrusive, 2½ ft. from the top (C.T.D. Pt. 2, No. 27). (O.S., Map of Neolithic Wessex, No. 157.)

'CELTIC' FIELDS, see p. 119, Group (72).

MONUMENTS (18–49), ROUND BARROWS

At least 37 round barrows formerly existed in the parish, but most of them are now levelled or damaged by cultivation. The majority (23–49) occur in three groups on Launceston Down ; many of them have been excavated.

Three barrows (18–20) on Blandford Race Down lie on the N.E. slope of a Chalk ridge, between 300 ft. and 360 ft. above sea-level.

(18) Barrow (92730924), within Settlement (14) comprises an oval mound, 50 ft. by 35 ft. and 2½ ft. high, now somewhat damaged.

(19) Bowl (92800903), S. of Settlement (14) has a hole dug in the centre of the mound; diam. 50 ft., ht. 4 ft., with a surrounding ditch.

(20) Barrow (93270889), now levelled by ploughing, is visible on an air photograph (N.M.R., ST 9510/1) as a well defined ring-ditch; diam. about 50 ft.

(21) Bowl (93250983), on the N. slope of a Chalk spur at 230 ft. above O.D., has now been levelled by ploughing, but is visible as a ring-ditch, about 40 ft. in diameter, on the air photograph noted in (20).

(22) Bowl (94841077), 200 yds. N.W. of Hyde Hill Plantation, lies at 350 ft. above O.D. on the shoulder of a westward-facing slope; diam. 60 ft., ht. 5 ft., with traces of a surrounding ditch. A low mound 35 yds. to the N., sometimes taken as a barrow, is almost certainly the remains of a 'Celtic' field angle.

The Hyde Hill Plantation Group comprises thirteen barrows (23–35) in two concentrations in and S.E. of the plantation; they lie between 340 ft. and 360 ft. above O.D. along the crest of a broad Chalk ridge between the Tarrant and Crichel Brooks. Most of them have been severely damaged by ploughing and (28), (29), (31) and (35) have been obliterated. Two barrows excavated by Warne in 1840 probably lay in this group; one of them yielded a primary cremation under a flint cairn, the other yielded only charcoal and ashes (C.T.D., Pt. 1, Nos. 39 and 40). The 'Launceston Sepulchralia' examined by Warne in 1840 probably lay in this area; it appears to have been a cremation cemetery, with the cremations in groups of holes in the chalk, each group being covered with a layer of closely packed flint nodules (C.T.D., Pt. 1, 57–8; Arch. J., CVIII (1951), 14, note 1).

(23) *Bowl* (95081041), in the plantation; diam. 45 ft., ht. 2½ ft., with traces of surrounding ditch.

(24) *Bowl* (95111043); diam. 40 ft., ht. 2½ ft., with traces of surrounding ditch.

(25) *Bowl* (95141043), immediately E. of the plantation, has been much denuded by ploughing; diam. about 30 ft., ht. less than 1 ft.

(26) *Bowl* (95111038), immediately S. of the plantation; diam. 40 ft., ht. 3½ ft.

(27) *Bowl* (95161040), now nearly levelled by ploughing; diam. about 28 ft.

(28) *Bowl* (95151042), now levelled by ploughing; former diam. about 25 ft.

(29) *Bowl* (95281032), now levelled by ploughing; former diam. about 21 ft.

(30) *Bowl* (95341024), heavily ploughed; diam. 40 ft., ht. 1 ft.

(31) *Bowl* (95401017), now levelled by ploughing; former diam. 44 ft.

(32) *Bowl* (95421020), a flat-topped mound; diam., diminished by ploughing, 48 ft., ht. 3½ ft.; traces of surrounding ditch.

(33) *Bowl* (95451019), a steep-sided mound; diam. 55 ft., ht. 8 ft.; with well-defined ditch (*Dorset Barrows*, Long Crichel, No. 24).

(34) *Bowl* (95441021), damaged by ploughing and by digging on the S.; diam. 36 ft., ht. 1½ ft.

(35) *Bowl* (95451024), now levelled by ploughing; former diam. 33 ft., ht. 1½ ft.

The *Launceston Down South Group* comprises thirteen barrows (36–44); four of them lie in the neighbouring parish of Long Crichel (see *Dorset V*). They are between 200 ft. and 250 ft. above O.D., and extend in an irregular line from W. to E. on the northward-facing slope of a dry combe which falls E. to the Crichel brook. All these barrows were excavated in 1938 by S. and C. M. Piggott (*Arch.*, XC (1944), 47–80); they are no longer visible on the ground and former dimensions, etc. are recorded.

(36) *Bowl* (95381067), covering a primary cremation, associated with a calcite double-spaced bead, in a circular grave cut into the chalk; diam. 25 ft., ht. 1 ft. (Piggott, 18).

(37) *Bowl* (95501069), disturbed in the past, yielded a cremation, probably primary, under an inverted cinerary urn in a shallow pit in the chalk; diam. 35 ft., ht. 1½ ft. (Piggott, 12).

(38) *Bowl* (95621064), with a primary crouched inhumation near the centre associated with a leaf-shaped arrowhead; diam. 40 ft., ht. 1 ft. (Piggott, 13).

(39) *Bowl* (95731061), covering a primary cremation in a pit cut into the chalk; diam. 12 ft., ht. 1 ft. (Piggott, 15).

(40) *Bowl* (95741058), containing a primary crouched inhumation with a trephined skull, associated with a bell beaker, in a central grave cut into the chalk, and a secondary cremation near it; diam. 17 ft., ht. less than 1 ft. (Piggott, 14).

(41) *Bowl* (95771060), apparently disturbed by earlier digging, probably had contained a primary inhumation associated with a small long-necked beaker; diam. 25 ft., ht. 1 ft. (Piggott, 16).

(42) *Bowl* (95711050), containing a primary crouched inhumation, associated with a bronze awl and a long-necked beaker, in a large grave cut into the chalk. An urn of 'degenerate food-vessel' type was found in a secondary position in this grave. Diam. 18 ft., ht. 1 ft. (Piggott, 17).

(43) *Bowl* (95891056), yielding a primary cremation and four secondary cremations, one of them associated with an inverted sub-biconical urn (*Arch. J.*, CXIX (1962), 41, 62). An intrusive crouched inhumation near the edge of the mound was probably Romano-British or pagan Saxon. Diam. 40 ft., ht. 2 ft., with a horseshoe-shaped ditch with a causeway on the E. (Piggott, 9; *Dorset Barrows*, Long Crichel, No. 22).

(44) *Bowl* (95901060), with three extended inhumations, perhaps intrusive and probably of pagan Saxon origin, in a shallow scraping in the chalk; diam. 20 ft., ht. less than 1 ft. (Piggot, 6; *Dorset Barrows*, Long Crichel, No. 19).

The *Launceston Down North Group* comprised a cluster of at least five small barrows located around 95451145, 220 ft. above O.D. on the southward-facing slope of a dry combe falling E. to the Crichel brook; all have now been levelled by cultivation, but each barrow was examined by J. H. Austen in 1864. One yielded nothing. Another yielded a cremation, probably secondary, in an urn now lost, together with 'the point of a bronze spear or dagger'. A third barrow yielded a primary cremation in a barrel urn of 'South Lodge' type, in a pit cut in the Chalk. A fourth barrow yielded a cremation, probably secondary, in a similar urn. A fifth barrow yielded a primary cremation in a pit, and two cremations, probably secondary, above it, one of the latter having a plain urn (*C.T.D.*, Pt. 2, nos. 36–40; *Ant. J.*, XIII (1933), 447; *Arch. J.*, CXIX (1962), 20, 54, 55). In 1938 four more urns, not covered by barrows but apparently part of an urnfield, were found in the vicinity of the barrow group; three of them contained cremations, one with a fragment of a bronze spearhead (*Arch.*, XC (1944), 50, 60, 61).

(45) *Bowl* (95821132), now levelled by ploughing, but visible as a ring-ditch soil-mark, lies at 230 ft. above O.D. on the northward-facing slope of a dry combe which falls E. to the Crichel brook. The first Dyke noted above (16) skirts it on the S. Diam. about 30 ft.

(46) *Disc* (95881133), 70 yds. E. of (45) and in a similar situation and condition, lies on the parish boundary with Long Crichel; it consists of a circular ditch, 150 ft. in diameter, with traces of an inner and an outer bank, and of a small mound S.E. of the centre. Dyke (16) appears to cut the outer bank on the S.

(47) *Bowl* (95731150), on the S.-facing slope of a dry combe, 220 ft. above O.D. and now levelled by ploughing; diam. about 30 ft.

(48) *Bowl* (95771153), 55 yds. N.E. of (47) and on the parish boundary with Long Crichel, is now levelled; former diam. 60 ft., ht. 1 ft. (*Dorset Barrows*, Long Crichel No. 4). Beaker sherds were found in a rabbit scrape on the mound in 1937 (note by C. D. Drew, D.C.M.).

(49) *Bowl* (95591190), in the extreme N. of the parish, on a gentle N. slope at 250 ft. above O.D., was excavated by S. and C. M. Piggott in 1938 (No. 10); it contained a primary cremation in a barrel urn (*Arch.*, XC (1944), 61–2, 72–3; *Arch. J.*, CXIX (1962), 55; *Helinium*, I (1961), 116).

29 TARRANT MONKTON (9408)

(O.S. 6 ins., ST 90 NW, ST 90 NE)

Tarrant Monkton, extending to a little over 2,000 acres, comprises a strip of land across the Tarrant valley, entirely on Chalk, at altitudes between 160 ft. and

400 ft. above sea-level. Until late in the 19th century it was combined with Tarrant Launceston. The village, one of the many Domesday Tarrants (*V.C.H., Dorset*, iii, 74, 83), has grown up on both sides of the Tarrant Brook. The church is the principal monument.

ECCLESIASTICAL

(1) THE PARISH CHURCH OF ALL SAINTS, on the W. of the village, has walls of banded ashlar and flint with ashlar dressings, and slated and tiled roofs. The *Chancel*, of *c.* 1400 in origin, was extensively restored in the 18th century. The *Nave* is of the 15th century, with 18th-century alterations; the *West Tower* also is of the 15th

aisle. Further W. the N. wall contains a 19th-century window of three trefoil-headed lights; the external face of the wall was largely restored in the 19th century, but the N.W. corner retains an original 15th-century square-set buttress with a chamfered plinth and three weathered offsets. The S. wall has, on the E., a 19th-century archway to the S. chapel; further W. is a square-headed doorway with a chamfered lintel and jambs, probably of the 16th century, now blocked. Adjacent on the W. is a square-headed 15th-century window of three trefoil-headed lights in a casement-moulded surround, and further W. is a similar window, except that the lights have plain two-centred heads and the surround is hollow-chamfered; this last window probably is of the early 16th century. The S.W. corner of the nave has a square-set buttress of two weathered stages.

The *West Tower* is of two stages, with chamfered plinths, an 18th-century plat-band between the stages, and a moulded

TARRANT MONKTON   *The Parish Church of All Saints*

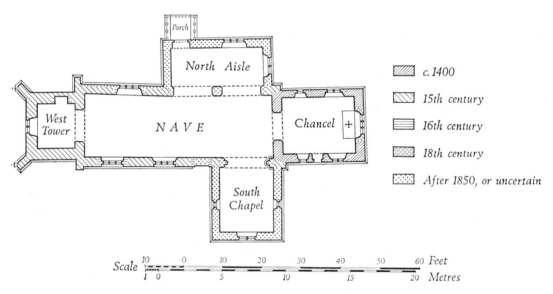

Scale (with legend):
- c. 1400
- 15th century
- 16th century
- 18th century
- After 1850, or uncertain

century, but the upper stage was rebuilt in the 18th century. Hutchins (III, 574) records that the *North Aisle* formerly had a ceiling dated 1624, but this has gone, probably in the 'restorations' of 1873; the *South Chapel* and the timber *North Porch* appear to be of 1873.

Architectural Description—The *Chancel* has a plain plinth and an 18th-century E. window of three gradated lancet lights. The N. wall has similar windows of two and of one lancet lights, that on the E. occupying a slightly wider mediaeval opening, the jambs of which are visible externally. The S. wall has windows as in the N. wall and, between them, a restored mediaeval doorway with a chamfered two-centred head, continuous jambs and run-out stops. The original chancel arch is two-centred and of two chamfered orders, the inner order dying into the responds and the outer order continuous. Externally on the E. gable of the nave is the creasing-course of a former chancel roof, slightly higher than the present slate-covered roof. Inside, the chancel has a plain 18th-century plaster barrel-vault and moulded cornices.

The N. side of the *Nave* has two 19th-century arches to the N.

string-course below a plain parapet; the remains of mediaeval gargoyles are reset at the corners of the string-course. In the lower stage the N.W. and S.W. corners have stout diagonal buttresses of two stages with weathered offsets. The tower arch is two-centred, with a plain chamfer on the E. side only, and with continuous jambs. The W. window is of two trefoil-headed lights in a square-headed surround; high in the lower stage is a small square-headed W. light with a chamfered surround. In the upper stage the E. side of the tower has an 18th-century belfry window of two square-headed lights flanked by reset mediaeval label-stops representing a human and a grotesque head. The W. side has a reset 15th-century window of two trefoil-headed lights with a central quatrefoil in a two-centred head with a moulded label. The N. and S. sides have no openings; reset in the S. side is a mediaeval head-stop.

Fittings—*Bells*: three; 1st by John Danton, with 'Prayse the Lord, 1629, J.D.': 2nd by Clement Tosier, inscribed in Roman capitals 'Thomas Isaacks and John Isaacks churchwardens of the parish of Tarrant Monkton: C.T. cast me in the year of 1694'; 3rd by John Wallis, with 'Feare the Lord I.W. 1610', badly cracked. *Font:* of Purbeck stone, with tapering square bowl with four round-headed panels on each side, on plain stout centre shaft and four plain corner shafts, and square base; bowl, 12th-century, shafts restored, base modern. *Graffito:* on S. doorway of chancel, 1757.

Plate: includes silver cup and cover-paten by 'Gillingham' silversmith (Plate 24), cup of usual pattern, cover-paten bowl-shaped and with inscription 'William Dashwood and Robert Tuffin Churchwardens 1607'. *Pulpit:* of oak, polygonal, four sides with fielded and enriched panelling in two heights, moulded cornice with strapwork frieze, and moulded base, late 17th century. *Royal Arms:* of George IV, on canvas in wood frame.

SECULAR

(2) Cross Base (94420887), of stone, probably part of a 14th-century wayside cross, lies some 50 yds. N.E. of the church. It is octagonal, some 4 ft. in diameter, and retains vestiges of a moulded nosing. A central socket is filled with the end of the former shaft, cut off level with the surface of the base and secured in position by lead grouting.

(3) Footbridge (94510904), across the R. Tarrant, of Heathstone ashlar and rubble, has three high segmental arches with chamfered voussoirs. It is probably of the 17th century.

(4) East Farm (946090), house, granary and barn, have walls of brick and of banded brick and flintwork, and thatched and slate-covered roofs. The farmhouse is two-storeyed and comprises a small class-I dwelling, with a larger class-U house added to it on the S. (see *Dorset* III, lviii). The original building is of the late 18th century; the addition is of *c.* 1840. A few paces W. of the house is a brick-built granary of *c.* 1840. Some 30 yds. N.W. is a large barn of 17th-century origin, partly reconstructed in the 18th century; it has brick and flint walls and a thatched roof. Another barn, adjacent on the N., with brick and flint walls and with a tiled roof, dates probably from *c.* 1700.

(5) Cottage (94480892), of one storey with an attic, has walls of rubble and flint with heavy squared rubble quoins, and a thatched roof; it dates probably from *c.* 1600. Inside, the plan resembles that of class S, but with the stairs adjacent to the partition between the two ground-floor rooms. The roof rests on stout trusses with cambered collar-beams.

(6) Cottage (94340895), of one storey with an attic, has walls partly of cob, partly of banded brick and flintwork, and partly of timber-framework; the roof is thatched. The building probably is of 17th-century origin and it may formerly have comprised two tenements. Inside, one room has a chamfered beam with shaped stops.

(7) Cottage (94510869), of one storey with an attic, has walls of rubble, flint, brick and cob, and a thatched roof; it probably is of the 17th century. Inside, the plan is of class S, and the plank-and-muntin partition between the two ground-floor rooms is original. The living room has two stop-chamfered beams.

(8) Apple Tree Cottage (94850848), of one storey with an attic, has rendered walls and a thatched roof; it probably is of 17th-century origin. Inside, the class-S plan has been modified by the addition of a room at each end of the range, and by the removal of the original ground-floor partition.

MONUMENTS (9–18)

Unless otherwise described the monuments in this group are of the 18th century and are two-storeyed, with cob walls and thatched roofs.

(9) *Inn* (94390887), about 30 yds. N. of the church, has walls of brickwork and of banded brick and flint. The S. front has a brick plat-band. Inside, the plan has been much changed and it is possible that the range originally comprised two dwellings.

(10) *Cottages* (94450887), pair, of one storey with attics, have each a large stop-chamfered beam in the living room.

(11) *Cottages* (94470889), two adjacent, have been altered and the division between the tenements no longer corresponds with the structural division. The S.W. tenement is single-storeyed with an attic; that on the N.E. is of banded brick and flint and probably is of the 19th century.

(12) *Cottage* (94430894), of one storey with an attic, is of the early 18th century. The N. room is an addition and the plan was originally of class S. The living room has a stop-chamfered beam.

(13) *Cottages* (94560909), range of three, are of one storey with attics. The E. tenement has recently been rebuilt.

(14) *Cottage* (94740873), of one storey with an attic, has a class-S plan. Inside, the original plank partition between the ground-floor rooms is preserved.

(15) *House* (94750869), formerly single-storeyed and recently heightened to two storeys, has brick walls and a tiled roof.

(16) *Bay Farm* (94570857), house, with a tiled roof, is of *c.* 1820. The plan is of class T3 (*Dorset* II, lxiii), with an additional room at the S. end of the range. Loose in the garden are two late 12th or early 13th-century respond capitals, with volute corners and ovolo-moulded necking bands; their provenance is unknown.

(17) *Cottage* (94540866), probably with a plan originally of class I or J, but altered.

(18) *Cottage* (94470878), originally with a class-S plan, was at one time extended at each end and converted into two tenements. Recently, however, the building has been remodelled as one tenement, the two original rooms being combined.

MEDIAEVAL AND LATER EARTHWORKS

(19) Settlement Remains (947089), on the E. side of High Street, now almost entirely destroyed, comprise seven or more long closes at right-angles to the street, with traces of house platforms at the upper ends (R.A.F., V.A.P., CPE/UK 1934 : 5151). Some of the sites still had cottages in the early 19th century (O.S., 1811).

ROMAN AND PREHISTORIC

(20) Enclosures (938083), perhaps representing an Iron Age or Romano-British settlement, appear as soil-marks on air photographs (C.U.A.P., AQY 91; N.M.R., ST 9308/1, 2; ST 9408/1). At least three subrectangular ditched enclosures, up to 600 ft. by 170 ft., associated with other ditches of uncertain length, occur in an area of about 20 acres; they lie on the summit and on the S. slope of a Chalk spur between 250 ft. and 290 ft. above sea-level.

(21) Dyke, on the S.W. edge of Blandford Camp, runs W.N.W. to E.S.E. (91240755–91410752) for some 200 yds. across the top of a N.–S. Chalk ridge, at over 350 ft. above O.D.

The W. end lies in Langton Long Blandford and it has been much disturbed by tracks and roads and by trees growing on it. The bank is 12 ft. across and up to 1½ ft. high with a ditch on its N. side 12 ft. across and 2 ft. deep.

ROMAN ROAD from Badbury Rings to Bath, see *Dorset* V.

LINEAR DYKE on Luton Down, see TARRANT KEYNESTON (19).

'CELTIC' FIELDS, see pp. 118-19, Groups (70, 72).

MONUMENTS (22–24), ROUND BARROWS

Three barrows remain, but ten others have been destroyed since 1914 in the construction of Blandford military camp (*Dorset Barrows*, 136). Three of the destroyed monuments (*Dorset Barrows*, Nos. 2–4) lay around 914080, in an E.–W. line at the W. end of Monkton Down; two (Nos. 5 and 6) lay on the W. of Pond Bottom Plantation, around 920076, forming a compact group with (23) and (24); five (Nos. 9–13) lay W. of Blackland Plantation, between 929086 and 930081. None of these barrows is known to have been excavated and all references to early excavations in Tarrant Monkton concern barrows in Launceston, which until the 19th century was part of Monkton parish. Certain barrows, however, which were excavated 'on Keynston Down' in 1846, may have been inside the boundary of Monkton (see TARRANT KEYNESTON, Round Barrows). Air photographs (C.U.A.P., ANC 73, 74) show soil-marks of four ring-ditches, probably the remains of barrows, in a tight cluster at 95480934.

(22) *Bowl* (91360836), 370 ft. above O.D., lies on top of a broad Chalk ridge in the extreme N.W. of the parish; diam. 50 ft., ht. 6 ft.; surrounding ditch too ill-defined for measurement.

(23) *Bowl* (92090767), 310 ft. above O.D., lies at the S.E. end of a broad Chalk spur on the W. of Pond Bottom Plantation; diam. 50 ft., ht. 6 ft.; ditch as in (22).

(24) *Bowl* (92100763), 40 yds. S. of the foregoing; diam. 50 ft., ht. 7½ ft.; ditch as in (22).

UNDATED

(25) ENCLOSURE (913083), immediately S. of (22), occupies the summit of a flat-topped Chalk ridge, 370 ft. above sea-level. Now largely destroyed, the earthwork formerly was a circle, 450 ft. in diameter, bounded by a low scarp. It may be associated with the race-course formerly on Blandford Down, and probably is of recent date.

30 TARRANT RAWSTON (9306)

(O.S. 6 ins., ST 90 NW, ST 90 NE)

This small parish, covering less than 700 acres, is a narrow strip of ground extending from side to side of the Tarrant valley. The land is entirely Chalk, at altitudes between 150 ft. and 300 ft. The village com-prises little more than the church and the manor-house, but earthworks indicate that it formerly was larger; doubtless it is one of the unidentified Tarrants of Domesday (*V.C.H., Dorset*, iii, 107). Eyton (p. 131) suggests correspondence with the two-hide manor of Radulfus, the recorded population of which was six. In 1327 nine taxpayers were listed, and in 1333 six. In 1435 the vill was granted tax relief on account of poverty (P.R.O., E. 179/103/79). In 1662 there were four households (Meekings, 67).

ECCLESIASTICAL

(1) THE PARISH CHURCH OF ST. MARY, near the middle of the parish, has walls of squared stone, rubble and flint, with ashlar dressings; the roofs are tiled, with stone-slate verges (Plate 5). The building was enlarged and restored towards the end of the 18th century and its original date is hard to determine; the list of rectors goes back to the early 14th century and the *Nave* probably is of that date. The *South Chapel* and *South Porch* were added in the 16th century; the *Chancel* and *North Chapel* are of the 18th century. A gallery was inserted at the W. end of the nave, probably early in the 19th century.

Architectural Description—The *Chancel* has a plain plinth and a square-headed E. window of three trefoil-headed lights. The chancel arch is semicircular, with moulded imposts.

In the *Nave*, the 18th-century archway to the N. chapel is a

TARRANT RAWSTON
The Parish Church of St. Mary

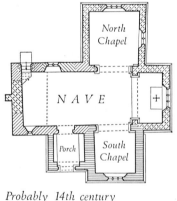

▨ *Probably 14th century*	
▧ *Late 14th or 15th century*	
▤ *16th century*	
▨ *18th century*	▨ *19th century*

Scale 10   0   10   20   30 *Feet*
1   0   5   10 *Metres*

copy of that on the S.; it has a chamfered semicircular head, hollow-chamfered imposts and chamfered jambs; the E. jamb has been cut back. To the W. of the chapel is a blocked doorway, with a square head and a mediaeval headstop reset above the lintel; adjacent is a late 14th or early 15th-century window of two trefoil ogee-headed lights; near the N.W. corner is a 19th-century square-headed doorway to the W. gallery. The 16th-century archway of the S. chapel has a chamfered semicircular head, hollow-chamfered imposts and chamfered jambs. The S. doorway is of the 14th century, with a chamfered two-centred head and continuous jambs with broach stops; further W. is an original window of one trefoil-headed light. The W. wall of the nave has original masonry at the base and at the N.W. and S.W. corners, but the central part has been rebuilt in rough flintwork with an ashlar buttress; this work is probably associated with the construction of the W. gallery. The W. gable contains a small 19th-century trefoil-headed light.

The *North Chapel* has a plain plinth and an E. window similar to that of the chancel, but of two lights. Reset in the N. wall is a 14th-century window with three trefoil ogee-headed lights in a square-headed surround.

The *South Chapel* has a chamfered plinth and a S. window of three lights, with restored trefoil heads in a square-headed surround.

The *South Porch* has a plinth continuous with that of the S. chapel, and an archway with chamfered jambs and a chamfered semicircular head. Above the archway, a 14th-century window of one trefoil-headed light opens into a bellchamber.

The *Roofs* are masked internally by plain plaster barrel vaults with moulded cornices, probably of the 18th century.

Fittings—*Bell:* inscribed '1588 GL' in reverse. *Coffin Stools:* pair, with beaded legs and stretchers; late 18th century. *Communion Rails:* of pine, with turned balusters, fluted column-shaped newels, moulded and enriched rail swept up at each end to continue as dado-capping on chancel walls, and hinged central part; late 18th century. *Gallery:* in W. part of nave, of pine, with panelled and moulded front; early 19th century. *Graffiti:* on stone in angle between nave and N. chapel, symbols arranged in vertical column.

Monument: In nave, on N. wall, of Radford Gundrey, 1788, and Thomas Gundrey, 1805, marble inscription tablet with stone surround having skull and crossbones on apron, side pieces with scrollwork and drapery, cornice and broken pediment; above, shield-of-arms of Gundrey.

Plate: includes silver cup, without assay marks, inscribed 'The gift of Mꜱ. Katherine Radford Widdow to the Parrish of Rawston 1639', with lozenge-of-arms of Uvedale.

Pulpit: of oak, polygonal, with four sides panelled in three heights, top panels carved, lower panels moulded, with enriched cornice and carved brackets to desk; early 17th century (Plate 13). *Seating:* in nave includes six seats made out of late 17th-century oak panelling; others, of pine, early 19th century. *Tables of Decalogue:* flanking E. window of chancel, with rounded heads and painted lettering by G. Stevens, Blandford, 1836. *Tiles:* reset in nave, slip-tiles with beasts and other devices, 14th century.

SECULAR

(2) RAWSTON FARM (93860666), house, some 20 yds. S.W. of (1), is two-storeyed with attics, and has walls partly of rubble and flint with ashlar dressings, and partly of brick. In the H-shaped plan the centre range, extending E.–W., is of late 16th or early 17th-century date; the E. range is of the 18th century, and the W. range is of the 19th century.

The 18th-century brick E. front is symmetrical and of five bays, with uniform segmental-headed sashed windows, and a central doorway with a rusticated ashlar surround and a pedimented hood. The ends of the façade are marked by french quoins; the centre bay is defined by plain pilasters. The pilasters formerly supported a pediment-like gable and the central window in the upper storey had a round head (photograph in N.M.R.), but these features have recently been eliminated.

The S. elevation of the original range is of squared rubble and flint; in it each storey has a stone casement window of four square-headed lights under a moulded label. The N. elevation retains the lower part of a large chimneybreast with a chamfered ashlar plinth. The 19th-century W. range has brick walls and plain casement windows.

Inside, the ground-floor room in the original range has 17th-century panelling, perhaps reset. The fireplace surround is modern. The E. range has a class-T plan; the stairs in the central compartment have close strings and turned balusters.

Adjacent to the house on the S. is a large *Barn*, with walls of coursed rubble and brickwork, and with a thatched roof; it is probably of the late 18th or early 19th century.

MEDIAEVAL AND LATER EARTHWORKS

(3) SETTLEMENT REMAINS (937064), formerly part of Rawston village, lie S.W. of (2) on the W. bank of the Tarrant. They comprise at least eight closes, up to 60 yds. long and 30 yds. wide, bounded by low banks. Well-defined building platforms, up to 40 ft. by 25 ft., are cut back into the slope at the S.E. ends of the closes.

PREHISTORIC AND ROMAN

The ROMAN ROAD to Bath from Badbury Rings crosses the E. end of the parish (see *Dorset* V).

'CELTIC' FIELDS, see pp. 118–19. Groups (70, 71).

(4) SETTLEMENT SITE (932066), of Iron Age or Romano-British date, lies at 275 ft. above O.D. on the crest, and on the E. slope at the S.E. end of a broad flat-topped Chalk spur which projects towards the Tarrant. Air photographs (N.M.R., ST 9306/1–5) show the soil-marks of a roughly circular enclosure some 700 ft. in diameter, bounded by a narrow ditch with traces of an inner bank; about two-thirds of the circle remain. Approaching the enclosure from the S.W. and traceable for 170 yds. are two parallel ditches, 20 ft. apart, perhaps representing a track; they appear, however, to butt against the ditch and there is no indication of an entrance. Soil-marks inside the enclosure indicate short lengths of narrow ditch, a ditched circular feature about 60 ft. in diameter, and a roughly triangular enclosure of just under ¼ acre, bounded on the W. by the main ditch and on the N. and E. by lesser ditches. Immediately W. of the main enclosure are traces of a smaller, subrectangular ditched enclosure, about 120 ft. across.

(5) LINEAR DITCH (92920651–93250693), 150 yds. W. of (4), can be traced as a soilmark on air photographs (N.M.R., ST 9306/3, 4); it extends for some 600 yds. from S.W. to N.E. across a broad Chalk ridge. For other linear ditches, see TARRANT KEYNESTON (18), (19).

(6) LONG BARROW (91560667), in the extreme W. of the parish, lies some 340 ft. above O.D. on the N.E. crest of a Chalk ridge, with which it is parallel in an orientation of 327°. The barrow is slightly wedge-shaped, 138 ft. long, 60 ft. wide at the

S.E. end, 50 ft. wide at the N.W. end, and 6½ ft. high. Well-defined side ditches are 30 ft. to 35 ft. wide and up to 3 ft. deep. An inconclusive excavation in 1896 yielded only two sherds and three pieces of bone (*Dorset Procs.*, XVIII (1897), pp. xxxiv and l; O.S., *Map of Neolithic Wessex*, No. 156).

MONUMENTS (7–13), ROUND BARROWS

Of four barrows found on Rawston Down in the W. of the parish, either (7) or (8) was excavated by Cunnington, yielding three crouched inhumations in one grave, apparently primary, and three secondary inhumations (*Dorset Procs.*, XXXVII (1916), 46 ; Cunnington MS., No. 42). An unidentified barrow, excavated 'on Keynston Down' in 1840, may have been in Rawston (see TARRANT KEYNESTON, pp. 104–5).

(7) *Bowl* (91590669), about 20 yds. N.E. of (6), has been much reduced by ploughing; former diam. 40 ft., ht. 2 ft.; hole dug in centre.

(8) *Bowl* (91560664), immediately S. of (6); diam. 28 ft., ht. 2 ft.; hole dug in centre.

(9) *Bowl* (92030634), on Rawston Down, 325 ft. above O.D., lies on the E. crest of a Chalk ridge extending N.W.–S.E.; diam. 74 ft., ht. 7 ft.; surrounding ditch 15 ft. wide and 1½ ft. deep.

(10) *Bowl* (91920612), 270 yds. S.W. of the foregoing and similarly situated; diam. 36 ft., ht. 2 ft.

Three barrows are found on The Cliff, in the E. of the parish, about 300 ft. above O.D. ; they lie on the crest of a steep N.W. slope overlooking the Tarrant valley. All three have been much reduced by ploughing.

(11) *Bowl* (94900717); diam. formerly 60 ft., ht. 2 ft.

(12) *Bowl* (95140730), 300 yds. N.E. of (11); diam. formerly 68 ft., ht. 2½ ft.

(13) *Bowl* (95270745), 220 yds. N.E. of (12); diam. formerly 55 ft., ht. 2 ft.

31 TARRANT RUSHTON (9305)

(O.S. 6 ins., ST 90 NW, ST 90 SW, ST 90 NE, ST 90 SE)

The parish, covering 2,073 acres, lies on the E. side of the Tarrant valley, all on Chalk ; the land slopes gently down from a maximum altitude of 310 ft. in the N., south-westwards to the R. Tarrant and south-eastwards to dry tributary valleys of the R. Allen.

The parish contains two mediaeval settlements, Preston Farm in the S., formerly part of Tarrant Crawford, and the present village of Tarrant Rushton in the N., comprising a scatter of cottages along the R. Tarrant. The scarcity of buildings earlier in date than the 18th century is explained by a note in the 1664 Hearth-Tax Returns : ' this thithing the dwelling houses were burnt down and not yet rebuilt' (Meekings, 104, 122).

ECCLESIASTICAL

(1) THE PARISH CHURCH OF ST. MARY, on the N. of the village, has walls of rubble and flint with ashlar dressings of Greensand and Heathstone, and tiled roofs. The *Nave* and chancel arch preserve the form and part of the structure of an early 12th-century building, which appears to have been extended westwards later in the 12th century. In the first half of the 14th century the *Chancel* was rebuilt, the *North* and *South Transepts* were added, and a small *West Tower* was erected over the western extension of the nave. The *South Porch* was added in the 15th century ; the N. vestry is modern.

TARRANT RUSHTON
The Parish Church of St. Mary

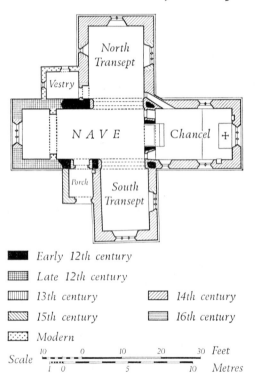

Early 12th century
Late 12th century
13th century 14th century
15th century 16th century
Modern

Scale

Architectural Description—The *Chancel* has a chamfered plinth in which is incorporated some reused 12th-century ashlar. The restored 14th-century E. window is of three trefoil ogee-headed lights with curvilinear tracery in a two-centred head; the N. and S. walls have similar two-light windows, that on the S. extensively restored. Further W. in the S. wall is a 14th-century window of one trefoil-headed light. The restored 12th-century chancel arch is round-headed and of one plain order with continuous jambs and chamfered plinths; it is flanked by small openings, probably of the 14th century, that on the N. with circular tracery with sexfoil cusping (Plate 10), that on the S. with a stone slab with a sexfoil perforation.

In the *Nave*, the 14th-century archway to the N. transept has a two-centred head of two chamfered orders, the inner order dying into the responds; the E. respond has been cut back. The archway to the S. transept is similar. The S. doorway, rebuilt in the 16th century, has its head formed from a 12th-century sculptured lintel, with the lower edge reshaped to give it a triangular 'Tudor' form. On the N. side the lintel retains original carving representing a large Agnus Dei flanked by small seated figures (Plate 8); that on the E. faces the spectator with hands raised, one hand holding an open book; that on the W., seen in profile, has a curule chair and holds a bird in one hand and in the other a tablet inscribed GREGOR. The rear-arch of the doorway is a reused 13th-century coffin-lid. Externally, the W. part of the S. wall has a chamfered plinth and a roll-moulded string-course, probably of the late 12th century. The W. wall has a chamfered plinth, but no string-course; the W. window, similar to the E. window of the chancel, is of the 14th century.

The *North Transept* has a square-headed 15th-century E. window of three trefoil-headed lights under a label with beast-head stops. Further S. in the E. wall is a square-headed 14th-century squint with a pierced closure slab (Plate 10) with three ogee-headed lights and curvilinear tracery; the N.E. side of the embrasure rests on a trefoil squinch. The 14th-century N. window is of two trefoil-headed lights with a quatrefoil spandrel light in a two-centred head. The W. wall has a reset 13th-century lancet window, and a 16th-century doorway with a chamfered segmental-pointed head and rear-arch.

The *South Transept* has an E. window similar to that of the N. transept; in the S. wall is a 14th-century window similar to the E. window in the chancel, but with the upper part cut down to the middle of the tracery and finished with a square head.

The *West Tower* has but one stage, and no buttresses. The tower arch is modern. The belfry has chamfered square-headed single-light N. and S. windows. The tiled roof is hipped and there is no parapet.

The *South Porch* has an archway with a moulded two-centred head and continuous jambs; the rear-arch, of depressed ogee form, is reused.

The early 17th-century *Roof* of the N. transept has three trusses, each with arched braces to the collar and a shaped pendant at the apex of the braces; the braces spring from moulded timber brackets. The S. transept roof has a chamfered tie beam.

Fittings—*Bell:* inscribed 'William Barns, Richard Arner Chvrchwardens, 1675, R.F.', with vine-scroll border, probably by Richard Hovey of Salisbury. *Bracket:* reset in S. transept, in E. wall, circular stone, 12th century. *Chest:* of oak, with panelled sides, early 18th century. *Coffin-lids:* Reused as rear-arch of S. doorway, slab with double hollow-chamfered edge, 13th century; reset in S. wall of tower, tapering fragment with cross-stem, probably 13th century; loose in chancel, fragment with foliate cross-head, 13th century; reset in churchyard wall on S., tapering slab, mediaeval. *Coffin Stools:* of oak, pair, with turned legs, 17th century. *Communion Rails:* of oak, with turned balusters, early 18th century. *Communion Table:* of oak, with cabriole legs, mid 18th century.

Monument: in chancel, on E. wall, behind communion table; of Richard Lawrence, 1765, rector, and others of his family, slate slab with bold Roman lettering.

Niche: in chancel, in E. wall, recess with moulded jambs, trefoil two-centred head, and label with ball-flower stops, base with three-sided chamfered corbel; early 14th century. *Piscina:* in chancel, in S. wall, recess (Plate 12) with moulded jambs, cinquefoil ogee head, and label with returned stops, projecting bowl with moulded corbel and sexfoil outlet; early 14th century.

Plate: includes silver cup and paten, each inscribed 'Rushton Church Plate Dorset 1756'. *Royal Arms:* of George IV, on painted panel, with moulded border inscribed with churchwardens' names and date 1825 (Plate 27). *Stoup:* in porch, recess with round bowl, probably 15th century. *Sundial:* scratched on S. wall of transept, mediaeval. *Tables of Decalogue:* on painted panels, by G. Stevens of Blandford, 1825. *Miscellanea:* in recesses above chancel arch, earthenware vases of uncertain date, probably intended to increase resonance. Loose, volute capital, 12th century, recut to form basin; also Purbeck marble slab with hollow-chamfered under-edge and two square recesses filled in with marble, mediaeval. Built into S. face of tower, stone cross 2½ ft. high, mediaeval.

SECULAR

(2) BRIDGE (93670579), over the Tarrant, of ashlar and brickwork with one segmental arch, is of the late 18th or early 19th century.

(3) THE OLD RECTORY (93770690), of two storeys with attics, has walls of banded rubble and flint, with ashlar and brick quoins; the roofs are tiled. The original range is of the 18th century, comprising a class-T house with an approximately symmetrical three-bay S. front, with a central doorway flanked by windows with horizontally sliding sashes, and with two-light casement windows in the upper storey. Early in the 19th century a service bay was added at the E. end of the range. In c. 1820 a lofty drawing-room was added at the W. end, and a study was added on the N. Further additions on the N.W. are of c. 1880.

(4) RUSHTON MILL (93710598), a water-driven corn mill of two storeys with an attic, has brick walls and a tiled roof; it dates probably from c. 1800 and was in use until 1920. Much of the machinery remains in good condition (drawings and photographs in R.C.H.M. files). Adjacent on the E. is a two-storeyed cottage of c. 1850, with banded brick and flint walls and with a slated roof.

(5) COTTAGES (93780594), range of three, of one storey with attics, have rendered walls and thatched roofs. The middle dwelling is probably of the early 18th century; those to E. and W. are somewhat later.

(6) COTTAGE (94990651), with cob walls and a tiled roof, is of the early 19th century. The plan is of class S.

(7) COTTAGE (93750534), of one storey with an attic, has cob walls and a thatched roof; it is of the early 18th century and has a class-S plan. The living room has a stop-chamfered beam.

(8) COTTAGE (93760528), of one storey with attics, has cob walls and a thatched roof; it is perhaps of the late 17th century and has a class-T plan. Inside, stop-chamfered beams are exposed.

(9) PRESTON FARM (93700500), house, of two storeys with brick walls and slate-covered roofs, has a class-U plan. The back rooms, now service rooms, are of the late 18th century; the front rooms were added early in the 19th century.

MEDIAEVAL AND LATER EARTHWORKS

(10) MOAT (937061), about 50 yds. N.W. of (1), is of class A1(b), (see *West Cambridgeshire*, lxii). The site, in the floodplain of the Tarrant, was formerly thought to represent a mediaeval chapel of St. Leonard and is noted by this name on the Ordnance Survey, but this has been disproved; it more probably surrounded Tarrant

Rushton manor house (*Dorset Procs.*, 64 (1942), 34–42). An approximately rectangular island, 130 ft. by 160 ft., is bounded on the W. by the Tarrant and on the other sides by a ditch, up to 40 ft. wide and 4 ft. deep. On N. and S. are low external and internal banks; on the S. the ditch has partly gone. The island has a large depression 2½ ft. deep near the S.W. corner, and two platforms at right angles to one another on the internal bank at the N.E. corner.

ROMAN AND PREHISTORIC MONUMENTS

The alignment of the ROMAN ROAD from Badbury Rings to Bath crosses the parish (see *Dorset* V).

MONUMENTS (11–15), ROUND BARROWS

(11) *Bowl* (94110380), in the S.E. of the parish, lies on an E.–W. spur about 240 ft. above O.D.; diam. 45 ft., ht. 1 ft.

(12) *Bowl* (94220385), or possibly *Bell*, 130 yds. N.E. of (11), has been damaged by ploughing and by a modern structure placed on top of it; diam. 70 ft., ht. 5 ft.

(13) *Barrow?* (94300383), 100 yds. E.S.E. of (12), has been ploughed almost flat; diam. about 45 ft.

(14) *Bowl* (94620440), 700 yds. N.E. of (13), lies on a ridge top at 250 ft. above O.D. It was formerly a small mound with a pit dug in the centre, but has now been destroyed by cultivation.

(15) *Bowl* (95240477), over 200 ft. above O.D., occupies an eastward-facing spur on the edge of Tarrant Rushton Airfield. Now being reduced by cultivation, it was formerly 60 ft. in diameter and 5 ft. high, with distinct traces of a ditch and of a pit dug in the centre.

UNDATED

(16) ENCLOSURE (939046), some 6 acres in extent and roughly oval in shape, lies 225 ft. above O.D., at the W. end of a spur overlooking the Tarrant. The site, seen only as a soil-mark on air photographs (C.U.A.P., AQY 92, 94), is defined by two ditches, 80 ft. apart or more on the S., but drawing closer together on the E. and W.; the N. side is concealed by a hedge. There are traces of a ditch which approached the enclosure on the S., but no entrance is visible.

32 TODBER (8020)

(O.S. 6 ins., ST 72 SE, ST 71 NE, ST 82 SW, ST 81 NW)

This small parish, of less than 379 acres, slopes gently southwards from 250 ft. down to 150 ft. above sea-level. The land in the S.E. is Kimmeridge Clay; that in the N.W. is Corallian Limestone, extensively quarried for building material. The topographical relationship of Todber with the large adjacent parish of Marnhull (*Dorset* III, 148), together with the irregularity of the W. boundary, suggest that Todber may have originated as a secondary settlement based on Marnhull; nevertheless separation appears to have occurred at an early date, for Todber is recorded in Domesday Book

(*V.C.H.*, *Dorset*, iii, 92) and the church retains fragments of a pre-conquest cross-shaft. Apart from the church the parish contains only a few scattered houses and cottages.

ECCLESIASTICAL

(1) THE PARISH CHURCH (dedication unknown) consists of *Chancel*, *Nave* and *South Tower*; the chancel and nave were rebuilt in 1879. A window of two trefoil ogee-headed lights reset in the N. wall of the chancel is of 15th-century origin. The tower was largely rebuilt in 1879, but the walls appear to be partly mediaeval; they are of rubble with ashlar dressings. The archway on the S. has a chamfered two-centred head and continuous jambs. Above, at the level of the belfry floor, two weathered string-courses are reset, one on top of the other.

Fittings—Altar: (4½ ft. by 2½ ft., by ⅔ ft. thick) of stone, with chamfered sides; mediaeval, on modern oak support. *Bells:* two, by William Cockey; 1st inscribed 'W.C. 1736 Mr Thomas Hiscock Ch. Wd.', recast 1879; 2nd inscribed 'W.C. 1737 Mr James Hatcher Ch. Wdn'. *Cross:* see below, Monument (2). *Coffin Stools:* of oak, with turned legs, moulded and fretted rails, moulded stretchers and beaded tops, 17th century. *Font:* octagonal, with plain sides, hollow-chamfered under side and octagonal stem with roll-moulding, 15th century, recut. *Glass:* in E. window of chancel and N.E. window of nave, reset fragments, 15th century. *Piscina:* reset in chancel, with octagonal bowl on moulded corbel, in rectangular recess with hollow-chamfered ogee-head with fleur-de-lis finial; 15th century.

Plate: includes Elizabethan silver cup resembling that of Gillingham, but without marks, stand paten with hallmark of 1713, inscribed 'Todber', and secular tray with pie-crust edge and three feet, hall-marked in 1743 and inscribed 'Todbere, Dorsetshire, 1746'. *Pulpit:* of oak, with five panelled sides, 17th century, restored; former sounding-board, panelled, with moulded edge and strapwork enrichment, now reset as reredos to communion table. *Royal Arms:* painted on lozenge-shaped wood panel, with monogram C.R. and inscription 'Feare God Honour the King', 17th century.

(2) CROSS-SHAFT (Plate 2). Three fragments of a carved stone block of late 10th or early 11th-century origin were discovered in 1879 during the rebuilding of the church. Reassembled, they compose a rectangular monolithic shaft, 4 ft. 4 ins. high, 1 ft. 7 ins. by 1 ft. 2 ins. at the base and 1 ft. 3 ins. by 9 ins. at the top. The decoration is in two heights: in the lower height each face of the stone retains a complete panel of interlacing leaf and scroll-work in low relief; the upper height is similarly decorated, but more than half of it has gone. The restored shaft has been set up in the churchyard, some 15 yds. S. of (1), with a modern base and finial.

SECULAR

(3) MANOR FARM (80202018), house, of two storeys with walls of ashlar and of rubble, and with slate-covered roofs, is of

18th-century origin, with 19th-century additions. The 19th-century S. front is symmetrical and of three bays, with a round-headed central doorway and square-headed sashed windows. Inside, the plan is of class T, the original building constituting a service wing on the N.

(4) PARSONAGE FARM (80452026), house, of two storeys, with rubble walls and a tiled roof, dates from the middle of the 19th century. Reset in the N. gable is the monolithic two-centred head of a small two-light window, with cusped two-centred heads under a circular tracery light with quatrefoil cusping; it is perhaps of 14th-century origin.

(5) TEMPLE'S COTTAGE (80462062), of two storeys, with rubble walls and a thatched roof, appears to be largely of the 17th century, but the N. wall is part of an earlier, probably 15th-century building, reused. The plan is of class S., with N. and S. doorways into the unheated W. room. In the S. front the doorway is modern; beside it on the E., a casement window of three square-headed lights with hollow-chamfered stone mullions gives light to the heated E. room; in the upper storey are three similar windows of one and of two lights. In the N. front a mediaeval stone doorway, now blocked, has a chamfered two-centred head and continuous jambs; adjacent on the W. is a square-headed loop with a chamfered surround; a large stone in the eastern part of the wall is part of another window. The gabled E. wall has a two-light window, as before, in the upper storey; the masonry is of large rubble blocks, but the chimneystack is modern. The gabled W. wall is partly masked by an adjacent building, but projecting at first-floor level are two rounded stone corbels, such as might originally have supported the plate of a lean-to roof.

(6) COTTAGES (80422050), range of three, are two-storeyed and have rubble walls and tiled roofs. The two eastern tenements are of the 18th century; that on the W. is later.

33 WEST ORCHARD (8216)
(O.S. 6 ins., ST 81 NW)

This small parish, extending over some 750 acres, lies entirely on Kimmeridge Clay at altitudes between 150 ft. and 200 ft. above the sea. The land is drained by the Manston Brook and its tributary the Key Brook. Until the latter part of the 19th century the parish was a chapelry of Fontmell Magna. For evidence of pre-conquest settlement, see EAST ORCHARD (p. 15).

ECCLESIASTICAL

(1) THE CHURCH (dedication unknown) has walls of squared rubble with ashlar dressings, and tile-covered roofs. The *Chancel* is of the second half of the 15th century ; the *Nave*, *North* and *South Aisles*, *Vestry* and *Porch* were wholly rebuilt in 1876, on a larger plan than before, to the design of T. H. Wyatt (Sarum Dioc. Regy.).

Architectural Description—The E. wall of the *Chancel* has a chamfered plinth and diagonal N.E. and S.E. buttresses of two weathered stages; at the centre, below the windowsill, is a single-stage square-set buttress. At the foot of the E. gable is a weathered string-course. The square-headed E. window has three cinque-

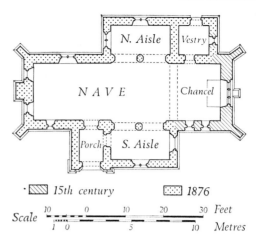

15th century ▨   1876 ▦

Scale

10   0   10   20   30   Feet

1   0   5   10   Metres

foil-headed lights under vertical tracery in a casement-moulded surround with a moulded label. The sill of the middle light is more than 1 ft. higher than those of the side lights, forming a plain panel in the lower part of the light. The S. wall of the chancel has two single-light windows with trefoil two-centred heads, casement-moulded surrounds and moulded labels. The N. wall has a 19th-century doorway to the vestry. Reset in the E. wall of the vestry is a 15th-century window, uniform with those on the S. of the chancel; it probably was originally in the N. wall of the chancel.

Fittings—*Chest:* of cast iron, for registers, 19th century. *Coffin Stools:* pair, with turned legs, plain stretchers, moulded rails and beaded tops, early 18th century. *Fonts:* two, disused and set against churchyard gate piers; one of tub form with plain round bowl with roll-moulding at base, 12th century; the other octagonal, much worn, 15th century. *Plate:* includes silver cup with assay mark of 1788, inscribed 'W.O. Chapel'.

SECULAR

(2) BRIDGE (82441735), over the Key Brook, is of Greensand ashlar and has four arches, the two central arches segmental, the others semicircular. The middle pier has a weathered cut-water at each end, its head level with the springing. The parapets have rounded capping. The bridge appears to be of the late 18th century.

(3) HAY BRIDGE (82571629), over the Manston Brook, is of Greensand ashlar and has three semicircular arches. Weathered cutwaters on the two piers rise nearly to parapet level. Reset in the N. parapet is a carved stone of uncertain date; an inscription stone in the S. parapet records that the bridge was built in 1824.

(4) NAISH'S FARM (82461626), house, is single-storeyed with dormer-windowed attics. The original range has rendered walls and a thatched roof and is of late 17th-century origin; at the E. end is a late 19th-century addition with brick walls and a tiled roof. The ground-floor room at the E. end of the 17th-century range has two intersecting deeply chamfered beams. The through-passage on the W. of this room has original plank-and-muntin partitions, much decayed.

(5) COTTAGE (82331672), single-storeyed with dormer-windowed attics, has walls of rubble dating from the 17th century, and of timber-framework comprising an 18th-century extension; a date-stone in the chimneystack is inscribed G.C. 1712. Inside, the living room has intersecting chamfered beams.

MEDIAEVAL AND LATER EARTHWORKS

(6) CULTIVATION REMAINS. Ridge-and-furrow of the former open fields, arranged in curving furlongs, is seen on air-photographs of the land E. and N.E. of the village (R.A.F., V.A.P. CPE/UK 1974 : 2158–9). The date of enclosure is not known.

34 WEST STOUR (7822)
(O.S. 6 ins., ST 72 SE)

The parish lies on the W. bank of the R. Stour and has an area of 1,070 acres. The N.E. part, on a low escarpment of Corallian Limestone which slopes E. to the river, lies between 200 ft. and 350 ft. above sea-level. Below the limestone scarp the S.W. part of the parish is on Oxford Clay, sloping gently south-westwards from 250 ft. to 180 ft., to the R. Cale which forms the parish boundary. At the Domesday survey the parish contained two settlements : West Stour, a narrow strip of land running S.W. from the R. Stour, and Little Kington, a shorter strip of land on the N., parallel with the first ; the combination of the two strips causes the irregular shape of the N.W. boundary. Little Kington was never more than a small settlement, but West Stour developed into a village, with open fields on the S.W. These fields were enclosed in 1779 (Enclosure Act), but no Award exists. Roadside cottages in the S.W. of the village reflect growth subsequent to enclosure.

ECCLESIASTICAL

(1) THE PARISH CHURCH OF ST. MARY stands in the N. of the village ; it has walls of squared and coursed rubble with ashlar dressings, and roofs covered with stone-slates and slates. The *Chancel* is of the 13th century with late 18th-century alterations ; the *Nave* and *South Tower* were rebuilt in 1840, following the original plan (contract in parish records).

Architectural Description—The *Chancel* has a chamfered plinth. In the E. wall is an 18th-century window of three trefoil-headed lights with vertical tracery in a square head under a moulded label. In the N. wall are two restored 13th-century lancets, each with a chamfered and rebated two-centred head, continuous jambs, a segmental rear-arch and widely splayed reveals. In the S. wall, on the E., is a 13th-century window of one light, wider than those on the N. and with a 16th-century trefoil head; to the W. is a 14th-century window of two cinque-foil-headed lights with a plain spandrel light in a two-centred head; between the windows is an original S. doorway with a chamfered two-centred head, continuous jambs and a two-centred rear-arch. The chamfered, two-centred chancel arch is of 1840.

The *Nave* has diagonal buttresses of two weathered stages at each corner. In the N. wall are three windows with plain two-centred heads; in the S. wall two similar windows flank a central doorway with a chamfered two-centred head; the W. window is uniform with those on the N. and S. The *South Tower* is of

one stage, with an ashlar plinth and with an embattled and moulded ashlar parapet above a moulded string-course; the walls are of rubble with ashlar dressings. The base of the tower forms the *South Porch*, and in the S. wall is a chamfered two-centred archway with a moulded label. Above, each face of the tower contains a chamfered lancet-shaped belfry window.

The nave *Roof* has a panelled ceiling, four-centred in cross-section, with hollow-chamfered and moulded wall-plates, and moulded transverse and longitudinal ribs forming six bays, each of four square panels, with plaster infilling.

WEST STOUR
The Parish Church of St. Mary

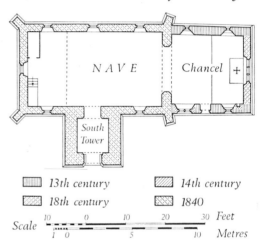

▥ 13th century	▨ 14th century
▧ 18th century	▩ 1840

Scale [10 0 10 20 30 Feet / 1 0 5 10 Metres]

Fittings—*Bells:* three; treble by John Danton, inscribed 'Reioyce in God 1635 ID', 2nd inscribed 'Mr Robert Hannam Ch Wd Wm Cockey bell founder 1733', tenor inscribed in black-letter 'sunt mea spes hii tres xpe. maria johes', late 15th century. *Communion Table:* (Plate 22), of oak, with heavy turned legs, moulded stretchers, shaped braces and carved rails, 17th century; top modern. *Font:* comprises hexagonal stone bowl, hollow-chamfered below, on large centre shaft and six small corner shafts, on chamfered hexagonal base; probably of 13th-century origin, recut. *Monuments* and *Floorslab. Monuments:* In churchyard, 5 paces S. of tower, (1) of . . . Cox, table-tomb with rusticated central and corner pilasters, and moulded top, 18th century; further S., (2) of . . . Ransom, table-tomb with plain pilasters and moulded top, 18th century. *Floorslab:* In nave, at W. end, with incised architectural surround enclosing inscription of . . . Meatyard and Margret Meatyard, 171. . *Piscina:* In chancel, in S. wall, recess with trefoil two-centred head, 14th century; bowl modern. *Plate:* now in Salisbury Museum, pewter flagon, early 18th century, and pewter stand-paten, late 18th century ('Connoisseur', June 1949). *Pulpit:* of oak, polygonal, panelled, with guilloche frieze and moulded cornice, 17th century. *Woodwork:* Reset in parapet of W. gallery, twenty-one trefoil-headed oak panels carved with finials and fleurs-de-lis, similar to those noted in Gillingham parish church; reset to form frontal-chest, six similar panels and, above, six panels with cusped ogee heads with traceried spandrels; reset in door to vesting cubicle, two fragments of oak tracery with cinquefoil two-centred heads and pierced spandrels, 16th century.

SECULAR

(2) CAUSEWAY (75812150), at the W. end of the parish and nearly 2 m. S.W. of (1), carrying the road from Shaftesbury to Sherborne across the flood plain of the R. Cale (see also KINGTON MAGNA (28)), is probably of late 18th-century origin. The structure is of rubble, squared rubble and ashlar, and comprises five arches of roughly two-centred form. The arches are now linked by walls, but originally were separate from one another, witness vertical joints in the masonry at the abutments of each arch. The connecting walls are of the early 19th century; the parapets are later.

(3) LITTLE KINGTON FARM (77522318), house, about ⅔ m. N.W. of (1), is of two storeys, but originally was of one storey with attics. It has rubble walls and tiled roofs and dates from the end of the 17th century. The E. front is of four bays, the entrance being in the second bay from the S. On the ground floor the N. and S. bays have original stone casement windows of four lights with chamfered surrounds and moulded labels. The doorway is modern and the window in the adjacent bay is a modern replica of those to N. and S. Between the doorway and the modern window is a small original loop. On the first floor each bay has a modern three-light casement window.

(4) MANOR FARM (78402251), house, 400 yds. S. of (1), is of two storeys with attics and has walls of coursed rubble, and roofs covered with stone-slates (Plate 30); it dates from c. 1800. The S. front is symmetrical and of three bays, with a central doorway on the ground floor and with uniform three-light casement windows in both storeys; the attic has dormer windows with sashed lights. To the W. is a single-storeyed service annex similar in construction to the main block.

(5) COTTAGE (78372313), 270 yds. N. of (1), is two-storeyed and has rubble walls and tiled roofs. It was built in the 18th century and formerly was two tenements.

(6) COTTAGES (78432295), pair, 50 yds. N.W. of (1), are two-storeyed, with rubble walls and metal-covered roofs; until recently they were single-storeyed with attics and had thatched roofs. They date from the mid 18th century.

(7) HOUSE (78502283), 90 yds. S.W. of (1), is two-storeyed and has rubble walls and slated roofs. It dates from the end of the 17th century, but has been much altered. To the S.E. is an 18th-century addition. The W. front has been largely rebuilt in modern brickwork. The E. front, of rubble, appears originally to have been single-storeyed, the upper part being added in coursed rubble. Inside, the main room is lined with 17th-century panelling, probably reset and now painted; the doorway has fluted pilasters and a pedimented head. Similar reset woodwork is seen in the staircase. Two rooms have stop-chamfered beams.

(8) THE SHIP INN (78482256), 150 yds. E. of (4), is two-storeyed, with coursed rubble and ashlar walls, and slate-covered roofs. It is of the early 19th century.

(9) COTTAGES (78422245), pair, 500 yds. S. of (1), are two-storeyed, but were originally of one storey with attics; they have rubble walls and metal-covered roofs and are of 17th-century origin although considerably altered. Inside, the E. tenement retains some oak panelling and a blocked fireplace surround with a stone four-centred head.

(10) HOUSE (78222245), 550 yds. S.W. of (1), is two-storeyed with squared rubble walls and tiled roofs; it dates from the 18th century. The N. front is symmetrical and of three bays, with a central doorway under a pedimented hood on moulded brackets, and with large sashed windows in each storey.

(11) COTTAGE (78262248), 520 yds. S.W. of (1), is single-storeyed with dormer-windowed attics, and has brick walls and a thatched roof; it is of the 18th century. On the S. front, which is of two bays with a central doorway, the first-floor level is marked by a strongly projecting plat-band; the same feature continues on the gabled W. wall.

Of the late 18th or early 19th century is a house at *Stour Farm* (78202244), some 550 yds. S.W. of (1), with carved stone panels on the W. front representing a swan and a ship. Seven early 19th-century *Cottages* are dispersed along the village street between 78352321 and 78262245.

MEDIAEVAL AND LATER EARTHWORKS

(12) CULTIVATION REMAINS. Nothing remains of the open fields of West Stour, which were enclosed by 1779 (D.C.R.O.). It is not certain if the settlement of Little Kington had open fields apart from those of West Stour, but angular field boundaries and two ploughed-down strip lynchets, S.E. of Little Kington Farm (778228), suggest that this was the case.

'CELTIC' FIELD GROUPS

See introductory notes to 'Celtic' Field Groups of Central Dorset (*Dorset* III, 318).– The
Field Groups of North Dorset are numbered consecutively with those of *Dorset* III.

INTRODUCTION

The 'Celtic' fields described in *Dorset* II and *Dorset* III survive in condition varying from well-preserved earthworks to the merest traces on air photographs. Those in the area covered by the present volume have almost without exception been severely damaged, chiefly by later cultivation.– From the mediaeval period onwards, ploughing has made inroads into the 'Celtic' fields, altering or obliterating them, a process of destruction which has reached a climax in the last few decades under the impact of the efficient machinery of modern arable farming. Large blocks of fields have been totally flattened and are now scarcely visible on the ground, though they still survive on air photographs. But even on photographs, particularly those taken in recent years, 'Celtic' fields are often only faintly discernible— the last vestiges of a lengthy process of attrition.

The fields all lie on the Chalk and can be detected over substantial areas of former downland (see general map of prehistoric and Roman sites in end-pocket). Their distribution, like that of so many earthworks, coincides to a notable extent with the areas of former downland as recorded, for example, in O.S., 1811; areas in which post-Roman ploughing has usually been of limited intensity, if it took place at all, until comparatively recent times. This suggests that the 'Celtic' fields were formerly much more widespread than now appears and that many have been obliterated in areas where arable activity has been intensive and continuous. Where the fields are certainly or probably related to settlements, the latter appear to be of the Iron Age or Romano-British periods. The small square fields forming an irregular pattern on Pimperne Down (Group (73)) are associated with an early Iron Age enclosure, Pimperne (15). A series of elongated, but somewhat irregular, fields and closes in the same group occupies the area between the probable Iron Age enclosure, Pimperne (18), and the double-enclosure settlement of Iron Age and Romano-British date, Tarrant Hinton (18). 'Celtic' fields (Group (70)) are integrated with the Iron Age and Romano-British settlement of Buzbury Rings and, in part, with a series of linear boundary dykes (Tarrant Keyneston (17–21)) in their vicinity. The fields of Group (74) adjoin the Iron Age and Romano-British settlement on Tarrant Hinton Down (19), and at their S. limit are cut by a linear dyke, Tarrant

Launceston (16). The Romano-British settlements on Chettle Down (Chettle (14)) and on Blandford Down (Tarrant Launceston (14)) lie among 'Celtic' fields (Groups (72) and (75)), but direct relationship can now be established only at the former settlement.

Among the 'Celtic' fields, virtually no trackways have been found leading to and from settlements, except on Manor Hill, Tarrant Gunville, where nearly half a mile of track associated with a probable settlement is visible as a soil-mark among contemporary fields (Group (76)). On Monkton Down (Group (72)) and on Gunville Down (Group (73)) two small areas of elongated and notably rectangular fields are conspicuous ; their form suggests that they were laid out in the Roman period, rather than earlier.

INVENTORY

GROUP (69) : TARRANT CRAWFORD. Air photographs indicate the former existence of 'Celtic' fields, now almost totally obliterated by ploughing, on the spur top S.E. of Tarrant Crawford (around 926030).

Air photographs : CPE/UK 1893 : 3091–2.

GROUP (70) : KEYNESTON DOWN, RAWSTON DOWN AND LUTON DOWN (*Langton Long Blandford, Tarrant Keyneston, Tarrant Monkton, Tarrant Rawston*). 'Celtic' fields (916047—914074—936075—935060), now largely flattened by ploughing, and discontinuous, cover some 500 acres on the top and sides of the interfluve between the Stour and the Tarrant, around the Iron Age and Romano-British settlement of Buzbury Rings (Tarrant Keyneston (16)).– They incorporate at least one other settlement, Tarrant Rawston (4), and are associated with a number of dykes, Tarrant Keyneston (18–21). See map in end pocket.

Traces of a number of fields, up to 60 yds. wide and of uncertain length, are detectable in Langton Long Blandford just W. of Buzbury Rings, around 915060. Clearly they are laid off the linear dyke (Tarrant Keyneston (18)), between which and dyke (19) are at least four large rectangular fields, measuring up to 85 yds. by 130 yds.

To the S. of Buzbury Rings heavy ploughing has totally flattened the fields, but traces are visible as far S. as 916047. Air photographs suggest that fields have been relaid near the linear earthwork, Tarrant Keyneston (20) ; some appear to be related to it, others to be cut by it.– A ploughed out hollow-way or dyke, apparently integrated with 'Celtic' fields, runs N.E. from 920050 to a roughly circular enclosure about 130 ft. across at 92150565.

'Celtic' field lynchets, but few complete fields, extend E. from Buzbury Rings towards Tarrant Rushton, along the steep slope N. of Keyneston Down, as far as 933060. Air photographs show traces of former 'Celtic' fields on Rawston Down, especially around 924067. Farther N., in Tarrant Monkton, traces are visible on Luton Down, around 915071, and also over an extensive area around, but mostly N. of Luton Drove, between 921074 and 936076. Within this area, soil-marks indicate the existence of a probable settlement at 913076, comprising at least one small enclosure approached by a long, narrow funnel and associated with further ditches.

Air photographs : CPE/UK 1934 : 1129, 3155-8, 5156-7 ; CPE/UK 1893 : 3068 ; 58/3250 : 0064-6, 0077-8 ; HSL/UK/ 62/263 : 2593, 2596 ; N.M.R. ST 9307/1-6.

GROUP (71) : THE CLIFF (*Tarrant Rawston*). Vestiges of 'Celtic' fields are traceable on the shoulder of The Cliff, a steep river cliff rising to 300 ft. above O.D. and facing N.W. over the Tarrant valley.– Because of destruction by strip cultivation and later ploughing no complete field survives.

Air photographs : CPE/UK 1934 : 3151-3.

GROUP (72) : SOUTH TARRANT HINTON DOWN— RACE DOWN—MONKTON DOWN (*Tarrant Hinton, Tarrant Launceston, Tarrant Monkton*).– 'Celtic' fields, now almost entirely destroyed by cultivation, are visible on air photographs over much of the western parts of these parishes. They are not demonstrably continuous, but they may once have been so, and some at least were almost certainly associated with the extensive settlement on Blandford Down (Tarrant Launceston (14)).

On S. Tarrant Hinton Down very faint traces of 'Celtic' fields are visible between 919100 and 929097 on the top of a ridge and extending down its E. slope into Tarrant Launceston. They lie close to the settlement on Blandford Down and to the enclosure in Tarrant Hinton (21), but the remains are so disturbed that no certain physical connections are determinable.

S.W. of Tarrant Hinton village (around 931106) air photographs reveal traces of 'Celtic' fields on a low spur overlooking the Tarrant valley.

Remains of 'Celtic' fields, severely damaged by recent development, survive within the area of the military camp on Race Down, around 918086. Further E. (around 934090) air photographs indicate the former existence of 'Celtic' fields, now totally flattened by ploughing, on the N.E. slope of a dry valley.

On Monkton Down (926080), 'Celtic' fields of markedly rectangular and rather elongated form, measuring up to 60 yds. across and 120 yds. long, are traceable on the W.-facing slope of a spur overlooking Pond Bottom. Faint traces are visible extending E. to the soil-mark enclosures Tarrant Monkton (20), and S.E. towards Group (70).

Air photographs : CPE/UK 1845 : 4064-5 ; 58/3250 : 0077-9, 0112-3 ; HSL/UK/62/263 : 2593 ; N.M.R. ST 9307/3, 9308/5.

GROUP (73) : PIMPERNE DOWN—HINTON BUSHES (*Pimperne, Tarrant Gunville, Tarrant Hinton*). 'Celtic' fields are traceable over much of the northern part of Pimperne parish and in the adjacent parts of Tarrant Gunville and Tarrant Hinton. They cover some 350 acres and are not continuous, though they may formerly

have been so. Enclosures in the area, some of them certainly settlements of Iron Age and/or Romano-British date, are likely to be associated with the 'Celtic' fields. (Map in end pocket.)

'Celtic' fields, now much damaged by ploughing, survive on Pimperne Down between 275 ft. and 380 ft. above O.D., on the S.E. slope of a dry valley. They extend in a narrow band N.E. from the Iron Age enclosure, Pimperne (15), towards Pimperne Fox Warren (900109). Most of those fields which are complete vary in area between ¼ and ½ acre.

To the S.W. of the foregoing, faint traces of 'Celtic' fields are discernible on Camp Down (around 881089), but they have been much altered by strip ploughing and later cultivation.

To the N., on Gunville Down and extending into Pimperne (904117), are further remains of 'Celtic' fields, now heavily ploughed. They are notably rectangular and elongated (though some internal divisions may have disappeared) with the long axes aligned N.W.–S.E. Faint traces of fields are also visible E. of Pimperne Wood.

E. of Pimperne Down, towards and around Ferns Plantation (910106), 'Celtic' fields now almost totally flattened by cultivation occupy the slopes and summit of a spur. Even the smallest of these fields is as much as 1 acre in area.

Further E., S. of Hinton Bushes and mainly in Tarrant Hinton parish, a series of elongated 'Celtic' fields and angular closes, now largely flattened, occupy the area between enclosure Pimperne (18) and settlement Tarrant Hinton (18), and almost certainly are associated with them. The boundary dyke extending S.W. from Tarrant Hinton (18) appears to delimit these fields on the S. One of the few complete fields measures 130 yds. by 33 yds.

Air photographs : CPE/UK 1845 : 4069-71, 6065-70 ; CPE/UK 1934 : 2159-60, 4154-8 ; CPE/UK 1944 : 2136-8, 2318-20, 3320 ; 58/3250 : 0111, 0136-8.

GROUP (74) : TARRANT HINTON DOWN AND LAUNCESTON DOWN (*Tarrant Hinton, Tarrant Launceston*). 'Celtic' fields formerly covered much of Tarrant Hinton Down in the N.E. of that parish (946126—950111), but they have been levelled by ploughing and for the most part are visible only as faint traces on air photographs. On the N. they adjoin and appear to be associated with an Iron Age and Romano-British settlement, Tarrant Hinton (19). Further S. they surround and incorporate a small group of round barrows, Tarrant Hinton (46–50) ; their relationship to the dyke (952119) extending W. from Long Crichel is uncertain. At their S. limit the fields are clearly cut by the W. end of another dyke Tarrant Launceston (16,*a*).

Air photographs : CPE/UK 1845 : 4149-50 ; 6059-61 ; F22/58/1090 : 0094-5 ; CPE/UK 1934 : 2150-1 ; HSL/UK/62/263 : 2589 ; C.U.A.P. AMO 9, 10.

Remains of 'Celtic' fields on the S. of Hyde Hill Plantation in Tarrant Launceston form part of a Group which lies mainly in Long Crichel ; they are, therefore, reserved for treatment in *Dorset* V.

GROUP (75) : CHETTLE DOWN AND HOOKSWOOD COMMON (*Chettle* and *Farnham*). 'Celtic' fields formerly covered much of the N. and W. of Chettle parish, between 940152 and 940135, but the majority have been severely damaged by ploughing and now are visible only on air photographs. They survive in old pasture on Chettle Common, around 940145, and may be traced into Chettle Chase Coppice, but these examples have been damaged by later digging and are partly obscured by scrub. They lie on a gentle S. slope and are defined by lynchets or low spread banks, rarely more than 2 ft. in height; though ploughed, they are visible to the E., up to and S. of the settlement in Chettle (14). Several of the fields or closes near the settlement are irregular in shape. Traces of fields extend as far E. as Hookswood Common (945152). Further traces, detached from the main block, occur N. of Farnham near Half Hide Coppice (955162) and also to the N.W. in Tarrant Gunville, just S. of enclosure (33).

Air photographs: CPE/UK 2038: 3065-9; C.U.A.P. ANC 4, 6.

GROUP (76): STUBHAMPTON DOWN AND MANOR HILL (*Tarrant Gunville*). 'Celtic' fields cover much of the N.W. part of Tarrant Gunville, but have largely been flattened by intensive cultivation, especially in recent years. They lie between 300 ft. and 500 ft. above O.D. on a series of spurs separated by dry combes at the head of the Tarrant valley (903143—923157).

In the area of Stubhampton Down 'Celtic' fields covered much of Earl's Hill and the slopes of the dry combe immediately S. of it (907142). Few complete fields remain visible, even on air photographs. On the lower slopes mediaeval and later strip cultivation had largely removed the 'Celtic' lynchets before the destructive effects of more recent ploughing.

Immediately to the N.E. 'Celtic' fields covered most of the spur between Stubhampton Bottom and Ashmore Bottom (around 914147). Though much damaged by later ploughing, a number of large fields, up to 150 yds. by 80 yds., appear to have existed, as well as smaller ones.

To the E., on the spur of Manor Hill, air photographs indicate an irregular pattern of earthworks associated with a track and probably representing a settlement, all now flattened by ploughing. The track, which appears to lie among 'Celtic' fields, runs N. from 922015 04 for some 400 yds. to the probable settlement area around 921154 and then turns sharply E.N.E.; after 200 yds. it turns N. again and after a further 200 yds. is lost. The presumed settlement incorporates what appears to be an almond-shaped enclosure, some 400 ft. by 300 ft. overall.

Air photographs: CPE/UK 1944: 4319-22; CPE/UK 2038: 3071-77.

GROUP (77): SUTTON HILL AND BAREDEN DOWN (*Fontmell Magna, Iwerne Minster, Sutton Waldron*). 'Celtic' fields appear formerly to have covered much of the summit and the slopes of the Chalk escarpment in these parishes. Subsequent destruction has left dis-

continuous areas of remains, all levelled by ploughing except on the steeper slopes, and visible only on air photographs.

Air photographs show 'Celtic' fields at the top of the escarpment in Fontmell Magna, between 877167 and 887165 on either side of the old Blandford–Shaftesbury road, and on the spur of Fontmell Down around 878180. A few lynchets survive on the upper slopes of the spur immediately S. of Littlecombe Bottom, with later strip lynchets below them. To the S. further remains are detectable on Sutton Hill, between 877157 and 892157, and on the steep slope overlooking Coombe Bottom (876160). In Iwerne Minster remains of 'Celtic' fields lie around the head of a dry combe on Bareden Down (885153).

Air photographs: CPE/UK 1934: 4324-6; CPE/UK 2038: 4082-3.

GROUP (78): ASHMORE. Evidence of 'Celtic' fields survives both N. and S. of the village. On the slopes of the combe head above Boyne Bottom (905185), near the N. edge of the parish, are at least four large 'Celtic' fields; they measure up to 130 yds. by 80 yds. and are defined by low lynchets. Air photographs suggest traces of other fields, now ploughed flat, adjacent to and S. of the village at 911172 and 910166. The lyncheted angles of 'Celtic' fields, much reduced by ploughing and in the past mistaken for barrows, survive on the spur immediately N. of Well Bottom (916167).

Air photographs: CPE/UK 1811: 1078-9; CPE/UK 2038: 4073-7; N.M.R. ST 9018/1-3.

GROUP (79): MELBURY DOWN AND COMPTON DOWN (*Compton Abbas* and *Melbury Abbas*). 'Celtic' fields have survived in the vicinity of Melbury Down, on the slopes of the deep and narrow dry valley which extends E. from Melbury Abbas village. Remains seen on air photographs S. and S.E. of Breeze Hill have now been levelled by ploughing or are obscured by the conifers of Gardiner Forest. They cover at least 100 acres on the often steep slopes of the spurs and re-entrants forming the N. side of the valley, between 500 ft. and 800 ft. above O.D. (894196—905196). Other remains occur to the S., around 891189, at a similar height on the northward-facing side of the valley; presumably they formerly extended on to the higher, more level ground to the S. Across the spur to the S.W., in Compton Abbas, remains of 'Celtic' fields occur on the steep slopes around the head of the combe E. of the village (884187); scarps are seen, but no complete fields. Ploughing above and below has removed all indication of their former extent.

Air photographs: CPE/UK 1811: 1079-81, 3078-80.

GLOSSARY

ABACUS—The uppermost member of a capital.

ACANTHUS—A plant represented in classical ornament, used particularly in the Corinthian and Composite Orders.

ACHIEVEMENT—In heraldry, the shield accompanied by the appropriate external ornaments, helm, crest, mantling, supporters, etc. In the plural the term is also applied to the insignia of honour carried at the funerals and suspended over the monuments of important personages, comprising helmet and crest, shield, tabard, sword, gauntlets and spurs, banners and pennons.

ACROTERIA—In classical architecture, blocks on the apex and lower ends of a pediment, often carved with honeysuckle or palmette ornament.

AEDICULE—A small temple or shrine, or a miniature representation of the same.

AGGER—The earthen ridge carrying a Roman road.

ALTAR—The name used in the Inventory to distinguish pre-reformation stone altars from post-reformation *Communion Tables* of wood.

ALTAR-TOMB—A modern term for a tomb of stone or marble resembling, but not used as, an altar. See also TABLE-TOMB.

ANTEFIXES—In classical architecture, small ornamental blocks fixed at intervals along the lower edge of a roof to conceal the ends of the roofing-tiles.

ANTHEMION—Honeysuckle or palmette ornament in classical architecture.

APRON—A plain or decorated panel below a window, or at the base of a wall-monument.

APSE—The semicircular or polygonal end of a chancel or chapel.

ARABESQUE—Decoration, in colour or low relief, with fanciful intertwining of leaves, scroll-work, etc.

ARCADE—A range of arches carried on piers or columns. *Blind arcade*, a series of arches, sometimes interlaced, carried on shafts or pilasters against a solid wall.

ARCH—The following are some of the most usual forms:
Equilateral—A pointed arch struck with radii equal to the span.
Flat or straight—Having the soffit horizontal.
Four-centred—A pointed arch of four arcs, the two outer and lower arcs struck from centres on the springing line and the two inner and upper arcs from centres below the springing line. For want of a better expression the term is also used of pointed door-heads, etc., in which the upper arcs are replaced by straight lines, the centres then being at infinity.
Lancet—A pointed arch, struck at the level of the springing, with radii greater than the span.
Nodding—An ogee arch curving also forward from the plane of the wall-face.
Ogee—A pointed arch of four or more arcs, the two uppermost being reversed, *i.e.*, convex instead of concave to the base line.
Pointed or two-centred—Two arcs struck from centres on the springing line, and meeting at the apex with a point.
Relieving—An arch, generally of rough construction, placed in the wall above the true arch or head of an opening, to relieve it of the superincumbent weight.

Segmental—A single arc struck from a centre below the springing line.
Segmental-pointed—A pointed arch, struck from two centres below the springing line.
Skew—An arch spanning between responds not diametrically opposite one another.
Stilted—An arch with its springing line raised above the level of the imposts.
Three-centred, elliptical—Formed with three arcs, the middle or uppermost struck from a centre below the springing line.

ARCHITRAVE—The lowest member of an entablature (*q.v.*); often adapted as a moulded enrichment to the jambs and head of a door-way or window-opening.

ARRIS—The sharp edge formed by the meeting of two surfaces.

ASHLAR—Masonry wrought to an even face and with square edges.

ASSARTING—The grubbing up of trees and bushes from forest land, to make it arable.

AUMBRY—Wall-cupboard, usually for sacred vessels in a church.

BAGSHOT BEDS—A Tertiary geological formation consisting mainly of sands and grits with seams of clay.

BAILEY—The courtyard of a castle.

BALL-FLOWER—In architecture, a decoration, peculiar to the first quarter of the 14th century, consisting of a globular flower of three petals enclosing a small ball.

BALUSTER—A vertical support to a handrail or parapet coping, usually turned, with a vase-shaped or column-shaped profile.

BARGE-BOARD—A board, often carved, fixed to the edge of a gabled roof a short distance from the face of the wall.

BARREL-VAULT—See VAULTING.

BARROW—A burial mound. *Long barrow*: an elongated burial mound of the Neolithic period. *Bank barrow*: a long barrow of exceptional length, resembling a length of bank. *Round barrow*: a burial mound, circular in plan, usually of the Bronze Age. For explanation of different types of round barrow see *Dorset* II, p. 422.

BASTION—A projection from the general outline of a fortress, from which the garrison is able to see, and defend by a flanking fire, the ground before the ramparts.

BAYS—The main vertical divisions of the façade of a building; the archways of an arcade or the intercolumniations of a colonnade; also the divisions of a roof, marked by its principals (*q.v.*) which usually correspond with the bays of the façade, etc., below it.

BEADING—A small rounded moulding.

BEAKER—A pottery vessel or jar, characteristic of a culture introduced into Britain towards the end of the Neolithic period; hence *Beaker culture* or *Beaker people*. *Bell beaker* or '*B*' *beaker*: the type of British beaker which most closely resembles widespread continental prototypes and which first appears here soon after 2000 B.C. *Long-necked* or '*A*' *beaker*: an insular development first appearing c. 1800 B.C.

BERM—In earthworks, a ledge between a bank and its accompanying ditch or scarp.

BICONICAL URN—A pottery vessel of the Middle Bronze Age, roughly biconical in outline, which in Dorset appears to be derived from Cornish biconical urns of the Early Bronze Age.

BILLET—In architecture, an ornament used in the 11th and 12th centuries, consisting of short attached cylinders or rectangles with intervening spaces. In heraldry, a small upright oblong charge.

BOLECTION-MOULDING—A bold moulding raised above the general plane of the framework of a doorway, fireplace or panelling.

BOND—See BRICKWORK.

BOSS—A square or round projecting ornament, often covering the intersections of the ribs in a vault, panelled ceiling, roof, etc.

BRACE—In roof construction, a subsidiary timber designed to strengthen the framing of a truss. *Wind-brace* : a subsidiary timber between the purlins and principals of a roof, designed to resist the pressure of the wind.

BRACKET—A projecting flat-topped support, usually decorated on the underside ; also, in open-string stairs, the spandrel or exposed triangular end of a step.

BRATTISHING—Ornamental cresting on the top of a screen, cornice, etc.

BRESSUMMER—A beam supporting an upper wall.

BRICKWORK—The following terms are used :
Header—A brick laid so that the end appears on the face of the wall.
Stretcher—A brick laid so that the long side appears on the face of the wall.
English Bond—A method of laying bricks so that alternate courses on the face of the wall are composed of headers and stretchers.
Flemish Bond—A method of laying bricks so that alternate headers and stretchers appear in each course on the face of the wall.

BROACH-STOP—A half-pyramidal stop against a chamfer, effecting the change from chamfer to arris.

BRONZE AGE—The period which in Britain is divided and dated roughly as follows : Early Bronze Age, 1650 to 1350 B.C. ; Middle Bronze Age, 1350 to 800 B.C. ; Late Bronze Age, 800 to 600 B.C.

BUCKET URN—A pottery vessel of the Middle to Late Bronze Age with sides tapering downwards and often incurving at the top. The true bucket shape, with straight sides, is rare.

BUTTRESS—Masonry or brickwork projecting from, or built against a wall to give additional strength.
Angle-buttresses—Two meeting, or nearly meeting, at an angle of 90° at the corner of a building.
Clasping-buttress—One that clasps or encases an angle.
Diagonal-buttress—One placed against the right-angle formed by two walls, and more or less equiangular with both.
Flying-buttress—An arch or half-arch transmitting the thrust of a vault or roof from the upper part of a wall to an outer support.

CABLE-MOULDING—A moulding carved in the form of a rope or cable.

CANONS—The metal loops by which a bell is hung.

CANOPY—A projection or hood over a door, window, etc., and the covering over a tomb or niche.

CARSTONE—See HEATHSTONE.

CARTON-PIERRE—A patent composition cast in moulds to form fine decorative details for application to the surfaces of joinery, thus simulating carved woodwork ; the process was introduced into Britain by Robert Adam, *c.* 1780.

CARTOUCHE—In Renaissance ornament, a tablet, often imitating a scroll with partly rolled borders, used ornamentally or bearing an inscription or a shield-of-arms.

CARYATID—Sculptured figure used as a column or support.

CASEMENT MOULDING—A wide and deep hollow moulding on the jambs and head of a window or doorway ; usually characteristic of the 15th or 16th century.

CASEMENT WINDOW—One closed with a hinged lattice.

CASTOR WARE—A colour-coated ware made in potteries near Castor, Northants, and elsewhere from the late 2nd century A.D.

CAUSEWAYED CAMP—A Neolithic enclosure bounded by a bank or banks, each with an external ditch interrupted at intervals by ' causeways ' or lengths of undisturbed ground.

' CELTIC ' FIELDS—Small, rectangular fields, usually bounded by lynchets, originating in the Bronze Age, but widespread in Romano-British times, especially in the south of England.

CHAÎNAGE—Bricks of contrasting colour bonded into a brick façade to form decorative vertical bands. As bonding requires the use of headers and stretchers in alternate courses the feature resembles a chain.

CHALCOLITHIC—That period which in Britain is characterised by the first use of copper tools in a predominantly stone-age society, roughly 1800 to 1650 B.C.

CHALICE—The name used in the Inventory to distinguish the pre-reformation type of communion cup with a small shallow bowl from the post-reformation cup with a larger and deeper bowl.

CHAMFER—The small plane formed when an arris of stone or wood is cut away, usually at an angle of 45°. When the plane is concave it is termed a *hollow chamfer*.

CHANTRY—A foundation, usually supporting a priest, for the celebration of mass for the soul of the founder and of such others as he may direct.

CHARGE—In heraldry, the representation of an object or device upon the field.

CHEVAUX-DE-FRISE—Iron spikes, originally set in timber to repel cavalry, now usually along the tops of walls to protect property.

CHEVRON—In heraldry, a charge resembling an inverted V. In architecture, a decorative form similar to the heraldic chevron and often used in a consecutive series.

CHIP-CARVING—Simple geometrical patterns gouged on the surface of joinery ; the work is characteristic of the 17th century.

CINQUEFOIL—See FOIL.

CIST—A small burial chamber lined with stones or cut in natural sub-soil, above or below ground level ; it has no entrance.

CLEARSTOREY—In a church that has colonnades, an upper storey with windows rising above the aisle roof. The term is applicable in secular architecture.

CLOSE—Enclosure. In earthworks, an area enclosed by banks.

CLUNCH—Hard stratum of the Lower Chalk used for building and sculpture.

COFFERS—Sunk panels in ceilings, vaults, domes and arch-soffits.

COLLAR-BEAM—In a roof, a horizontal beam framed to and serving to tie together a pair of rafters, some distance above wall-plate level.

COLLARED URN—A type of pottery vessel with a deep rim, frequently found in association with cremation burials ; it first appears in the Early Bronze Age (c. 1550 B.C.) and is largely a development of late Neolithic (Fengate) pottery.

CONSOLE—A bracket with a compound curved outline.

CORALLIAN LIMESTONE—An oolitic limestone of the Upper Jurassic system, often containing much comminuted shell.

CORBEL—A projecting stone or piece of timber for the support of a superincumbent feature. *Corbel-table*—A row of corbels, usually carved.

CORNBRASH—In geology, a calcareous formation of the Middle Jurassic system consisting of a rubbly ferruginous limestone and clayey marl.

CORNICE—A crowning projection. In classical architecture, the crowning portion of the entablature.

COUNTERSCARP—The outer face or slope of the ditch of a fortification. *Counterscarp bank*—a small bank immediately beyond the counterscarp of a hill-fort or defensive work.

COVE—A concave moulding at the junction of wall and ceiling, or masking the eaves of a roof.

COVER-PATEN—A cover to a communion cup, used as a paten when inverted.

CRENELLES—The openings in an embattled parapet.

CROCKETS—Carvings projecting at regular intervals from the sloping sides of spires, canopies, hood-moulds, etc.

CROP-MARK—A trace of a buried feature revealed by differential growth of crops, best seen from the air.

CROSS—In heraldry, a pale combined with a fesse, as St. George's Cross. Of many varieties the following are the most common : *Crosslet*—with a smaller arm crossing each main arm ; *Fitchy*—having the lowest arm spiked or pointed ; *Flowered* or *Flory*—having the arms headed with fleurs-de-lis ; *Formy*—having arms widening from the centre, and square at the ends ; *Moline* (or *mill-rind*)—with the arms split or forked at the ends ; *Paty*—as a cross *formy*, but with the arms notched in two places at the ends, giving them something of the form of a fleur-de-lis ; *Pommy*—with the arms ending in balls ; *Potent*—having a small transverse arm at the extreme end of each main arm ; *Quadrate*—with a small rectangular projection at each angle as though the crossing was surcharged with a square ; *Saltire* (or *St. Andrew's*)—an X-shaped cross ; *Tau* (or *Anthony*)—in the form of a T ; *Trefly*—with the arms terminating in trefoils.

CROSS-RIDGE DYKE—A bank and ditch, or sometimes a ditch between two banks, crossing a ridge or a spur of high ground.

CRUCK TRUSS—See ROOFS.

CURTAIN—The connecting wall between the towers or bastions of a castle.

CUSHION CAPITAL—A capital cut from a cube, with its lower angles rounded off to adapt it to a circular shaft.

CUSPS—The projecting points forming the foils in Gothic windows, arches, panels, etc. ; they are sometimes ornamented at the ends (*cusp-points*) with leaves, flowers, berries, etc. *Sub-cusps*—cusps within the foils formed by larger cusping.

CYMA—A moulding with an S-shaped profile consisting of two contrary curves.

DADO—The protective or decorative treatment applied to the lower part of a wall-surface to a height, normally, of 3 to 4 feet. *Dado-rail*—the moulding or capping at the top of the dado.

DENTILS—Small rectangular tooth-like blocks used decoratively in cornices.

DIAPER—All-over decoration of surfaces with reticulate and other patterns.

DIE—The part of a pedestal between its base and its cornice.

DIP-SLOPE—Land surface developed on dipping strata ; the rear slope of an escarpment.

DOG-TOOTH ORNAMENT—A typical 13th-century carved ornament consisting of a series of pyramidal flowers of four petals ; used to cover hollow mouldings.

DORMER—A sleeping recess contrived as a projection from the slope of a roof and having a roof of its own ; it usually is unlighted, but occasionally it has small lights in the cheeks.

DORMER-WINDOW—A vertical window projecting from the slope of a roof, and having a roof of its own, as in a dormer.

DORTER—A monastic dormitory.

DOUBLE LYNCHET TRACK—A trackway running through fields on a slope and defined on either side by their lynchets ; frequently associated with ' Celtic ' fields.

DRESSINGS—The stone or brickwork used about an angle, window, or other feature, when worked to a finished face, whether smooth, tooled or rubbed, moulded, or sculptured.

EARED (or LUGGED) ARCHITRAVE—Enrichment of an opening wherein the horizontal mouldings of the head continue beyond the sides of the vertical mouldings of the jambs and are returned to form a π-shaped feature.

EASTER SEPULCHRE—Aedicule or recess, usually on the N. side of the chancel, in which the sacrament, chalices and reliquaries were enshrined during the three days before Easter, in commemoration of Christ's entombment.

EMBATTLED—In architecture, a parapet with an indented outline, comprising *merlons* separated by *crenelles*, is said to be embattled.

EMBRASURES—The recesses for windows, doorways, etc.

ENTABLATURE—In classical architecture, the moulded horizontal capping of a wall, colonnade or opening. A full entablature consists of *architrave, frieze* and *cornice*.

ENTASIS—The convexity or swelling in the shaft of a classical column or pilaster, designed to correct the optical illusion of concavity when the sides are straight.

FAN-VAULT—See VAULTING.

FASCIA—A plain or moulded facing board.

FIELDED PANEL—A panel, usually of woodwork, with recessed and bevelled margins.

FINIAL—An ornament at the top of a pinnacle, gable, canopy, etc.

FLUTING—Ornament consisting of narrow concave striations, the reverse of reeding.

FOIL (*trefoil*, *quatrefoil*, *cinquefoil*, *multifoil*, etc.)—A leaf-shaped space defined by the curve of the cusping in an opening or panel.

FOLIATE (of a capital, corbel, etc.)—Carved with leaf ornament.

FOREST MARBLE—A Middle Jurassic geological formation comprising a hard flaggy oolitic limestone alternating with bands of shaley clay or marl.

FOUR-CENTRED ARCH—*See* ARCH.

FRATER—The refectory or dining-hall of a monastery.

FRIEZE—The middle division in an entablature, between the architrave and the cornice ; generally any band of ornament or colour below a cornice.

FURLONG—An area of the Open Fields (*q.v.*) containing a number of adjacent strips extending in the same direction.

GABLE—The wall at the end of a ridged roof, generally triangular, sometimes semicircular, or with an outline of various curves, then called *curvilinear* or *Dutch*. A *stepped* gable has an outline formed of a series of steps.

GADROON ORNAMENT—A series of convexities and/or concavities forming the edge of a prominent moulding in stone, wood or metalwork.

GARB—In heraldry, a sheaf, usually of wheat.

GARDEROBE—Wardrobe. Antiquarian usage applies the word to a latrine.

GARGOYLE—A carved projecting figure pierced or channelled to carry off rainwater from the roof of a building.

GAUGING—In brickwork, bringing every brick exactly to a certain form by cutting and rubbing.

GLOBULAR URN—A type of pottery vessel of the Middle or Late Bronze Age, probably of foreign derivation and regarded as intrusive into southern England ; it has a spherical body with a constriction above, and a more or less vertical neck.

GREENSAND—A Cretaceous sandstone containing the green iron-bearing mineral glauconite.

GRISAILLE—Formal patterns painted in greyish tints, on wall surfaces or on glass windows.

GROINED VAULT—See VAULTING.

GUILLOCHE—A geometrical ornament consisting of two or more intertwining bands forming a series of circles or other shapes.

GUTTAE—Small stud-like projections under the triglyphs and mutules of the Doric entablature.

HALL—The principal room of a mediaeval house, normally open to the roof.

HAM HILL STONE—An oolitic freestone found within the Upper Lias (Lower Jurassic) ; it takes its name from a major quarry area near Yeovil.

HATCHMENT—Square or lozenge-shaped tablet displaying the armorial bearings, usually painted, of a deceased person ; it is first hung outside the house and then laid up in the church.

HEATHSTONE—A brown, ferruginous gritstone found within the Bagshot Beds ; also called *Carstone*.

HELM—Complete barrel or dome-shaped head-defence of plate. Not used in warfare after the middle of the 14th century, it continued in use in the tilt-yard into the 16th century.

HILL-FORT—A defensive enclosure of the Iron Age, fortified with rampart and ditch, single or multiple, usually on dominant ground.

HIPPED ROOF—A roof with sloped instead of vertical ends. *Half-hipped*, a roof in which the ends are partly vertical and partly sloped.

HOLD-WATER BASE—A column base with a deep concave moulding in the upper surface.

HOLLOW WAY—A sunken track, caused either by wear or by the raising of the ground on each side.

HOOD-MOULD—A projecting moulding on the face of a wall above an arch, doorway, or window ; it may follow the form of the arch or it may be square in outline. Also called *Label*.

HORNWORK—An outwork of an earthwork enclosure, such as a hill-fort, often consisting of a single arm thrown out to protect an entrance.

HUT CIRCLE—Footings or other remains of the walls of a circular dwelling, usually prehistoric.

IMPOST—The projection, often moulded, at the springing of an arch, upon which the arch appears to rest.

INCENSE CUP—A very small ritual or symbolic vessel, often found in association with urn burials of the Early Bronze Age and particularly of the Wessex culture.

INDENT—The sinking in a tomb slab for a monumental brass.

INTERLACE—Stone decoration in relief simulating woven or entwined bands, in England usually associated with the period before the Norman Conquest.

IRON AGE—The period which in Britain is taken to date from *c.* 600 B.C. to the Roman Conquest, A.D. 43.

JAMB—The side of an archway, doorway, window or other opening.

JETTY—The projection of the upper storey of a building beyond the vertical plane of the lower storey.

JEWELLED—With prism-like decoration in relief.

JOGGLING—The method of cutting the adjoining faces of the voussoirs of an arch with rebated, zigzagged or wavy surfaces to provide a key.

KEEL MOULDING—A stone moulding, in profile resembling the cross-section through the keel of a boat.

KEYSTONE—The middle stone in an arch.

KING-POST—The middle vertical post in a roof-truss. See ROOFS.

KNEELER—The stone at the foot of a gable, on which the inclined coping stones rest.

LABEL—See HOOD-MOULD.

LANCET—A narrow window with a pointed head, typical of the 13th century.

LIERNE-VAULT—See VAULTING.

LIGHT—Perpendicular division of a mullioned window.

LINTEL—Horizontal beam or stone, bridging an opening.

LOMBARDIC LETTERING—Lettering, based on N. Italian manuscripts, often used by mediaeval bellfounders.

LOOP—A small narrow window, usually unglazed.

LOUVRE—A lantern-like structure on the roof of a hall or other building, with openings for ventilation or for the escape of smoke ; it is usually fitted with sloping slats (called louvre-boards), to exclude rain. Louvre-boards are also used in belfry windows.

LYNCHETS—Cultivation scarps and terraces on hillsides, the *positive* element comprising the accumulation of plough soil from uphill, the *negative* element being cut away by the plough and moved downhill.

MATHEMATICAL TILES—Revetment for walls of timber or cob, consisting of hung tiles wherein each tile is so shaped that, when pointed with mortar, the exposed surface resembles brickwork.

MERLON—The solid part of an embattled parapet between the crenelles.

METOPES—The panels, sometimes carved, filling the spaces between the triglyphs of the Doric entablature.

MILL-RIND—The iron affixed to the centre of a millstone. A heraldic charge.

MISERICORD—A bracket, often elaborately carved, on the underside of the hinged seat of a choir-stall. When the seat is turned up the bracket comes into position to support the occupant during long periods of standing.

MODILLIONS—Brackets under the cornice in classical architecture.

MOTTE—In earthworks, a steep flat-topped mound, forming the main feature of an 11th or 12th-century castle ; originally often surmounted by a timber tower and usually associated with a BAILEY.

MULLION—A vertical post, standard, or upright dividing a window into lights.

MUNTIN—In joinery or carpentry, an intermediate upright between panels, tenoned into or stopping against upper and lower rails.

MUTULES—Shallow blocks under the corona of the cornice in classical architecture.

NAIL-HEAD—Architectural ornament of small pyramidal form used extensively in 12th-century work.

NARROW RIG—A form of ridge-and-furrow (*q.v.*) with ridges up to 5 yds. across ; it is usually of 18th or 19th-century date.

NECKING OR NECK-MOULDING—The narrow moulding around the bottom of a capital.

NEOLITHIC—Of the later Stone Age ; in Britain probably from about 3400 to 1800 B.C.

NEWEL—The central post in a circular staircase ; also the principal posts at the angles of a dog-legged or well staircase.

NODDING ARCH—See under ARCH.

OGEE—A compound curve of two parts, one convex, the other concave ; a *double-ogee moulding* has two ogee profiles side by side, the convexities adjacent to one another.

OPEN FIELDS—Large unenclosed fields of mediaeval and later date, usually held in common and cultivated on a strip system.

ORDERS—In an arch, the receding concentric rings of voussoirs.

ORIEL—A projecting bay-window, sometimes carried upon corbels or brackets ; also a compartment or embrasure with a large window opening off one side of a mediaeval Hall.

OVOLO MOULDING—A convex moulding of rounded profile.

PALLADIAN WINDOW—A three-light window with a round-headed middle light and square-headed lights on either side, the side lights having flanking pilasters, and small entablatures which form the imposts to the arch of the centre light. See also VENETIAN WINDOW.

PALMETTE—In classical architecture, a stylised palm-leaf ornament.

PARK PALE—A fence around a park. Mediaeval park pales usually survive as banks with inner ditches.

PATEN—A shallow vessel for holding the bread or wafer at the celebration of the Holy Communion.

PATERA—A flat disc-shaped ornament applied to a frieze, moulding, or cornice ; in Gothic work it commonly takes the form of a four-lobed leaf or flower.

PEDIMENT—A low-pitched gable used in classical architecture above a portico, at the end of a building, or above doors, windows, niches, etc. ; sometimes the apex is omitted, forming a *broken pediment*, or the horizontal members are omitted, forming an *open pediment*.

PELICAN-IN-PIETY—A pelican shown, according to the mediaeval legend, feeding her young upon drops of blood which she pecks from her own breast.

PISCINA—A basin in a church for washing the sacred vessels and provided with a drain ; it is generally set in or against the S. wall of the chancel, but sometimes is sunk in the pavement.

PLANK-AND-MUNTIN PARTITION—A wooden division between two rooms, composed of vertical planks alternating with, and tongued into, grooved upright posts.

PLAT-BAND—A projecting horizontal band of plain masonry or brickwork, as distinct from a moulded string-course.

PLINTH—The projecting base of a wall or column, often chamfered or moulded at the top.

PODSOLISATION—A leaching process in sandy soils, resulting in impoverishment of the top-soil and the deposit of iron salts at a lower level.

POPPY-HEAD—Type of finial commonly found at the heads of bench-standards or desks in churches ; generally it is carved with foliage and flowers and resembles a fleur-de-lis.

PORTLAND STONE—A fine white oolitic limestone of the Upper Jurassic system.

PRESBYTERY—The part of a church, usually reserved for priests, in which is placed the communion table.

PRINCIPALS—The main as opposed to the common rafters of a roof.

PULPITUM—A screen in a monastic church, dividing the monastic choir from the nave.

PULVINATED FRIEZE—In Classical and Renaissance architecture, a frieze having a convex or bulging profile.

PURBECK MARBLE—A shelly limestone of the Upper Jurassic system, quarried in S. Dorset and capable of being polished.

PURLIN—In roof construction, a horizontal timber resting on the principal rafters or trusses and forming an intermediate support for the common rafters. For *Collar-purlin*, see *King-post* under ROOFS.

QUARRY—In windows, a small pane of glass, often lozenge-shaped. In pavements, a square tile.

QUATREFOIL—A four-petalled flower. See also FOIL.

QUEEN-POSTS—A pair of vertical posts in a roof-truss, equidistant from the centre line of the roof. See also under ROOFS.

QUOIN—The dressed stones at the angle of a building, or distinctive brickwork in this position. Normally the quoin stones are long and short in alternate courses ; if they are of equal length it is called a french quoin.

RAFTERS—Inclined timbers supporting a roof-covering. See also under ROOFS.

RAIL—A horizontal member in the framing of a door, screen, panelling or other woodwork.

READING BEDS—A Tertiary geological formation consisting of sand and mottled red and white clay, with bands of concretionary ironstone and of flints.

REAR-ARCH—The arch, on the inside of a wall, spanning a doorway or window-opening.

REBATE—A continuous rectangular notch cut on an edge.

REEDING—Ornament consisting of narrow convex striations, the reverse of fluting.

REREDORTER—A monastic latrine.

REREDOS—A screen of stone or wood at the back of an altar, usually enriched.

RESPONDS—The half-columns or piers at the ends of an arcade, or abutting a single arch.

REVEAL—The internal side surface of a recess, doorway or window opening.

RIDGE (or RIG)-AND-FURROW—Remains of cultivation of mediaeval and later date ; initially strips of arable land, usually 3 to 12 yds. wide, thrown into ridges by the action of ploughing, leaving furrows between them.

RINCEAUX—Decoration composed of a sinuous stem between parallel margins, with a coiled branch in each interstice, usually with acanthus enrichment.

ROLL-MOULDING—A continuous convex moulding cut upon the edges of stone, woodwork, etc.

ROOD (*Rood-beam, Rood-screen, Rood-loft*)—A cross or crucifix. The *Great Rood* was set up at the E. end of the nave with accompanying figures of St. Mary and St. John ; it was generally carved in wood, and fixed on the loft or head of the rood-screen, or on a special beam (the *Rood-beam*), reaching from wall to wall. Sometimes the rood was merely painted on the wall above the chancel-arch or on a closed wood partition or typanum in the upper part of the arch. The *Rood-screen* is the open screen spanning the E. end of the nave, shutting off the chancel ; in the 15th century a narrow gallery was often constructed above the cornice to carry the rood and other images and candles, and it was also used as a music-gallery. This loft was approached by a staircase (and occasionally by more than one), either of wood or built in the wall, wherever most convenient, and, when the loft was carried right across an aisled building, the intervening walls of the nave were often pierced with narrow archways. Many roods were destroyed at the Reformation and their removal, with the rood loft, was ordered in 1561.

ROOFS—*Collar-beam*—a principal-rafter roof with collar-beams (*q.v.*) connecting the principals.
Cruck—having a truss with principals springing from below the level of the wall-plate. The timbers are usually curved, but examples with straight timbers are recorded.
Hammer-beam—in which cantilevered beams instead of tie-beams, braced from a level below the wall-plates, form the basis of construction.
King-post and Collar-purlin—a trussed-rafter roof with king-posts standing on the tie-beams to carry a centre purlin supporting the collars.
King-post and Ridge—in which king-posts standing on tie-beams or collar-beams directly support the ridge.
Mansard—characterised in exterior appearance by two pitches, the lower steeper than the upper.
Principal Rafter—with rafters at intervals, of greater scantling than the common rafters and framed to form trusses ; they are normally called by the name of the connecting member used in the truss, *tie-beam* or *collar-beam*.
Queen-post—with two vertical or nearly vertical posts standing on the tie-beam of a truss and supporting a collar-beam or the principal rafters.
Scissors-truss—as trussed-rafter, but with crossed braces instead of collars.
Tie-beam—a principal rafter roof with a simple triangulation of a horizontal beam linking the lower ends of the pairs of principals to prevent their spread.
Trussed-rafter—in which all the timbers in the slopes are common rafters of uniform size, and each pair of rafters is connected by a collar-beam, which is often braced. At intervals, pairs of rafters may be tenoned into a tie-beam.
Wagon—a trussed-rafter roof with curved braces, forming a semi-circular arch, springing from wall-plate level. The soffit is usually plastered over and the ridge member, other longitudinal members, and transverse members at intervals are usually decorated with mouldings which project below the plaster to form coffers.

RUBBLE—Walling of rough unsquared stones or flints. *Coursed Rubble*—rubble walling with the stones or flints very roughly dressed and levelled up in courses.

RUSTICATION—Masonry in which only the margins of the stones are worked ; the word is also used for any masonry where the joints are emphasised by mouldings, grooves, etc. Rusticated columns are those in which the shafts are interrupted by square blocks of stone, or by broad projecting bands.

SACRISTY—A room, generally in immediate connection with a church, in which the holy vessels are kept.

SAMIAN WARE—A common table ware of the Roman period, mostly of Gaulish origin, with a glossy surface, generally red in colour. Also known as *terra sigillata*.

SCALLOPED CAPITAL—A development of the cushion capital in which the single cushion is elaborated into a series of truncated cones.

SCARP—A short, abrupt slope, usually artificial. In earthwork fortifications, the downward slope in front of the defenders. See also *Strip Lynchets*.

SCREEN—In secular buildings, the wooden partition separating the main space of a hall from the service end. *Screens-passage*, the space at the service end of a hall between the screen and the end wall.

SEDILIA—The seats, on the S. side of the chancel, used by the ministers during the Mass.

SILL—The lower horizontal member of a window or door-frame ; the stone, tile or wood base below a window or door-frame, usually with a weathered surface projecting beyond the wall-face to throw off water. In timber-framed walls, the lower horizontal member into which the studs are tenoned.

SITULATE—A term used to describe the form of vessels, chiefly of pottery, with straight tapering sides, high shoulders and short everted necks, characteristic of the earlier phases of the Iron Age in Britain.

SLIP-TILES—Tiles moulded with a design in intaglio which is filled in, before burning, with clay of a different colour.

SOFFIT—The under-side of an arch, staircase, lintel, cornice, canopy, vault, etc.

SOIL-MARK—A trace of a levelled or buried feature revealed by differences in colour or texture of the soil, usually in ploughed land.

SOLAR—In a mediaeval house, a chamber occupied by the master, usually adjoining the dais end of the hall.

SPANDREL—The space between the outside curve of an arch and the surrounding rectangular framework or moulding, or the space between the outside curves of two adjoining arches and a moulding above them. Also, in open-string staircases, the bracket or triangular exposed end of a step, often decorated with a scroll.

SPLAT—A flat board with shaped sides used in place of a turned and moulded member, often having the outline of a baluster.

SPRINGING-LINE—The level at which an arch springs from its supports.

SQUINCH—An arch thrown across the angle between two walls to support an obliquely set superstructure, such as the base of a dome or spire.

SQUINT—An aperture pierced through a wall to allow a view of an altar from places whence it could otherwise not be seen.

STAGES—The divisions (*e.g.* of a tower) marked externally by horizontal string-courses.

STAIRCASES—A *close-string* staircase is one having a raking member into which the treads and risers are morticed. An *open-string* staircase has the raking member cut to the shape of the treads and risers. A *dog-legged* staircase has adjoining flights running in opposite directions, with a common newel. A *well-staircase* has stairs rising round a central opening more or less as wide as it is long.

STILE—The vertical member of a timber frame, into which are tenoned the ends of the rails or horizontal pieces.

STOPS—Blocks terminating mouldings or chamfers in stone or wood ; stones at the ends of labels, string-courses, etc., against which the mouldings finish, frequently carved to represent shields, foliage, human or grotesque masks ; also, plain or decorative, used at the ends of a moulding or a chamfer to form the transition from the angle to the square.

STOUP—A receptacle to contain holy water ; those remaining are usually in the form of a deeply-dished stone set in a niche or on a pillar near a church doorway.

STRAPWORK—Decoration consisting of strap-like bands, often interlaced ; characteristic of the late 16th and early 17th century.

STRING-COURSE—A projecting horizontal band in a wall, usually moulded.

STRIP FIELDS—Narrow fields characteristic of mediaeval and later open-field agriculture.

STRIP LYNCHETS—Long, narrow cultivation terraces (*treads*), usually open-ended, with scarps (*risers*) above or below. They are of mediaeval and later date and represent the extension of strip cultivation, usually the open fields, on to hillsides.

STUDS—The common posts or uprights in timber-framed walls.

SWAG—An architectural ornament ; a festoon suspended at both ends and carved to represent cloth, or flowers and fruit.

TABLE-TOMB—A chest-like funeral monument, usually with panelled sides and a flat top, sometimes with a recumbent effigy on top ; occasionally without sides, the top being supported on legs. See also ALTAR-TOMB.

TAS-DE-CHARGE—The lower courses of a vault or arch, laid in horizontal courses.

TESSERA—A small cube of stone, glass, or marble, used in mosaic.

THUMB-GAUGING—An ornamental top-edge to a ridge-tile, made with the thumb before the tile is baked.

TIE-BEAM—The horizontal transverse beam in a roof, tying together the feet of opposed rafters to counteract thrust.

TIMBER-FRAMED BUILDING—A building in which the walls are built of open timbers and the interstices are filled in with brickwork or lath and plaster (' wattle and daub ') ; the whole often covered with plaster or boarding.

TOOLING—Dressing or finishing a masonry surface with an axe or other tool, usually in parallel lines.

TORUS—In classical architecture, a convex moulding, generally rounded in profile.

TOUCH—A soft black marble quarried near Tournai.

TRACERY—The ornamental work in the head of a window, screen, panel, etc., formed by curving and interlacing of bars of stone or wood, grouped together, generally over two or more lights or bays.

TRANSOM—A horizontal bar of stone or wood across a window-light.

TREFOIL—See FOIL.

TRELLIS, TREILLAGE—Lattice-work of light wood or metal bars.

TRIFORIUM—In larger churches, an arcaded wall-passage at about mid-wall height, between the aisle arcades and the clearstorey. A large gallery the full width of the aisle below is termed a *Tribune*.

TRIGLYPHS—Blocks with vertical channels, placed at intervals along the frieze of the Doric entablature.

TRUSS—A number of timbers framed together to bridge a space, designed to be self-supporting and to carry other timbers. The *trusses* of a roof are generally named after a peculiar feature in their construction, such as *King-post, Queen-post, Hammer-beam, Cruck* ; see ROOFS.

TUFA (Calcareous)—Spongy deposit formed by the action of water on limestone and resembling volcanic lava ; often used in vaulting on account of its light weight.

TUSKING—Bricks or stones in alternate courses left projecting beyond the wall-face of a building to facilitate the bonding in of an extension.

TYMPANUM—The triangular or segmental field in the face of a pediment or in the head of an arch.

VAULTING—An arched ceiling or roof of stone or brick, sometimes imitated in wood and plaster. *Barrel Vaulting* is a continuous vault unbroken in its length by cross-vaults. A *Groined Vault* (or *Cross-vaulting*) results from the intersection of simple vaulting surfaces. A *Ribbed Vault* is a framework of arched ribs carrying the cells that cover in the spaces between them. One bay of vaulting, divided into four quarters or compartments, is termed *quadripartite*; but often the bay is divided longitudinally into two subsidiary bays, and the vaulting bay is thus divided into six compartments and is termed *sexpartite*. Increased elaboration is given by *Tiercerons*, secondary ribs springing from the wall-supports and rising to a point other than the centre, and *Liernes*, tertiary ribs that do not spring from the wall-supports, but cross from main rib to main rib. In *fan-vaulting* numerous ribs rise from the springing in equal curves, diverging equally in all directions, giving fan-like effects when seen from below.

VENETIAN WINDOW—Similar to Palladian window.

VESICA PISCIS—An oval frame, pointed at top and bottom, common in mediaeval art.

VICE—A small circular stair.

VOUSSOIRS—The stones forming an arch.

WAGON-ROOF—See under ROOFS.

WALL-PLATE—A timber laid lengthwise on the wall to receive the ends of the rafters and other joists. In timber-framing, the studs are tenoned into it.

WAVE-MOULDING—A compound moulding formed by a convex curve between two concave curves.

WEATHERING (to sills, tops of buttresses, etc.)—A sloping surface for casting off rainwater.

WESSEX CULTURE—A group of rich Early Bronze Age burials, largely confined to the Wessex area, found almost entirely in round barrows and associated with exotic grave goods of gold, amber, faience, etc.

WINDMILL HILL—A causewayed camp in Wiltshire; a type-site of the earlier Neolithic period which gives its name to a culture and to a family of pottery, characterised by several regional types, *e.g.* Hembury, Abingdon, Whitehawk, etc.

INDEX

In the **Index** the letters 'a' and 'b' indicate the left-hand and
right-hand columns on the page to which reference is made.